D1553705

Gideon Lewis-Krauss

The Extended Mind

Life and Mind: Philosophical Issues in Biology and Psychology
Kim Sterelny and Robert A. Wilson, editors

Cycles of Contingency: Developmental Systems and Evolution, Susan Oyama, Paul E. Griffiths, and Russell D. Gray, editors, 2000

Coherence in Thought and Action, Paul Thagard, 2000

Evolution and Learning: The Baldwin Effect Reconsidered, Bruce H. Weber and David J. Depew, 2003

Seeing and Visualizing: It's Not What You Think, Zenon Pylyshyn, 2003

Organisms and Artifacts: Design in Nature and Elsewhere, Tim Lewens, 2004

Molecular Models of Life: Philosophical Papers on Molecular Biology, Sahotra Sarkar, 2004

Evolution in Four Dimensions, Eva Jablonka and Marion J. Lamb, 2005

The Evolution of Morality, Richard Joyce, 2006

Maladapted Psychology: Infelicities of Evolutionary Psychology, Robert Richardson, 2007

Describing Inner Experience? Proponent Meets Skeptic, Russell T. Hurlburt and Eric Schwitzgebel, 2007

The Native Mind and the Cultural Construction of Nature, Scott Atran and Douglas Medin, 2008

The Extended Mind, Richard Menary, editor, 2010

The Extended Mind

edited by Richard Menary

A Bradford Book
The MIT Press
Cambridge, Massachusetts
London, England

MIT Press books may be purchased at special quantity discounts for business or sales promotional use. For information, please email special_sales@mitpress.mit.edu or write to Special Sales Department, The MIT Press, 55 Hayward Street, Cambridge, MA 02142.

This book was set in Stone Sans and Stone Serif by Westchester Book Composition and was printed and bound in the United States of America.

Library of Congress Cataloging-in-Publication Data

The extended mind / edited by Richard Menary.
    p.   cm.—(Life and mind)
"A Bradford book."
Includes bibliographical references and index.
ISBN 978-0-262-01403-8 (hardcover : alk. paper)
1. Externalism (Philosophy of mind).   2. Cognition—Philosophy.   3. Philosophy of mind.   I. Menary, Richard.
BD418.3.E86   2010
128'.2—dc22
                                                    2009037120

10   9   8   7   6   5   4   3   2

For my parents with thanks
Ab imo pectore

Contents

1 Introduction: The Extended Mind in Focus

Richard Menary

One of the most dangerous ideas for a philosopher is, oddly enough, that we think with or in our heads. The idea of thinking as a process in the head, in a completely enclosed space, gives him something occult.

—Wittgenstein, *Zettel*

In 1998, *Analysis* published an essay by Andy Clark and David Chalmers[1] which has excited vigorous debate about the nature and study of mind and cognition. This volume presents the best critical and reflective responses to the bold vision of mind and cognition set out in that essay. Before turning to the details of this debate, I want to briefly summarize the main proposals and arguments as laid out in the 1998 essay and highlight the main features that are criticized or developed by the essays in this volume. In this way we will be in a better position to understand the focus of the arguments and developments to be found in the essays presented here.

1 Active Externalism

The extended mind begins with the question "where does the mind stop and the rest of the world begin?" In answer to this question, C&C present an *active externalism*, which should be distinguished from the more traditional meaning externalism familiar from the writings of Putnam (1975) and Burge (1986). Active externalism is distinguished from traditional forms of externalism because it concerns *the active role of the environment in driving cognitive processes* (Clark and Chalmers 1998, this volume, p. 27). This statement of active externalism is ambiguous between two interpretations, and we must be careful about which is implied. First, there is a rather trivial reading of active externalism, where some causally active features of the environment influence cognitive processing in the brain. Second, there is the more robustly externalist reading, where some cognitive processing is *constituted* by active features of the environment. For example, C&C define an epistemic action as altering "the world so as to aid and augment cognitive processes such as recognition and search" (this volume, p. 28). I doubt that internalists will have any problem with actions that *aid* cognitive processes, just so long as those actions themselves are not constitutive of cognitive processes.

However, C&C explicitly endorse the constitutive version of active externalism: "In these cases, the human organism is linked with an external entity in a two-way interaction, creating a *coupled system* that can be seen as a cognitive system in its own right" (p. 29). The coupled system constitutes a cognitive system. It is not simply that the external features, to which the organism is interactively linked, have a causal influence on the cognitive processing of the organism; rather, the interactive link *is* the cognitive processing. Therefore, active externalism is a constitutive thesis, not a merely causal one, as encapsulated by the slogan "cognitive processes ain't (all) in the head" (p. 29). We should be aware that active externalism as a robustly constitutive thesis has been challenged by critics (Adams and Aizawa, this volume; Rupert 2004, this volume), who are inclined to think that the less robust causal version of the thesis is all that we are likely to get. I shall outline the reasons for this below.

Before turning to the nature of coupling we should attempt to understand the difference between active externalism and *passive* forms of externalism.

When I believe that water is wet and my twin believes that twin water is wet, the external features responsible for the difference in our beliefs are distal and historical, at the end of a lengthy causal chain. Features of the *present* are not relevant: if I happen to be surrounded by XYZ right now (maybe I have teleported to twin earth), my beliefs still concern standard water, because of my history. In these cases, the relevant external features are *passive*. Because of their distal nature, they play no role in driving the cognitive processes in the here-and-now. This is reflected by the fact that the actions performed by me and my twin are physically indistinguishable, despite our external differences. (C&C, p. 29)

Active externalism is to be distinguished from an externalism where the contents of beliefs are dependent on my history. The external features are distal, not having a synchronic effect on the organism. This opens up an important question about the role of content in extended cognitive processes, a question addressed in the essays by Adams and Aizawa and

Wilson. By contrast, active externalism focuses on active features of the environment in the here-and-now.

The active nature of this externalism is explicated in terms of the notion of causal coupling. Since the issue of coupling relations is a focal point for criticism of the extended mind (EM) in this volume and elsewhere (Adams and Aizawa 2001), we should be very clear about what it entails.

2 Causal Coupling

C&C define a coupled system in the following way: "In these cases, the human organism is linked with an external entity in a two-way interaction, creating a *coupled system* that can be seen as a cognitive system in its own right" (p. 29). C&C give something by way of criteria for this constitutive thesis (p. 29):

1. All the components in the system play an active causal role.
2. They jointly govern behavior in the same sort of way that cognition usually does.
3. If we remove the external component, the system's behavioral competence will drop, just as it would if we removed part of its brain.
4. Therefore, this sort of coupled process counts equally well as a cognitive process, whether or not it is wholly in the head.

The active features of the environment have an influence over us in the here-and-now. If we maintained the internal structure but varied the nature of the environment then our behaviors and competences might alter radically. Crucially, C&C claim that "the external features here are just as causally relevant as typical internal features of the brain" (p. 30).

There are two possible interpretations of causal coupling here, and it is important to be clear about which one is implied by C&C.

A. Asymmetric influence: environmental features have a causal influence over inner processes. It may still be the case that we can change the external environment and that affects competence and behavior of the subject. If you take my diary away from me I won't be able to remember all my engagements. The diary prompts my recall of memories, but there is no need to go further and say that because the diary has a causal influence on me that it is thereby part of my memory, or the cognitive processes that allow me to remember. It would be a mistake to make this claim simply on the basis of a causal connection.

B. Symmetric influence: the inner and outer features have a mutually constraining causal influence on one another that unfolds over time. It is not simply that the diary prompts or causes, as input, various cognitive processes to unfold in my brain; rather, the external process of retrieving the information from the diary and the concurrent processes in my brain jointly govern my future behavior. This is what Menary calls *cognitive integration* (2006, 2007, this volume).

This distinction is important because, critics of EM, such as Adams and Aizawa (2001, this volume) are working with interpretation A, but Clark is working with B. Hence there is a misunderstanding between exponents of EM and their critics. The critics may wish to claim that although EM is supposed to endorse B, very often A is what is endorsed, and A is not a constitutive thesis. Exponents of EM must be careful to indicate when and why they are using interpretation B.

C&C do not give an explicit example of a coupled process, nor do they explain how the internal and external features jointly govern behavior. However, in some of Clark's other work he does make the notion more explicit. In chapter 8 of *Being There*, Clark outlines the notion of continuous reciprocal causation, "the presence of continuous mutually modulatory influences linking brain, body and world" (Clark 1997, p. 163).[2]

Continuous reciprocal causation (CRC) occurs when some system S is both continuously affecting and simultaneously being affected by, activity in some other system O. Internally, we may well confront such causal complexity in the brain since many neural areas are linked by both feedback and feedforward pathways (e.g., Van Essen and Gallant 1994). On a larger canvass, we often find processes of CRC that criss-cross brain, body and local environment. Think of a dancer, whose bodily orientation is continuously affecting and being affected by her neural states, and whose movements are also influencing those of her partner, to whom she is continuously responding! (Clark 2008, p. 24)

Although we can identify the relevant components, and factorize them into internal and external components, the nature of reciprocal coupling makes it difficult to study the components as separate systems because they are continuously influencing and responding to one another. They are coordinating with one another to produce behavior. Insofar as brain, body, and world can be shown to be reciprocally coupled in this way, we can consider them to be a coupled system. However, we are still not in a position to definitively say when a coupled system is a cognitive system, because there might be coupled systems that are noncognitive. The parity principle is supposed to help us make such judgments.

3   The Parity Principle

The parity principle is stated in the following way:

If, as we confront some task, a part of the world functions as a process which *were it done in the head*, we would have no hesitation in recognizing as part of the cognitive process, then that part of the world *is* (so we claim) part of the cognitive process. (C&C, p. 29)

The parity principle (henceforth PP) should not be taken independently of active externalism and causal coupling. It is not the main pillar in support of the conclusion that cognitive and mental processes are extended. The PP has two roles in the argument. First, it is an intuition pump; it asks us to reconsider our Cartesian prejudices[3]. The location of a process should not, by itself, discount a process from being cognitive. Second, it introduces the functionalist credentials of EM. As long as a process has a cognitive *function* then it does not matter where it is located. If it plays the right sort of role and is causally integrated with other cognitive processes, then it is part of the system of processes that constitute a person's completion of a cognitive task. The functionalist credentials of EM will be evident again in section 6 below.

It is important to note that the parity principle has become the focus for some of the main criticisms leveled at EM. Some critics (e.g., Adams and Aizawa 2001, this volume) take the PP to have specific implications, which EM theorists have been at some pains to resist (Clark 2005, this volume; Menary 2006; Sutton, this volume). Some friends of EM even deny that the PP is a useful motivational tool and claim that it is apt to confuse rather than enlighten (see Menary 2006, this volume; Wilson, this volume; and see Sutton, this volume and Wheeler, this volume, for a qualified defense of the PP).

Problems arise because C&C's formulation of the PP does not rule out the misleading interpretation of the extended mind as "the externalizing of internal processes." Nor does it rule out identifying external processes/vehicles as cognitive because of the relevant similarity of the external with the internal.

My strategy is to focus on a specific kind of cognitive state, memory, and here the thrust of the discussion is twofold: I argue that the external portions of extended "memory" states (processes) differ so greatly from internal memories (the process of remembering) that they should be treated as distinct kinds; this quells any temptation to argue for HEC [hypothesis of extended cognition] from brute analogy (namely, extended cognitive states are like wholly internal ones; therefore, they are of the same explanatory cognitive kind; therefore there are extended cognitive states). (Rupert 2004, p. 407)

Clark and Chalmers' 1998 article leans heavily on the *parity argument,* which says that if a process counts as cognitive when it is performed in the head, it should also count as cognitive when it is performed in the world. (Dartnall 2005, pp. 135–136)

They [C&C] contend that the active causal processes that extend into the environment *are just like the ones found in intracranial cognition.* (Adams and Aizawa 2001, p. 56)

These critics think that the main argument for the extended mind is simply the claim that if external processes are sufficiently similar to internal ones, then they are cognitive. Is this really the argument for EM? I believe that the critics have reached this conclusion by misinterpreting the PP. It would have been better if C&C had made it clear that it is functionality and not location that matters when determining whether or not a process is cognitive. If a coupled process has the relevant functionality—for example, it meets the criteria set out in the previous section—then it doesn't matter whether that process is partly, or indeed, mostly external. Focus on the function, not the location, is the purpose of the PP.[4] It is not a simple comparative exercise; if external process X is sufficiently similar to internal process Y, then X is cognitive.[5]

This would be a bad way to argue for EM because external processes are often very different from internal ones. Internal process X may have properties a, b, and c and external process Y may have properties d, e, and f. They may differ radically in their physical properties; it is not the physical properties that matter to EM, however, but the functionality of the process. Internalist critics think that a knock-down argument against EM is available because it is easy enough to highlight these differences. Internal and external memories are so different, as Rupert argues, that they should not be counted as being members of the same cognitive kind. This would quell the temptation to argue for EM on the basis of similarity; but the argument for EM is not that external memories must be like internal memories for them to be counted as cognitive, *pace* Rupert and Adams and Aizawa.

This is an important point, because Rupert and Adams and Aizawa think that EM can be shown to be implausible because external processes are not susceptible to the same cognitive explanations as internal processes, and that, therefore, they cannot be considered to be members of the same cognitive kind. For example, biological memory, to use a less prejudicial term, is subject to a variety of effects such as recency, interference, and chunking. Nonbiological memories stored in notebooks, PDAs, and so on do not share these same effects; worse, they are not subsumable under the laws that apply to biological memories. Even if we don't argue for EM through explicit similarity of processes, the difference in explanatory approach to biological and nonbiological memories should tell us that there is a problem for EM.

Or is there? Theorists such as Sutton (this volume), Rowlands (1999), Wilson (2004), and Menary (2007) argue for a hybrid science of memory (and by extension cognition and mind) where the unit of study is the entire cognitive unit, including both bodily internal and bodily external processes. There is no assumption that the internal and external must be alike. Following Merlin Donald's work, the virtue of external memories is that they have different properties from internal ones; they allow us to do things that we cannot achieve with internal memory alone.[6] However, it is clear that internal and external memories complement one another and coordinate in completing cognitive tasks.

4 Portability, Reliability, and the Linguistic Surround

C&C raise a potential objection to EM that some commentators have picked up on, and that it is the issue of portability and reliability (Adams and Aizawa 2001, this volume). The brain and body constitute a package of cognitive capacities that are *portable* in that they can always be brought to bear on a cognitive task; they form the constant cognitive core of an individual. The coupling of these core cognitive resources to the local environment is *too* contingent: the cognitive core can be too easily decoupled from its environment. Two conclusions can be drawn from this observation. First, it is the core cognitive resources that are of real interest to cognitive scientists, who are largely interested in the cognitive processes to be found in the brain. Second, the contingency[7] of coupled cognitive resources shows that they are not really part of the reliable and portable cognitive resources that agents bring to bear on the world.

C&C respond with the idea that coupled cognitive systems can be both portable and reliable; it is reliable coupling that is important. If the resources in the environment are reliably available to me, then they can be reliably coupled to me. "In effect they are part of the basic package of cognitive resources that I bring to bear on the everyday world" (C&C, p. 31). The brain is subject to the dangers of damage and malfunction and even loss of specific capacities through intoxication or stress, so this cannot be a sufficient reason for rejecting externally coupled systems.

C&C go further by claiming that external coupling is part of our core cognitive resources because "the biological brain has in fact evolved and matured in ways which factor in the reliable presence of a manipulable external environment" (C&C, p. 31). For example, the visual system exploits various features of the external environment and bodily motion (Ullman and Richards 1984; Blake and Yuille 1992).

Another central example of reliable coupling with the surrounding environment is language.[8] We are surrounded by spoken and written language in our everyday lives; we develop ideas and plans in groups, we write down lists, we consult diaries, we look up train timetables. The capacity to produce the linguistic surround and manipulate and exploit it for our own cognitive ends is something we gain through a process of learning and psychological development (this is what Menary 2007 calls the *transformation thesis*):

> In such cases the brain develops in a way that complements the external structures, and learns to play its role in a unified, densely coupled system. Once we recognize the crucial role of the environment in constraining the evolution and development of cognition, we see that extended cognition is a core cognitive process, not an add-on extra. (C&C, p. 32)

The surrounding linguistic environment contains reliable structures, speech and text, that are available as cognitive resources to be coupled with. Our ability to reliably couple with this ever-present environment constitutes human cognition and thought.

5   From Cognition to Mind

The argument so far has focused on the extended nature of cognitive processes, but what of the mind? C&C provide an audacious argument to the conclusion "that *beliefs* can be constituted partly by features of the environment, when those features play the right sort of role in driving cognitive processes. If so the mind extends into the world" (C&C, p. 33). They argue to this conclusion largely through the use of an example, the case of Otto and his extended memory system.

Inga hears that there is a cool Rothko exhibition on at the Museum of Modern Art, and she decides to go to it. Inga recalls the location of the Museum of Modern Art from biological memory, which causes her to go to 53rd street. Thus, Inga makes use of a long-standing biological memory that MoMA is on 53rd street. Consider Otto: he has Alzheimer's and depends on a notebook for the retrieval of information. He has all sorts of useful information about places and people, addresses and names, and so on. Otto takes his notebook with him wherever he goes and refers to it frequently. Upon being told of the same exhibition as Inga he decides to go, but Otto retrieves information from his notebook concerning the location of MoMA. This causes him to go to 53rd street.

As such, the physical implementation of the causal role is irrelevant to the functional level of description—Otto's use of his notebook and Inga's pattern of activation in her brain. The two cases are on a par. "For Otto, his notebook plays the role usually played by a biological memory" (C&C, p. 33). This is the case only if Otto's notebook plays the same role for Otto that biological memory plays for Inga. We might be inclined to agree with C&C that the information in Otto's notebook is reliably available to him and guides his actions in just the sort of way that beliefs are usually supposed to. The information is available and functions just like the information that constitutes non-occurrent beliefs; the only difference is the location of the information. C&C's argument calls on their commitment to functionalism: as long as information plays the relevant role it is a belief, regardless of location. Hence, the mind extends into the world. However, we should note that we are identifying the functional role of belief at a level quite abstracted from the details of physical implementation. It is certainly debatable as to whether Otto and his notebook display the same causal profile as Inga and her biological memory—once again raising the problematic nature of the argument to EM from functional parity. As we shall see in the next section, Clark does not think that the Otto case is problematic in the way that I have described here. I shall now turn to the criticisms of EM concentrating on those formulated in Adams and Aizawa's, Rupert's, and Preston's essays for this volume.

6   Criticisms of the Extended Mind and Responses

Extended Beliefs

In "*Memento*'s Revenge: the Extended Mind Extended," Andy Clark responds to various criticisms that have been leveled at EM, bringing out clearly the central commitment to functionalism of EM, the challenge it poses to setting the boundary of the mind at the skin, and further refinement of the notion of a coupled system.

Clark reaffirms that the conclusion of EM is that "mental states, including states of believing, could be grounded in physical traces that remained firmly outside the head" (this volume, p. 43). Some of Otto's dispositional beliefs are stored in his notebook, because the information in Otto's notebook has the same functional poise as that stored in Inga's biological memory for the control of subsequent behavior; Otto and Inga's memories are on a par. An obvious objection to this claim is what Clark calls the "Otto two–step": "all Otto actually believes (in advance) is that the address is in the notebook. That's the belief (step 1) that leads to the looking (step 2) that then leads to the (new) belief about the actual street address" (ibid., p. 46).

Clark doesn't think that this objection works, because the notebook acts as transparent equipment for Otto as Inga's memory does for her. The Otto two-step introduces needless complexity into the account of Otto's memory system. However, this response does not really take into account what is potentially damaging about the objection. The point is that we don't normally have to remember that we remember something; Otto has to remember that the relevant information is in his notebook before looking it up. Inga, by contrast, just remembers where the address is. Thus, Otto and Inga do not appear to be on a par when considered in this way.

John Preston takes the criticism further in his essay (chapter 15) by addressing the issue of first-person authority. Beliefs are the kind of mental states over which we can be said to have first-person authority[9] "in utterance" (this volume, p. 359). One can *say* what one's beliefs are without fear of contradiction by others. We do not have a similar authority over "external" resources such as notebooks and diaries. Otto is not, according to Preston, an authority about the content of his notebook before he has consulted it. Otto has to find out what he believes, and such finding out is not included in the ordinary concept of belief.

Preston locates the problem with identifying Otto's notebook as being the location of his belief in the distinction between subpersonal cognitive systems and personal beliefs, avowals, intentions, and other mental states. We normally say that a person (such as Clark or Preston) remembers or believes something, and furthermore it is they who cognitively achieve things; Clark sees the subway entrance, Preston calculates that the $34 entrance fee to MoMA subtracted from his $50 bill leaves him with $16 for lunch. Say Clark wears strong eyeglasses to be able to see the signs in the subway station; is it Clark plus the prosthetic enhancement of the eyeglasses that sees? Preston uses a calculator to subtract 34 from 50; is it Preston plus calculator that achieves the calculation? If it is the subpersonal cognitive system that includes both Preston and calculator (reliably coupled, etc.) that makes the calculation, then, according to EM, epistemic credit for the cognitive achievement is spread across the system, which includes Preston's brain, body, and the calculator. Preston denies, though, that we attribute such achievements and therefore epistemic achievement to systems; he claims we do so only to persons— "Preston made the calculation using a calculator" would be the natural thing to say in this instance.

The Otto case may, though, be clouding the issue,[10] for, as Preston himself suggests, we often do remember what we think about an issue by making reference to an external record of our thoughts. In these cases it looks fair to say that the contents of our beliefs are stored externally, in books, notebooks, diaries, computer files, on beer mats, and so on, allowing for their easy retrieval when required—when we are asked to make an avowal of what we think about a subject, for example.[11] Therefore, although we don't say that our beliefs are in the notebooks, and so on, we do retrieve the contents of our beliefs to be able to make accurate and authoritative avowals about what we are committed to. There is a clear sense in which the vehicles and their contents stored in the notebook and our accessing those vehicles for a cognitive purpose are part of our completion of a cognitive task: they enable the cognitive achievement (see Menary and Hurley's essays in this volume for further discussion).

The Coupling-Constitution Fallacy (Fallacy)

Adams and Aizawa's primary criticism of the extended mind (chapter 4) is based on an alleged fallacy that the argument for the extended mind perpetrates, namely, the coupling-constitution fallacy. The fallacy is summed up in the following way:[12]

When Clark makes an object cognitive when it is connected to a cognitive agent, he is committing an instance of a "coupling-constitution fallacy." This is the most common mistake the extended mind theorists make. (Adams and Aizawa, this volume, pp. 67–68)

When some object or process is coupled to a cognitive agent in some way, Adams and Aizawa claim that the extended mind theorist slides to the conclusion that the object or process constitutes part of the agent's cognitive apparatus. The fallacy is based in the distinction between causal relations and constitutive relations and "the fact that object or process X is coupled to object or process Y does not entail that X is part of Y" (ibid., p. 68).

This alleged fallacy is the first line of attack in their strategy to draw the boundaries of cognition at the skin of the "individual." Schematically the strategy is as above: just because X is causally related to Y, it does not follow that X is a part of Y. The second line of attack is closely allied to the first: because we need to ask which processes are candidates for inclusion in the "kind" cognitive. Schematically the argument strategy runs like this:[13] neuronal (and therefore cognitive) processes have property X; nonneuronal processes do not have property X; therefore nonneuronal properties are not cognitive. This form of argument looks dangerously close to the fallacy of denying the antecedent: if a process has property X, then it is cognitive; this process does not have property X; therefore it is not cognitive. Let us focus on the first line of attack here.

Friends of the extended mind have begun to respond to the charge of committing the causal coupling fallacy (Menary 2006; Clark, this volume; Hurley, this volume; Ross and Ladyman, this volume). Menary's response is to deny the picture of causal coupling as presented by Adams and Aizawa. Rather than the picture of a cognitive agent causally related to an object, such as a notebook, the picture ought to be one that is integrated. Schematically: X is the manipulation of the notebook reciprocally coupled to Y—bodily processes, including neuronal ones—which together constitute Z, the process of remembering. Once we have this picture, it is easy to see that Adams and Aizawa have distorted the aim of the extended mind. The aim is not to show that artifacts get to be part of cognition just because they are causally coupled to a preexisting cognitive agent, but to explain why X and Y are so coordinated that they together function as Z, which causes further behavior. Take this analogous example: the input layer of units in a feed-forward neural network is coupled to the hidden layer of units, but nobody thinks that this makes the input layer part of the hidden layer. However, the coupling of the input units to the hidden layer units does make them part of a larger system, that is, the neural network.

Clark takes a similar line in his response to Adams and Aizawa in chapter 5 of this volume. The point of coupling isn't to make the notebook cognitive; "rather it is intended to make some object, that in and of itself is not usefully (perhaps not even intelligibly thought of as *either cognitive or non-cognitive*, into a *proper part of some cognitive system*, such as a human agent" (Clark, this volume, p. 83). The question that Clark proposes as the object of the extended mind theorist's inquiries is "when is some physical object or process part of a larger system?"—rather than the "murkier" question that Adams and Aizawa think the extended mind theorist is pursuing, "when should we say, of some such candidate part, that it is *itself* cognitive?" (ibid., p. 84). Therefore, the extended mind theorist needs to clarify the kind of coupling that allows for incorporation into a single system rather than use by that system. This is also the point of Menary's cognitive integration: we need to understand how bodily processes and the manipulation of external vehicles are coordinated in such a way that they jointly cause further behavior (see Menary 2006, 2007, this volume).

If Adams and Aizawa's answer to this were that the putative part of a cognitive system cannot be a candidate because it does not exhibit the mark of the cognitive (representations with nonderived content), then they may, as Clark points out, be subject to the fallacy of composition—assuming that the parts of a system must have the same properties as the whole. We do not, for example, expect the subsystems that support conscious thought to themselves be conscious.

Hurley (chapter 6) and Ross and Ladyman (chapter 7) are concerned about the very nature of the alleged fallacy. Hurley complains that philosophers employ the causal–constitutive distinction, on which the causal coupling fallacy trades, without motivating or explaining the distinction in detail. Ross and Ladyman argue that the distinction itself is not used in mature sciences such as economics and physics. Furthermore, the distinction is based on a metaphor ubiquitous in analytic metaphysics, that of "containment": "On this doctrine, the world is a kind of container bearing objects that change location and properties over time. These objects cause things to happen by interacting directly with one another" (Ross and Ladyman, this volume, p. 159). These objects are themselves containers, and their properties and causal dispositions are explained by the properties and dispositions of the objects they contain. The notion of composition in the sciences is different from that of the containment picture, they argue. For example, water is composed of oxygen and hydrogen in polymeric forms such as $(H_2O)2$, $(H_2O)3$, and so on, that are constantly forming, dissipating, and reforming over short time periods. As such, the properties of the macroscopic kind water, such as wetness, are emergent features of a complex dynamical system.

Therefore, the containment metaphor and the causal–constitutive distinction have no place in the mature sciences. Since mature sciences such as physics and economics have no need for the distinction, cognitive science should feel under no similar stricture.[14]

Fleeting versus Persistent Cognitive Systems
A related worry is explored by Rupert (chapter 14): "We want to understand how and why the capacities and abilities of individual persisting systems change over time, eventually taking a stable form" (Rupert, this volume, p. 330). The worry is that we cannot explain the developmental

differences between a child of two and one of five if there are only "ephem-
eral" coupled systems. There would be nothing stable and persisting, the
individual, to study. The problem is generated by the supposition that
coupled systems are fleeting; Otto, for example, is not constantly coupled
to his notebook, but only fleetingly so. However, Rupert looks to be working with a picture of extended systems similar to the problematical one
endorsed by Adams and Aizawa above. If cognition depends on factor X
in an especially strong or clear way, then X is part of the thinker's cognitive system (see also Preston, this volume). Rupert takes this to be an unreliable form of dependence reasoning, but it is the kind of reasoning that
has been used in work on supervenience for decades. Mental properties are
dependent on neuronal properties in an especially clear way; therefore the
brain instantiates mental properties.[15] Does it turn out for Rupert, Adams
and Aizawa, and others that mind–brain supervenience is based on an
unreliable form of inference? That would be a surprising and interesting
result.

Perhaps the unreliability of the dependence inference should be applied
only to cases where the factor in question is bodily external. If my capacity to walk is clearly dependent on a walking stick, then it does not follow
that the walking stick is part of my "walking system." This conclusion
does not always follow in the biological world; spiders are clearly dependent on their spider webs to catch prey—the spider's prey-catching system
consists of both spider and web (and spider's webs are fleeting systems if
anything is). The organismic process extends beyond the boundary of the
body of the organism in this case. Similarly, the caddis fly larva collects
small stones and shell fragments from the riverbed and binds them
together with a kind of secreted cement (Dawkins 1982). The caddis fly
larva then lives in and carries this new home around with it on the riverbed for its larval period. Humans with their linguistic surround, speech
and writing, are in a similar situation. They must create and maintain
delicate and intricate linguistic webs as part of their cognitive processing.

However that may be, Rupert still finds a fundamental difficulty in the
extended approach: "First, consider that the persisting nature of the capacities investigated by cognitive science cannot be squared with the often
fleeting nature of extended systems comprised of human organisms and
external linguistic resources (Wilson 2002, pp. 630–631); the latter do not
have the longevity or integrity to support the capacities of interest in cognitive science, for example, the capacity to use or to respond to language
systematically across a wide variety of contexts" (Rupert, this volume,

p. 325). This opens up an interesting question about the notion of capacity at work here. Rupert rejects extended cognitive systems because they have cognitive capacities only for as long as the "fleeting" extended system is coupled. It would then appear to follow that we lose our cognitive capacities when the extended cognitive system is decoupled. Otto has the capacity to remember only when he is coupled to his notebook and not when he is decoupled from it. Let's apply the same inference to an analogous case: the spider has a capacity to catch prey when it is coupled to its web; it loses this capacity when it is decoupled from its web. I suspect that no one would want to endorse this inference, because it is clear that the spider has a long-standing capacity to create, maintain, and manipulate its webs, and therefore it does not lose its capacity to catch prey.

Perhaps, then, the answer to Rupert's worry is to distinguish between long-standing dispositional capacities and the exercising of those capacities[16] on various occasions. To exercise its prey-catching capacity the spider must have a web in place and be able to maintain and manipulate that web—it is able to do so because it has a long-standing capacity to create webs. Similarly, humans have a long-standing capacity to create linguistic surrounds and then to maintain and manipulate them: Otto's cognitive "web" is created and maintained in his notebook, where he manipulates and exploits the written sentences for cognitive ends. The exercising of the capacity is, of course, fleeting, although the long-standing disposition is not.

Derived and Underived Content, or The Mark of the Cognitive

Adams and Aizawa (2001, this volume) base their second criticism of the extended mind on the need for a mark of the cognitive/mental. They propose, "A first essential condition on the cognitive is that cognitive states must involve intrinsic, non-derived content" (2001, p. 48). Cognition just is causal processing involving nonderived content.[17] They do, however, draw a fundamental distinction between vehicles with conventionally determined (derived) content and vehicles with naturalistically determined (nonderived) content. Adams and Aizawa further clarify the condition as follows: "Clearly, we mean that if you have a process that involves no intrinsic content, then the condition rules that the process is noncognitive" (Adams and Aizawa, this volume, p. 70).

Clark's initial response to this condition[18] is to provide an example of an image of a set of overlapping Venn diagrams. He suggests that the meaning of the overlaps of two Venn diagrams is determined by convention, but that we would not, consequently, wish to deny that the image could be a part of a cognitive process. The example is supposed to lead us to the conclusion that some mental and cognitive states have contents with conventional content.

Adams and Aizawa do not find this response convincing, because they think that there is an *important* difference between the way artifacts get their meanings determined and the way that mental representations get their meanings determined. Artifacts, such as "words, stop signs, warning lights and gas gauges mean what they do through some sort of social convention" (Adams and Aizawa, this volume, p. 70)—whereas mental representations of natural objects, "such as trees, rocks, birds, and grass mean what they do in virtue of satisfying some naturalistic conditions on meaning" (ibid.). Adams and Aizawa think that Clark has not noticed this difference; they accept that Venn diagrams on paper get their meanings determined by social convention, but images of Venn diagrams get their meanings determined by some naturalistic conditions.

The next move is to reject the *derivation* of the content of the image from the external Venn diagram, the social convention governing the intersection of Venn diagrams is "not a fact about the constitution of the content of a mental image of the intersections of [Venn diagrams]" (ibid., p. 72). The content of the image of the Venn diagram is *dependent* on the Venn diagram on the page in the same sense that an image of a car is dependent on there being cars that are contrived into existence (i.e., artifacts that do not occur naturally).

Finally, Adams and Aizawa reject the notion that cognitive content could be conventionally determined. They do this because agreement on what an artifact means is dependent on the artifact being publically accessible; for example, we can make "bad" or "cool" into positive adjectives by agreement. However, we cannot do this with neuronal states; we cannot agree that a group of neurons will mean something by agreement. This, Adams and Aizawa claim, gives us reason "to believe that cognitive content is not normally derived via any sort of social convention" (ibid., p. 73).

Before looking at Clark's response, it is worth noting that there are several puzzling features to the underived content condition as Adams and Aizawa set it up.[19] First, Adams and Aizawa make a great deal of the difference between conventional determination of meaning and naturalistic determination of meaning; but in the case Clark considers, this had better not make the meaning of the image different from the meaning of the overlapping Venn diagrams. Adams and Aizawa may be right that, strictly speaking, the content of an image of a car or a stop sign is directly caused by visual processing that has no access to conventional content. However, if all cognitive content were like the images in this case, then it would be unclear how we could deploy the content in inferences and related cognitive processing. Why? Because the image, naturalistically construed, does not constitute the concept of a Venn diagram, stop sign, or a car. Such concepts are derived from the conventions that determine what a Venn diagram, stop sign, or a car is and what they can be used for, how they can be acted on, and other useful information. Perhaps our concepts do have imagistic content of a naturalistically determined sort, but they also have content of a conventionally determined sort—at least in cases like these. If Adams and Aizawa restrict cognitive content to naturally determined contents and not conventionally determined ones then cognitive explanations will lose much of their explanatory power. If my concept of a stop sign does not contain any conventional content, then how will I know when to stop?

Clark responds[20] by drawing attention to the nature of Adams and Aizawa's proposed condition. They appear to claim that only processes that involve no intrinsic content can be considered cognitive (see above). However, on closer analysis Clark thinks that:

> Adams and Aizawa are committed to the usefulness of pressing a question that, to us, looks pretty clearly to be among the very reddest of possible herrings. That is the question whether Otto's notebook (to put the matter bluntly), is "cognitive." Since what is at issue is (to repeat) whether the notebook might now be part of the local supervenience base for some of Otto's dispositional beliefs (a putative systems-level fact if ever there was one) the status of the notebook itself, as "cognitive" or "noncognitive," is (to whatever extent that idea is even intelligible) simply irrelevant. By contrast, the *precise nature* of the coupling between the notebook and the rest of the Otto system seems absolutely crucial to how one then conceives of the overall situation. (Clark, this volume, p. 90)

Thus the question is being asked at the wrong level. It is not whether Otto's notebook, on its own, is cognitive or noncognitive, but whether Otto and his notebook, appropriately coupled, constitute a cognitive system. This leads Clark to reject the condition because "from the requirement (if it is a requirement) that every cognitive agent trade in intrinsic contents, it cannot follow that every proper part of such an agent must trade, and trade at all times, in such contents" (ibid., pp. 89–90).

If Clark is right about this, then Adams and Aizawa's question becomes: "do the parts of a system of type X have to share the essential properties that make it a system of that type?" Do all the parts of a cognitive system have to involve intrinsic content, for them to be parts of that system? It may turn out that this is not the right kind of question to ask, as Clark argues. Instead, it may be that there are more fine-grained questions concerning the roles that states and processes have to play in a cognitive system for them to be parts of that system, and how those states and processes are integrated as parts of the same system, even though some of them are not always spatially and temporally present as parts of the system.[21] Presumably it is incumbent upon extended mind theorists to provide empirical examples of such states and processes, rather than relying on imagined examples (as useful as they may be to begin articulating the position). This leads us to the next problem for the extended mind.

Scientific Kinds

Adams and Aizawa stipulate that "the cognitive must be discriminated on the basis of underlying causal processes" (Adams and Aizawa 2001, p. 52). The causal processes studied by psychology give rise to certain laws and regularities that are not found in other processes. Therefore, the scientific kind "cognitive" is discriminated on the basis of these causal processes. It turns out, as a matter of empirical fact, that the only lawlike regularities that psychology has so far offered are ones that apply to intracranial processes and not intercranial ones (see also Rupert 2004, this volume).

The critics claim that the natural kind "cognitive" is structured by a set of causal regularities that apply to processes of only one type. Hence effects such as recency and chunking in memory apply only to processes found in the brain. The critics are impressed by the differences between processes found in the head and those found in the surrounding environment, such that "the external portions of extended 'memory' states (processes) differ so greatly from internal memories (the process of remembering) that they should be treated as distinct kinds" (Rupert 2004, p. 407).

Clark (this volume), Sutton (this volume), and Menary (this volume, 2006, 2007) hold that this difference is irrelevant as long as external processes and internal processes exhibit a sufficient degree of complementarity and integration. Will this move satisfy the critics? Not unless complementarity and integration provide genuine cases of lawlike regularity—the test being that the move to extend cognition beyond the brain must yield genuine advances in scientific explanations. This is a reasonable request, but conclusions should not be too hastily drawn; the science of extended thought is, as yet, in its theoretical and empirical infancy—but a fair amount of empirical work has been done.

Clark also suggests another alternative (this volume, p. 93), which "to paraphrase Dennett, is that cognition is as cognition does. That is to say, we should individuate the cognitive by its characteristic effects, not by its characteristic causes." Hence, we should not look for a distinctly unified set of similar causal properties that give rise to causal regularities, but instead expect to see a "motley" crew of internal and external resources that produce regular effects because of a looser coordination "poised" in such a way that characteristically cognitive behavior is produced (cf. Otto and his notebook).

An alternative approach to Clark's conclusion can be found in Susan Hurley's remarkable essay in this volume. She presents a taxonomy of the varieties of externalism allowing us to see the relationships between more traditional versions of externalism and more radical ones such as the extended mind. She distinguishes between "what" and "how" varieties of externalism. "What" explanations explain mental states in terms of their personal-level content types or phenomenal quality types. "How" explanations explain the workings of the processes and mechanisms that enable mental states (that are of a content or quality type). "What" versions of externalism are familiar as the standard content externalism of Putnam and Burge, although less so in the "what" phenomenal sense. However, "how" externalism is the newer and more radical version of externalism, in that it is committed to enabling mechanisms, processes, and vehicles being external. In one obvious sense the extended mind falls within the "how" externalist camp, because it identifies external processes and vehicles as enabling cognitive processes and mental states.

Hurley's essay is split into two sections. In the first she gives a detailed account of "what" externalism in both its content and "quality" forms. In the second part she turns to "how" or enabling externalism. She makes the distinction between cultural and noncultural cases of extension (cf. Menary's taxonomy of different kinds of manipulation). In the cultural cases, an external artifact enables mental states or cognitive processes (Otto's notebook being the test case for C&C), whereas in noncultural cases extended sensorimotor dynamics extend enabling processes. This goes some way to answering Adams and Aizawa's charge that the extended mind creates an unscientific motley.

The remaining essays in the volume provide a variety of ways in which the extended mind project can be pursued.

7   The Second Wave of Extended Mind Arguments

Chapters 8 through 13 begin the process of looking at the different directions in which the extended mind project might be taken. Wilson's, Sutton's, and Menary's essays (chapters 8, 9, and 10) all point to the need for an approach that focuses on cognitive activity and practice. Rowlands's essay focuses in on the extended conception of consciousness. Wheeler's essay argues for a functionalist interpretation of the extended mind project. Spurrett and Cowley's essay indicates ways in which empirical research on child development fits very happily into an extended mind framework.

Wilson identifies intentionality as not being the problem of specifying essentialist criteria for mental representations—we should instead move from the essences of things to the specification of certain activities as cognitive:

The shift is one from a focus on "things," such as representations, to a concern with "activities," such as the act of representing. Such activities are often bodily, and are often world-involving in their nature. A version of the problem of intentionality formulated so as to apply to them—"In virtue of what is activity A the representation of C?"—seems hardly pressing at all. Rather, what cries out for discussion is the question of just what forms these activities take, and just how they bring about the effects they do. (Wilson, this volume, p. 183)

This defuses the coupling constitution error and the problem of underived content of Adams and Aizawa and discussed by Hurley. Instead Wilson echoes Sutton's call (this volume) for a more interdisciplinary approach to the study of cognitive practices.

The task is to understand a variety of representational practices, and wherein they are representational. The means we employ in doing so will be various: historical analysis of their emergence, sociological analysis of the conditions under which they operate, experimental psychological analysis of representational gaps and gluts, anthropological analysis of practices of symbolization, evolutionary analysis of social environments and our sensitivity to them. (Wilson, this volume, p. 183)

Sutton helpfully distinguishes between a first wave of arguments for the extended mind and a second wave. The first wave is based on the parity principle, where external processes "function in the same way as do unquestionably cognitive processes in the head" (this volume, p. 193). The second wave is based on what Sutton calls the complementarity principle, where external processes and vehicles can be radically unlike internal ones. Exograms (external memories) can have different properties and play different roles from engrams (internal memories); but nevertheless engrams and exograms can make complementary contributions to cognitive processes (this is what Menary calls *integration*).

Sutton indicates that in the move from parity-based to complementarity approaches there are yet some problems to be superseded. Menary (chapter 10) also attempts to begin this process, by specifying different cognitive activities, one of which, cognitive practices, is defined in terms of the normative practice of manipulating external representations to complete cognitive tasks. He indicates (in a similar way to Hurley) that there are two ways in which extension, or integration, can happen: one involves integration through sensorimotor activity, the other through the manipulation of external representations. What Menary adds to the discussion is the importance of normativity for any account of extension/integration, whether it is primarily biological or biocultural.

Wheeler (chapter 11) argues that the extended mind is a kind of extended functionalism. Wheeler points out that the extended mind is not simply a weak claim about the causal dependence of some cognition on external factors (cf. Adams and Aizawa's coupling-constitution fallacy). It is a stronger claim involving the constitution of cognition, at least in part, by external factors. Therefore, the extended mind is not simply an embodied-embedded thesis that treats external props and tools as causally relevant features of the environment. It is a thesis that takes the bodily manipulation of external vehicles as constitutive of cognitive processes. Wheeler argues that this commits us to a functionalist account of cognition, where cognitive processes and vehicles are multiply realizable, insofar as the stuff in which the processes are realized allows for the function to be discharged. Wheeler argues that such multiple realization of functions is often found in nature, in which case, contra Adams and Aizawa, extended functionalist minds may turn out to be actual. He then goes on to argue that certain objections to the extended mind can be dealt with by providing a high-level liberal grain of functional analysis—such as that raised by Rupert (2004) and Sprevak (forthcoming).

Wheeler's extended functionalism complements the arguments of Clark (chapters 3 and 5) in giving a functionalist reading of the parity principle and showing that the extended mind is the next logical step in the development of a functionalist theory of mind. This emphasis on the functionalist credentials of the extended mind differs from the focus on activity found in the essays of Wilson, Sutton, Menary, and Rowlands (see below), who all take a more enactive approach to the extended mind, focusing on how the manipulation of environmental vehicles constitutes cognitive processes. It may turn out that a liberal functionalist account of cognition will provide a way of determining which manipulations are part of cognition and which are not, in which case there may not be any great tension between the enactive and functionalist approaches to the extended mind.

However, the details of this proposed rapprochement are yet to be worked out in any depth.

Rowlands (chapter 12) provides a way of thinking about consciousness as extended and therefore connects up with Hurley's quality-enabling externalism. He argues for an extended account of conscious states that are intentional. He argues that conscious experiences that are intentionally directed are a form of revealing or disclosing activity and that such an activity "typically straddles neural processes, bodily processes and things we do to and in the world" (this volume, p. 271). Rowlands begins this process by considering two interpretations of Frege's conception of sense: the first is sense as an intentional object, and the second is sense as determining reference. The first is Frege's claim that a sense, or thought, can be apprehended in an act of consciousness and that the act of consciousness is aimed at the sense or thought. Rowlands claims that this is analogous to the way that physical objects can be the objects of mental acts; for example, they can be perceived. However, it is the second conception of sense that is primary for Rowlands, the picking out of a referent, and it is this role of sense that can only be *shown* and not *said*—in this role, sense is not an object of apprehension. From this position Rowlands goes on to show that "what it is like to have an experience does not supervene on what is going on inside the head of a conscious subject" (this volume, p. 274). He does this by showing that there is a parallel between Fregean sense as an object of apprehension and as a determinant of reference and the mode of presentation of an intentional object[22] and a mode of presentation that enables aspects of an object to be presented. Just as the role of sense as a determinant of reference cannot itself be an object of apprehension, so the enabling role of a mode of presentation cannot itself be an aspect of experience for a subject.

The noneliminable core of intentional experience, according to Rowlands, consists in a *disclosure* or *revelation* of the world. Intentional acts disclose or reveal aspects of intentional objects at which they are directed, and it follows that this form of disclosing activity does not supervene exclusively on what is inside the head. Rowlands goes on to argue that it follows from this that consciousness is extended into the world via disclosing and revealing activities that are intentional acts.

The focus of Wilson, Menary, and Sutton on cognition as an activity, on cognitive practices, finds its corollary in Rowlands's extended account of the intentional directedness of conscious experience.

Cowley and Spurrett give an embodied account of language in terms of what they dub *utterance-activity*. Rather than think of language as a formal system of arbitrary symbols, we should think of language as developing out of utterance-activity, which is "the full range of kinetic, vocal and prosodic features of the behavior of interacting humans" (this volume, pp. 295–296). Cowley and Spurrett develop an account of how we come to be symbol-using creatures through the kind of "robust real-time embodied responsiveness" (this volume, p. 303) that the extended mind affords.

In providing some detailed examples of developmental research, they conclude that infant–caregiver dyads are examples of extended cognition at work. The caregiver provides the linguistic scaffolding for the infant in the cases that Cowley and Spurrett describe: "The types of embodied coordination noted above thus permit a particular type of extended mind, in which infant's cognitive powers are augmented by those people with whom they interact" (this volume, p. 316). Cowley and Spurrett's arguments can be usefully contrasted with Rupert's arguments that language does not extend cognition.

The essays collected together in this book present a comprehensive analysis of the hypothesis of the extended mind. Many of them provide the most recent criticisms of the position, and others move the debate in new and exciting directions. They provide reference points for a debate that is sure to continue for many years to come.

Notes

1. Henceforth, C&C. Unless otherwise noted, all page references are to the essay as reprinted in this volume.

2. See also Wheeler, this volume.

3. A clearer statement of the intuition is as follows: "But if an inner mechanism with this functionality would intuitively count as cognitive, then (skin-based prejudices aside) why not an external one?" (Clark 2005, p. 7).

4. Michael Wheeler makes this clear in his chapter in this volume, he thinks that there is longevity in the PP *only* as an articulation of EM's functionalist credentials.

5. Clark denies that this is the point of the PP in this volume, pp. 44–45.

6. See Sutton's essay in this volume for an especially clear statement of this point.

7. Or to coin an uglier word: the *decouplability*.

8. Rupert is a strong critic of the view that language extends cognition; see his essay in this volume.

9. Preston admits that the extent of this authority is a matter of debate.

10. Because Otto has Alzheimer's and has impaired biological memory, whereas Preston has a normal biological memory but still manipulates diaries and lists to remember things properly.

11. I'm inclined to think that we don't just store passive chunks of text in this way; we also construct narratives, which are retrieved as embodied enactments. Memory and belief may have narrative and embodied (or felt) structuring elements and therefore may be very different from the classical image of passive chunks of data that are stored away in memory registers to be retrieved or accessed at a later date.

12. Rupert sees the problem as involving a form of 'dependence reasoning' that is unreliable. See his essay, this volume, for further discussion and below.

13. This argument strategy is also being run by Ron Chrisley (in preparation) as a phenomenological objection to the extended mind: neuronal properties are not directly available to consciousness; nonneuronal processes are directly available to consciousness; therefore nonneuronal processes are not cognitive.

14. Ross and Ladyman note that the metaphor of the mind extending, or pushing out into the world, is similarly subject to the same metaphorical problem.

15. Noticeably, Clark takes Otto's notebook to be part of his supervenience base for beliefs because of a special form of dependence (see his essays in this volume); so if this form of dependence reasoning is unreliable, then so is the reasoning behind mind–brain supervenience.

16. A distinction that goes all the way back to Aristotle.

17. Adams and Aizawa are cagey about the extent to which a cognitive process must involve nonderived, or as they sometimes refer to it, *intrinsic* content. They do not, therefore, make the claim that cognitive processes involve only nonderived content, just that there must be some.

18. In "*Memento*'s Revenge," this volume.

19. See Menary 2006 for further discussion.

20. In "Coupling, Constitution, and the Cognitive Kind: A Reply to Adams and Aizawa," this volume.

21. This alone is reason for suspicion, argue some critics (see Rupert, this volume, and discussion above): if parts of a system are fleeting, how can they be considered as genuine parts? Won't the system be unstable and liable to break down when these parts are not present?

22. Where a mode of presentation presents an aspect of an object, such as the redness of a tomato.

References

Adams, F., and Aizawa, K. (2001). The bounds of cognition. *Philosophical Psychology, 14*, 43–64.

Blake, A., and Yuille, A. (eds.) (1992). *Active Vision*. Cambridge, MA: MIT Press.

Burge, T. (1986). Individualism and psychology. *Philosophical Review, 94*, 1, 3–45.

Clark, A. (1997). *Being There: Philosophy, Cognitive Science and Parallel Distributed Processing*. Cambridge, MA: MIT Press.

Clark, A. (2005). Intrinsic content, active memory, and the extended mind. *Analysis, 65*, 1–11.

Clark, A. (2008). *Supersizing the Mind: Embodiment, Action, and Cognitive Extension*. Oxford: Oxford University Press.

Clark, A., and Chalmers, D. (1998). The extended mind. *Analysis, 58*, 7–19.

Dartnall, T. (2005). Does the world leak into the mind? Active externalism, "internalism," and epistemology. *Cognitive Science, 29*, 135–143.

Dawkins, R. (1982). *The Extended Phenotype*. Oxford: Oxford University Press.

Menary, R. (2006). Attacking the bounds of cognition. *Philosophical Psychology, 19*, 329–344.

Menary, R. (2007). *Cognitive Integration: Mind and Cognition Unbounded*. Basingstoke: Palgrave Macmillan.

Putnam, H. (1975). *Mind, Language, and Reality*. Cambridge: Cambridge University Press.

Rowlands, M. (1999). *The Body in Mind: Understanding Cognitive Processes*. Cambridge: Cambridge University Press.

Rupert, R. (2004). Challenges to the hypothesis of extended cognition. *Journal of Philosophy, 101*, 389–428.

Sprevak, M. (forthcoming). Extended cognition and functionalism. *Journal of Philosophy*.

Ullman, S., and Richards, W. (1984). *Image Understanding*. Norwood, NJ: Ablex.

Wilson, M. (2002). Six views of embodied cognition. *Psychonomic Bulletin and Review, 9*, 625–636.

Wilson, R. A. (2004). *Boundaries of the Mind: The Individual in the Fragile Sciences: Cognition*. New York: Cambridge University Press.

2   The Extended Mind

Andy Clark and David J. Chalmers[1]

Introduction

Where does the mind stop and the rest of the world begin? The question invites two standard replies. Some accept the demarcations of skin and skull, and say that what is outside the body is outside the mind. Others are impressed by arguments suggesting that the meaning of our words "just ain't in the head," and hold that this externalism about meaning carries over into an externalism about mind. We propose to pursue a third position. We advocate a very different sort of externalism: an *active externalism*, based on the active role of the environment in driving cognitive processes.

1   Extended Cognition

Consider three cases of human problem-solving:

(1) A person sits in front of a computer screen which displays images of various two-dimensional geometric shapes and is asked to answer questions concerning the potential fit of such shapes into depicted "sockets." To assess fit, the person must mentally rotate the shapes to align them with the sockets.

(2) A person sits in front of a similar computer screen, but this time can choose either to physically rotate the image on the screen, by pressing a rotate button, or to mentally rotate the image as before. We can also suppose, not unrealistically, that some speed advantage accrues to the physical rotation operation.

(3) Sometime in the cyberpunk future, a person sits in front of a similar computer screen. This agent, however, has the benefit of a neural implant which can perform the rotation operation as fast as the computer in the previous example. The agent must still choose which internal resource to

use (the implant or the good old-fashioned mental rotation), as each resource makes different demands on attention and other concurrent brain activity.

How much *cognition* is present in these cases? We suggest that all three cases are similar. Case (3) with the neural implant seems clearly to be on a par with case (1). And case (2) with the rotation button displays the same sort of computational structure as case (3), although it is distributed across agent and computer instead of internalized within the agent. If the rotation in case (3) is cognitive, by what right do we count case (2) as fundamentally different? We cannot simply point to the skin/skull boundary as justification, since the legitimacy of that boundary is precisely what is at issue. But nothing else seems different.

The kind of case just described is by no means as exotic as it may at first appear. It is not just the presence of advanced external computing resources which raises the issue, but rather the general tendency of human reasoners to lean heavily on environmental supports. Thus consider the use of pen and paper to perform long multiplication (McClelland, Rumelhart, and Hinton 1986; Clark 1989), the use of physical rearrangements of letter tiles to prompt word recall in Scrabble (Kirsh 1995), the use of instruments such as the nautical slide rule (Hutchins 1995), and the general paraphernalia of language, books, diagrams, and culture. In all these cases the individual brain performs some operations, while others are delegated to manipulations of external media. Had our brains been different, this distribution of tasks would doubtless have varied.

In fact, even the mental rotation cases described in scenarios (1) and (2) are real. The cases reflect options available to players of the computer game Tetris. In Tetris, falling geometric shapes must be rapidly directed into an appropriate slot in an emerging structure. A rotation button can be used. David Kirsh and Paul Maglio (1994) calculate that the physical rotation of a shape through 90 degrees takes about 100 milliseconds, plus about 200 milliseconds to select the button. To achieve the same result by mental rotation takes about 1,000 milliseconds. Kirsh and Maglio go on to present compelling evidence that physical rotation is used not just to position a shape ready to fit a slot, but often to help *determine* whether the shape and the slot are compatible. The latter use constitutes a case of what Kirsh and Maglio call an "epistemic action." *Epistemic* actions alter the world so as to aid and augment cognitive processes such as recognition and search. Merely *pragmatic* actions, by contrast, alter the world because some physical change is desirable for its own sake (e.g., putting cement into a hole in a dam).

Epistemic action, we suggest, demands spread of *epistemic credit*. If, as we confront some task, a part of the world functions as a process which, *were it done in the head*, we would have no hesitation in recognizing as part of the cognitive process, then that part of the world *is* (so we claim) part of the cognitive process. Cognitive processes ain't (all) in the head!

2 Active Externalism

In these cases, the human organism is linked with an external entity in a two-way interaction, creating a *coupled system* that can be seen as a cognitive system in its own right. All the components in the system play an active causal role, and they jointly govern behavior in the same sort of way that cognition usually does. If we remove the external component the system's behavioral competence will drop, just as it would if we removed part of its brain. Our thesis is that this sort of coupled process counts equally well as a cognitive process, whether or not it is wholly in the head.

This externalism differs greatly from standard variety advocated by Putnam (1975) and Burge (1979). When I believe that water is wet and my twin believes that twin water is wet, the external features responsible for the difference in our beliefs are distal and historical, at the other end of a lengthy causal chain. Features of the *present* are not relevant: if I happen to be surrounded by XYZ right now (maybe I have teleported to Twin Earth), my beliefs still concern standard water, because of my history. In these cases, the relevant external features are *passive*. Because of their distal nature, they play no role in driving the cognitive process in the here-and-now. This is reflected by the fact that the actions performed by me and my twin are physically indistinguishable, despite our external differences.

In the cases we describe, by contrast, the relevant external features are *active*, playing a crucial role in the here-and-now. Because they are coupled with the human organism, they have a direct impact on the organism and on its behavior. In these cases, the relevant parts of the world are *in the loop*, not dangling at the other end of a long causal chain. Concentrating on this sort of coupling leads us to an *active externalism*, as opposed to the passive externalism of Putnam and Burge.

Many have complained that even if Putnam and Burge are right about the externality of content, it is not clear that these external aspects play a causal or explanatory role in the generation of action. In counterfactual cases where internal structure is held constant but these external features are changed, behavior looks just the same; so internal structure seems to be doing the crucial work. We will not adjudicate that issue here, but we note that active externalism is not threatened by any such problem. The external features in a coupled system play an ineliminable role—if we retain internal structure but change the external features, behavior may change completely. The external features here are just as causally relevant as typical internal features of the brain.[2]

By embracing an active externalism, we allow a more natural explanation of all sorts of actions. One can explain my choice of words in Scrabble, for example, as the outcome of an extended cognitive process involving the rearrangement of tiles on my tray. Of course, one could always try to explain my action in terms of internal processes and a long series of "inputs" and "actions," but this explanation would be needlessly complex. If an isomorphic process were going on in the head, we would feel no urge to characterize it in this cumbersome way.[3] In a very real sense, the rearrangement of tiles on the tray is not part of action; it is part of *thought*.

The view we advocate here is reflected by a growing body of research in cognitive science. In areas as diverse as the theory of situated cognition (Suchman 1987), studies of real-world robotics (Beer 1989), dynamical approaches to child development (Thelen and Smith 1994), and research on the cognitive properties of collectives of agents (Hutchins 1995), cognition is often taken to be continuous with processes in the environment.[4] Thus, in seeing cognition as extended one is not merely making a terminological decision; it makes a significant difference to the methodology of scientific investigation. In effect, explanatory methods that might once have been thought appropriate only for the analysis of "inner" processes are now being adapted for the study of the outer, and there is promise that our understanding of cognition will become richer for it.

Some find this sort of externalism unpalatable. One reason may be that many identify the cognitive with the conscious, and it seems far from plausible that consciousness extends outside the head in these cases. But not every cognitive process, at least on standard usage, is a conscious process. It is widely accepted that all sorts of processes beyond the borders of consciousness play a crucial role in cognitive processing: in the retrieval of memories, linguistic processes, and skill acquisition, for example. So the mere fact that external processes are external where consciousness is internal is no reason to deny that those processes are cognitive.

More interestingly, one might argue that what keeps real cognition processes in the head is the requirement that cognitive processes be *portable*. Here, we are moved by a vision of what might be called the Naked Mind: a package of resources and operations we can always bring to bear on a cognitive task, regardless of the local environment. On this view, the trouble with coupled systems is that they are too easily *decoupled*. The true cognitive processes are those that lie at the constant core of the system; anything else is an add-on extra.

There is something to this objection. The brain (or brain and body) comprises a package of basic, portable, cognitive resources that is of interest in its own right. These resources may incorporate bodily actions into cognitive processes, as when we use our fingers as working memory in a tricky calculation, but they will not encompass the more contingent aspects of our external environment, such as a pocket calculator. Still, mere contingency of coupling does not rule out cognitive status. In the distant future we may be able to plug various modules into our brain to help us out: a module for extra short-term memory when we need it, for example. When a module is plugged in, the processes involving it are just as cognitive as if they had been there all along.[5]

Even if one were to make the portability criterion pivotal, active externalism would not be undermined. Counting on our fingers has already been let in the door, for example, and it is easy to push things further. Think of the old image of the engineer with a slide rule hanging from his belt wherever he goes. What if people always carried a pocket calculator, or had them implanted? The real moral of the portability intuition is that for coupled systems to be relevant to the core of cognition, *reliable* coupling is required. It happens that most reliable coupling takes place within the brain, but there can easily be reliable coupling with the environment as well. If the resources of my calculator or my Filofax are always there when I need them, then they are coupled with me as reliably as we need. In effect, they are part of the basic package of cognitive resources that I bring to bear on the everyday world. These systems cannot be impugned simply on the basis of the danger of discrete damage, loss, or malfunction, or because of any occasional decoupling: the biological brain is in similar danger, and occasionally loses capacities temporarily in episodes of sleep, intoxication, and emotion. If the relevant capacities are generally there when they are required, this is coupling enough.

Moreover, it may be that the biological brain has in fact evolved and matured in ways which factor in the reliable presence of a manipulable external environment. It certainly seems that evolution has favored onboard capacities which are especially geared to parasitizing the local environment so as to reduce memory load, and even to transform the nature of the computational problems themselves. Our visual systems have evolved to rely on their environment in various ways: they exploit contingent facts about the structure of natural scenes (e.g., Ullman and Richards

1984), for example, and they take advantage of the computational short-cuts afforded by bodily motion and locomotion (e.g., Blake and Yuille 1992). Perhaps there are other cases where evolution has found it advantageous to exploit the possibility of the environment being in the cognitive loop. If so, then external coupling is part of the truly basic package of cognitive resources that we bring to bear on the world.

Language may be an example. Language appears to be a central means by which cognitive processes are extended into the world. Think of a group of people brainstorming around a table, or a philosopher who thinks best by writing, developing her ideas as she goes. It may be that language evolved, in part, to enable such extensions of our cognitive resources within actively coupled systems.

Within the lifetime of an organism, too, individual learning may have molded the brain in ways that rely on cognitive extensions that surrounded us as we learned. Language is again a central example here, as are the various physical and computational artifacts that are routinely used as cognitive extensions by children in schools and by trainees in numerous professions. In such cases the brain develops in a way that complements the external structures, and learns to play its role within a unified, densely coupled system. Once we recognize the crucial role of the environment in constraining the evolution and development of cognition, we see that extended cognition is a core cognitive process, not an add-on extra.

An analogy may be helpful. The extraordinary efficiency of the fish as a swimming device is partly due, it now seems, to an evolved capacity to couple its swimming behaviors to the pools of external kinetic energy found as swirls, eddies, and vortices in its watery environment (see Triantafyllou and Triantafyllou 1995). These vortices include both naturally occurring ones (e.g., where water hits a rock) and self-induced ones (created by well-timed tail flaps). The fish swims by building these externally occurring processes into the very heart of its locomotion routines. The fish and surrounding vortices together constitute a unified and remarkably efficient swimming machine.

Now consider a reliable feature of the human environment, such as the sea of words. This linguistic surround envelops us from birth. Under such conditions, the plastic human brain will surely come to treat such structures as a reliable resource to be factored into the shaping of on-board cognitive routines. Where the fish flaps its tail to set up the eddies and vortices it subsequently exploits, we intervene in multiple linguistic media, creating local structures and disturbances whose reliable presence drives our ongoing internal processes. Words and external symbols are thus paramount among the cognitive vortices which help constitute human thought.

3   From Cognition to Mind

So far we have spoken largely about "cognitive processing," and argued for its extension into the environment. Some might think that the conclusion has been bought too cheaply. Perhaps some *processing* takes place in the environment, but what of *mind*? Everything we have said so far is compatible with the view that truly mental states—experiences, beliefs, desires, emotions, and so on—are all determined by states of the brain. Perhaps what is truly mental is internal, after all?

We propose to take things a step further. While some mental states, such as experiences, may be determined internally, there are other cases in which external factors make a significant contribution. In particular, we will argue that *beliefs* can be constituted partly by features of the environment, when those features play the right sort of role in driving cognitive processes. If so, the mind extends into the world.

First, consider a normal case of belief embedded in memory. Inga hears from a friend that there is an exhibition at the Museum of Modern Art, and decides to go see it. She thinks for a moment and recalls that the museum is on 53rd Street, so she walks to 53rd Street and goes into the museum. It seems clear that Inga believes that the museum is on 53rd Street, and that she believed this even before she consulted her memory. It was not previously an *occurrent* belief, but then neither are most of our beliefs. The belief was sitting somewhere in memory, waiting to be accessed.

Now consider Otto. Otto suffers from Alzheimer's disease, and like many Alzheimer's patients, he relies on information in the environment to help structure his life. Otto carries a notebook around with him everywhere he goes. When he learns new information, he writes it down. When he needs some old information, he looks it up. For Otto, his notebook plays the role usually played by a biological memory. Today, Otto hears about the exhibition at the Museum of Modern Art, and decides to go see it. He consults the notebook, which says that the museum is on 53rd Street, so he walks to 53rd Street and goes into the museum.

Clearly, Otto walked to 53rd Street because he wanted to go to the museum and he believed the museum was on 53rd Street. And just as Inga had her belief even before she consulted her memory, it seems reasonable to say that Otto believed the museum was on 53rd Street even before consulting his notebook. For in relevant respects the cases are entirely analogous:

the notebook plays for Otto the same role that memory plays for Inga. The information in the notebook functions just like the information constituting an ordinary non-occurrent belief; it just happens that this information lies beyond the skin.

The alternative is to say that Otto has no belief about the matter until he consults his notebook; at best, he believes that the museum is located at the address in the notebook. But if we follow Otto around for a while, we will see how unnatural this way of speaking is. Otto is constantly using his notebook as a matter of course. It is central to his actions in all sorts of contexts, in the way that an ordinary memory is central in an ordinary life. The same information might come up again and again, perhaps being slightly modified on occasion, before retreating into the recesses of his artificial memory. To say that the beliefs disappear when the notebook is filed away seems to miss the big picture in just the same way as saying that Inga's beliefs disappear as soon as she is no longer conscious of them. In both cases the information is reliably there when needed, available to consciousness and available to guide action, in just the way that we expect a belief to be.

Certainly, insofar as beliefs and desires are characterized by their explanatory roles, Otto's and Inga's cases seem to be on a par: the essential causal dynamics of the two cases mirror each other precisely. We are happy to explain Inga's action in terms of her occurrent desire to go to the museum and her standing belief that the museum is on 53rd street, and we should be happy to explain Otto's action in the same way. The alternative is to explain Otto's action in terms of his occurrent desire to go to the museum, his standing belief that the Museum is on the location written in the notebook, and the accessible fact that the notebook says the Museum is on 53rd Street; but this complicates the explanation unnecessarily. If we must resort to explaining Otto's action this way, then we must also do so for the countless other actions in which his notebook is involved; in each of the explanations, there will be an extra term involving the notebook. We submit that to explain things this way is to take *one step too many*. It is pointlessly complex, in the same way that it would be pointlessly complex to explain Inga's actions in terms of beliefs about her memory. The notebook is a constant for Otto, in the same way that memory is a constant for Inga; to point to it in every belief/desire explanation would be redundant. In an explanation, simplicity is power.

If this is right, we can even construct the case of Twin Otto, who is just like Otto except that a while ago he mistakenly wrote in his notebook that the Museum of Modern Art was on 51st Street. Today, Twin Otto is a physical duplicate of Otto from the skin in, but his notebook differs. Consequently, Twin Otto is best characterized as believing that the museum is on 51st Street, where Otto believes it is on 53rd. In these cases, a belief is simply not in the head.

This mirrors the conclusion of Putnam and Burge, but again there are important differences. In the Putnam/Burge cases, the external features constituting differences in belief are distal and historical, so that twins in these cases produce physically indistinguishable behavior. In the cases we are describing, the relevant external features play an active role in the here-and-now, and have a direct impact on behavior. Where Otto walks to 53rd Street, Twin Otto walks to 51st. There is no question of explanatory irrelevance for this sort of external belief content; it is introduced precisely because of the central explanatory role that it plays. Like the Putnam/Burge cases, these cases involve differences in reference and truth conditions, but they also involve differences in the dynamics of *cognition*.[6]

The moral is that when it comes to belief, there is nothing sacred about skull and skin. What makes some information count as a belief is the role it plays, and there is no reason why the relevant role can be played only from inside the body.

Some will resist this conclusion. An opponent might put her foot down and insist that as she uses the term "belief," or perhaps even according to standard usage, Otto simply does not qualify as believing that the museum is on 53rd Street. We do not intend to debate what is standard usage; our broader point is that the notion of belief *ought* to be used so that Otto qualifies as having the belief in question. In all *important* respects, Otto's case is similar to a standard case of (non-occurrent) belief. The differences between Otto's case and Inga's are striking, but they are superficial. By using the "belief" notion in a wider way, it picks out something more akin to a natural kind. The notion becomes deeper and more unified, and is more useful in explanation.

To provide substantial resistance, an opponent has to show that Otto's and Inga's cases differ in some important and relevant respect. But in what deep respect are the cases different? To make the case *solely* on the grounds that information is in the head in one case but not in the other would be to beg the question. If this difference is relevant to a difference in belief, it is surely not *primitively* relevant. To justify the different treatment, we must find some more basic underlying difference between the two.

It might be suggested that the cases are relevantly different in that Inga has more *reliable* access to the information. After all, someone might take away Otto's notebook at any time, but Inga's memory is safer. It is not implausible that constancy is relevant: indeed, the fact that Otto always uses his notebook played some role in our justifying its cognitive status. If Otto were consulting a guidebook as a one-off, we would be much less likely to ascribe him a standing belief. But in the original case, Otto's access to the notebook is very reliable—not perfectly reliable, to be sure, but then neither is Inga's access to her memory. A surgeon might tamper with her brain, or more mundanely, she might have too much to drink. The mere possibility of such tampering is not enough to deny her the belief.

One might worry that Otto's access to his notebook *in fact* comes and goes. He showers without the notebook, for example, and he cannot read it when it is dark. Surely his belief cannot come and go so easily? We could get around this problem by redescribing the situation, but in any case an occasional temporary disconnection does not threaten our claim. After all, when Inga is asleep, or when she is intoxicated, we do not say that her belief disappears. What really counts is that the information is easily available when the subject needs it, and this constraint is satisfied equally in the two cases. If Otto's notebook were often unavailable to him at times when the information in it would be useful, there might be a problem, as the information would not be able to play the action-guiding role that is central to belief; but if it is easily available in most relevant situations, the belief is not endangered.

Perhaps a difference is that Inga has *better* access to the information than Otto does? Inga's "central" processes and her memory probably have a relatively high-bandwidth link between them, compared to the low-grade connection between Otto and his notebook. But this alone does not make a difference between believing and not believing. Consider Inga's museum-going friend Lucy, whose biological memory has only a low-grade link to her central systems, due to nonstandard biology or past misadventures. Processing in Lucy's case might be less efficient, but as long as the relevant information is accessible, Lucy clearly believes that the museum is on 53rd Street. If the connection was too indirect—if Lucy had to struggle hard to retrieve the information with mixed results, or a psychotherapist's aid were needed—we might become more reluctant to ascribe the belief, but such cases are well beyond Otto's situation, in which the information is easily accessible.

Another suggestion could be that Otto has access to the relevant information only by *perception*, whereas Inga has more direct access—by introspection, perhaps. In some ways, however, to put things this way is to beg the question. After all, we are in effect advocating a point of view on which Otto's internal processes and his notebook constitute a single cognitive system. From the standpoint of this system, the flow of information between notebook and brain is not perceptual at all; it does not involve the impact of something outside the system. It is more akin to information flow within the brain. The only deep way in which the access is perceptual is that in Otto's case, there is a distinctly perceptual phenomenology associated with the retrieval of the information, whereas in Inga's case there is not. But why should the nature of an associated phenomenology make a difference to the status of a belief? Inga's memory may have some associated phenomenology, but it is still a belief. The phenomenology is not visual, to be sure. But for visual phenomenology consider the Terminator, from the Arnold Schwarzenegger movie of the same name. When he recalls some information from memory, it is "displayed" before him in his visual field (presumably he is conscious of it, as there are frequent shots depicting his point of view). The fact that standing memories are recalled in this unusual way surely makes little difference to their status as standing beliefs.

These various small differences between Otto's and Inga's cases are all *shallow* differences. To focus on them would be to miss the way in which for Otto, notebook entries play just the sort of role that beliefs play in guiding most people's lives.

Perhaps the intuition that Otto's is not a true belief comes from a residual feeling that the only true beliefs are occurrent beliefs. If we take this feeling seriously, Inga's belief will be ruled out too, as will many beliefs that we attribute in everyday life. This would be an extreme view, but it may be the most consistent way to deny Otto's belief. Upon even a slightly less extreme view—the view that a belief must be *available* for consciousness, for example—Otto's notebook entry seems to qualify just as well as Inga's memory. Once dispositional beliefs are let in the door, it is difficult to resist the conclusion that Otto's notebook has all the relevant dispositions.

4   Beyond the Outer Limits

If the thesis is accepted, how far should we go? All sorts of puzzle cases spring to mind. What of the amnesic villagers in *100 Years of Solitude*, who forget the names for everything and so hang labels everywhere? Does the information in my Filofax count as part of my memory? If Otto's notebook has been tampered with, does he believe the newly installed information? Do I believe the contents of the page in front of me before I read it? Is my cognitive state somehow spread across the Internet?

We do not think that there are categorical answers to all of these questions, and we will not give them. But to help understand what is involved in ascriptions of extended belief, we can at least examine the features of our central case that make the notion so clearly applicable there. First, the notebook is a constant in Otto's life—in cases where the information in the notebook would be relevant, he will rarely take action without consulting it. Second, the information in the notebook is directly available without difficulty. Third, upon retrieving information from the notebook he automatically endorses it. Fourth, the information in the notebook has been consciously endorsed at some point in the past, and indeed is there as a consequence of this endorsement.[7] The status of the fourth feature as a criterion for belief is arguable (perhaps one can acquire beliefs through subliminal perception, or through memory tampering?), but the first three features certainly play a crucial role.

Insofar as increasingly exotic puzzle cases lack these features, the applicability of the notion of "belief" gradually falls off. If I rarely take relevant action without consulting my Filofax, for example, its status within my cognitive system will resemble that of the notebook in Otto's. But if I often act without consultation—for example, if I sometimes answer relevant questions with "I don't know"—then information in it counts less clearly as part of my belief system. The Internet is likely to fail on multiple counts, unless I am unusually computer-reliant, facile with the technology, and trusting, but information in certain files on my computer may qualify. In intermediate cases, the question of whether a belief is present may be indeterminate, or the answer may depend on the varying standards that are at play in various contexts in which the question might be asked. But any indeterminacy here does not mean that in the central cases, the answer is not clear.

What about socially extended cognition? Could my mental states be partly constituted by the states of other thinkers? We see no reason why not, in principle. In an unusually interdependent couple, it is entirely possible that one partner's beliefs will play the same sort of role for the other as the notebook plays for Otto.[8] What is central is a high degree of trust, reliance, and accessibility. In other social relationships these criteria may not be so clearly fulfilled, but they might nevertheless be fulfilled in specific domains. For example, the waiter at my favorite restaurant might act as a repository of my beliefs about my favorite meals (this might even be construed as a case of extended desire). In other cases, one's beliefs might be embodied in one's secretary, one's accountant, or one's collaborator.[9]

In each of these cases, the major burden of the coupling between agents is carried by language. Without language, we might be much more akin to discrete Cartesian "inner" minds, in which high-level cognition relies largely on internal resources. But the advent of language has allowed us to spread this burden into the world. Language, thus construed, is not a mirror of our inner states but a complement to them. It serves as a tool whose role is to extend cognition in ways that on-board devices cannot. Indeed, it may be that the intellectual explosion in recent evolutionary time is due as much to this linguistically enabled extension of cognition as to any independent development in our inner cognitive resources.

What, finally, of the self? Does the extended mind imply an extended self? It seems so. Most of us already accept that the self outstrips the boundaries of consciousness; my dispositional beliefs, for example, constitute in some deep sense part of who I am. If so, then these boundaries may also fall beyond the skin. The information in Otto's notebook, for example, is a central part of his identity as a cognitive agent. What this comes to is that Otto *himself* is best regarded as an extended system, a coupling of biological organism and external resources. To consistently resist this conclusion, we would have to shrink the self into a mere bundle of occurrent states, severely threatening its deep psychological continuity. Far better to take the broader view, and see agents themselves as spread into the world.

As with any reconception of ourselves, this view will have significant consequences. There are obvious consequences for philosophical views of the mind and for the methodology of research in cognitive science, but there will also be effects in the moral and social domains. It may be, for example, that in some cases interfering with someone's environment will have the same moral significance as interfering with their person. And if the view is taken seriously, certain forms of social activity might be reconceived as less akin to communication and action, and as more akin to thought. In any case, once the hegemony of skin and skull is usurped, we may be able to see ourselves more truly as creatures of the world.

Notes

This essay was originally published in *Analysis* 58 (1998): 10–23. Reprinted in P. Grim (ed.), *The Philosopher's Annual*, vol. 21 (1998); reprinted in D. Chalmers (ed.), *Philosophy of Mind: Classical and Contemporary Readings* (Oxford University Press, 2002).

1. The authors are listed in order of degree of belief in the central thesis.

2. Much of the appeal of externalism in the philosophy of mind may stem from the intuitive appeal of active externalism. Externalists often make analogies involving external features in coupled systems, and appeal to the arbitrariness of boundaries between brain and environment. But these intuitions sit uneasily with the letter of standard externalism. In most of the Putnam/Burge cases, the immediate environment is irrelevant; only the historical environment counts. Debate has focused on the question of whether mind must be in the head, but a more relevant question in assessing these examples might be: is mind in the present?

3. Herbert Simon (1981) once suggested that we view internal memory as, in effect, an external resource upon which "real" inner processes operate. "Search in memory," he comments, "is not very different from search of the external environment." Simon's view at least has the virtue of treating internal and external processing with the parity they deserve, but we suspect that on his view the mind will shrink too small for most people's tastes.

4. Philosophical views of a similar spirit can be found in Haugeland 1995, McClamrock 1995, Varela, Thompson, and Rosch 1991, and Wilson 1994.

5. Or consider the following passage from a fairly recent science fiction novel (McHugh 1992, p. 213): "I am taken to the system's department where I am attuned to the system. All I do is jack in and then a technician instructs the system to attune and it does. I jack out and query the time. 10:52. The information pops up. Always before I could only access information when I was jacked in, it gave me a sense that I knew what I thought and what the system told me, but now, how do I know what is system and what is Zhang?"

6. In the terminology of Chalmers's "The Components of Content" (2002): the twins in the Putnam/Burge cases differ only in their *relational* content, but Otto and his twin can be seen to differ in their *notional* content, which is the sort of content that governs cognition. Notional content is generally internal to a cognitive system, but in this case the cognitive system is itself effectively extended to include the notebook.

7. The constancy and past-endorsement criteria may suggest that history is partly constitutive of belief. One might react to this by removing any historical component (giving a purely dispositional reading of the constancy criterion and eliminating the past-endorsement criterion, for example), or one might allow such a component as long as the main burden is carried by features of the present.

8. Might this sort of reasoning also allow something like Burge's extended "arthritis" beliefs? After all, I might always defer to my doctor in taking relevant actions concerning my disease. Perhaps so, but there are some clear differences. For example, any extended beliefs would be grounded in an existing active relationship with the doctor, rather than in a historical relationship to a language community. And on the current analysis, my deference to the doctor would tend to yield something

like a true belief that I have some other disease in my thigh, rather than the false belief that I have arthritis there. On the other hand, if I used medical experts solely as terminological consultants, the results of Burge's analysis might be mirrored.

9. From the *New York Times*, March 30, 1995, p. B7, in an article on former UCLA basketball coach John Wooden: "Wooden and his wife attended 36 straight Final Fours, and she invariably served as his memory bank. Nell Wooden rarely forgot a name—her husband rarely remembered one—and in the standing-room-only Final Four lobbies, she would recognize people for him."

References

Beer, R. (1989). *Intelligence as Adaptive Behavior*. New York: Academic Press.

Blake, A., and Yuille, A. (eds.) (1992). *Active Vision*. Cambridge, MA: MIT Press.

Burge, T. (1979). Individualism and the mental. *Midwest Studies in Philosophy, 4*, 73–122.

Chalmers, D. J. (2002). The components of content. In David J. Chalmers (ed.), *Philosophy of Mind: Classical and Contemporary Readings*. Oxford: Oxford University Press.

Clark, A. (1989). *Microcognition*. Cambridge, MA: MIT Press.

Haugeland, J. (1995). Mind embodied and embedded. In Y. Houng and J. Ho (eds.), *Mind and Cognition*. Taipei: Academia Sinica.

Hutchins, E. (1995). *Cognition in the Wild*. Cambridge, MA: MIT Press.

Kirsh, D. (1995). The intelligent use of space. *Artificial Intelligence, 73*, 31–68.

Kirsh, D., and Maglio, P. (1994). On distinguishing epistemic from pragmatic action. *Cognitive Science, 18*, 513–549.

McClamrock, R. (1995). *Existential Cognition*. Chicago: University of Chicago Press.

McClelland, J. L., Rumelhart, D. E., and Hinton, G. E. (1986). The appeal of parallel distributed processing. In J. L. McClelland, D. E. Rumelhart, and PDP Research Group, *Parallel Distributed Processing* (vol. 2). Cambridge, MA: MIT Press.

McHugh, M. (1992). *China Mountain Zhang*. New York: Tom Doherty Associates.

Putnam, H. (1975). The meaning of "meaning." In K. Gunderson (ed.), *Language, Mind, and Knowledge*. Minneapolis: University of Minnesota Press.

Simon, H. (1981). *The Sciences of the Artificial*. Cambridge, MA: MIT Press.

Suchman, L. (1987). *Plans and Situated Actions*. Cambridge: Cambridge University Press.

Thelen, E. and Smith, L. (1994). *A Dynamic Systems Approach to the Development of Cognition and Action.* Cambridge, MA: MIT Press.

Triantafyllou, M., and Triantafyllou, G. (1995). An efficient swimming machine. *Scientific American, 272*(3), 64–70.

Ullman, S., and Richards, W. (1984). *Image Understanding.* Norwood, NJ: Ablex.

Varela, F., Thompson, E., and Rosch, E. (1991). *The Embodied Mind.* Cambridge, MA: MIT Press.

Wilson, R. (1994). Wide computationalism. *Mind, 103,* 351–372.

3   *Memento*'s Revenge: The Extended Mind, Extended

Andy Clark

In the movie *Memento*, the hero, Leonard, suffers from a form of antero-grade amnesia that results in an inability to lay down new memories. Nonetheless, he sets out on a quest to find his wife's killer, aided by the use of notes, annotated polaroids, and (for the most important pieces of information obtained) body tattoos. Using these resources he attempts to build up a stock of new beliefs and to thus piece together the puzzle of his wife's death. At one point in the movie, a character exasperated by Leonard's lack of biological recall shouts:

"*You* know? What do *you* know. *You* don't know anything. In ten minutes' time *you* won't even know you had this conversation!"

Leonard, however, believes that he does, day by day, come to know new things. But only courtesy of those photos, tattoos, tricks and ploys. Who is right?

These are the kinds of question addressed at length in the essay (coau-thored with David Chalmers) "'The Extended Mind'" (1998 and this volume). Is the mind contained (always? sometimes? never?) in the head? Or does the notion of thought allow mental processes (including believings) to inhere in extended systems of body, brain, and aspects of the local environment? The answer, we claimed, was that mental states, including states of believing, could be grounded in physical traces that remained firmly outside the head. As long as a few simple conditions were met (more on which below), Leonard's notes and tattoos could indeed count as new additions to his store of long-term knowledge and dispositional belief.

In the present treatment I revisit this argument, defending our strong conclusion against a variety of subsequent observations and objections. In particular, I look at objections that rely on a contrast between the (puta-tively) intrinsic content of neural symbols and the merely derived content of external inscriptions, at objections concerning the demarcation of scientific domains via natural kinds, and at objections concerning the ultimate locus of agentive control and the nature of perception versus introspection. I also mention a possible alternative interpretation of the argument as (in effect) a reductio of the very idea of the mind as an object of scientific study. This is an interesting proposal, but one whose full evaluation must be left for another time.

First, though, it will help to briefly review the original argument from Clark and Chalmers (1998 and this volume).

1 Tetris and Otto

Two examples animated the original essay. The first involved a human agent playing the arcade game Tetris. The human player has the option of identifying the falling pieces (1) by mental rotation or (2) by the use of the onscreen button that causes the falling zoid to rotate. Now imagine (3) a future human with both normal imaginative rotation capacities and also a retinal display that can fast-rotate the image on demand, just like using the rotate button. Imagine too that to initiate this latter action the future human issues a thought command straight from motor cortex.[1]

Now let us pump our intuitions. Case (1) looks, we argue, to be a simple case of mental rotation. Case (2) looks like a simple case of nonmental (merely external) rotation. Yet case (3) now looks hard to classify. By hypothesis, the computational operations involved are the same as in case (2). Yet our intuitions seem far less clear. But now add the Martian player (case 4) whose natural cognitive equipment includes (for obscure ecological reasons) the kind of biotechnological fast-rotate machinery imagined in case (3). In the Martian case, we would have no hesitation in classifying the fast rotations as a species of mental rotation.

With this thought experiment as a springboard, we offered a parity principle as a rule of thumb:

The Parity Principle
If, as we confront some task, a part of the world functions as a process which, were it to go on in the head, we would have no hesitation in accepting as part of the cognitive process, then that part of the world is (for that time) part of the cognitive process.[2]

The parity principle invites us to treat the players' use of the external rotate button, the cyberpunk implant, and the Martian native endowment as all on a cognitive par. But of course there are differences. Most strikingly, in case (2) the fast-rotate circuitry is located outside the head and the results are read in by perception, whereas in cases (3) and (4) the circuitry is all bounded by skin and skull and the results are read off by introspection. I return to these issues below. Nonetheless there remained, we argued, at least a prima facie case for parity of treatment based on the deep computational commonalities rather than simple prejudices about skin and skull, inner and outer. The most important difference, we felt, concerned not the arbitrary barriers of skin and skull, or the delicate (and potentially question-begging) call between perception and introspection, but the more basic functional issues of portability and general availability for use. The standard player's use of the fast-rotate button is limited by the availability of the Tetris console, whereas the cyberpunk and Martian players exploit a resource that is part of the general equipment with which they confront the world.

Taking the argument one step further, we then considered a second example, one designed to address the portability issue and to extend the treatment to the more central case of an agent's beliefs about the world. This was the case of Otto and Inga.

Inga hears of an intriguing exhibition at MoMA (the Museum of Modern Art in New York). She thinks, recalls it's on 53rd Street, and sets off. Otto suffers from a mild form of Alzheimer's, and as a result he always carries a thick notebook. When Otto learns useful new information, he always writes it in the notebook. He hears of the exhibition at MoMA, retrieves the address from his trusty notebook and sets off. Just like Inga, we claimed, Otto walked to 53rd Street because he *wanted* to go to the museum and *believed (even before consulting his notebook)* that it was on 53rd Street. The functional poise of the stored information was, in each case, sufficiently similar (we argued) to warrant similarity of treatment. Otto's long-term beliefs just weren't all in his head.

In the paper we showed, in detail, why this was not equivalent to the more familiar Putnam/Burge-style externalism, arguing that what was at issue was more like an environmentally extended case of narrow content than a case of broad content. The idea was that the causally active physical vehicles of content and of cognitive processes could be spread across the biological organism and the world. This was quite different, we claimed, from any form of passive, reference-based externalism.

Further, we allowed that (as far as our argument was concerned) conscious mental states might well turn out to supervene only on local processes inside the head. But insofar as the scope of the mental is held to outrun that of conscious, occurrent contents (to include, for example, my long-term dispositional beliefs as well as my current conscious believings) there was no reason to restrict the physical vehicles of such nonconscious mental states to states of the brain or central nervous system.

In response to the more serious (in our opinion) concerns about availability and portability, we offered a rough-and-ready set of additional criteria to be met by nonbiological candidates for inclusion into an individual's cognitive system. They were:

1. That the resource be reliably available and typically invoked. (Otto always carries the notebook and won't answer that he "doesn't know" until after he has consulted it).
2. That any information thus retrieved be more or less automatically endorsed. It should not usually be subject to critical scrutiny (unlike the opinions of other people, for example). It should be deemed about as trustworthy as something retrieved clearly from biological memory.
3. That information contained in the resource should be easily accessible as and when required.

Applying the three criteria yielded, we claimed, a modestly intuitive set of results for putative individual cognitive extensions. A book in my home library would not count. The cyberpunk implant would. Mobile access to Google would not (it would fail condition (2)). Otto's notebook would. Other people typically would not (but could in rare cases)—and so on.

There is one reply which we consider in the essay that I choose to repeat here, just because it is still the most common response to our story. I call it the Otto two-step, and it goes like this:

all Otto actually believes (in advance) is that the address is in the notebook. That's the belief (step 1) that leads to the looking (step 2) that then leads to the (new) belief about the actual street address.

Despite its initial plausibility, we do not think this can work. Suppose we now ask why we do not depict Inga in similar terms? Why don't we say that Inga's only antecedent belief was that the information was stored in her memory, and depict her retrieval as an Inga two-step?

Intuitively, the reason seems to be that in the case of Inga, the two-step model adds spurious complexity: "Inga wanted to go to MoMA. She believed that her memory held the address. Her memory yielded 53rd Street. . . ." What's more, it seems likely that in the normal course of events Inga relies on no beliefs about her memory as such. She just uses it, transparently as it were. But *ditto* (we may suppose) for Otto: Otto is so used to using the book that he accesses it automatically when bio-memory fails. It is transparent equipment for him, just as biological memory is for Inga. And in each case, it adds needless and psychologically unreal complexity to introduce additional beliefs about the book or biological memory into the explanatory equations.

In the original essay we consider a few variants on this theme, but all go the same way in the end. Inga's biological memory systems, working together, govern *her* behaviors in the functional ways distinctive of believing. Otto's biotechnological matrix (the organism and the notebook) governs his behavior in the same sort of way. So the explanatory apparatus of mental state ascription gets an equal grip in each case, and what looks at first like Otto's action (looking up the notebook) emerges as part of Otto's thought. Mind, we conclude, is congenitally predisposed to seep out into the world.

2   Intrinsic Content

Adams and Aizawa (2001) present a variety of considerations meant to undermine a position they dub "transcranialism," the view that "cognitive processes extend in the physical world beyond the bounds of the brain and the body" (Adams and Aizawa 2001, p. 43). This is a view they associate, in varying degrees, with the work of Merlin Donald, Daniel Dennett, Ed Hutchins, and Clark and Chalmers. While conceding that transcranialism is "logically and nomologically possible" (and might thus be true of, for example, some alien species on a different planet), they maintain that it is false in the case of human cognition. They thus opt for a "contingent intracranialism about the cognitive" (ibid.).

At the top of their list of reasons for this oddly mixed judgment is that in the human case (though not, presumably, in some imaginable alien case) the external media (Adams and Aizawa focus almost entirely on simple external symbolic media such as Otto's notepad) support only *derived* content. Inner symbols, on the other hand, are said to have *intrinsic* content. Thus we read that:

strings of symbols on the printed page mean what they do in virtue of conventional associations. . . . The representational capacity of orthography is in this way derived from the representational capacities of cognitive agents. By contrast, the cognitive states in normal cognitive agents do not derive their meanings from conventions or social practices. (Ibid., p. 48)

And later on:

Whatever is responsible for non-derived representations seems to find a place only in brains. (Ibid., p. 63)

Suppose we grant, for the sake of argument, something I am actually fundamentally inclined to doubt, namely, that there is a clear and distinct sense in which neural representations get to enjoy "intrinsic contents" of some special kind, quite unlike the kinds of content that figure in external inscriptions. The most obvious way to unpack this, still following Adams and Aizawa, is in terms of a fundamental distinction between inscriptions whose meaning is conventionally determined and states of affairs (e.g., neural states) whose meaning-bearing features are thus not parasitic. The question is, must everything that is to count as part of an individual's mental processing be composed solely and exclusively of states of affairs of this latter (intrinsically content-bearing) kind? I see no reason to think that they must.

For example, suppose we are busy (as part of some problem-solving routine) imagining a set of Venn diagrams/Euler circles in our mind's eye. Surely the set-theoretic meaning of the overlaps between, say, two intersecting Euler circles is a matter of convention. Yet this image can clearly feature as part of a genuinely cognitive process.

To this, Adams and Aizawa might reply as follows: "Ah, but the image, when understood, must be triggering neural goings-on with intrinsic content: and it is in that that the understanding eventually consists." But so what? When Otto reads the notebook, neural goings-on with intrinsic content are likewise triggered. To which (perhaps) the reply is: "OK, but what about before that, when the inscription is simply in the notebook? Surely Inga's stored beliefs must continuously have intrinsic content too, not just her occurrent ones."

Now, this is a harder question, and one which might even begin to suggest the ultimate fragility of the very idea of intrinsic content. But we can sidestep that discussion with a simple thought experiment that builds on the original parity principle rehearsed in section 1. What if we found Martians whose biological routines stored *bitmapped images* of printed words that they could later access (and interpret) via bitmapped signals sent to visual cortex? Surely we would have no hesitation in embracing that kind of bitmapped storage as part of the Martian system? It is not unlike, in fact, the case of those human memory masters who are able to recall a passage from a text by first recalling, then imaginatively inspecting, a photolike image of the original page.

In light of all this, the fair demand is (at most) that we should somehow link those stored representations whose contents are derived (conventionally) to ones whose contents, at least when occurrent, are "intrinsic" (by whatever standards of intrinsicness Adams and Aizawa imagine may prevail). But such linking can be (and is) routinely achieved for representations stored outside the head. The inscriptions in Otto's notebook, I conclude, can be properly poised in any larger cognitive economy that includes states with intrinsic content.

In fact, after a long discussion of all this, Adams and Aizawa actually concede that:

Having argued that, in general, there must be non-derived content in cognitive processes, it must be admitted that it is unclear to what extent every cognitive state of each cognitive process must involve non-derived content. (Adams and Aizawa 2001, p. 50)

At which point there is really no case (concerning intrinsic content) left to answer.

3 Scientific Kinds and Functional Similarity

In the same paper, Adams and Aizawa also raise a very different kind of worry. This concerns the nature and feasibility of the scientific enterprise implied by taking transcranialism seriously. The worry, in its simplest form, is that "science tries to carve nature at its joints" (Adams and Aizawa 2001, p. 51). But (they argue) the various types of neural and extraneural goings-on that the trancranialist lumps together as "cognitive" seem to have little or nothing in common by way of underlying causal processes. The causal arrangements whereby external stuff contributes to considered action look to be very different to those whereby internal stuff does. As a result, the argument continues, there can be no unified science of the extended mind. Better, then, to keep the domains apart and settle for a unified science of the inner (properly mental) goings-on, and another science (or sciences) of the (nonmental) rest.

To make this concrete, we are invited to consider the process that physically rotates the image on the Tetris screen. This, they correctly note, is nothing like any neural process. It involves firing electrons at a cathode ray tube! It requires muscular activity to operate the button. Similarly, "Otto's extended 'memory recall' involves cognitive-motor processing not found in Inga's memory recall" (Adams and Aizawa 2001, p. 55). And so on. More generally, they suggest, just look at the range of human memory augmenting technologies (photo albums, tattoos [for Memento], rolodexes, palm pilots, notepads, and the like):

what are the chances of there being interesting regularities that cover humans interacting with all these sorts of things? Slim to none, we speculate. (Ibid., p. 61)

By contrast, biological memory systems are said to

display a number of what appear to be law-like regularities, including primacy effects, recency effects, chunking effects and others. (Ibid.)

And, unlike the biological memory processes,

transcranial [extended] processes are not likely to give rise to interesting scientific regularities. There are no laws covering humans and their tool-use over and above the laws of intercranial [inner] human cognition and the laws of the physical tools. (Ibid.)

The first thing to say in response to all this is that it is unwise to judge, from the armchair, the chances of finding "interesting scientific regularities" in any domain, be it ever so superficially diverse. Consider, for example, the recent successes of complexity theory in unearthing unifying principles that apply across massive differences of scale, physical type, and temporality. There are power laws, it now seems, that compactly explain aspects of the emergent behavior of systems ranging from the size distribution of cities to word-occurrence frequencies to the frequency of avalanches in sandpiles.

In a similar vein, it is quite possible that despite the bottom-level physical diversity of the processes that write to, and read from, Otto's notebook, and those that write to, and read from, Otto's biological memory, there is a level of description of these systems that treats them in a single unified framework (for example, how about a framework of information storage, transformation, and retrieval?). The mere fact that Adams and Aizawa can find *one* kind of systemic description at which the underlying processes look wildly different says very little, really, about the eventual prospects for an integrated scientific treatment. It is rather as if an opponent of rule and symbol models of mental processing were simply to cite the deep physical differences between brains and von Neumann computers as proof that there could be no proper science that treated processes occurring in each medium in a unified way. Or, to take a different kind of case, as if one were to conclude from the fact that chemistry and geology employ distinct vocabularies and techniques, that the burgeoning study of geochemistry is doomed from the outset. But neither of these, I presume, is a conclusion that Adams and Aizawa would wish to endorse.

The bedrock problem thus lies with the bald assertion that "the cognitive must be discriminated on the basis of underlying causal processes" (Adams and Aizawa 2001, p. 52). For it is part of the *job* of a special science to establish a framework in which superficially different phenomena can be brought under a unifying explanatory umbrella. To simply cite radical differences in some base-level physical story goes no way at all toward showing that this cannot be done. Moreover, it is by no means clear that acceptable forms of unification require that all the systemic elements behave according to the same laws. As long as there is an intelligible domain of convergence, there may be many subregularities of many different kinds involved. Think, for example, of the multiple kinds of factor and force studied by those interested in creating better home audio systems. Even if "home audio" is rejected as any kind of unified science, it certainly names a coherent and proper topic of investigation. The study of mind might, likewise, need to embrace a variety of different explanatory paradigms whose point of convergence lies in the production of intelligent behavior.

It is quite possible, after all, that the *inner* goings-on that Adams and Aizawa take to be paradigmatically cognitive themselves will turn out to be a motley crew, as far as detailed causal mechanisms go, with not even a family resemblance (at the level of actual mechanism) to hold them together. It is arguable, for example, that conscious seeing and nonconscious uses of visual input to guide fine-grained action involve radically different kinds of computational operation and representational form (Goodale and Milner 1992; Milner and Goodale 1996).

Adams and Aizawa to the contrary, some kinds of mental rehearsal (such as watching sports, or imagining typing a sentence) do seem to reinvoke distinct motor elements, whereas others (imagining a lake) do not (Decety and Grezes 1999). Some aspects of biological visual routines even use a form of table look-up (Churchland and Sejnowski 1992).

In the light of all this, my own suspicion is that the differences between external-looping (putatively cognitive) processes and purely inner ones will be *no greater than those between the inner ones themselves*. But insofar as they all form parts of a flexible and information-sensitive control system for a being capable of reasoning, of feeling, and of experiencing the world (a "sentient informavore," if you will) the motley crew of mechanisms have something important in common. It may be far less than we would require of any natural or scientific kind. But so what?

The argument-from-scientific-kinds is thus doubly flawed. It is flawed in virtue of its rather limited conception of what makes for a proper scientific or explanatory enterprise. And it is flawed in its assessment of the potential for some form of higher-level unification despite mechanistic dissimilarities. It is, above all else, a matter of empirical discovery, not armchair speculation, whether there can be a full-fledged science of the extended mind.

It is also perhaps worth noting that nascent forms of just such a science have been around for quite some time. The field of HCI (human–computer interaction) and its more recent cousins HCC (human-centered computing) and HCT (human-centered technologies) are ongoing attempts to discover unified scientific frameworks in which to treat processes occurring in (and between) biological and nonbiological information-processing media (see, e.g., Norman 1999, Rogers et al. 2002). Likewise, the existence of academic bodies such as the Cognitive Technology Society (and their excellent new journal) likewise attests to the viability of the attempt[3] to understand minds and technologies as aspects of an integrated whole.

Adams and Aizawa try to parlay the misconceived appeal to scientific kinds into a kind of dilemma. Either (the argument goes) Clark and Chalmers are radically mistaken about the causal facts or (more likely) they are closet behaviorists. On the one horn, if our claim is that "the active causal processes that extend into the environment are just like the ones found in intracranial cognition" (Adams and Aizawa 2001, p. 56), we are just plain wrong. On the other horn, if we don't care about that, and claim only that "Inga and Otto use distinct sets of capacities in order to produce similar behavior" (ibid.), then we are behaviorists.

This is surely a false dilemma. To repeat, our claim is not that the processes in Otto and Inga are identical, or even similar, in terms of their detailed implementation. It is simply that, in respect of the role that the long-term encodings play in guiding current response, both modes of storage can be seen as supporting dispositional beliefs. It is the way the information is poised to guide reasoning (such as conscious inferences that nonetheless result in no overt actions) and behavior that counts. This is not behaviorism but functionalism. It is systemic role that matters, not brute similarities in public behavior (though the two are of course related). Perhaps Adams and Aizawa believe that functionalism just *is* a species of behaviorism. If so, we plead guilty to the charge but find it less than damning.

A related concern has been raised by Terry Dartnall (pers. comm.). Dartnall worries that the plausibility of the Otto scenario depends on an outmoded image of biological memory itself: the image of biological memory as a kind of static store of information awaiting retrieval and use. This image, Dartnall claims, cannot do justice to the active nature of real memory. It is somewhat ironic, Dartnall adds, that the present author (in particular) should succumb to this temptation, given my long history of interest in, and support for, the connectionist alternative to classical (text-and rule-based) models of neural processing. By way of illustration (though the illustration may actually raise other issues too, as we shall see) he offers the following example: suppose I have a chip in my head that gives me access to a treatise on nuclear physics. That doesn't make it true that *I know* about nuclear physics. In fact, the text might even be in a language I don't understand. "Sterile text," Dartnall concludes, cannot support cognition (properly understood). In a sense, then, the claim is (once again) that text-based storage is so unlike biological memory that any claim of role-parity must fail.

This is an interesting line of objection but one that ultimately fails for reasons closely related to the discussion of intrinsic content in section 1. Certainly, biological memory is an active process. And retrieval is to a large extent reconstructive rather than literal: what we recall is influenced by our current mood, our current goals, and by information stored after the time of the original experience (Roediger and McDermott 1995; Roediger et al. 2001). It is possible, in fact, that biological memory is such an active process as to blur the line between memory systems and reasoning systems. All this I happily accept. But to repeat, our claim is not (ridiculously) that the notebook considered alone would constitute any kind of cognitive system. It would not; but in this respect it is no worse off than a single neuron, or neural population. Rather, the claim is that in the special context of the rest of Otto's information-processing economy, the notebook is co-opted into playing a real cognitive role. And the informal test for this is, just supposing some inner system provided the functionality that Otto derives from the reliable presence of the notebook, would we hesitate to classify that inner system as part of Otto's cognitive apparatus?

The reader must here rely on her own intuitions. But ours are clear. There would be no such hesitation. To cement the intuition, I considered (section 1) the Martians with their additional bitmap memories, or humans with quasi-photographic recall. To add one more case to the pot, consider now the act of rote learning. When we learn a long text by rote, we create a memory object that is in many ways unlike the standard case. For example, to recall the sixth line of the text we may have to first rehearse the others. Moreover, we can rote learn a text we do not even understand (e.g., a Latin text, in my case). Assuming that we count rote learning as the acquisition of some kind of knowledge (even in the case of the Latin text) it seems that we should not be bothered by the consequences that Dartnall unearths. The genuine differences that exist between the notebook-based storage and standard cases of biological memory do not matter, since our claim was not one of identity in the first place.

The question is how to balance the parity principle (which makes no claims about process-level identity at all, and merely identifies a state or process as cognitive) against the somewhat stronger claim of "sufficient functional similarity" that underpins treating Otto's notebook as a contributor to Otto's long-term store of dispositional beliefs. But the answer emerges as soon as we focus on the role the retrieved information will play in guiding current behavior. It is at that point (and there are, of course, all kinds of active and occurrent processing coming into play as well) that the functional similarity becomes apparent.

It is true, that which is stored in Otto's notebook won't shift and alter while stored away. It won't participate in the ongoing underground reorganizations, interpolations, and creative mergers that characterize much of biological memory. But *when called upon*, its immediate contributions to Otto's behavior still fit the profile of a stored belief. Information retrieved from the notebook will guide Otto's reasoning and behavior in the same way as information retrieved from biological memory.

The fact that *what* is retrieved may be different is unimportant here. Thus, had Otto stored the information about the color of the car in the auto accident in biological memory, he may be manipulated into a false-memory situation by a clever experimenter. The notebook storage is sufficiently different to be immune to that manipulation (though others will be possible). But the information recalled (veridical in one case but not the other) will nonetheless guide Otto's behavior (the way he answers questions and the further beliefs he forms, etc.) in exactly the same kind of way.

As a final thought hereabouts, reflect that for many years the classical "text- and rule-based" image of human cognition was widely accepted. During that time, no one (to my knowledge) thought that an implication of this was that humans were not cognizers. It might have turned out that all our memory systems operated as sterile storage, and that false memory cases and the like were all artifacts of retrieval processes. This shows, again, that there is nothing intrinsically "noncognitive" about less active forms of storage.

There is, however, a much bigger issue bubbling beneath the surface of this last discussion. It is the question of how to extend the notion of cognition and cognitive processes beyond the normal human case. Should we fix the domain of the cognitive by reference to the actual (detailed) processing profiles of normal human agents (deferring, I suppose, to our best final science of the normal human brain)? Or should we count ourselves as already commanding an understanding capable of extension to new cases?

The argument by Clark and Chalmers assumes that we do possess some such understanding, and that it is rooted, roughly speaking, in our implicit knowledge of the distinctive functional role of cognitive processes in guiding intelligent behavior. It is this knowledge that allows us to count alien processes in nonhuman animals as properly cognitive, and on which we must rely when applying the informal test embodied in the parity principle. The alternative (making everything depend on identity with processing in the normal human case) strikes us as both anthropocentric and ultimately unworkable. But this is a very large topic indeed and one that I cannot fruitfully pursue much further in the present essay (see the end of section 6 for a few additional comments).

4 On Control

Keith Butler raises the following worry:

there can be no question that the locus of computational and cognitive control resides inside the head of the subject [and involves] internal processes in a way quite distinct from the way external processes are involved. If this feature is indeed the mark of a truly cognitive system, then it is a mark by means of which the external processes Clark and Chalmers point to can be excluded. (Butler 1998, p. 205)

Butler's suggestion is that even if external elements sometimes participate in processes of control and choice (the knot in the hanky, the entry in the notebook) still it is always the biological brain that has the final say, and that here we locate the distinction that (cognitively speaking) really makes a difference. The brain is the controller and chooser of actions in a way that all that external stuff is not, and so the external stuff should not count as part of the *real* cognitive system.

In fact, there are at least two issues here. One concerns the functional poise of the neural computations, and the claim that they (alone) are the "locus of computational and cognitive control." The other concerns the nature of the processes, which are said (echoing Adams and Aizawa and Dartnall) to act "in a way quite distinct from the way external processes are involved." I think this latter worry has already been laid to rest. What of the former: the worry about ultimate choice and control?

The worry is interesting because it again highlights the deceptive ease with which critics treat the inner realm itself as scientifically unified. Thus, suppose we reapply the "locus of control" criterion *inside the head*. Do we now count as *not part of my mind or myself* any neural subsystems that are not the ultimate arbiters of action and choice? Suppose only my frontal lobes have the final say—does that shrink the real mind to just the frontal lobes? What if (as Dan Dennett sometimes suggests, most recently in Dennett 2003) no subsystem has the "final say"? Have the mind and self just disappeared?

There is a sense, I think, in which much opposition to the idea of non-biological cognitive extension trades on a deeply mistaken view of the thinking agent as some distinct inner locus of final choice and control. This is a view that I argue against at length in Clark 2003. But for now, let us simply notice that even if there *were* some distinct inner locus of final choosing, there would be no reason at all to identify that with the mind or the "cognitive agent." Thus my long-term stored knowledge is often called upon in my decision routines, but the long-term storage itself is no more an ultimate decision routine than is Otto's notebook. But (and this is the crunch) to discount all that long-term stored knowledge as partially constitutive of my mind and self is to divorce my identity as an agent from the whole body of memories and dispositional beliefs that guide and shape my behaviors. And this, I maintain, is to shrink the mind and self beyond recognition, reducing me to a mere bundle of control processes targeted on occurrent mental states.

The argument from ultimate control does not reveal the mark of the mental, or the source of the self.

5   Perception and Development

A common worry is that the role of perception, in "reading in" the information from the notebook, marks a sufficient disanalogy to discount the notebook as part of Otto's cognitive apparatus. We made a few brief comments on this issue in the original essay, noting that whether the "reading in" counts as perceptual or introspective depends, to a large extent, on how one classifies the overall case. From our perspective the systemic act is more like an act of introspection than one of perception. As a result each side is here in danger of begging the question against the other.

Thus Butler complains that:

In the world-involving cases, the subjects have to *act* in a way that demands of them that they perceive their environment [whereas Inga just introspects] . . . the very fact that the results are achieved in such remarkably different ways suggests that the explanation for one should be quite different from the explanation for the other. . . . Otto has to look at his notebook while Inga has to look at nothing. (Butler 1998, p. 211)

But from our point of view, Otto's inner processes and the notebook constitute a single, extended cognitive system. Relative to *this* system, the flow of information is wholly internal and functionally akin to introspection (for more on this, see section 6 following).

One way to try to push the argument is to seek an independent criterion for the perceptual. With this in mind, Martin Davies (pers. comm.) has suggested that it is revealing that Otto could misread his own notebook. This opening for error may, Davies suggests, make the notebook seem more like a perceived part of the external world than an aspect of the agent. But parity still prevails: Inga may misremember an event not as the result of an error in her memory store but because of some disturbance during the act of retrieval. The opening for error does not yet establish that the error is, properly speaking, perceptual. It only establishes that it occurs during retrieval.

A slight variant, again suggested by Martin Davies (pers. comm.), is that perception (unlike introspection) targets a potentially public domain. Notebooks and databases are things to which other agents could in principle have access. But (the worry goes) my beliefs are essentially the beliefs to which *I* have a special kind of access, unavailable to others.

There is, of course, something special about Otto's relation to the information in the notebook, in that (as we commented in the original essay) Otto more or less automatically endorses the contents of the notebook. Others, depending on their views of Otto, are less likely to share this perspective. But this is not a special kind of access so much as a special kind of cognitive relationship.

But why suppose that uniqueness of access is anything more than a contingent fact about standard biological recall? If, in the future, science devises a way for you to occasionally tap into my stored memories, would that make them any less *mine*, or part of my cognitive apparatus? Imagine, for that matter, a form of MPD (multiple personality disorder) in which two personalities have equal access to some early childhood memories. Here we have (at least arguably) a case where two distinct persons share access to the same memories. Of course, one may harbor all kinds of reasonable doubts about the proper way to conceptualize MPD in general. But the point is simply that it seems to be at most a contingent fact that I and I alone have a certain kind of access to my own biologically stored memories and beliefs.

Before leaving this topic, I want to briefly mention a very interesting worry raised by Ron Chrisley (pers. comm.). Chrisley notes that as a child, we do not begin by experiencing our biological memory as any kind of object or resource. This is because we do not encounter our own memory perceptually. Instead, it is just part of the apparatus through which we relate to (and experience) the world. Might it be this special developmental role that decides what is to count as part of the agent and what is to count as part of the (wider) world?

Certainly, Otto first experiences notebooks (and even his own special notebook) as objects in his world. But I am doubtful that this genuine point of disanalogy can bear the enormous weight that Chrisley's argument requires. First of all, consider the child's own bodily parts. It is quite possible, it seems to me, that these are first experienced (or at least simultaneously experienced) as objects in the child's world. The child sees its own hand. It may even want to grab the toy and be unable to control the hand well enough to do so. The relation here seems relatively "external," yet the hand is (and is from the start) a proper part of the child.

Perhaps you doubt that there is any moment at which the child's own hand is really experienced (or at any rate conceptualized) as an object for the child. But in that case we can surely imagine future nonbiological (putatively cognitive) resources being developmentally incorporated in just the same way. Such resources would be provided so early that they, too, are not first conceptualized as objects (perhaps spectacles are like this for some of us already). Contrariwise (as Chrisley himself helpfully points out), we can imagine beings who from a young age are taught to experience even their own *inner* cognitive faculties as objects, courtesy of being plugged into bio-feedback controllers and trained to monitor and control their own alpha rhythms, and so on.

The developmental point, though interesting, is thus not conceptually crucial. It points only to a complex of contingent facts about human cognition. What counts in the end, though, is the resource's current role in guiding reasoning and behavior, not its historical positioning in a developmental nexus.

6   Perception, Deception, and Contested Space

In a most interesting and constructive critique of the extended mind thesis, Kim Sterelny (2004) worries that Clark and Chalmers underplay the importance of the fact that our epistemic tools (our diaries, Filofaxes, compasses, and sextants) operate in a "common and often contested" space. By this, he means a shared space apt for sabotage and deception by other agents. As a result, when we store and retrieve information from this space, we often deploy strategies meant to guard against such deception and subversion.

More generally still, the development and functional poise of perceptual systems are, for this very reason, radically different from the development and functional poise of (biologically) internal routes of information flow. The intrusion of acts of perception into Otto's information-retrieval routine thus introduces a new set of concerns that justify us in not treating the notebook (or whatever) as a genuine part of Otto's cognitive economy.

Sterelny does not mean to deny the importance of "epistemic artifacts" (as he calls them) in turbo-charging human thought and reason. Indeed, he offers a novel and attractive coevolutionary account in which our ability to use such artifacts both depends on, and further drives, a progressive enrichment of our internal representational capacities. In this way,

Our use of epistemic artifacts explains the elaboration of mental representation in our lineage and this elaboration explains our ability to use epistemic artifacts. (Sterelny 2004, p. 241)

What he does mean to deny, however, is that the use of such artifacts reduces the load on the naked brain, and that the brain and the artifacts can coalesce into a single cognitive system. Instead, he sees increased load and a firm boundary between the biological integrated system and the array of props, tools, and storage devices suspended in public space. I tend to differ on both counts, but will here restrict my comments to the point about the boundary between the agent and the public space.

Within the biological sheath, Sterelny argues, information flow occurs between a community of cooperative and coadaptive parts that are under selection for reliability (Sterelny 2004). Over both evolutionary and developmental time, the signals within the sheath should become clearer, less noisy, and less and less in need of constant vetting for reliability and veridicality. As soon as you reach the edge of the sheath, however, things change dramatically. Perceptual systems may be highly optimized for their jobs. But it is still the case that the signals they deliver have their origins in a public space populated in part by organisms under pressure to hide their presence, to present a false appearance, or to otherwise trick and manipulate the unwary so as to increase their own fitness at the other's expense. Unlike internal monitoring, Sterelny says,

perception operates in an environment of active sabotage by other agents [and] often delivers signals that are noisy, somewhat unreliable and functionally ambiguous. (Sterelny 2004, p. 246)

One result of all this is that we are forced to develop strategies to safeguard against such deceptions and manipulations. The cat moves gingerly across the lawn and may stop and look very hard before trusting even the clear appearance of a safe passage to the other side. Though at a higher level by far, we may even deploy the tools of folk logic and consistency checking (here, Sterelny cites Sperber 2001).

The point about vulnerability to malicious manipulation is well taken. Many forms of perceptual input are indeed subject, for that very reason, to much vetting and double checking. I do not think, however, that we treat all our perceptual inputs in this highly cautious way. Moreover, *as soon as we do not do so,* the issue about extended cognitive systems seems to open up (see below). As a result, I am inclined to think that Sterelny has indeed hit on something important here, but something that may in the end be helpful, rather than harmful, to the extended mind account.

Take the well-known work on magic tricks and so-called change blindness (for a review, see Simons and Levin 1997). In a typical example of such work you might be shown a short film clip in which major alterations to the scene occur while you are attending to other matters. Often, these alterations are simply not noticed. Once they are drawn to your attention, however, it seems quite amazing that you ever missed them. The art of the stage magician, it is often remarked, depends on precisely such manipulations. We are, it seems, remarkably vulnerable to certain kinds of deception. But this, I want to suggest, may be grist for the extended mind mill. For the reason we are vulnerable in just those kinds of cases is, I would argue, because we are relying on an ecologically sound strategy of treating the external scene as a stable, reliable substitute for internally stored memory traces. In short, our brains have decided (if you will allow such loose talk for a moment) that on a day-to-day basis the chances of these kinds of espionage are sufficiently low that they may be traded against the efficiency gains of treating the perception-involving loop as if it were an inner, relatively noise-free channel, thus allowing them to use the world as "external memory" (O'Regan 1992; O'Regan and Noë 2001).

It is important, in our story about Otto, that he too treats the notebook as a typically reliable storage device. He must not feel compelled to check and double-check retrieved information. If this should change (perhaps someone carefully does begin to mess with his external stored knowledge base), and Otto should notice the change and become cautious, the notebook would at that point cease to count as a proper part of his individual cognitive economy. Of course, Otto might wrongly become thus suspicious. This would parallel the case of a person who begins to suspect that aliens are inserting thoughts into his or her head. In these latter cases, we begin to treat biologically internal information flow in the cautious way distinctive of perception.

In sum, I think Sterelny is right to pursue this kind of issue. But what emerges is not so much an argument against the extended mind as a way of further justifying our claim that in some contexts signals routed via perceptual systems are treated in a way more typical of internal channels (and vice versa, in the case of standard thought-insertion). To decide, in any given case, whether the channel is acting more like one of perception or more like one of internal information flow, look (in part) to the larger functional economy of defenses against deception. The lower the defenses, the closer we approximate to an internal flow.

Sterelny might reply to this by shifting the emphasis from the extent to which an agent actually does guard against deception and manipulation to the extent to which he or she is, as a matter of fact, vulnerable to it. Thus the fact that we are vulnerable to the magician's art may be said to count for more than the fact that in being thus vulnerable we treat (as I tried to argue) the perceptual route as a quasi-internal one. But this seems unprincipled, since given the right "magician" (say, an alien able to directly affect the flow of energy between my synapses), all routes seem about equally vulnerable. Recall also that false beliefs can (as noted earlier in this essay) be generated in biological memory by many a good psychologist. Or consider, for that matter, the many rather bizarre ways in which biological memory and reason can be systematically impaired (for example, the patients whose memories, like their ongoing experience, exhibit hemispatial neglect [Bisiach and Luzzatti 1978; Cooney and Gazzaniga 2003]). What seems (to me) to count is not vulnerability as such but rather something like our "ecologically normal" level of vulnerability. And our actual practices of defense and vetting are, I claim, rather a good guide to this. If Otto doesn't worry about tricksters copying his writing and adding false entries, maybe that is because the channel is as secure as it needs to be.

There is, finally, a large and I suspect unresolvable issue still waiting in the wings. For present purposes I am happy to have shown (or tried to show) that the very large differences that Sterelny highlights do not in fact obtain in the kinds of case Chalmers and I meant to imagine. But nonetheless I must concede (to Sterelny and to others) that the functional poise of information stored in public space is probably never *quite* the same as that of information stored using our inner biological resources. Might this itself secure the conclusion that information thus stored cannot count toward an agent's stock of dispositional beliefs? To do so would require a strong intervening premise. One such premise would be, for example, the claim that perfect identity of functional poise is essential if nonbiologically stored information is to count. But such a requirement is surely too strong. For all we know, the fine details of functional poise differ from person to person and hour to hour. This point is merely dramatized by those alien beings whose recall is (let's imagine) not subject to hemispatial neglect, crosstalk, or error: do these differences make a difference? Is the alien whose recall is fractionally slower than ours, or fractionally faster, or much less prone to loss and damage, to be banned from the ranks of true believers? To demand identity of functional poise is surely to demand too much.

But just what *aspects* of the functional poise of stored information are essential if the information is to count toward an individual's stock of dispositional beliefs, and what aspects merely mark contingent features of current, standard human belief systems? Chalmers and I tend to favor a rather coarse notion of the required functional role in which all that matters is that the information be typically trusted and that it guide gross choice, reason, and behavior in roughly the usual ways. To unpack this just a tiny bit further, we can say that it should guide behavior, reason, and choice in ways that would not cause constant misunderstandings and upsets if the agent were somehow able to join with, or communicate with, a human community. I do not see how to make this requirement any clearer or stronger without undue anthropocentricity. But nor do I see how to further argue this case with anyone whose intuitions differ.

7   An Alternative Ending?

Recall Adams and Aizawa's worry that the inner/outer elements form at best a motley, not the kind of causally unified set needed to support a real science, and their insistence that "the cognitive must be discriminated on the basis of underlying causal processes" (Adams and Aizawa 2001, p. 52). In reply (section 3 above) I mooted that there might be great variety among the inner, and paradigmatically cognitive, elements themselves: fully as much variation, perhaps, as between the inner and outer. This raises, however, the possibility of an alternative reading of the Clark and Chalmers argument itself. Perhaps the real moral of the story is that the realm of the mental is itself too disunified to count as a scientific kind?

This idea was first suggested to me by Jesse Prinz and was to be investigated in a joint project (Clark and Prinz, unpublished). The claim of that paper was to be that:

there is no unified, coherent understanding of the very *idea* of "mind" at work in various philosophical and scientific projects all of which claim to be studying aspects of the mental

and that:

not only is there no satisfying definition available, there is not even a useful shared scientific understanding, guiding prototype, or loosely connected web of salient properties and features. . . . there are no signs that we are here dealing with any natural kind . . . nor . . . with anything perhaps more nebulous, but nonetheless capable of legitimating the mind as a proper object of scientific study.

Evidence for this rather dramatic claim could be found, we hoped to suggest, in the endless philosophical debates over the applicability of mental predicates to an incredibly wide variety of cases, such as: thermostats (Dennett 1987), paramecia (Fodor 1986), language-less animals (McDowell 1994), swampmen, computers (Searle 1980), subpersonal "cognitive" activity in general (Searle 1992). Not to mention nonhuman animals, fetuses, prelinguistic infants, comatose patients, and now, of course, *extended cognitive systems* such as Otto and his trusty notebook. The point we wanted to make was that there was no easy consensus among "suitably trained observers" concerning the distribution of minds and mentality in nature and artifice. We just don't know a mind when we see one. Could the reason for this be that there simply aren't any there? Might the extended mind debate form part of a reductio of the very notion of mind in cognitive science?

In response to this suggestion, I would concede that the notion of "mind" as it is now used is torn between its roots in the idea of conscious experience and occurrent thoughts, and its extension into the realm of nonconscious processes and long-term stored knowledge. It is this latter extension that opens the door to the extended mind argument. One good way of reading that argument, I have long thought, is as a demonstration that if you allow nonconscious processes to count as properly mental, the physical basis of the mental cannot remain bound by the ancient barriers of skin and skull. Nor should it be thus bound since (as argued in section 4), attempted defenses that stress occurrent processes (there, of ultimate control and choice) will surely shrink mind too small, ruling out much that we want to count as mental and cognitive even inside the head. But since for many tastes, the extended mind story bloats mind too large, could we not conclude that the idea of the mental is terminally unstable? Couldn't we just *eliminate the mind*?

I don't think so (hence the perhaps permanently stalled status of the Clark and Prinz paper). For as I noted in section 3, despite the mechanistic motley, we may still aspire to a science of the mind. Granted, this will be a science of varied, multiplex, interlocking, and criss-crossing causal mechanisms, whose sole point of intersection may consist in their role in informing processes of conscious reflection and choice. It will be a science that needs to cover a wide variety of mechanistic bases, reaching out to biological brains, and to the wider social and technological milieus that (I claim) participate in thought and reason. It will *have* to be that accommodating, since that very mix is what is most characteristic of us as a thinking species (see Clark 2003). If we are lucky, there will be a few key laws and regularities to be defined even over such unruly coalitions. But there need not be. The science of the mind, in short, won't be as unified as physics. But what is?

In sum, I am not ready to give up on the idea of minds, mentality, and cognition any day soon. The extended mind argument stands not as a reductio but as originally conceived: a demonstration of the biotechnological openness of the very ideas of mind and reason.

Conclusions

The notion of the extended mind draws strong reactions. Many feel it is patently false. These same people tend to feel that the mind is simply and obviously just the activity of the brain. Others regard it as patently true, and they tend to be those who identify the mind with an essentially socially and environmentally embedded principle of informed agency (i.e., the fans of situated cognition). My own feeling is that we have not yet reached the philosophical or scientific bottom of this debate. There is something important to be said, for example, about the role of emotion in constantly coloring and informing cognition, and something (perhaps along the lines of Damasio 1994, 1999) about the way our ongoing sensing of our own biological body-state informs our sense of self. There is much to be said about the way our sense of what we know is, at bottom, a sense of what kinds of information we can easily and reliably exploit in the pursuit of our daily goals and projects (for a detailed meditation on this theme, see Clark 2003). The critical role of conscious awareness and occurrent thought in the overall debate over what is mental and what is not is worrisomely unclear, and will probably remain so until we have a better understanding of the neural roots of qualitative experience. Finally, the consistent (though to my mind unattractive) option of simply restricting the realm of the mental to that of occurrent conscious processing probably bears further thought and investigation, though not, I expect, by me.

So does Leonard (the protagonist of *Memento*) really increase his stock of beliefs every time he gets a new body tattoo? Better wait for the sequel.

Notes

1. This is the same technology as actually used in so-called thought control experiments—see, e.g., Graham-Rowe 1998.

2. This is a slight variation on the parity principle as originally stated in "The Extended Mind," this volume, p. 29.

3. Though it is, of course, no guarantee of ultimate success.

References

Adams, F and Aizawa, K (2001). The bounds of cognition. *Philosophical Psychology 14*, 1, 43–64.

Bisiach, E., and Luzzatti, C. (1978). Unilateral neglect of representation space. *Cortex, 14*, 129–133.

Butler, K. (1998). *Internal Affairs: A Critique of Externalism in the Philosophy of Mind.* Dordrecht: Kluwer.

Churchland, P. S., and Sejnowski, T. (1992). *The Computational Brain.* Cambridge, MA: MIT Press.

Clark, A. (2003). *Natural-Born Cyborgs: Minds, Technologies, and the Future of Human Intelligence.* Oxford: Oxford University Press.

Clark, A., and Chalmers, D. (1998). The extended mind. *Analysis, 58*, 10–23. Reprinted in this volume.

Clark, A., and Prinz, J. (unpublished). The absence of mind.

Cooney, J., and Gazzaniga, M (2003). Neurological disorders and the structure of human consciousness. *Trends in Cognitive Sciences, 7*(4), 161–165.

Damasio, A. (1999). *The Feeling of What Happens: Body and Emotion in the Making of Consciousness.* New York: Harcourt Brace.

Damasio, A. (1994). *Descartes' Error: Emotions, Reason, and the Human Brain.* New York: Avon Books.

Decety, J., and Grezes, J. (1999). Neural mechanisms subserving the perception of human actions. *Trends in Cognitive Sciences, 3*(5), 172–178.

Dennett, D. C. (1987). *The Intentional Stance.* Cambridge, MA: MIT Press.

Dennett, D. C. (2003). *Freedom Evolves*. New York: Viking.

Fodor, J. (1986). Why paramecia don't have mental representations. *Midwest Studies in Philosophy, 10,* 3–23.

Goodale, M. A., and Milner, A. D. (1992). Separate visual pathways for perception and action. *Trends in Neurosciences, 15,* 20–25.

Graham-Rowe, D. (1998). Think and it's done. *New Scientist* (October): 17.

McDowell, J. (1994). *Mind and World*. Cambridge, MA: Harvard University Press.

Milner, A. D., and Goodale, M. A. (1996). *The Visual Brain in Action*. Oxford: Oxford University Press.

Norman, D. (1999). *The Invisible Computer*. Cambridge, MA: MIT Press.

O'Regan, J. K. (1992). Solving the "real" mysteries of visual perception: the world as an outside memory. *Canadian Journal of Psychology, 46*(3), 461–488.

O'Regan, J. K., and Noë, A. (2001). A sensorimotor account of vision and visual consciousness. *Behavioral and Brain Sciences, 24*(5).

Roediger, H. L., and McDermott, K. B. (1995). Creating false memories: Remembering words not presented in lists. *Journal of Experimental Psychology. Learning, Memory, and Cognition, 4,* 803–814.

Roediger, H. L., Watson, J. M., McDermott, K. B., and Gallo, D. A. (2001). Factors that determine false recall: A multiple regression analysis. *Psychonomic Bulletin and Review, 8,* 385–407.

Rogers, Y., Brignull, H., and Scaife, M. (2002). Designing dynamic interactive visualisations to support collaboration and cognition. In *Proceedings of IEEE Sixth International Conference on Information Visualization (IV '02)* (pp. 39–50). Piscataway, NJ: IEEE Press.

Searle, J. (1980). Minds, brains, and programs. *Behavioral and Brain Sciences, 3,* 417–457.

Searle, J. (1992). *The Rediscovery of the Mind*. Cambridge, MA: MIT Press.

Simons, D., and Levin, D. (1997). Change blindness. *Trends in Cognitive Sciences, 1*(7), 261–267.

Sperber, D. (2001). An evolutionary perspective on testimony and argumentation. *Philosophical Topics, 29,* 401–413.

Sterelny, K. (2004). Externalism, Epistemic Artefacts and the Extended Mind. In R. Schantz (ed.), *The Externalist Challenge: New Studies on Cognition and Intentionality*. Berlin: de Gruyter.

4 Defending the Bounds of Cognition

Fred Adams and Ken Aizawa

Introduction

Question: Why did the pencil think that 2 + 2 = 4?
Clark's answer: Because it was coupled to the mathematician.

That about sums up what is wrong with Clark's extended mind hypothesis. Clark apparently thinks that the nature of the processes internal to a pencil, Rolodex, computer, cell phone, piece of string, or whatever, has nothing to do with whether that thing carries out cognitive processing.[1] Rather, what matters is how the thing interacts with a cognitive agent; the thing has to be coupled to a cognitive agent in a particular kind of way. Clark (this volume) gives three conditions that constitute a rough or partial specification of the kind of coupling required:

1. The resource has to be reliably available and typically invoked.
2. Any information retrieved from/with the resource must be more or less automatically endorsed. It should not usually be subject to critical scrutiny (unlike the opinions of other people, for example). It should be deemed about as trustworthy as something retrieved clearly from biological memory.
3. Information contained in the resource should be easily accessible as and when required (Clark, this volume, p. 46).

Granted condition 3 doesn't fit the use of a pencil very well, since the mathematician is not really extracting information from the pencil, but blame Clark for that. After all, he likes the idea that the use of pencil and paper in computing sums constitutes part of an agent's cognitive processing; hence it's up to him to make his story work there.[2]

When Clark makes an object cognitive when it is connected to a cognitive agent, he is committing an instance of a *coupling-constitution fallacy.*

This is the most common mistake that extended mind theorists make.[3] The fallacious pattern is to draw attention to cases, real or imagined, in which some object or process is coupled in some fashion to some cognitive agent. From this, one slides to the conclusion that the object or process constitutes part of the agent's cognitive apparatus or cognitive processing. If you are coupled to your pocket notebook in the sense of always having it readily available, use it a lot, trust it implicitly, and so forth, then Clark infers that the pocket notebook constitutes a part of your memory store. If you are coupled to a rock in the sense of always having it readily available, use it a lot, trust it implicitly, and so forth, Clark infers that the rock constitutes a part of your memory store. Yet coupling relations are distinct from constitutive relations, and the fact that object or process X is coupled to object or process Y does not entail that X is part of Y. The neurons leading into a neuromuscular junction are coupled to the muscles they innervate, but the neurons are not a part of the muscles they innervate. The release of neurotransmitters at the neuromuscular junction is coupled to the process of muscular contraction, but the process of releasing neurotransmitters at the neuromuscular junction is not part of the process of muscular contraction. (That's a quick and dirty run through the coupling-constitution fallacy. For a less quick and dirty treatment, see Adams and Aizawa 2008.)

So, if the fact that an object or process X is coupled to a cognitive agent does not entail that X is a part of the cognitive agent's cognitive apparatus, what does? The nature of X, of course. One needs a theory of what makes a process a cognitive process rather than a noncognitive process. One needs a theory of the "mark of the cognitive." It won't do simply to say that a cognitive process is one that is coupled to a cognitive agent, since this only pushes back the question. One still needs a theory of what makes something a cognitive agent. This is another weakness of extended mind theories. Yet, in all fairness to Clark and other extended mind theorists, it must be admitted that one of the shortcomings of contemporary cognitive psychology is that there is no well-established theory of just exactly what constitutes the cognitive. Be this as it may, Adams and Aizawa (2001) set out a rather familiar proposal, namely, that cognition is constituted by certain sorts of causal processes that involve nonderived content. We motivated this proposal in two ways, by appeal to examples in other sciences, such as chemistry and physics, and by appeal to what appear to be psychological laws. We mentioned in particular psychophysical laws, such as Weber's law, and psychological laws governing memory formation and recall. We might well have extended our examples by appeal to further examples to be found in cognitive psychology textbooks. What we, there-fore, proposed is that the weight of empirical evidence supports the view that, as a matter of contingent empirical fact, there are processes that (a) are recognizably cognitive, (b) take place in the brain, (c) do not take place outside of the brain, and (d) do not cross from the brain into the external world.

We think that Clark has not yet come to grips with what we are getting at with the view that cognition is a species of causal processing involving nonderived content. Our paper did not provoke him to address what seems to us to be the two most widespread problems with extracranial and tran-scranial theories of tool use. That is to say, Clark provides no response to the coupling-constitution fallacy, and he provides little more than a hint at what *he* thinks distinguishes the cognitive from the noncognitive. Further, we are disappointed that we were unable to convey our objections clearly enough to forestall Clark's criticisms.

1   The Intrinsic Content Condition[4]

In Adams and Aizawa 2001, we proposed that "A first essential condition on the cognitive is that cognitive states must involve intrinsic, non-derived content" (p. 48). This hypothesis has some calculated openness in it.[5] Sup-pose that during the course of a cognitive process an agent entertains the thought that John loves Mary. This cognitive agent might thus pass through a cognitive state containing the representation JOHN LOVES MARY. Then, our proposed condition would be satisfied. But, suppose that instead the cogni-tive agent passed through a cognitive state that has JOHN LOVES MARY fol-lowed by a period or maybe some parentheses thrown in. Still, our proposed condition on the cognitive would be satisfied. The hypothesis has this lati-tude, since we think that although we have good reasons to believe in the existence of intrinsic content, we have no good reasons to think that cogni-tive states must consist entirely of intrinsic representations or that cognitive states must be, in their entirety, content bearing.[6] This is why we said that "it is unclear to what extent each cognitive state of each cognitive process must involve non-derived content" (Adams and Aizawa 2001, p. 50).

Despite our attempts to present the foregoing position clearly, Clark criticizes us both for being too demanding and too lenient on the role we think nonderived content plays in cognition. Early in his section on intrinsic content he writes, "The question is, must everything that is to count as part of an individual's mental processing be composed solely and exclusively of states of affairs of this latter intrinsically content-bearing kind? I see no reason to think that they must" (Clark, this volume, p. 48). Here Clark tars us with the overly strong view which we explicitly rejected, then proceeds to critique the overly strong view. (We shall return to this critique, which we find unconvincing.) Later, when Clark comes to our claim about the extent to which each cognitive state of each cognitive process must involve nonderived content, he treats the qualification as rendering the condition vacuous. But this is not a very serious attempt to understand what we are after. Clearly, we mean that if you have a process that involves no intrinsic content, then the condition rules that the process is noncognitive. In fact, that is exactly what the condition is used to show in our 2001 essay. The images on the CRT screen of the Tetris video game are not representations of blocks to be rotated; they are the blocks to be rotated.[7]

Although Clark attributes to us a view we rejected, we find that his case against this misinterpretation is unconvincing. We want to review this here simply to clarify, where we can, features of the distinction between derived and nonderived content. So, what is Clark's case against thinking that not all of an individual's cognitive states must be exhaustively constituted by nonderived representations? It is the following:

suppose we are busy (as part of some problem-solving routine) imaging a set of Venn diagrams/Euler circles in our mind's eye. Surely the set-theoretic meaning of the overlaps between, say, two intersecting Euler circles is a matter of convention. Yet this image can clearly feature as part of a genuinely cognitive process. (Clark, this volume, p. 48)

Evidently the problem here is supposed to be that there are some mental states that have contents in virtue of a social convention. So, Clark implies that there are bona fide cognitive processes that involve derived content. Clark explores a line of response he thinks we might try. That line, however, strikes us as very weak. We'll bother with none of it. Our view is that Clark's analysis of the Euler circles case is superficial and confused.

To begin, let us draw a rough-and-ready distinction between mental representations of natural objects and mental representations of objects with derived content.[8] The idea is that there are mental representations of things like trees, rocks, birds, and grass, on the one hand, and mental representations of words, stop signs, warning lights, and gas gauges, on the other. Perhaps a better terminology can be chosen, but the names are really inessential. By our lights, words, stop signs, warning lights, and gas gauges mean what they do through some sort of social convention. By our lights, mental representations of natural objects, such as trees, rocks, birds, and grass, mean what they do in virtue of satisfying some naturalistic conditions on meaning. Many of the essays in Stich and Warfield 1994 present some of the options that philosophers have proposed in these latter cases. Clark's example of the Euler circles draws attention to a muddier case, the case of mental representations of items with derived content. How do these get their meanings?

As noted above, Clark suggests that mental representations of items with derived content get their content by social convention. Now, it is common ground that social convention is in some sense involved in the meaning of the overlap of Euler circles. But that is a logically separate matter from what makes an imagistic mental representation of intersecting Euler circles mean what they do. Intersecting Euler circles on paper getting their meaning is one thing; intersecting Euler circles in mental images getting their meaning is another. Clark apparently overlooks this difference, and hence does not bother to provide a reason to think that Euler circles in mental images get their meaning via social convention. For all Clark says, mental items that have Euler circles as their content could mean what they do by some naturalistic theory of content, just as we suppose that mental representations of natural objects do. So, for all Clark says, a mental image of an intersection of two Euler circles means what it does in virtue of satisfying the conditions of Fodor's (1994) asymmetric causal dependency theory of content. Moreover, what we have just said about Euler circles applies just as well to mental representations of words, stop signs, white flags, and warning lights. It can be a matter of convention that "dog" means dog, that a stop sign means that you should stop, that a person raising a white flag means to surrender, and that a flashing red light means that something is overheating. But that does nothing to show that it is not the satisfaction of some set of naturalistic conditions on nonderived content that gets something in the head to have the meanings of "dog," a stop sign, a white flag, and a warning light.

But suppose Clark acknowledges that there is a conceptual difference between how mental objects get their contents and how artifacts outside the mind get theirs. He might give the following argument for his view. He might still think that there cannot be mental images in which intersecting Euler circles mean set-theoretic overlap unless there were a social convention according to which intersecting Euler circles meant set-theoretic overlap. He might say that this is a kind of derivation of meaning. The meaning of the mental image derives in part from the prior existence of the meaning of physical pictures. The meaning of the mental image might be said to depend on the existence of a prior meaning.

At first blush this argument may seem compelling, but in reality the argument merely trades on an ambiguity in the notions of derivation and dependency.[9] Insofar as there must be a social convention regarding the intersections of Euler circles in order to have a mental representation regarding the intersections of Euler circles, this is not a fact about the constitution of the content of a mental image of the intersections of Euler circles. It is, if anything, a kind of historical fact.[10] One would not have a mental image involving the intersection of Euler circles meaning set-theoretic overlap without having had at some prior time the social convention involving the intersection of Euler circles meaning set-theoretic overlap. It is like this: The dependence of meaning of the mental image of intersecting Euler circles on the social contrivance regarding the intersection of Euler circles is just like the dependence of the meaning of a mental representation of a car on the contrivance of a car. Had the car not been invented, there would not have been mental images of cars. Had the usage of Euler circles not been invented, there would not have been mental images of Euler circles for set-theoretic purposes. This sort of historical truth, if it is a truth, does not show what Clark might want it to show, namely, that the content of certain mental items derives (in the relevant sense) from a social convention.

Suppose, now, that Clark concedes that there is a conceptual difference between how mental objects get their meaning and how physical objects outside the mind get their meaning and admits that he has no argument for the former having derived content, but then demands some reason to think that mental objects do not have derived content. Maybe he has no argument in support of his view, but what reason is there against his view? In the arrangement of social conventions, we have some access to the items bearing the content we want. A community might get together and decide that a yellow flag, rather than a white flag, means surrender, that "bad" or "cool" makes a positive commentary on a thing, or that "WC" is a symbol for the facilities. To do these things, there has to be some way to specify or access the would-be syntactic item that is to figure in the semantic convention. Yet, with the brain, we have no such access to the syntactic items we would like to have bear a particular content. We cannot make, say, the firing of a particular set of neurons mean what it does simply by an agreement that it does. We cannot do this because we have no way to identify particular tokens of brain states qua syntactic items in order to affix contents to them. Given the state of current science, we only identify a person's brain states via inferences to the content of those states. We think that Jones wants to go to that restaurant in Philly because she said she wants to go to that restaurant and is looking up the address in the phone book. Even when we know that Jones wants to go to that restaurant in Philly, we don't know what specific syntactic item in the brain bears that content. This is not how conventional meanings work.

So, as far as we can tell, Clark gives no reason to doubt what we think is false, namely, that all cognitive states must be exhaustively constituted by content-bearing items. Much less does he give any reason to doubt what we think is true, namely, that cognitive states must involve nonderived content. Further, there are reasons to believe that cognitive content is not normally derived via any sort of social convention. Perhaps there are futuristic science-fiction scenarios in which humans have sufficient access to brain states that this situation could change, but then maybe it will be the case that cognitive content can at times be socially controlled. Maybe. After all, can a mental image of Abraham Lincoln really mean George Washington?

2   The Causal Processing Condition

Our appeal to scientific categorization via causal principles is meant to do two sorts of things for us. First, it is supposed to draw attention to what appears to be one of the principal differences between processes that occur in the brain and processes that occur outside of the brain. Second, it is supposed to draw attention to the unruly collection of processes that might fall under the rubric of a would-be "brain-tool science." Although both of these contentions undermine transcranial theories of cognition, Clark directs most of his attention to the second use of the causal processing condition. He thinks that this argument is doubly flawed. We shall address each of these alleged flaws in turn.

The First Flaw
Clark begins his critique with the following:

The first thing to say in response to all this is that it is unwise to judge, from the armchair, the chances of finding "interesting scientific regularities" in any domain, be it ever so superficially diverse. Consider, for example, the recent successes of complexity theory in unearthing unifying principles that apply across massive differences of scale, physical type, and temporality. There are power laws, it now seems, that compactly explain aspects of the emergent behavior of systems ranging from the size distribution of cities to word-occurrence frequencies to the frequency of avalanches in sandpiles.

In a similar vein, it is quite possible that despite the bottom-level physical diversity of the processes that write to, and read from, Otto's notebook, and those that write to, and read from, Otto's biological memory, there is a level of description of these systems that treats them in a single unified framework (for example, how about a framework of information storage, transformation, and retrieval?) (Clark, this volume, p. 50)

We find this passage indicative of a number of respects in which we have failed to make our argument sufficiently clear.

Let's begin by clarifying what we take to be the epistemic status of our view. Clark claims that "it is unwise to judge, from the armchair, the chances of finding 'interesting scientific regularities' in any domain, be it ever so superficially diverse." This may be just a generic rejection of anything like "armchair philosophy." We don't endorse armchair philosophy and we don't see that we are guilty of it. We think that the available empirical evidence provides good reason to think that the chances of finding interesting cognitive regularities covering brains and tools is low. Bear in mind that we side with what is by all accounts scientific orthodoxy. Note as well that Clark does not respond to us by marching out an interesting scientific or cognitive regularity we didn't see from our "armchairs."[11] Alternatively, Clark may be giving an argument for the conclusion that it is unwise to judge the chances of finding interesting scientific regularities that might constitute a "brain-tool science." Clark's argument may be that, just as we have found surprising new regularities through complexity theory, so we might find interesting new regularities in "brain-tool science"; perhaps they will be information-processing regularities. This argument, however, is hardly compelling. Are we to think that a judgment is unwise simply because it could be wrong? More compelling would be to argue that a particular judgment is unwise because it flies in the face of weighty empirical evidence. More compelling would be to show us an interesting cognitive brain-tool regularity that we have overlooked. Yet Clark provides no such case.

Think of the foregoing this way. We maintain that the weight of empirical evidence supports the view that there are processes that (a) are plausibly construed to be cognitive, (b) occur within the brain, (c) do not occur outside of the brain, and (d) do not cross the bounds of the brain. One can challenge the evidence and the argumentation, but it is a bit much to suggest, as does Clark, that there is no evidence whatsoever. We are, after all, siding with scientific orthodoxy. Since it is orthodoxy, there is at least some prima facie reason to think it is not scientifically groundless. Further, the fact that it sides with scientific orthodoxy suggests that the position is defeasible. So it hardly helps Clark to point out that we could be wrong.

The observation that *it is possible that* there are higher-level information-processing regularities that cross the boundary of the brain does nothing to challenge our position, which is concerned with what the evidence shows. However, let's see what happens if we grant Clark a much stronger premise. Suppose we detach the modal operator. Suppose that there really are information-processing regularities that cross the boundary of the brain.[12] Perhaps processing information is what Clark thinks constitutes the mark of the cognitive, a condition other than being connected to a cognitive agent.[13] Does this much stronger, nonmodal premise suffice to establish that the mind extends beyond the bounds of skin and skull? No. The problem is that the empirical evidence we have indicates that the brain processes information according to different principles than do common brain-tool combinations. Think of consumer electronics devices. We find that DVD players, CD players, MP3 players, tape recorders, caller ID systems, personal computers, televisions, AM/FM radios, cell phones, watches, walkie talkies, inkjet printers, digital cameras, and so forth, are all information processors. The preponderance of scientific evidence, however, indicates that they process information differently than does the brain. That is why, for example, the brain is capable of linguistic processing, whereas these other devices are not. That is why, for example, the brain is capable of facial recognition over a range of environmental conditions, whereas these other devices are not. This is why the brain is crucial for humans' ability to drive cars, whereas these other devices are not. The differences in information-processing capacities between the brain and a DVD or CD player is part of the story of why you can't play a DVD or CD with just a human brain. These differences are part of the reason you need a radio to listen to AM or FM broadcasts. It is these differences that support the defeasible view that there is a kind of intracranial processing, plausibly construed as cognitive, that differs from any extracranial or transcranial processing. This is the first kind of work we take our appeal to causal processing to do.

We appeal to the nature of causal processing to do more work when we observe that consumer electronics devices and other tools differ among themselves in how they process information. DVD players process information differently than do digital cameras. Digital cameras and DVD players process information differently than do FM radios. This, after all, is what differentiates these tools from each other. What information-processing principles do string, a rock, and DVD players have in common?

When we press this point, we suppose that tools constitute an open-ended set of objects. Tools do not constitute a natural kind; tools are, after all, artifacts. It is for this reason that, a would-be brain-tool science would have to cover more than just a multiplicity of causal processes. It would have to cover a genuine motley. A brain-tool science would not have to cover a mere disjunction of things; it would have to cover an open disjunction. In our 2001 paper, we noted the existence of areas of scientific investigation where there was an apparent fragmentation of a domain.[14] The reason, we argued, that brain-tool science will not go the way of these other investigations is that a would-be brain-tool science would have to cover too broad a collection of processes. It would have to cover a motley of processes, not just a multiplicity of processes.

Clark has hinted that information processing constitutes the mark of the cognitive, but we have argued that this is implausible. What, then, of the possibility that Clark thinks that some other higher-level processes constitute the mark of the cognitive? Perhaps the higher-level processes that extend the mind are of some other nature. Okay; but what are these principles and what is the evidence for their existence? Clark gives us no clue. Note as well that it is not enough for Clark to show that "there is a level of description of these systems that treats [intracranial and extracranial processes] in a single unified framework." Physics provides a reasonable approximation to such a thing. Biology and chemistry might also provide levels of description at which there are processes that are continuous across the boundary of the brain. What Clark needs is a *cognitive* level of description of these systems that treats them in a single unified way. That is, he needs a plausible theory of what constitutes the cognitive. That is where our theory of nonderived content and causal processes supports intracranialism.

The Second Flaw

What, now, of the second way in which Clark thinks our appeal to causal processing is doubly flawed? Clark observes that cognition might fragment into a motley of causally distinct processes without even a family resemblance. Perhaps the folk notion of visual processing will break down into two subtypes: visual processing that eventuates in perceptual experiences and visual processing that guides action independently of perceptual experiences. Extrapolating from what Clark writes, we might add that memory might break down into distinct kinds: short-term memory, long-term memory, visual memory, and so on. A folk notion of auditory processing could fragment into auditory processing and linguistic processing. Olfaction could have a generic smell component alongside a system for processing pheromones. If cognition is a motley, then Adams and Aizawa's standard will judge intracranial cognitive science just as much a bust as a would-be brain-tool science.

To address this objection, we can apply much of what we said above. To begin with, we do not suppose that the decomposition of the cognitive into a motley is in any sense impossible. We made this epistemic point above. We think that the weight of argumentation supports our view. So, insofar as Clark cares to address our position, he evidently needs at least the non-modal conclusion that cognition fragments into a motley collection of principles. This, however, we are not prepared to concede. In our earlier discussion we drew a distinction between a multiplicity of principles being at work in some domain and a genuinely motley, open-ended collection of principles being at work. We think that the available scientific evidence makes it plausible that there are distinct sorts of cognitive processing occurring in the brain: processing corresponding to many distinct forms of visual processing, memory processing, and so forth. Yet, we see no reason to extrapolate to the conclusion that there is an open-ended collection. The brain is at least in the running to be a natural kind, whereas brain-tool combinations are hybrids of natural kinds and artifacts. Outside the realm of science fiction, the brain is constrained to develop only a limited set of distinct structures with a bounded range of plasticity. An organism's genome and environmental interactions limit what can be done with neurons and glial cells. Clark appeals to the wide diversity of organisms that might be capable of cognitive processing, but this does not show that there is an open-ended range of things that can constitute cognitive processing. By contrast, tools can be made of anything and can work according to any number of distinct principles. They are clearly artifacts and not natural kinds. That is good grounds for saying that intracranial processing is a collection of disparate mechanisms, whereas brain-tool combinations form an open-ended collection.

Finally, suppose that Clark is right about cognition breaking down into a genuinely open-ended collection of principles. Even that would not necessarily vindicate extracranialist or transcranialist theories of cognition. As long as the multiplicity or motley collection of plausibly cognitive intracranial causal processes is distinct from the set of extracranial and transcranial processes, there will be a basis on which to say that cognition is intracranial. Even if we were to concede the idea that there could be a science of the motley, a science of the motley would not vindicate extra-cranialism. So, as far as we can tell, Clark has said nothing that challenges our original analysis of the role of causal processing and nonderived content in the demarcation of the cognitive.

Conclusion

In our essay "The Bounds of Cognition" we thought that the principal weakness in extracranialist theories of tool use was inadequate attention to the mark of the cognitive. Since then, however, we have been impressed with the extent to which this inattention appears to have been involved in so many process externalists' succumbing to one or another version of the coupling-constitution fallacy. It would certainly do much to advance the transcranial theories of cognition were Clark not only to address our theory of the mark of the cognitive, but to address the pervasive coupling-constitution fallacy and set out a plausible theory of what distinguishes the cognitive from the noncognitive.

Notes

1. Clark does shy away from this from time to time, but more on this below.

2. Cf. Clark and Chalmers, this volume, p. 28; Clark 2001, pp. 133–134.

3. Van Gelder and Port (1995), Clark and Chalmers (1998, this volume), Clark (2001), Gibbs (2001), and Haugeland (1998) all make this mistake in one way or another.

4. In a conference presentation in which he responds, in part, to Adams and Aizawa 2001, Clark alludes to Dennett 1990 as providing an argument against non-derived content. Clark does not refer to this argument in this volume, so we have produced an independent critique of Dennett's paper in Adams and Aizawa 2005.

5. See Adams and Aizawa 2001, pp. 50–51.

6. If you think that a cognitive state is a total computational state of a computer, such as a Turing machine, then you will have another reason to doubt the view that a cognitive state must be representational in its entirety. In such views of cognition, at least some of the program states are not representational. That is, for at least some Turing machines, the read-write head of a Turing machine in state S_0, or whatever, is not representational.

7. See Adams and Aizawa 2001, p. 54.

8. We might run what follows using a different terminology. We might talk about states in which the contents are natural objects and states in which the contents

are objects with derived content. We choose to write about mental representations simply for convenience.

9. See Dennett 1990, and our discussion of it in Adams and Aizawa 2005, for another instance of this kind of problem.

10. There is room here to challenge the historical claim that had the use of Euler circles not been invented, there would not have been the use of the mental images of Euler circles. For present purposes, however, we will not pursue this.

11. In truth, when Clark starts "pumping intuitions" (p. 44), talking about Martians (p. 44), and drawing attention to what could happen in science (p. 50), it begins to sound as if he is the one doing armchair philosophy.

12. This is what Rowlands (1999) clearly thinks constitutes a basis for a version of the extended mind hypothesis.

13. This harks back to our opening paragraph.

14. Adams and Aizawa 2001, pp. 60–61.

References

Adams, F., and Aizawa, K. (2001). The bounds of cognition. *Philosophical Psychology*, *14*, 43–64.

Adams, F., and Aizawa, K. (2005). Defending non-derived content. *Philosophical Psychology*, *18*, 661–669.

Adams, F., and Aizawa, K. (2008). *The Bounds of Cognition*. Oxford: Blackwell.

Clark, A. (2001). Reasons, robots, and the extended mind. *Mind and Language, 16*, 121–145.

Clark, A., and Chalmers, D. (1998). The extended mind. *Analysis, 58*, 7–19.

Dennett, D. (1990). The myth of original intentionality. In K. A. Mohyeldin Said, W. H. Newton-Smith, R. Viale, and K. V. Wilkes (eds.), *Modeling the Mind*. Oxford: Oxford University Press.

Fodor, J. (1994). A theory of content, II: The theory. Reprinted in Stich and Warfield 1994 (pp. 180–222).

Gibbs, R. W. (2001). Intentions as emergent products of social interactions. In Bertram F. Malle, Louis J. Moses, and D. A. Baldwin (eds.), *Intentions and Intentionality* (pp. 105–122). Cambridge, MA: MIT Press.

Haugeland, J. (1998). Mind embodied and embedded. In J. Haugeland (ed.), *Having Thought*. Cambridge, MA: Harvard University Press.

Rowlands, M. (1999). *The Body in Mind*. Cambridge: Cambridge University Press.

Stich, S., and Warfield, T. (eds.) (1994). *Mental Representation: A Reader*. Cambridge, MA: Blackwell.

van Gelder, T. and Port, R. (1995). It's about time: An overview of the dynamical approach to cognition. In R. Port and T. van Gelder (eds.), *Mind as Motion: Explorations in the Dynamics of Cognition*. Cambridge, MA: MIT Press.

5 Coupling, Constitution, and the Cognitive Kind: A Reply to Adams and Aizawa

Andy Clark

1 Introduction: Crossed Wires

Adams and Aizawa, in a series of recent and forthcoming essays (2001, 2009, this volume) seek to refute, or perhaps merely to terminally embarrass, the friends of the extended mind. One such essay begins with the following illustration:

Question: Why did the pencil think that 2 + 2 = 4?
Clark's answer: Because it was coupled to the mathematician. (Adams and Aizawa, this volume, p. 67)

"That," the authors continue, "about sums up what is wrong with Clark's extended mind hypothesis." The example of the pencil, they suggest, is just an especially egregious version of a fallacy said to pervade the literature on the extended mind. This fallacy, which they usefully dub the "coupling-constitution fallacy," is attributed,[1] in varying degrees and manners, to Van Gelder and Port (1995), Clark and Chalmers (1998), Haugeland (1998), Dennett (2000), Clark (2001), Gibbs (2001), and Wilson (2004). The fallacy, of course, is to move from the causal coupling of some object or process to some cognitive agent, to the conclusion that the object or process is part of the cognitive agent, or part of the agent's cognitive processing (see, e.g., Adams and Aizawa, this volume, p. 68). Proponents of the extended mind and related theses, Adams and Aizawa repeatedly assert, are prone to this fallacy in part because they either ignore or fail to properly appreciate the importance of "the mark of the cognitive," that is, the importance of an account of "what makes something a cognitive agent" (ibid., p. 68). The positive part of Adams and Aizawa's critique then emerges as a combination of the assertion that this "mark of the cognitive" involves the idea that "cognition is constituted by certain sorts of causal process that involve non-derived contents" (ibid.) with the claim that these processes look to be characterized by psychological laws that turn out to apply to many internal goings-on but that do not currently apply (as a matter of contingent empirical fact) to any processes that take place in nonbiological tools and artifacts.

In what follows, I show why these arguments display nothing so much as mutual failures of communication: crossed wires concealing a couple of real, but rather more subterranean, disagreements. In particular, I show why the negative considerations advanced by Adams and Aizawa fail to successfully engage the argument for the extended mind, and why their more radical positive story, unless supplemented by implausible additional claims, does nothing to undermine the conclusion that minds like ours can (without the need for any radically new techniques, technologies, or interventions) extend into the world.

Before embarking on this, a word about the intended force of the argument. Adams and Aizawa make much of their concession (see, e.g., Adams and Aizawa 2009) that mental extension is *possible*, just not, they claim, actual. Theirs, they insist, is a "contingent intercranialism" applicable to human agents in the current state of technology. But they seem to imply that our view, if it is to stand in contrast to theirs, must be that such extension is rampant, and that "in ordinary tool use we have instances in which cognitive processes span the cranial boundary and extend into intercranial space" (ibid., p. 79). Whatever the truth of such a claim (of rampant extension), it was not the claim made by Clark and Chalmers (1998, reprinted in this volume). Our claim was that in fairly easily imaginable circumstances—ones that involved no giant leaps of technology or technique—we would be justified in holding that certain mental and cognitive states extended (in a sense to be explained later) into the nonbiological world. This leaves it open whether there are such extensions and (if there are) exactly how widespread they are. But it is far stronger than the mere claim of "logical possibility" that Adams and Aizawa suggest as the alternative to rampant actual extension.

2   The Odd Coupling

Consider the following exchange, loosely modeled on Adams and Aizawa's opening "reductio":

Question: Why did the V4 neuron think that there was a spiral pattern in the stimulus?
Answer: Because it was coupled to the monkey.

Now clearly, there is something wrong here. But the absurdity lies not in the appeal to coupling but in the idea that a V4 neuron (or even a group of V4 neurons, or even a whole parietal lobe . . .) might *itself* be some kind of self-contained locus of thinking. It is crazy to think that a V4 neuron thinks, and (just as Adams and Aizawa imply) it is crazy to think that a pencil might think. Yet the thrust of Adams and Aizawa's rhetoric is, again and again, to draw attention to the evident absence of cognition *in the putative part* as a way of "showing" that coupling (even when properly understood—see below) cannot play the kind of role it plays in the standard arguments for cognitive extension. Thus we read that:

When Clark *makes an object cognitive* when it is connected to a cognitive agent, he is committing an instance of a "coupling-constitution fallacy. (Adams and Aizawa, this volume, p. 67; my emphasis)

But this talk of an object's being or failing to be "cognitive" seems to me almost unintelligible when applied to some putative *part* of a cognitive agent or of a cognitive system. What would it mean for the neuron *or* the pencil to be, as it were, brute factively "cognitive"? Nor, I think, is this merely an isolated stylistic infelicity on the part of Adams and Aizawa. For the same issue arose many times during personal exchanges[2] concerning the vexed case of Otto and his notebook (the example used, with a great many riders and qualifications, in Clark and Chalmers 1998). And it arises again and again, as we shall later see, in the various parts of their recent challenge to engage the issue of "the mark of the cognitive."

Let us first be clear then about the precise role of the appeal to coupling in the arguments for the extended mind. The appeal to coupling is not intended to make any external object "cognitive" (insofar as this notion is even intelligible). Rather, it is intended to make some object, which in and of itself is not usefully (perhaps not even intelligibly) thought of as *either cognitive or noncognitive*, into a *proper part of some cognitive system*, such as a human agent. It is intended, that is to say, to ensure that the putative part is poised to play the kind of role that *itself* ensures its status as part of the agent's cognitive routines.

Now, it is certainly true (and this, we think, is the important fact to which Adams and Aizawa's argument might successfully draw the reader's attention) that not just any old kind of coupling will achieve even this result. But probably no one in the literature, and certainly not Chalmers and I, ever claimed otherwise. Hence the presence of the conditions of (broadly speaking) "glue and trust" pursued at length in the original essay, and briefly summarized in various other places, including the target essays by Adams and Aizawa. There is no need to repeat the conditions, even summarily, here, as the present focus is on the overall shape of our argument and on issues concerning coupling and the mark of the cognitive, rather than on these aspects of the original content. But it is worth noting that the bulk of our (Clark and Chalmers 1998) treatment was devoted to the isolation and defense of these very features.

The biggest of the crossed wires in the exchange with Adams and Aizawa, we now believe, lies quite close by. For Adams and Aizawa often fail to fully appreciate that the conditions speak to the question (which we deem intelligible) "when is some physical object or process part of a larger cognitive system?" and not to the much murkier question "when should we say, of some such candidate part, that it is *itself* cognitive?" The only question at issue, then, was what kind of coupling makes *for incorporation into* a single cognitive system rather than simple *use by* a cognitive system.

In outlining an answer, we chose to be guided by a set of intuitions derived from reflection on the ordinary use of talk of non-occurrent, dispositional beliefs. In essence, we took these intuitions and systematically showed that the kind of functional poise (poise to guide various forms of behavior) associated with such dispositional believings might be supported by a nonstandard physical realization in which a notebook (for example) acted as the medium of long-term storage. The right kind of coupling to make the external resource into a part of the cognitive system, we argued, was one that poised the information contained in the notebook for sufficiently easy, reliable, and automatic "use" (deployment would be a better word) in much the same way as is typically (though not always) achieved by biological encoding.

Chalmers and I thus offered an argument (which one may accept or reject: that is, of course, another matter) concerning conditions not of "being cognitive" but for incorporation into a cognitive system. In so doing we were not even close, as far as we can see, to committing any simple coupling-constitution fallacy.

We must be cautious, however, for it is not, strictly speaking, that Adams and Aizawa fail to see that the real issue concerns cognitive incorporation. Indeed, they are well aware that the conclusion we were aiming for is that the object or process be part of the agent's cognitive apparatus (see, e.g., Adams and Aizawa, this volume, p. 68). The misunderstanding is more complex, and ultimately more interesting, than that. Adams and Aizawa seem to think that some objects or processes, *in virtue of their own nature* (see section 3 below) are, as we shall now put it, *candidate parts* (for inclusion in a cognitive process), whereas other objects or processes, still in virtue of their own nature, are not. This, I think, must be the way to give sense to that otherwise baffling question "is some X cognitive?" when asked of some putative part. This then is the link between the skirmish concerning a putative coupling-constitution fallacy and the subsequent positive story concerning the "mark of the cognitive." Thus the authors ask:

if the fact that an object or process X is coupled to a cognitive agent does not entail that X is a part of the cognitive agent's cognitive apparatus, what does? *The nature of X, of course.* One needs a theory of what makes a process a cognitive process. . . . One needs a theory of the "mark of the cognitive." (Adams and Aizawa, this volume, p. 68, my emphasis)

It is to this (vexed and vexing) issue that we now turn.

3   On Your Marks . . .

So wait a moment: maybe that V4 neuron *is*, in some intelligible sense, cognitive? Maybe it is cognitive in the sense (identified above) of being, *in virtue of its own nature*, at least a *candidate* for becoming a proper part of a genuinely cognitive process. Such, we are at least tempted to think, must be the underlying belief driving much of Adams and Aizawa's otherwise mystifying critique. This slightly puzzling thought thus brings us to the (marginally) more positive part of their discussion, namely their appeal to the "mark of the cognitive."

Notice first that this way of displaying the debate, if correct, already suggests a major concession to the role of coupling. For assume we find some such acceptable (in virtue of its own nature) candidate part. Then what settles the question of whether that part belongs to this cognitive system, or to that one, or (currently) to no cognitive system at all? It is hard to see just what, apart from appeal to some kind of coupling, at some time in the causal-historical chain, could motivate an answer to this subsequent question.

But let's now stick, as Adams and Aizawa insist we should, to the topic of the "mark of the cognitive," and hence to the question (as we see it) of cognitive candidacy rather than actual cognitive incorporation. What could it be that, as they put it, "makes a process a cognitive process" (this volume, p. 68)? The question is nontrivial and has, as Adams and Aizawa somewhat reluctantly admit, no well-established answer within cognitive science or philosophy of mind. But they happily tie their colors to what they depict as "a rather orthodox theory of the nature of the cognitive"

(Adams and Aizawa 2001, p. 52). According to this theory (ibid., p. 53), "cognition involves particular kinds of processes involving non-derived representations." This is the line also pursued in Adams and Aizawa (this volume, 2009). It comprises two distinct elements, just as presented in the quote—namely, an appeal to nonderived content and an appeal to "particular kinds of process."

Despite its prominence in their account, Adams and Aizawa really tell us very little about what nonderived content is. We learn that it is content that is in some sense intrinsic (Adams and Aizawa 2001, p. 48). We learn that this is to be contrasted with, for example, the way a public language symbol gets its content by "conventional association" (ibid.). We are told, in the same place, that Dretske, Fodor, Millikan, and others are (sometimes) in search of an adequate theory of such content, and that the combination of a language of thought with some kind of causal-historical account is a hot contender for such an account. Toward the end of all this, however, the authors make a concession which, I elsewhere argue (chapter 3 of this volume), takes much of the sting out of the tail of the appeal to nonderived content, however (if at all) that elusive concept is to be unpacked. This is the concession that

Having argued that, in general, there must be non-derived content in cognitive processes, it must be admitted that it is unclear to what extent every cognitive state of each cognitive process must involve non-derived content. (Adams and Aizawa 2001, p. 50)

As I understand it, this concession allows that an external resource, none of whose states or processes or stored representations are themselves intrinsically contentful (assuming we are able to make sense of that notion in some way) might nonetheless be a proper part of some cognitive process. Otto's notebook, to take the obvious example, might be just such a resource, since it is full of inscriptions written in (let's assume) English. Yet Otto's notebook, in the light of this concession, might still figure as part of the supervenience base for some of Otto's dispositional beliefs even while failing itself to be a repository of states with intrinsic content.

Of course, we do not *have* to think of Otto's notebook this way. A more radical response would be to argue that what makes *any* symbol or representation (internal or external) mean what it does is just something about its behavior-supporting role (and maybe its causal history) within some larger system. We might then hold that when we understand enough about that role (and, perhaps, history) we will see that the encodings in Otto's notebook are in fact on a par with those in his biological memory.

In other words, just because the symbols in the notebook happen to look like words of English and require some degree of interpretative activity when retrieved and used, that need not rule out the possibility that they have also come to satisfy the demands on being, given their role within the larger system, among the physical vehicles of intrinsic content.

Nonetheless, there is something quite compelling, I want to agree, about the idea that there is something conventional about the notebook encodings and even about the thought that some parts of any genuinely cognitive system need to trade in representations that are not thus conventional. To accept this, however, is not to give up on the extended mind unless one also accepts (what seems to be an independent and far less plausible assertion) that *no proper part of a properly cognitive system can afford, at any time, to trade solely in conventional representations*. It was this additional claim that, I thought, was being rejected (and, I felt, quite rightly so) in the above quoted passage from Adams and Aizawa.

It seems, however, that I was wrong, and that Adams and Aizawa do in fact endorse something like this additional claim. Thus (this volume, p. 70) the authors accuse me of not seriously attempting to understand the point of their actual concession, and hence of (incorrectly) taking it as rendering the appeal to nonderived content argumentatively vacuous, at least in the case of the debate concerning extended cognition.

So what went wrong? The original concession was followed by an example to which I paid insufficient attention. The example involved possible nonrepresentational elements in a language-of-thought encoding, such as punctuation marks and parentheses (see Adams and Aizawa 2001, p. 50). Such potential elements, they concede, need not count as "intrinsic representations" or even as content-bearing, yet they would still be proper parts of a properly cognitive process. I confess that I simply did not (and still do not) understand this suggestion regarding a language-of-thought encoding (it is repeated in this volume, p. 69, without appearing to me to be any clearer). Nonetheless, it is now clear that whatever it may mean, it was not intended to concede the possibility (given only the considerations concerning intrinsic content) of Otto's notebook counting in the same way. For the authors now clarify their original claim thus:

Clearly, we mean that if you have a process that involves no intrinsic content, then the [intrinsic content] condition rules that the process is noncognitive. (Adams and Aizawa, this volume, p. 70)

As I now understand it, their position regarding the role of intrinsic content is this: there may be a process that is a genuinely cognitive process that has as proper parts some goings-on (such as, presumably, the token-ing of the punctuation mark in the LOT, puzzling as this still sounds to me) that themselves do not themselves involve intrinsic, nonderived con-tents (presumably because those parts-of-the-part do not involve contents at all). But such a process (the part, not the part-of-a-part!) must still involve at least *some* intrinsic content on pain of failing to be genuinely "cognitive." And Otto's notebook (I presume they must then wish to assert) fails even this very slightly weakened test, as here (they think) we have a process that involves *no intrinsic content at all*.

But in what sense do we, in the case of Otto's notebook, confront a *pro-cess* that involves *no intrinsic content at all*? It helps to be careful about tim-ing here. The time at which the notebook looks most clearly to be part of some real *process* is during the retrieval and use phase, and at that point in time, there are clearly plenty of states in play, in the larger notebook-including system, that count as intrinsically contentful, even on the Adams and Aizawa model. At run time, the process is not one that trades solely in representations whose contents are derived or conventionally determined.

What about at other times? Well, at such other times the claim is just that the notebook is part of the supervenience base for some of Otto's disposi-tional beliefs. What demands does this make on process? We can at least say this: the very notion of a dispositional belief already makes implicit refer-ence to what would happen in possible run-time situations. So here there is implicit reference to everything that those run-time processes would involve. The poise of the encodings in the notebook is such that, in the appropri-ate whole-system run-time circumstances, those encodings participate in extended processes that involve (let's assume) states with intrinsic contents.

But suppose, Adams and Aizawa may insist, we put all that run-time process talk aside and look solely at the (putative) part itself. Surely here we find a resource all of whose contentful states are derived, and doesn't that contravene the requirement concerning intrinsic content? In Clark 2003 and 2005b, I offered a thought experiment meant to show that Adams and Aizawa's requirement, as applied to some storage resource considered out of the context of its run-time role in a larger system, was too strong and ought to be rejected. The thought experiment concerned beings ("Mar-tians") endowed with an extra biological routine that allowed them to store *bit-mapped images* of important chunks of visually encountered text. Later on, at will, they could access (and then interpret) this stored text. Surely, I argued, we would have no hesitation in embracing that kind of bit-mapped storage, even prior to an act of retrieval, as part and parcel of the Martian cognitive equipment. But what is stored is just a bit-mapped image of a fully conventional form of external representation. If we accept the Martian memory into the cognitive fold, surely only skin-and-skull-based prejudice stops us extending the same courtesy to Otto.

Despite spending significant time on what I presented as a weaker and more complex example (the one involving reasoning with imagined Venn diagrams/ Euler circles[3]), Adams and Aizawa do not comment on this case. Yet it raises, I still believe, exactly the right issues. Even if we demand the involvement, in any cognitive process, of at least some items that bear their contents intrinsically, it is quite unclear how we should distribute this requirement across time and space. The Martian encodings are poised, here and now, to participate in processes that invoke intrinsic contents. So are those in Otto's notebook. Since it is arguably poise that matters, at least where dispositional believing is concerned, it seems that any reasonably plausible form of the requirement involving intrinsic content is met.

The notebook, I am happy to concede, is not, considered all on its own (and as far as we understand this notion at all) "intrinsically cognitive." But it *is* a resource whose encodings, at appropriate run-time moments, inform Otto's behavior in the way characteristic (we claimed) of dispositional beliefs. And this, we claim, is all that matters. Perhaps it is indeed essential that any truly cognitive *activity* (and hence any genuinely cognitive *agent*) draw on at least some states with intrinsic content. But we have been given no reason at all to accept the further (and crucial) claim that *no proper part* of such a properly cognitive system, considered now in splendid isolation from those crucial run-time wholes in which it participates, can afford to contain only representations lacking intrinsic content.

Indeed, I see no reason why we should accept (or even be tempted by) such a further condition. In general, for some X to be part of the supervenience base of some Y, where that Y must (to count as a Y at all, let's assume) exhibit some property Z, there is no requirement *that Z be in addition a property of the putative part X*. Thus suppose it were essential, for any system to count as properly cognitive, that the system be capable of conscious awareness. We would not want to insist (indeed, we would be crazy to insist) that every proper part of that system be capable of such awareness. We would not even insist (to draw even closer to the case in hand) that every proper part *of the subsystems that support conscious awareness* need be such as to exhibit such awareness when considered in isolation. Or suppose that we think that any genuinely moral agent must be able to reason about the good of others. Still, we should not think that every proper part of that agent (not even every proper part essential to the agent's moral reasoning) must be capable of so doing. Just so, from the requirement (if it is a requirement) that every cognitive agent trade in intrinsic contents, it cannot follow that every proper part of such an agent must trade, and trade at all times, in such contents.

This, to be sure, cuts both ways. As Adams and Aizawa point out (in Adams and Aizawa 2009, p. 84) "it does not follow from the fact that one has an 'X system' that every component of the system does X." Consider, they suggest, a sound system:

> Not every component produces sounds. The speakers do, but lasers in CD players, amplifiers, volume controls and tone controls do not. Again, not every component of an X system does X. (Ibid., p. 85)

But what this actually shows, I think, is pretty much the opposite of what Adams and Aizawa intend it to show. Agreed, the mere fact that the notebook and bio-Otto "form a system" establishes nothing. Perhaps Otto also forms some kind of a system with his garden tools, but that does not make the garden tools part of Otto. But the way to then proceed is surely *not* by asking, of the candidate part, whether it somehow "possesses" the characteristic that we now want to ascribe to the resultant overall system. What the point about sound systems shows, yet again, is simply the surprising extent to which Adams and Aizawa are committed to the usefulness of pressing a question that, to us, looks pretty clearly to be among the very reddest of possible herrings. That is the question whether Otto's notebook (to put the matter bluntly) is "cognitive." Since what is at issue is (to repeat) whether the notebook might now be part of the local supervenience base for some of Otto's dispositional beliefs (a putative systems-level fact if ever there was one), the status of the notebook itself, as "cognitive" or "noncognitive," is (to whatever extent that idea is even intelligible) simply irrelevant. By contrast, the *precise nature* of the coupling between the notebook and the rest of the Otto system seems absolutely crucial to how one then conceives of the overall situation.

4 That Cognitive Kind

Consider now the second major part of Adams and Aizawa's challenge. Recall that their suggestion concerning the "mark of the cognitive" is that "cognition involves particular kinds of processes involving non-derived representations" (Adams and Aizawa 2001, p. 53). We have, I think, now said all that needs to be said concerning the appeal to nonderived representation. But what about the other part of the clause, the appeal to "particular kinds of process" involving such representations? It is at this point that another kind of consideration comes into play. This concerns the possible existence of a characteristic set of causal processes found, by painstaking empirical investigation, to pervade the internal, biologically supported aspects of human cognitive architecture. The operation of these signature causal processes, the authors claim, gives rise to a number of laws and regularities that seem to apply to (these known) cognitive processes, but that do not apply elsewhere (for example, to Otto's notebook). In light of this, Adams and Aizawa ask, shouldn't we judge that the notebook falls outside the class of the cognitive? We should indeed do so, they claim, because "the cognitive must be discriminated on the basis of underlying causal processes" (ibid., p. 52). Here too, then, we must unfortunately grapple with the murky appeal to some kind of apparently self-standing (i.e., nonsystemic) notion of "the cognitive." Only this time the notion is linked to the specific laws and regularities characteristic of the internal, biological routines running in earthly cognitive agents.

The kinds of law and regularity the authors have in mind here include the pervasiveness, in human (biological) memory systems of the effects of chunking, priming, recency, and so on (ibid., p. 61), and in human perceptual systems of various psychophysical laws (such as Weber's law; ibid.). Given that science has uncovered these (undeniably important and interesting) regularities, what does this imply concerning the nature of cognition? According to Adams and Aizawa, the proper conclusion is that

the weight of empirical evidence supports the view that, as a matter of empirical fact, there are processes that (a) are recognizably cognitive, (b) take place in the brain, (c) do not take place outside of the brain, and (d) do not cross from the brain into the external world. (Adams and Aizawa, this volume, p. 69)

Quite so. Or rather, quite so up until (d), where we again confront the thorny issue of processes, parts, and the "nature" of parts. For whereas specific neural processes and their characteristic properties clearly do not cross over into the nonbiological world, there may exist (according to friends of the extended mind) overarching processes that include (some of the) neural ones and that play the right kind of role in guiding and enabling behavior to count as part of the physical base for cognition.

Thus recall that opening salvo concerning the mathematician's pencil. Their very next sentence reads:

Clark apparently thinks that the nature of the processes internal to a pencil, Rolodex, computer, cell phone, piece of string, or whatever, has nothing to do with whether that thing carries out cognitive processing. (Ibid., p. 68)

It is now clear what is at stake. Adams and Aizawa think that empirical investigations have turned up a number of features (e.g., priming effects in the case of memory) that reflect the operation, in some parts of the physical universe, of processes internal to those parts. Since these concern our paradigm cases of terrestrial cognition, we should believe (defeasibly, but on the basis of current evidence) that these kinds of causal process are essential to the cognitive status (again, we may need to try hard if we are to understand something by this notion) of such parts. It is *the nature of the processes internal to the part* that, so the argument insists, must determine whether it meets the conditions for inclusion into the ranks of the cognitive.

But this is something the extended mind theorist might very reasonably deny. It seems very plausible, for example, that there is no part of the physical universe so devoid of potentially computationally useful properties that that part could not, under some conceivable circumstances, participate as a crucial element in some extended, recognizably computational process, on which some cognitive state of some being supervenes. Whether a candidate part has the "right nature" seems, in such cases, to have more to do with the rest of the system (and what it can and can't do in the absence of that part) than with any intrinsic properties of the part itself.

Perhaps Adams and Aizawa will press the question, how do we know the state, in the scenario above, to be cognitive? On their account, we do so by asking to what extent it shares in the casual processes so far identified as characteristic of terrestrial biological cognition. But they surely cannot hold this as a general model of "cognition-spotting" since it rules out the discovery of *new* signature processes, even of the internal, earthbound, biological kind. Nor, I would have thought, can they hold that what goes for internal, biological, earth-bound cognition need be true of cognition tout court. The notion of the cognitive is surely bigger than that. If that special bit-mapped Martian memory, or even the whole of Martian memory, does not exhibit priming and recency effects, should we conclude that it is not memory at all or that Martian remembering (if it is some more generic kind of memory) is "not cognitive"?

But what, Adams and Aizawa will by now be screaming in frustration, *makes* a process cognitive? I haven't said. What makes a process cognitive, it seems to me, is that it supports intelligent behavior. This is obviously unhelpful, though it is almost certainly just the reply that would be given by, say, the average neuroscientist or cognitive psychologist. Surely no psychologist or neuroscientist would instead assert, for example, that what makes some candidate process cognitive is that it supports effects of recency and priming. To identify cognitive processes as those processes, however many and varied, that support intelligent behavior may be the best we can do. To argue from the other direction, and to identify cognitive processes as those that happen to characterize the neural activity of human agents, is to risk an unwarranted narrowing of focus (to the neural) and a dangerous and unappealing chauvinism to boot.

The alternative, to paraphrase Dennett, is that cognition is as cognition does. That is to say, we should individuate the cognitive[1] by its characteristic effects, not by its characteristic causes. The notion of a cognitive process, if that is correct, is best unpacked as the notion of a process that supports certain kinds of behavior (actual and counterfactual). This is the notion that allows Otto's notebook, in virtue of its gross functional poise, to count as part of the local supervenience base for Otto's cognizings, and, more specifically, for some of his dispositional believings. Why ask for more?

We are now circling what may be the intractable nub of the problem. For Adams and Aizawa[5] are mightily impressed by the clear differences that exist between many of the goings-on found (so far) inside the bounds of skin and skull and the kinds of goings-on found in artifacts such as notebooks. And they invite us, repeatedly, to focus our attention on *the nature of the notebook* (to stick with that example) and thus hope to persuade us that it is "not cognitive," that it fails to partake of the "mark of the cognitive," and so on. That such differences (between, let's say, the notebook and the neocortex) exist, no one should deny. But some of us are *equally* impressed by our apparent capacity to form extended computational systems that profoundly factor in both sets of distinctive contributions, creating wholes that look to support new kinds of cognitive capacities. In the case of Otto, the new capacity is just a coarse functional simulacrum of his damaged biological memory capacity. In other cases, the new capacities might be more genuinely novel. But what matters, in every instance, is (1) the degree of complementarity (between the different contributions) and (2) the degree of integration achieved. Given sufficient complementarity and integration, it becomes plausible (many of us believe) to treat the resultant system as a cognitive whole, with cognitive properties that supervene on more than the biological components alone.

As a brief aside, I tend to believe, though nothing in the argument for the extended mind hangs on it, that large chunks of the internal, biological processing that goes on in us humans (though not in other animals) consist not in the manipulation of items bearing intrinsic content but in the manipulation of a variety of pointers and markers inherited from public language itself. These would be direct neural encodings of public-language words and symbols that act, within the inner realm itself, in many of the same ways as external public-language encodings act on, and empower, us. As a result, I believe that the kind of complementarity that, on the extended mind model, explains the power of integrated systems of internal and external resources *also* explains much of the apparently unique power of purely internal human cognition. (For more on this idea, see Clark 1998, 2005a.)

Returning to the main matter of complementary internal and external (nonbiological) resources, it is important to notice that attention to larger systemic wholes in no way precludes a proper investigation of the special features of various parts, aspects, and components. A useful comparison is with the move toward systems-level neuroscience.[6] For much of the century, most serious neuroscientific knowledge concerned the responses and behaviors of single cells. Then, with the advent of new techniques of recording, intervention, and investigation, some attention began to be devoted to understanding the neural dynamics of whole populations of cells and the distinctive processing styles of different gross anatomical elements (such as the hippocampus). Contemporary neuroscience, courtesy of still-newer techniques of imaging and analysis, and by using increasingly bio-realistic neural network simulations, is just beginning to make progress in understanding some of the key features and properties of larger-scale neural systems, whole processing cycles that involve the temporally evolving, often highly reentrant, activity of multiple populations of neurons spanning a variety of brain areas. Note that the advent of true systems-level neuroscience will not (and should not) imply the inappropriateness of investigations that target the special properties and features of distinct cell-types or of distinct populations, or of distinct neural areas. But it must add to these investigations a new sensitivity to the added value created by processing cycles that include multiple complementary operations, performed using various kinds of neural resource, and whose integrated action is responsible for much of the power and scope of an individual human intelligence.

The notion of the extended mind is nothing other than the notion of systems-level cognitive (rather than neuro-) science. All it adds to that notion is some discussion, adverting to the details of biological–artifactual coupling, meant to make it plausible to treat some of these larger-scale systems as the local supervenience base for the knowledge and cognitive capacities of a specific agent. This added wrinkle was not necessary in the move toward systems-level neuroscience, as the old prejudices concerning the bounds of skin and skull there worked in favor of the "obvious" appropriateness of the larger-scale investigation.

Imagine a world (call it Hippo-world) in which for half a century, all neuroscientific attention is focused on the hippocampus, regarded (for some historical reason let's assume) as the obvious locus of all human cognitive activity. Specific features of hippocampal processing and encoding are discovered and publicized. One day, a few researchers turn their attention to the rest of the brain. They discover many new and interesting features, and begin to talk about the larger processing circuits that link (for example) hippocampal and neocortical processing, and the way certain memory phenomena seem to depend on the complex interactions between the two components. But there is a problem. Some philosophers in Hippo-world believe that in discovering the characteristic causal processes that operate in the hippocampus, they are discovering *the essential characteristics of cognition itself*. Better, they now insist, to view *what the hippocampus does as cognitive* and the rest of the brain as merely sending inputs to, or receiving outputs from, that "truly cognitive part." These other parts, after all, just don't do the same things as the hippocampus, so why regard what they do as cognitive? Others demur, for much of what they see as gross intelligent human behavior seems to depend as much on the special features and properties of the other parts as on the (important but limited) contribution of the hippocampus itself. Hippo-world begins a public debate on what they clumsily dub "the extended brain." The jury remains out.

One important challenge, for those Hippo-worlders who want to treat the whole brain as a cognitive organ, concerns the question of "added value." What do we gain, they are asked, by challenging common sense and starting to speak of extrahippocampal activity as part of the physical base for cognition? Can't we explain all that anyone actually does by treating what the hippocampus does as cognitive and the rest as (perhaps instrumentally useful but) noncognitive? As long as we note what actually gets done, and are sensitive to how information flows through the system, this will work fine, won't it? Isn't all we need, to paraphrase Rupert (2004), the "hypothesis of the embedded hippocampus"?

I think the answer to this question must be "yes." We could, if we so wished, carve up the contributions in the way suggested. And this may well have the advantage of not challenging common sense (as it had apparently developed on Hippo-world). But by the same token, if we accept the vision of the whole brain as a locus of processing cycles that include multiple complementary operations, performed using various kinds of neural resource, and whose integrated action is responsible for much of the power and scope of an individual human intelligence, there is a clear case for accusing Hippo-world common sense of displaying a needlessly restricted vision of cognitive processing. Yet the description just given works every bit as well for the case of the extended mind. There, the idea is that the brain–body–world system is sometimes (when the right coupling conditions are met) the locus of processing cycles that include multiple complementary operations, performed using various kinds of neural resource, and whose integrated action is responsible for much of the power and scope of an individual human intelligence.

The challenge of added value thus cuts both ways. For what is the added value, one may ask, in *not* embracing these visions of larger systemic wholes? No one, after all, is suggesting that such larger visions preclude investigation of the special features and properties of any of the parts. Just as systems-level neuroscience should not be seen as a threat to single-cell neuroscience or to the study of the hippocampus, so systems-level cognitive science should not be seen as a threat to neuroscience or to the study of the special features and properties of the biological brain. In fact, one of those special features and properties, neural plasticity, is probably crucial to the brain's astounding ability to enter into the most profound forms of cognitive extension[7] in the first place.

Conclusions: Watering the Landscape

Adams and Aizawa's challenge to the extended mind is rather like a challenge that might be posed to a theorist of irrigation. Take some putative part of a process of irrigation and ask yourself, is that part *irrigative*? To push the question, demand of the theorist of irrigation an account of the "mark of the irrigative" and then ask whether some putative part of some process of irrigation shares in that mark.

We should not, I think, like to approach the matter of an irrigation system in this way. What we want to know, of some putative proper part of such a system, is whether it contributes to the functional whole. We may ask ourselves, for example, whether it enables that functional whole to irrigate land that it could not otherwise reach. To the extent that the answer is positive, the part (ceteris paribus, of course) looks to be part of the system of irrigation, regardless of whether water drizzles out of it.

Just so, there is surely no value in pursuing the question, asked of Otto's notebook, "is it cognitive?" Instead, we must attend (and Chalmers and I did attend, in the published essays) to the role of the notebook in the larger organization of which biological Otto is a part. Then we can ask questions such as, does the notebook enable this larger system to exhibit the kinds of behavioral regularity characteristic of an individual's dispositionally believing that such and such?

This move toward a larger systemic focus is familiar and oftentimes helpful. The study of the extended mind presents, I suggest, no *greater* theoretical or practical difficulties than those, significant as they were, that attended the move toward a systems-level neuroscience. And it is justified (or so I believe) in very much the same way. In each case, we confront densely integrated larger-scale organizations that support some of the kinds of intelligent behavior most characteristic of our species. Systems-level neuroscience, however, could for the most part simply help itself to the idea of an individual, sufficiently unified cognizer. Extended mind theorists cannot. Instead, the incorporation of a nonbiological resource into the cognitive processing of an individual requires that certain kinds of coupling between biological and nonbiological resources be present. Absent these, even inner biological goings-on, replete with any available "marks of the cognitive," would not count as part of the cognitive activity *of that very agent*. When such couplings are in place, however, the bounds of skin and skull are rendered functionally irrelevant, and cognition extends gracefully into the world.

Notes

1. These attributions are all fully explicit, but are spread across the three essays (2001, 2008, this volume) mentioned at the start.

2. Thus Ken Aizawa, after a long series of exchanges, asks "so, you really agree with us that the notebook is noncognitive?" as if an affirmative answer were incompatible with the extended mind thesis. Yet insofar as the question is even intelligible, we would indeed reply that the notebook, considered alone, is "noncognitive," *just like a neuron or group of neurons*.

3. Adams and Aizawa (this volume) devote much space to arguing that the case of the Euler circles fails to meet their condition, properly understood, and they are right to do so. I offered it only as a case where *some* proper aspects of a genuinely mental process seem to trade in representations whose meanings are conventional. This, after all, was how I saw the case of Otto's notebook (more on which in the text).

4. Note that the cognitive is a much broader notion than that of the conscious, which may be individuated in ways that appeal to much more than characteristic effects or (what comes to the same thing) characteristic kinds of functional poise.

5. See also Rupert 2004.

6. For a useful survey, see Bechtel 2001.

7. See Clark 2003.

References

Adams, F., and Aizawa, K. (2001). The bounds of cognition. *Philosophical Psychology,* *14*(1), 43–64.

Adams, F., and Aizawa, K. (2009). Why the mind is still in the head. In P. Robbins and M. Aydede (eds.), *The Cambridge Handbook of Situated Cognition.* Cambridge: Cambridge University Press.

Bechtel, W. (2001). Cognitive neuroscience: Relating neural mechanisms and cognition. In P. Machamer, P. McLaughlin, and R. Grush (eds.), *Philosophical Reflections on the Methods of Neuroscience.* Pittsburgh, PA: University of Pittsburgh Press.

Clark, A. (1998). Magic words: How language augments human computation. In P. Carruthers and J. Boucher (eds.), *Language and Thought: Interdisciplinary Themes* (pp. 162–183). Cambridge: Cambridge University Press.

Clark, A. (2001). Reasons, robots, and the extended mind. *Mind and Language, 16,* 121–145.

Clark, A. (2003). *Natural-Born Cyborgs: Minds, Technologies and the Future of Human Intelligence.* New York: Oxford University Press.

Clark, A. (2005a). Word, niche, and super-niche: How language makes minds matter more. *Theoria, 20,* 255–268.

Clark, A. (2005b). Intrinsic content, active memory, and the extended mind. *Analysis, 65*(285), 1–11.

Clark, A. (2007). Re-inventing ourselves: The plasticity of embodiment, sensing, and mind. *Journal of Philosophy and Medicine, 32,* 263–282.

Clark, A., and Chalmers, D. (1998). The extended mind. *Analysis 58*:1: 7–19. Reprinted as chapter 2 of this volume.

Dennett, D. (2000). Making tools for thinking. In D. Sperber (ed.), *Metarepresentations: A Multidisciplinary Perspective* (pp. 43–62). Oxford: Oxford University Press.

Gibbs, R. (2001). Intentions as emergent products of social interactions. In B. F. Malle, L. J. Moses, and D. Baldwin (eds.), *Intentions and Intentionality* (pp. 105–122). Cambridge, MA: MIT Press.

Haugeland, J. (1998). Mind embodied and embedded. In J. Haugeland (ed.), *Having Thought: Essays in the Metaphysics of Mind.* Cambridge, MA: Harvard University Press.

Rupert, R. (2004). Challenges to the hypothesis of extended cognition. *Journal of Philosophy, 101*(8), 389–428.

Van Gelder, T., and Port, R. (eds.) (1995). *Mind as Motion.* Cambridge, MA: MIT Press.

Wilson, R. A. (2004). *Boundaries of the Mind: The Individual in the Fragile Sciences— Cognition.* Cambridge: Cambridge University Press.

6 The Varieties of Externalism

Susan Hurley

Externalism comes in varieties. While the landscape isn't tidy, I offer an organizing framework within which many of the forms it has taken (though perhaps not all) can be located. This taxonomy should be useful in itself. I'll also use it to survey and compare arguments for different kinds of externalism, while probing related intuitions.[1]

1 Taxonomy and Preliminaries

1.1 What versus how and content versus quality My taxonomy consists in a two-by-two matrix: *what-externalism* contrasts with *how-externalism*, and content-related versions of each contrast with phenomenal quality-related versions. (I often say "quality" as short for "phenomenal quality.")

Some forms of externalism invoke external factors to explain the "what" of mental states, whereas other forms invoke external factors to explain the "how" of mental states. The what–how distinction isn't always sharp; how a thing works can determine what type of thing it is. For present purposes, the distinction is used as follows. *What-explanations* explain the mental types of mental states—their personal-level content types or phenomenal quality types. For example, they explain why an intention is an intention to look inside the box on the left, rather than to look inside a different box, or to do something else entirely. Or they might why an experience is one of how something looks rather than of how it feels or sounds, or is an experience of red rather than of green. *How-explanations* explain how the processes or mechanisms work that enable mental states of a given content or quality type (see and cf. McDowell 1994 on the "enabling" language). They explain, for example, what processes or mechanisms enable a given intention to look inside the box on the left, or a given visual experience of a certain surface as blue. If token mental states of the same type (content or quality) are implemented in different ways (reflecting neural plasticity), we can ask whether their 'how'-explanations are fundamentally different, or also display commonality at the right level of description (Hurley and Noë 2003a; see also below).

What-externalism is also called *taxonomic externalism* (Wilson 2004). The content externalism familiar to philosophers from traditional debates about wide versus narrow content and Twin Earth is one variety of it; another variety applies to phenomenal quality rather than (or as well as) intentional content (Dretske 1996; Hurley and Noë 2003b).

How-externalism is a more recent arrival. I christened it *vehicle externalism* (Hurley 1998a), but here I'll also call it *enabling externalism.*[2] How-explanations can be given at different or mixed levels of description, including subpersonal neural, information-processing, dynamical systems, and ecological descriptions. Talk of "vehicles" of content here does not imply that vehicles must be subpersonal representations—that only representational accounts of enabling processes are in the running; my use of "vehicle" is neutral between representational and any nonrepresentational accounts there may be of enabling processes. Some dynamical accounts of enabling processes may not count as representational, for example, while others do (e.g., Wheeler and Clark 1999; Clark 1997; Wheeler 2001; van Gelder 1999b, 1995, 1998).[3] My usage of the term "cognitive" (as in "cognitive processes" and "cognitive science") is similarly neutral between representational and any nonrepresentational accounts there may be of how mental states are enabled (see Wheeler and Clark 1999). No assumptions about these empirical issues are implied by my terminology. Of course, the content of my arguments doesn't depend on this labeling, if someone prefers another.

In the rest of this section I sketch the landscape my taxonomy generates, to orient readers and introduce some general issues; the following sections focus on each category of externalism in turn.

1.2 What-content externalism *What-content externalism* is the most well-established variety: externalism about the intentional content of mental states. Just as the meaning of "water" is determined in part by the external world, on this view the content of mental states about water is determined in part by the external world. Arguments for content externalism typically derive from intuitions that content does not supervene internally in "Twin Earth" or supervenience thought experiments (STEs), supplemented by various positive externalist accounts of content that explain such intuitions. These intuitions are supposedly widely shared (though I'm not aware of empirical work verifying this) and widely accepted as appropriate data for philosophical theorizing and thus as support for externalist theories of content that predict such intuitions, such as causal or teleosemantic theories.

In this section I'll distinguish "mere" internal supervenience from the possibility of STEs. The latter but not the former requires explanatory separability of internal and external factors. "Mere" internal supervenience requires that when internal factors are duplicated, so are mental contents. This can be true even when internal factors cannot be "unplugged" from external, so that internal and external factors vary together and are not explanatorily separable. But STEs assume that internal factors can be so unplugged. The issue about internalism and externalism, I argue, is one about explanation, not "mere" internal supervenience—which is compatible with externalist explanation. Internal supervenience is necessary but not sufficient for internalist explanation. Internalism can fail either because external factors are needed for explanation in an STE, or because the relevant STE is not possible and internal and external factors are not explanatorily separable.

1.3 What-quality externalism and the magical membrane problem *What-quality externalism* is analogous to what-content externalism, but applies to the phenomenal quality of mental states. This is less widely accepted, but it has proponents, especially among those who link the phenomenal qualities of experience to its intentional content. If content is partly externally determined, and content determines phenomenal quality, then phenomenal quality is partly externally determined (Dretske 1996; Harman 1990).

Note two contrasts between what-content externalism and what-quality externalism. First, widespread intuitions favor what-content externalism, whereas what-quality externalism is often regarded as counterintuitive. The results of STEs for phenomenal character are controversial, but probably evoke more phenomenal-internalist than phenomenal-externalist intuitions. (Again, these are merely informed impressions about intuitions; I'm not aware of empirical work confirming them.) Rather, what-quality externalism is often regarded as a bullet to be bitten, a price to be paid, in order to have the courage of one's what-content externalist convictions.

A second, metaintuitive contrast should be distinguished from the first, intuitive contrast; it concerns the status rather than the content of intuitions. Do intuitions provide competent data to resolve the internalism–externalism issue, or are they merely expressions of opinion or predictions? Metaintuition says that intuitions STEs provide appropriate data to resolve what-content issues, but could simply be wrong about what-quality issues.

To elaborate: Regardless of what intuitions say about content in STEs, they provide competent data for theories of content. What-content metaintuitions say that intuitions about content under various hypothetical suppositions provide the right kind of data, to which the issue between internalist and externalist what-content explanations are ultimately responsible. Content-intuitions provide the observations or evidence that what-content explanations must explain.

What-quality metaintuitions contrast strikingly. Regardless of what intuitions say about phenomenal quality in STEs, it is not at all clear that such intuitions provide data competent in principle to resolve the issue between internalist and externalist what-quality explanations. Oddly, although intuitions here may be more strongly internalist, they are also metaintuitively less competent to determine the issue. The question of whether phenomenal qualities can vary with external factors when internal factors are held constant appears to be an empirical question, ultimately responsible to experience itself rather than our intuitions about thought experiments. Such intuitions merely express our opinions or predictions about what experience would be like in such cases; but we could simply be wrong. This *autonomy metaintuition for phenomenal qualities* is an expression of the intuition that there is an intractable explanatory gap between physical or functional properties and phenomenal qualities. Autonomy metaintuitions provide resistance to views that tie phenomenal qualities tightly to intentional contents, since qualities are ultimately autonomous in relation to data to which contents are ultimately responsible. Although autonomy and explanatory gap intuitions are often held alongside internalist intuitions, the combination is paradoxical: If someone really has no conception of how neural or internal functional properties—or indeed any others—could explain phenomenal qualities, then how can he be so confident that *if* phenomenal qualities can be explained, it must be internal factors that do the job? What is so magical about the boundary around internal factors? I discuss this "magical membrane problem" below.

Why are intuitions favoring what-quality internalism so prevalent? Why, that is, is it so widely assumed that qualities of experience cannot vary with external factors, when internal factors are fully controlled for? I'll reflect below on two responses, appealing to hallucinations and to brains in vats. First, specific localized hallucinations and illusions can have phenomenal qualities that do not depend on external factors. It's tempting to generalize from this point, by postulating neural twins in different environments, to what-quality internalism. Second, suppose it were technically possible to transfer a brain from vivo to vitro in such a way that neural processes continue undisrupted in established patterns during and after the envatting process, relying on computer-generated inputs and feedback. It's widely assumed the transition would be phenomenally seamless: the subject–brain would experience no global or local phenomenal changes simply as a result of the envatting process, despite changes in external factors and/or intentional contents. This supposition may also seem to support what-quality externalism.

1.4 Enabling externalism for content and for quality So far we have two varieties of *what*-externalism, concerned respectively to explain the content and the phenomenal quality of persons' mental states. Other varieties of externalism aim to explain *how*—by what processes or mechanisms or "vehicles"—mental states are enabled. Enabling processes can be explained in terms of computation, neural networks, dynamical systems, and so on. What are the boundaries of the relevant enabling processes? Can enabling processes extend beyond exclusively internal neural processes into the body and its environment? Enabling externalism (or how-externalism, or vehicle externalism) answers "yes."

We should distinguish externalism about processes that enable intentional content from externalism about processes that enable phenomenal quality. Arguments for *content-enabling externalism* have often proceeded under the headings of "extended mind" or "embodied, situated cognition." For example, an Alzheimer's patient's cognitive processes arguably extend to a notebook he uses in place of reliable neural memory processes (Clark and Chalmers 1998); an accountant's cognitive processes may include her use of pen and paper in complex calculations. Arguments for *quality-enabling externalism* have tended to appeal to embodied, situated interactions with natural environments, often under the heading of "sensorimotor dynamics."

1.5 What–how relations and the "causal–constitutive error" error What- and how-explanations needn't coincide, of course. What-externalism doesn't require how-externalism; indeed, most what-content externalists are probably internalists about enabling processes. On the other hand, how-externalism may require what-externalism (see Wilson 2004, p. 179). More generally, externalist what- and how-explanations can overlap significantly, or constrain one another.[4] In particular, externalist what-quality explanations and externalist quality-enabling explanations tend to converge in their worldly portions, since both appeal directly to dynamic sensorimotor interactions with natural environments (see, e.g., Noë 2004).

The distinction between what- and how-explanations in philosophy of psychology should not be confused with a distinction between explanations of something's constitution as opposed to its causes. The what–how distinction doesn't align cleanly with either a causal–constitutive distinction or an external–internal distinction.

In philosophy of psychology, explanations tend to be treated as causal or constitutive with no independent justification,[5] in accord with prior assumptions or intuitions about boundaries, which often themselves have no clear basis and do not illuminate the distinction. For example, prevalent externalist what-content explanations appeal to causal relations between an organism and its environment, understood to provide constitutive rather than merely causal explanation of mental content type, even though in many illusions and hallucinations, tokens of content types do not participate in the type of causal process that is nevertheless taken to explain, constitutively, their content. By contrast, externalist what-quality explanations and enabling explanations may be accused of committing a "causal-constitutive error" if they regard extended explanations as constitutive rather than merely causal (Block 2005), and illusions and hallucinations are widely taken to support what-quality internalism and enabling internalism. Why are externalist explanations allowed to be constitutive in the former case but assumed to be "merely causal" in the latter? The answer presumably turns on some theoretical account of content, or phenomenal quality, or their enabling processes—but this is just what is at issue between internalism and externalism. The *"causal–constitutive error" error* is the error of objecting that externalist explanations give a constitutive role to external factors that are "merely causal" while assuming without independent argument or criteria that the causal–constitutive distinction coincides with some external–internal boundary. To avoid thus begging the question, we should not operate with prior assumptions about where to place the causal–constitutive boundary, but wait on the results of explanation. I understand externalism as in the first instance a claim about explanation rather than about metaphysics or constitution.

Some internalist critics of the "causal–constitutive error" do provide a criterion of the mental that doesn't evidently beg the question against externalism, and thus don't commit the "causal–constitutive error" error. For example, the criterion of underived content motivates Adams and Aizawa to argue that extended processes are not constitutive but merely causal. My reply to them is different but related. Criteria of the mental or the cognitive vary widely (if not wildly) across theorists; it isn't even clear what agreed-on work such criteria should do. Yet psychology continues on its way with a rough-and-ready sense of what it wants to explain, generating good explanations. The issues between internalism and externalism should be resolved bottom up by such scientific practice, not by advance metaphysics: by seeing whether any good psychological explanations are externalist, not by deciding on a criterion of the mental and using it to sort explanations as constitutive or not. In this context, I'm aware of no appropriate criterion independent of good explanations; to the extent good explanations reveal constitution, a criterion of the constitutive cannot be used to select among good explanations. As I understand it, externalism predicts that some good psychological explanations of the "what" or "how" kinds will be externalist.

1.6 The intuitive landscape Widespread intuitions resist the extension of externalist explanation from content to quality and from "what" to "how." As we've seen, intuitions tend to favor what-content externalism and resist what-quality externalism. Content-enabling externalism, about the vehicles of intentional content, is also regarded as counterintuitive (Adams and Aizawa 2001). And quality-enabling externalism, about the vehicles of phenomenal quality, seems to be the most counterintuitive of all (when it is even registered as a possibility).

Why do intuitions about varieties of externalism differ in these ways, resisting moves from "what" to "how" and from content to quality? Quite different arguments have been offered for these different forms of externalism. Some of the arguments may be more plausible than others, though intuitions about the different forms of externalism may be influenced by unexamined assumptions as well as by the plausibility of arguments. Continuing to take a lofty view of the landscape, let's compare the arguments and assumptions at work.

Table 6.1

Varieties of Externalism	*Concerning Intentional Content (More Intuitive)*	*Concerning Phenomenal Quality (Less Intuitive)*
What-externalism (more intuitive)	What-content externalism (most intuitive)	What-quality externalism (less intuitive)
How-externalism (less intuitive)	Content-enabling externalism, about vehicles of content (less intuitive)	Quality-enabling externalism, about vehicles of phenomenal qualities (least intuitive)

I   What-Externalism

2   What-Content Externalism and Supervenience Thought Experiments
Arguments for what-content externalism typically take the form of STEs
in which the supervenience of mental content on internal factors intuitively fails.[6] Internal supervenience requires that when internal factors are
constant—duplicated or twinned—across some range of cases, then mental content is also constant. Hence, the supervenience counterfactual: if
mental content were different across such cases, internal factors would
have to differ also.

The duplication or "Twin Earth thought experiments that test supervenience requirements are so familiar that it is worth holding them up with
a pair of tweezers and taking a detached look at them, to articulate the
assumptions that are being made. In this section I will first explain the
sense in which STEs are controlled thought experiments that seek to separate out the explanatory roles of internal and external factors. Explanatory separability requires that internal factors can be unplugged from
external factors. Second, I will distinguish the truth of a supervenience
claim from the possibility of a corresponding STE. Internal supervenience
can hold even though the relevant STE is not possible because internal
factors cannot be unplugged from external. Third, the mere truth of
internal supervenience provides no support for internalist explanation, if
the relevant STE is not possible. Internalist explanation requires explanatory separability.

**2.1   Supervenience thought experiments as controlled thought experi-
ments**   Let's begin with the general idea of a controlled experiment. Suppose we want to explain X. The method of controlled experimentation
requires us to hold certain potentially explanatory factors constant while
we vary others, in a systematic effort to separate out the factors that actually do the work of explaining X. So we divide potentially explanatory
factors into two sets, A and B, and hold the B factors constant while
manipulating the A factors. If we then observe that X varies if and only if
the A factors vary, this suggests that the A factors are needed to explain X.
On the other hand, if X holds constant with the B factors when the A factors vary, this suggests that A factors are not needed to explain X.

The method of controlled experiment seeks factors that are *explanatorily separable.* If the A and the B factors are explanatorily separable, then
either the contribution made by A factors to explaining X is independent
of the level of or relations among B factors, or vice versa. But if the contri-

bution of A factors to explaining X depends on the level of or relations among B factors, and the contribution of B factors to explaining X also depends on the level of or relations among A factors, then A and B factors are not explanatorily separable. In coupled dynamic systems, for example, the parameters of one system are the variables of the other system, and vice versa. Or, consider the nonseparability of bodily phenotype and extended phenotype in explaining the presence of a certain genotype (Dawkins 1982). If X depends not just on the factors that are varied but also on the levels of and relations among the factors that are "controlled," whichever way around we allocate variation and control to the A and B factors, then explanatory separability fails. Explanatory separability also fails if the A and B factors vary together in the relevant possible worlds, so that the factors in one set cannot hold constant while the others vary and their contributions to explaining X thus cannot be separated.

Perhaps we can reindividuate sets of potentially explanatory factors, so that they are explanatorily separable. But perhaps not. X may depend non-separably on all the potentially explanatory factors and relations among them; they may be interdependent so as to form an explanatory unit.[7]

The ideas of control and explanatory separability can be extended from actual experiments to thought experiments about hypothetical cases. Supervenience thought experiments are in effect controlled thought experiments, which seek to separate out explanatory factors. STEs in philosophy of mind usually divide potentially explanatory factors into an internal set and an external set, relative to some boundary such as the skull or the skin; internal factors (neural or functional) are held constant by supposition while external factors vary. STEs thus assume that internal and external factors do not vary together in relevant possible worlds—that internal factors can be unplugged from one array of external factors and plugged into another. If internal factors are not unpluggable, but rather internal and external factors vary together across the relevant worlds, then they are not explanatorily separable.

Under the suppositions of a STE, does intentional content vary? What-content externalists answer "yes." This intuition provides evidence that suggests that external factors are needed to explain content, though it assumes unpluggability. The explanatory role of external factors is characterized in different ways by different versions of what-content externalism. Some appeal to direct causal interactions, some to causal history, others to teleology and evolutionary function, others to expertise in the social community; different versions can apply to different content types. STEs provide the evidence such what-content explanations aim to explain.

Note that externalist what-content explanations explain the content type of mental states; they are thus *type-explanatory* (Hurley 1998b). Not all tokens of the type need engage the external factors that explain the type in the same way. For example, an externalist what-explanation, in terms of certain normal causal interactions or normal functions, can be given of the content of a token illusory experience, even though the token itself does not participate in those type-explanatory processes (as in the well-known cracks and shadows example in Burge 1986, or in Millikan's 1984, 1993 account, of how tokens can fail to perform their proper function, which determines their type). So what-content explanations of token mental states can be parasitic on absent causal processes, in which the token is not engaged.

2.2   Supervenience on internal factors is necessary but not sufficient for internalist what-explanation   The truth of internal supervenience claims should be distinguished from the possibility of controlled STEs. Internal supervenience merely requires that mental content does not vary *if* the relevant internal factors are duplicated across different environments: unplugged and replugged. But the truth of this conditional claim does not require that the relevantly controlled STEs are possible: it may not be possible for the internal factors to remain constant while external factors vary, to be unplugged from one environment and replugged into another. They may vary together in the relevant possible worlds, so that they are not explanatorily separable.

Internalist what-explanation requires not merely the truth of internal supervenience, but that controlled STEs are possible; internal supervenience is necessary but not sufficient for internalist what-explanation. Internal supervenience without unpluggability provides no support for internalist explanation; mere supervenience is compatible with the explanatory non-separability of internal and external factors. In effect, there are two generic ways for internalism to fail: because *given* unplugging and replugging, external factors are needed to explain intuitions about content, or because unplugging and replugging are not possible in the first place. What-content externalism has focused on the first type of argument against internalism, but has largely ignored the second (but see Hurley 1998a, chap. 8; Wilson 2004).

The possibility of unplugging internal factors from one environment and plugging them unchanged into another is normally taken for granted when discussing internal supervenience. It shouldn't be. Whether it's possible depends on several matters:

A. On the range of possible worlds across which the corresponding supervenience claim operates. The modal strength of supervenience claims varies with the range of cases at issue: they may extend through this world only, through near possible worlds, or through all possible worlds. For example, the near-worlds counterfactual reading says that, in all near worlds in which mental content differs from that in the actual world, internal factors also differ; any worlds in which mental content differs while internal factors don't are far-out worlds, such as worlds where the laws of nature differ. A stricter modal reading of supervenience applies not just to near worlds but to all worlds.

Suppose near possible worlds don't permit unplugging and replugging, though far worlds with different laws do.[8] If so, a near-worlds supervenience counterfactual is trivially true: in near worlds where internal factors are the same, external factors are also the same, hence mental content is also the same. However, the relevant STE, controlled across near worlds, is not possible; this is what could provide evidence for internalism, understood as a naturalistic explanatory claim. STEs that rely on far, merely logically possible worlds where laws differ can't provide evidence for naturalistic internalist explanations. So, from the truth of the near-worlds supervenience counterfactual it doesn't follow that external factors are not needed to explain content. The supervenience counterfactual could be true even though internal and external factors were not explanatorily separable.

B. On the specific contents and environmental variations in question. Unplugging and replugging may be possible in some specific cases but not others, with different implications for internalist explanation in those cases (for an example in which unplugging and replugging is not possible, see my discussion of El Greco worlds, Hurley 1998a, chap. 8).

C. On whether the mental "states" are dynamic and extend through time. Consider the perceptual "states" of an agent who moves body, hands, head, and eyes continually as she probes and samples her environment through multiple informational channels, generating multiple feedback loops both wide and narrow. Unplugging and replugging is less likely to be possible for such dynamic cases than for static "snapshot" cases. Temporal extension leads to spatial extension; Dennett (1991) famously made the intracranial version of this point in his arguments against a Cartesian theater, but the point extends promiscuously across the boundaries of skull and body.

D. On how the boundary between internal and external is understood. If the boundary is understood functionally, the bodily or environmental scaffolding (e.g., compensating lenses, or computers controlling brains in vats) needed to duplicate neural factors in a different environment may itself count as a functionally "internal" factor, so that the supervenience boundary should include it. If so, factors inside the relevant boundary are not duplicated after all (see Hurley 1998a, chap. 8).

In this subsection I've distinguished the truth of a supervenience claim from the possibility of a corresponding STE, with its further separability and unpluggability assumptions. I've argued that a supervenience claim is true if the corresponding STE is possible and supports it; but it can be trivially true (or at least not false) if the corresponding STE is not possible, since there will then be no relevant case in which the antecedent of the supervenience claim holds and the consequent fails. Moreover, when internal and external factors vary together across relevant possible worlds, mental content can supervene on internal factors even though it requires explanation in terms of nonseparable internal and external factors. The truth of an internalist supervenience claim is thus necessary but not sufficient for internalist explanation; internal supervenience per se does not *provide* an explanation of intentional content in terms of internal factors,[9] or even entail that there must *be* such an explanation. When internal factors are not unpluggable, external factors may be needed for explanation despite internal supervenience.

2.3   Reflective equilibrium between boundary intuitions and explanation: The explanatory role of supervenience claims depends on boundaries that are neither too wide nor too narrow   Supervenience claims owe much of their significance to the explanatory credentials of the boundaries they draw. They provide evidence favoring internalist explanation if and only if they express the results of a controlled STE. This requires drawing a supervenience boundary that avoids two errors, of redundancy and trivialization.

On the one hand, the boundary shouldn't be too wide. The supervenience of content on the global physical state of the world tells us nothing about what specific factors explain content. Many factors in the global state may be redundant: they may do no work in explaining content. Content might be unaffected if they were allowed to vary, while holding other physical factors constant. To avoid redundancy, the supervenience boundary should be narrow enough to separate out nonexplanatory factors.

On the other hand, the boundary shouldn't be too narrow. It should be wide enough to permit potentially explanatory factors on one side of it to be held constant while those on the other side vary, across relevant possible worlds. Not all boundaries do so, since some factors cannot be separated or "unplugged" from others for explanatory purposes. An overly narrow boundary runs a danger of trivializing supervenience: the danger is that when factors outside the boundary vary, nonseparable factors within the boundary will also vary, and when factors within it are constant, nonseparable factors outside it will also hold constant. As explained, supervenience cannot be falsified if the two sets of factors cannot come apart over relevant worlds. Supervenience boundaries should be wide enough to avoid cutting across explanatorily nonseparable factors.

For example, suppose we're trying to explain color experience. We draw a boundary around a subset of the cells in the color-processing area of the brain, within which a certain process sometimes occurs: call it process 1. Whenever process 1 occurs in these cells, color A is experienced; whenever color A is not experienced, process 1 is not occurring in these cells. So color experience supervenes on the state of the smaller group of cells. It doesn't follow that experience of color A can be explained by the occurrence of process 1 in these cells. For suppose process 1 can only occur in these cells when process 2 occurs within a wider group of cells that includes the first. The smaller group of cells may be so intricately embedded in the dynamics of the wider group that the narrower process and what is happening outside the narrower boundary are not explanatorily separable. Holding the narrower process constant while varying what is happening in surrounding cells, or vice versa, may not be possible. We lack the control needed to support explanation of experience of color A in terms of the narrower process. The explanation should instead be sought within a wider boundary. This point would not be disarmed if experience of color A could be induced by stimulating specific cells, since such stimulation could well induce processes in other cells that contribute to explaining experience of color A.

STEs provide controls for explanations of mental types; supervenience boundaries should be adjusted as needed for these purposes. The right supervenience boundary is the one that captures the factors that explain what we're interested in, avoiding false separability and unpluggability assumptions. To avoid the dangers of redundancy and trivialization, STEs should be part of a process of seeking reflective equilibrium, in which boundaries are revised—loosened or tightened in light of explanatory progress—rather than assumed exogenously.

More generally, I see no basis independent of explanatory success for regarding factors within some prespecified boundary as deeply or constitutively explanatory, while those outside it are explanatory only in some shallower or "merely causal" way. I take issues about internalism and externalism to be issues about explanation. Some boundaries, like the skin, are intuitively salient. But they may not capture the explanation we seek. Intuitive boundaries can cut between factors that are not explanatorily separable.

I'm largely in sympathy with STE arguments for what-content externalism. This section isn't intended as a general challenge to such views. Rather, its aim is to induce critical awareness of the unpluggability and boundary assumptions made by STEs, and to place them into a broader explanatory context, for purposes of comparison to other arguments for externalism.

3   What-Quality Externalism and Supervenience Thought Experiments

In the context of what-content externalism, the previous section distinguished supervenience claims from STEs and made claims about separability, unpluggability, boundaries, and explanation. These points also apply to issues about what-quality externalism. In particular, the supervenience of quality on internal factors is compatible with externalist what-quality explanation. This section does not rehearse the application of these points to quality as opposed to content. Rather, it pursues further issues, concerning the two dimensions of intuitive difference between what-content externalism and what-quality externalism. Recall: (1) STEs yield internalist intuitions for quality but externalist intuitions for content, whereas (2) metaintuition says that intuitions about quality in STEs have lesser standing, as evidence for internalism or externalism, than do intuitions about content.

3.1   Supervenience thought experiments for phenomenal quality type: The magical membrane problem   Consider an STE for phenomenal quality instead of content. Let's place the supervenience boundary around the central nervous system (CNS), so the STE postulates CNS twins in different environments. Moreover, it postulates dynamic CNS twins, not merely snapshot CNS twins: their CNS processes continue to match over time, as they interact with their different environments. The STE assumes that even so, unplugging and replugging are not problematic. Finally, the laws of nature are the same for both twins (if they weren't, their CNS processes arguably wouldn't be either). Granting all this, the STE asks: could these dynamic CNS twins experience different phenomenal qualities?

I hypothesize that a widespread intuitive response would be: "The CNS twins *could* experience different qualities, as a conceptual matter, but of course they *won't*." Intuitions about such cases typically combine strongly internalist predictions, that phenomenal qualities would in fact supervene

on internal factors, with autonomy metaintuitions, that phenomenal qualities are ultimately independent of our intuitive internalist predictions. Our
intuitions could simply turn out to be wrong, if qualities of experience just
did differ across the CNS twins.

The *autonomy metaintuition for phenomenal quality* says: "Phenomenal
qualities are ultimately independent of intuition, in a way that intentional
contents are not. If our intuitions about content in STEs were to support
internalist explanation, no unexpected brute facts about mental content in
CNS twins could overturn this result. But even if our intuitions about phenomenal quality in STEs do strongly support internalist explanation, unexpected brute facts about the experiences of CNS twins could in principle
overturn internalism. Qualities of experience aren't responsible to intuitions in STEs the way contents are."

The autonomy metaintuition allows that phenomenal qualities could
resist explanation in terms of internal physical or functional factors, including neural processes. It's an expression of the widespread view that there's
an explanatory gap between phenomenal qualities and such internal factors, since we have no idea how they could explain phenomenal qualities.
Yet at the same time, widespread intuitions strongly favor what-quality
internalism.

This prevalent combination, of strong internalist intuitions with the
autonomy metaintuition, is puzzling, even paradoxical. Given the strength
of internalist intuitions, this combination is more than just a matter of
hedging one's empirical bets. Why are intuitions favoring what-quality
internalism so strong, given the autonomy metaintuition? If we have no
understanding of how phenomenal qualities *could* be explained, why is
the conditional intuition so strong that *if* phenomenal qualities can be
explained at all, it could only be in terms of internal factors? Why does the
internal–external boundary sustain fiercely internalist intuitions about
what, if anything, must explain phenomenal qualities despite the general
admission of bafflement about *how anything could possibly* explain phenomenal qualities, including neural properties? This is what I call the *magical membrane problem.*[10]

I suspect internalist intuitions gain part of their strength from aversion
to the perceived alternative: dualism. The qualitative inscrutability of internal material factors, including neural processes, yields autonomy and
explanatory gap intuitions. These are usually interpreted to admit the conceptual possibility of dualism as the relevant alternative to materialism.
But the scrutiny that produces autonomy and explanatory gap intuitions is

usually internally focused. So we should also consider alternatives that reject internalism instead of materialism. Boundary-crossing interactionist explanations of phenomenal qualities are usually overlooked, but they provide a more promising, nondualistic response to the qualitative inscrutability of purely internal processes.

What-quality externalism avoids the mysteries of dualism without incurring the magical membrane problem of internalism. On this view, how far what-quality explanations extend is an empirical matter, case by case. In principle, what explains phenomenal qualities can be distributed within the brain, among brain and body, or among brain, body, and embedding environment, depending on the explanatory dynamics. We're familiar with the idea that explanatory processes can be distributed across disparate areas within the brain instead of being localized. But no magical membrane contains distributed processing; brains are in continuous causal interaction with their bodies and their environments. Why should dynamics distributed within a prespecified boundary be capable of explaining qualities, while those beyond in are in principle ineligible? The logical basis for externally extended explanation is no different in principle from that for internally distributed explanation (Hurley 1998a,b).

As explained in section 2, processes on either side of any given boundary can in principle vary together, whether we are thinking about internally distributed or externally extended processes. Changes in one area of the brain can induce changes in another; changes in the environment can induce changes in the brain. When local or internal factors vary with distributed or external factors in near possible worlds, it is trivially true that phenomenal quality supervenes on local or internal factors. But it doesn't follow that quality can be explained solely in terms of local or internal factors.

Why is the combination of intuitions that generate the magical membrane problem so widespread, if there's a better alternative to both internalism and dualism in the form of what-quality externalism? In the rest of this section I'll consider two responses on behalf of internalism: one that appeals to local illusions and hallucinations, and the other to brains in vats. I'll argue that neither succeeds. What-quality externalism deserves further attention.

3.2 Why local illusions and hallucinations don't support what-quality internalism   The first response generalizes a claim based on local illusions and hallucinations, which seems to support internalism in a CNS twin STE. Note the nod to explanatory gap intuitions at step 2:

1. Local illusions and hallucinations can share specific phenomenal qualities with veridical experiences, despite differences in the environment.
2. Given the external differences, there must be some purely internal way
to explain the sameness in specific quality of experience (even if we can't
at present understand how such an explanation would go).[11]
3. If external factors are not needed to explain specific qualities of experience, they aren't needed to explain global phenomenal state, either.
4 If global phenomenal state can be explained internally, it must supervene nontrivially on internal factors, as for CNS twins in different
environments.

This argument appears to support internalist intuitions in STEs despite
explanatory gap worries because it fails to probe the assumptions it makes
about internalist explanation. It doesn't succeed because the claim made
at step 2 is false. Sameness of quality despite external differences does not
require purely internal what-quality explanation. So the antecedents of
steps 3 and 4 aren't justified (there are also further problems with the generalization made at step 3, discussed below).

The problem with step 2's claim is that neural correlates can differ
between an illusory (or hallucinatory—I won't keep adding this) experience and a veridical experience with the same specific quality. Sameness of
phenomenal quality does not ensure sameness of neural correlate. But if
internal as well as external factors can differ between illusory and veridical
same-quality cases, it's an open question why these different combinations
of factors are associated with the same quality. In some cases, the best
what-quality explanation may be externalist, contra the claim at step 2.

The possibility of variable realizations of mental states in hypothetical
aliens has traditionally been used as an argument for functionalism as
against "tissue" views. But variable neural correlates of given quality types
aren't just for Martians—they begin at home. As well as varying across illusory and veridical experiences of the same quality type, neural correlates
can vary across instances of the same quality type before and after perceptual adaptation, and over normal development within one brain. Neural
plasticity extending from childhood well into adulthood is characteristic of
human brains. As a result, the neural correlates of childhood mental states
can be quite different from those of adult mental states of the same phenomenal quality type. In early development, some areas of a child's brain
can generate as many as 100,000 synapses a second; this early synaptic exu-
berance is subject to interaction-driven pruning throughout later development. Children's neural processes tend to be more distributed, within brains

that contain far more synapses, and adults' to be more localized, reflecting a long process of synaptic pruning (Huttenlocher 2002, p. 47 and *passim*). Such neural plasticity, yielding variable neural correlates of given types of experience, is part of the normal dynamics explanatory of human experience. It isn't an exceptional process that leads to a uniquely explanatory neural endpoint (see below on the "internal endpoint error"). And neural plasticity is disciplined and directed largely by the interactions of embodied nervous systems with their environments.

Such domesticated variable neural correlates (unlike imaginary Martian cases) are relevant to naturalistic explanations of phenomenal qualities. To explain quality type, we should explain why variable neural correlates are associated with the same quality type (when they are). What-quality externalism allows (whereas internalism denies) that such explanations can turn on the extended dynamics that embed neural processes: extended dynamics can have a characteristic underlying pattern that explains quality type, the neural components of which can be implemented or parameterized in different ways. In such cases, characteristic patterns of interaction between embodied nervous systems and their environments can explain what experience is like, not just the internal neural portion of such interactions.

I'll elaborate the argument from variable neural correlates against step 2 of the above internalist argument, in two steps. First, I'll give an example of variable neural correlates across illusory and veridical experiences of the same quality-type. Second, I'll explain how variable neural correlates can figure in an extended dynamical what-quality explanation of veridical cases, which I claim have explanatory priority.

3.2.1 Variable neural correlates: Example   For an example of how the neural correlate of a local illusion can differ from that of a veridical experience of the same quality type, we can compare an illusion of environmental movement with a perception of environmental movement. But to do this, we need first to consider an experience that does not involve environmental movement. When you move your eyes sideways, motor signals are associated with resulting changes in actual visual inputs and with precreated or simulated feedback in a certain dynamical pattern. This pattern correlates with your experience as of objects in your environment not moving, though your eyes have moved. By contrast, if your eye muscles are paralyzed so they don't move sideways when you try to move them, and objects in the environment don't move either, you nevertheless have an illusory experience as of the environment moving sideways. On a standard view, the neural correlate of this illusion includes motor signals and simulated feedback similar to those correlated with the no-movement experience, but lacks the changes in actual visual input correlated with the no-movement experience.

So far we've got a veridical no-movement experience with one neural correlate, and an illusory experience of movement with another neural correlate. Now let's consider a veridical experience of movement, qualitatively the same as the illusory experience of movement. This veridical experience might be had during a sideways earthquake, during which you neither move nor attempt to move your eyes (apologies to J. J. Gibson). In one case there is an earthquake, and in the other there is not; yet your specific experience of sideways movement is qualitatively the same. But the neural correlates of the experience are not the same in the illusory movement and earthquake cases. In the illusory movement case the neural correlate includes motor signals and simulated feedback relating to attempted eye movements that are not part of the neural correlate in the earthquake case; in the earthquake case the neural correlate includes actual visual input signals that are not part of the neural correlate in the illusory case. It's tempting to explain quality in the illusory movement case in terms of its neural correlate alone, since no actual sideways movement occurs. But this would not explain why the same quality type is present in both the illusory movement and the earthquake cases, despite their varying neural correlates.

The internalist argument from illusion we're considering compares illusory and veridical cases, failing to recognize that neural correlates can vary despite sameness of quality. To explain this, we should focus in the first instance on veridical cases, and try to explain why neural correlates of a given quality can vary *across veridical cases*. Only then will we be in a position to explain sameness of quality despite variable neural correlates when we compare veridical and illusory cases. The argument from variable neural correlates for what-quality externalism gives *explanatory priority to veridical cases* in which neural correlates of a given quality can vary.

3.2.2 Variable neural correlates within extended explanatory dynamics   So let's now consider how neural correlates can vary across veridical cases, despite sameness of quality. We get examples of this across normal development, given normal neural plasticity, and when illusions induced by distorting lenses adapt away over time, as the agent interacts with her environment. For example, each lens of Kohler's goggles are yellow to one side of the midline and blue to the other; they distort wavelengths reaching the eye as a function of eye movement or object movement across the midline, producing illusions about the colors of objects. But after a period of wearing Kohler's goggles, color experience adapts, so that veridical experience replaces illusory experience. However, the neural correlates of veridical experience of a given color presumably differ before wearing the goggles and after adaptation, as a function of, among other things, different wavelengths reaching the eye. So a given type of (veridical) experience can have different neural correlates before and after adaptation.[12]

What is the best explanation of sameness of experience type when neural correlates vary across veridical experiences? Does the explanans cross internal–external boundaries in some cases? This is an empirical question, to be settled by explanatory success, case by case. Moreover, although some illusions adapt away, deferring to reality, others do not. Why? To explain *what experience is like* we must explain why some experiences defer to *what the world is like*, whereas others do not (see Hurley and Noë 2003a on the dominance–deference distinction). What-quality externalism holds that, in principle, the needed what-explanatory factors can cross the internal–external boundary; it can do so in some cases, but not in others.

In general terms, explanations of mental types in terms of extended dynamic patterns go as follows. As an agent interacts with her environment, information flows from environment through nervous system along multiple sensory and motor channels and out into body, as embodied activity changes the environment and/or information flowing from the environment into the nervous system, along multiple channels of sensorimotor feedback. A complex multidimensional space results, which evolves through time in characteristic patterns. The nervous system also precreates or simulates feedback, anticipating the sensory consequences of movement, adding further loops to these complex dynamic patterns. Such complex patterns carry information about both agent and environment and enable the agent's practical perceptual skills. Some of the dimensions of these patterns are purely neural, while others extend beyond the neural. Feedback loops can rope in external factors; loopiness ("turbo drive," as Clark puts it) is crucial to dynamic extension. Degree of extension is governed not by ultimate causal sources of organismic inputs but by the orbit of feedback loops whereby organismic outputs produce organismic inputs via external factors. Nervous system and embedding environment are informationally coupled, via the body, as each affects the other. The parameters of a system express the way its variables interact; in coupled systems, variables of each system act as parameters of the other. Not only can variables in human nervous systems change environmental parameters, but environmental variables can also reparameterize the plastic nervous system.

Relevant dynamic patterns are often multimodal as well as extended. Experience of a given type often depends not simply on a single channel of interaction between external and internal factors that can easily be interrupted or "faked," but rather on relationships among multiple dimensions that develop in characteristic ways over time, as various modalities of sensory input and simulated feedback are followed by motor output with consequences that bounce off various features of the environment and generate multimodal feedback.[13] Such complex sensorimotor dynamics triangulate flexibly on environmental features. Single sensory channels can contribute to explaining experience type in the context of such extended patterns without being explanatorily separable from such context.

Such complex extended dynamics can be described in part subpersonally, but they enable personal-level perceptual know-how or skills, including implicit practical familiarity with both the sensory consequences of movement and the actions empowered or afforded by sensations: these aspects of practical perceptual skill are, in general, inseparably interdependent. Just as the subpersonal, enabling level of description essentially includes both input-to-output and output-to-input loops, the enabled personal-level skills essentially include practical knowledge of both the implications of movement for sensation and of sensation for movement (see Hurley 1998a,b on two-level interdependence; see Hurley and Noë 2006 on the hunter-gatherer approach).

When a single sensory modality is distorted (e.g., by goggles), characteristic dynamic multimodal patterns are disturbed, disabling the agent's practical perceptual skills and creating illusions; multiple types of experience can be affected. Conflicts between experiential modalities can be resolved by veridical adaptation of one modality (e.g., vision) or nonveridical adaptation of another (e.g., proprioception); when illusory experienced distinctions adapt away, other illusory distinctions can arise (see Hurley 1998a, chap. 9). Adaptation reestablishes practical perceptual skills and coherence between modalities and between experienced distinctions and constancies. This can involve the partial reimplementation of extended dynamic patterns at new neural locations or with new parameterizations of intraneural aspects of the patterns. As an agent reacquires perceptual skills and experience of color constancy while wearing Kohler's goggles, the underlying sensorimotor pattern characteristic of certain colors is reimplemented, reparameterized to reflect eye movements (see Gibson's account in Kohler 1964; Hurley and Noë 2006).

What-quality explanation is externalist if the dynamic pattern explanatory of an experience-type has boundary-crossing dimensions of embodiment and environmental embedding. Adaptive recovery of the same quality of experience can in some cases be best explained by the reemergence of its characteristic extended dynamic, reimplemented in some internal dimensions by a variant neural process. For example, adaptation to Kohler's goggles restores color constancy as objects or eyes move across the midline. The neural correlates of experiencing an object moving across the midline as white differ, before wearing the goggles versus while wearing them after adaptation. Why are both neural correlates of the whiteness quality of experience? Because both participate in a certain extended dynamic characteristic of color, which reflects, among many other things, the fact that external objects do not change color systematically as they move, or as eyes move, across the midline.[14] The embodied adapting agent needn't explicitly represent this extended dynamic pattern or the reimplementation of its neural portion, but his embodied perceptual skills are part of what sustain it. With time, as a seamless result of neural plasticity and the agent's reacquisition of such skills through interactions with his environment, the extended pattern characteristic of a certain experience type may reemerge, relocated in certain dimensions of its multidimensional space so as to compensate for the imposed distortion. An underlying higher-order dynamic pattern can obtain across changes in neural implementation, as adaptation realigns what experience is like with what the world is like (see McDowell 1994, de Gaynesford 2004, on the openness of experience to the world).

This account of extended multidimensional dynamics reveals further problems with the internalist generalization argument above: with step 3's generalization from local to global internalist explanation, leading to step 4's postulation of CNS twins in STE. The best explanation of some quality types may be internalist, whereas others are best explained by extended multidimensional dynamics. Thus, it may be possible for some neural correlates to hold constant across different environments such that quality-types supervene on neural correlates, but in other cases this may not be possible. In some cases internal factors may not be unpluggable and repluggable across near worlds, so that internal and external factors are not explanatorily separable. So the generalization from local internalist explanation to global internalist explanation is in some cases not warranted.

The argument from variable neural correlates in veridical cases does not assume that extended dynamical patterns, as opposed to purely internal dynamical patterns, must provide the best explanation. Even if neural correlates vary, they may both implement one purely internal functional pattern, rather than an extended functional pattern, which explains sameness of quality. The argument only assumes that extended patterns can provide explanations of quality type when neural correlates vary; it's an empirical question whether they do in any particular case.

However, it might be objected that there will always be an internal "shadow," at a functional level of description, of any extended dynamic pattern, and that this will always provide a better, internalist functionalist explanation of quality type even if neural correlates vary. In reply, we can suppose for the sake of argument that *some* internal functional shadow can be found to correlate with any extended dynamical pattern, even when neural correlates vary. But it doesn't follow that this internal functional pattern will have any independent explanatory role, let alone that it could provide a better explanation. It may be seriously disjunctive. In the absence of the extended explanation, it may be one nonsalient functional pattern among many, with no nonarbitrary significance. Given the extended explanation, it may be a *mere* shadow, projected in the light of the extended dynamic that does the real explanatory work. Again, it is an empirical question, to be answered case by case, whether an internal functional pattern or an extended dynamic provides a better explanation.

Note that the answer to this question does not turn on the truth of internal supervenience, which is necessary but not sufficient for internalist explanation. An extended dynamic can provide a better explanation, because internal and external factors are not explanatorily separable, even if an internal supervenience claim is true.[15] The issue is one of explanation, rather than a prior metaphysical issue.

Note that the plausibility of externalist explanation depends on allowing that some qualities of experience may be best explained dynamically, rather than as a series of snapshots strung together. Internalist intuitions too often turn on snapshot assumptions. It is the dynamic character of experience that makes active, embodied CNS twins problematic and that knits internal and external factors together. As Dennett (1991) has argued, temporal and spatial extension go hand in hand.

Thus, the first internalist response to the magical membrane problem fails. It tries to support internalist intuitions in STEs by arguing from illusion. But we cannot get from specific illusions to what-quality internalism for global phenomenal state, as the internalist generalization argument tries to do. Nor does what-quality externalism depend on violations of internal supervenience. What-quality internalism applies too narrow a boundary to would-be twins in STEs, one that cuts across potentially explanatory extended dynamics in cases involving variable neural correlates resulting from environmentally driven adaptation and/or neural plasticity. Extended what-quality explanations shouldn't be excluded a priori. If there's no magical membrane, then it's an empirical question, to be answered case by case, whether they succeed. I predict they will for some qualities, in particular where neural correlates vary, and not others. To explain quality type where neural correlates differ, we should give priority to comparison of veridical cases, and address illusory cases in the light of our understanding of veridical cases.

3.3 Why brains in vats don't support what-quality internalism The internalist may be tempted to appeal next to virtual reality devices. But active, embodied agents can probe, manipulate, remove, smash, or walk out of such devices. Embodied action creates extended dynamic patterns that triangulate on qualities of the environment flexibly and reliably, and that are sensitive to very small differences; it can outwit virtual reality as well as eliminate many illusions. The only action-proof virtual reality is a duplicate reality.

A second, more radical internalist response to the magical membrane problem removes the very embodiment that mediates such extended dynamics: brains in vats seem to be internalism's ultimate weapon. But, I'll argue, brains in vats don't secure what-quality internalism in STEs either.

In my argument from variable neural correlates, embodied dynamic interactions make trouble for the internalist argument from illusion to internalist explanation of the experiences of CNS twins in STEs. Perhaps the trouble can be avoided by arguing for internalism from disembodied CNS twins—twin brains in vats. Unlike embodied brains, envatted brains are helpless. They can be unplugged from one environment and replugged in another as freely as technology allows. They can't manipulate or smash their vats or walk out of them to eliminate the phenomenal qualities the vat conjures up. They can't probe and sample their environments to induce illusions to adapt away. Nor can they wear distorting goggles to induce neural reparameterizations that contribute to explaining quality type only as part of an extended dynamic. Duplicate neural processes in vats could in principle be sustained over time, despite being located in different environments—say, by means of computers that provide each brain with multimodal simulations of external input and of feedback in response to motor signals, and which cancel out any further influences their different environments might otherwise have on the brains. Of course, the envatted twin brains wouldn't actually be generating any movement or feedback from movement, but motor signals could be fed through their respective computers and generate sensory feedback along multiple channels, to create a simulation of the extended dynamic pattern resulting from active multimodal triangulation on external factors. But this simulated pattern needn't bear any relationship to the further different environments of each vat–computer pair.

If brains in vats have the last word, what do they tell us? Suppose internal supervenience holds; the duplicate brains "experience" the same quality. (The scare quotes indicate noncommitment to the thought that brains, as opposed to animals or people, have experiences; having registered that point, I'll drop the scare quotes.) Would their duplicated neural processes explain the shared experience type?

Not necessarily. A version of the argument from variable neural correlates applies again. Brains in vats are highly nonstandard in being disembodied. But if they are normal brains, they should still display neural plasticity. Their computers could thus simulate the external feedback loops of wearing distorting goggles, inducing twin neural reparameterizations in both twin brains. Each twin brain could thus have variable neural correlates of that quality type. What explains the sameness of quality type despite varying neural correlates within each brain?

For present purposes, this question is no different from the question of why the same quality can have different neural correlates for one interactive agent who sports an embodied, situated brain. The twinning and envatting are idle in answering the question about variable neural correlates within one brain, so they don't support internalism. In the embodied case, I appealed to possibility that a complex environment-involving dynamic with variable neural implementations could explain quality type. In the disembodied case, computers simulate such a dynamic, independently of the environment beyond the computers; but by doing so they provide the external part of an extended dynamic. Here, an extended explanation of quality type despite variable neural correlates would be in terms each brain's interactions with its computer rather than with its further environment. But such an explanation would nevertheless appeal to something beyond the brains themselves—to the extended dynamics provided by their computer-environments. Again, it's an empirical question whether an extended dynamic provides the best explanation of quality type given variable neural correlates.

Conceding that twin brains in vats must share quality types thus doesn't support what-quality internalism. Neural supervenience is not the touchstone of what-quality internalism.

3.4 Leaks in the magical membrane The magical membrane problem arises from combining strongly internalist intuitions with the autonomy metaintuition for phenomenal qualities. If we're genuinely modest about our understanding of how quality type could be explained, we should remain open minded about what-quality externalism, and consider externalist explanations on their empirical merits, case by case. We shouldn't assume that whatever could explain quality type must be located within a boundary that cuts between neural and external factors. What-quality internalism is not the only alternative to dualism. Neural processes are normally in continuous dynamical interaction with external factors; there's nothing magical about the boundary between them. In some cases it may be explanatorily transparent, so that internal and external factors make nonseparable contributions to explaining quality type. The qualities of the world we interact with may be part of what explains the qualities of our experience. Some of our bafflement about how to explain phenomenal quality may derive from boundary presuppositions that attempt to separate explanatorily inseparable factors and focus our scrutiny inward, when what is needed is a wider gaze, one that takes in extended dynamics with bodily and environmental *as well as* neural dimensions.

Here it may be objected that a causal-constitutive error is being committed: that external factors are merely causally, not constitutively, related to quality type. If this objection helps itself to an unargued assumption that a causal–constitutive distinction coincides with an external–internal distinction, then it makes the causal-constitutive error error. What non-question-begging criterion of constitutive explanation justifies this assumption? If extended multidimensional dynamic patterns provide the best explanation of quality type in some cases, why assume that external dimensions are merely causal while internal are constitutive? Moreover, it isn't clear how causal-constitutive talk can be mapped onto complex dynamical explanation, or even what work a criterion of the constitutive is supposed to do in this context. We don't have such a criterion here, and it isn't clear that the cognitive sciences need one in order to provide good explanations. We should proceed by seeking good explanations of qualities of experience case by case, then noticing whether any are externalist, rather than by trying to apply a prior criterion of the constitutive to select among potential explanations.

The overall shape of my argument about what-quality externalism in section 3 has been this. Two internalist responses to the magical membrane problem were considered, both of which attempt to support internalist intuitions in STEs: one on the basis of illusions, the other on the basis of brains in vats. I've argued that variable neural correlates of given qualities make trouble for both responses: what explains why different neural correlates are collected by the same quality type? In some cases, extended dynamics in which internal and external factors are not explanatorily separable can provide plausible answers. Externalism competes case by case with internalism to provide a better explanation. There's no shortcut to internalism via the claim that only internalist explanations are constitutive.

II How-Externalism

4 Content-Enabling Externalism

I turn now from what- to how-explanations, or enabling explanations. Externalism about how mental states are enabled has been referred to as *vehicle externalism*; I'll speak here of *enabling externalism*. This section focuses on content-enabling externalism, and the next on quality-enabling externalism.

Most discussions of the "extended mind" concern extended cognition—externalism about vehicles of intentional contents. They consider enabling explanations that cross internal–external boundaries, including body, environmental objects, or both. Arguments for boundary-crossing vehicles of contents tend to be of two overlapping types, appealing to agents' dynamic interactions with cultural artifacts or tools in particular, or with natural environments more generally.

4.1 Cultural extension: Artifacts plus parity Cultural arguments for extended cognition invoke artifacts that extend the powers of the mind, often involving language, plus a principle of parity. Parity says that the location per se of a process doesn't determine whether it counts as part of how the mind works. If processes relying on silicon chips, or notebooks, do enabling work relevantly similar to work done by neural assemblies or synaptic settings—so that they would count as mental processes if they were in the head—then they can count as vehicles of mental contents regardless of location.[16] If Otto's notebook "play the right sort of role in driving cognitive processes"—does work similar to internal memory in reliably enabling him to go to the museum—then, by parity, it's part of his extended mind, part of how it works (Clark and Chalmers 1998, p. 12, and this volume, p. 27). Continual interaction with artifacts isn't required for extended cognition; it could be enough for Otto automatically to check his notebook at critical points. But some cases of extended cognition do rely on continual dynamic interaction with artifacts, as when a skilled accountant performs complex calculations, her pencil flying across her notebook page, her eyes sampling just the pencil marks needed at each point of the calculation process. Accessible information doesn't need to be copied internally to be exploited in cognition (see Wilson 2004 on exploitative representation and wide computation).

4.1.1 Cultural extension: Objections and replies   Cultural extension arguments face various objections. Slippery-slope objections urge that extended minds leak into the world uncontrolledly, with absurd consequences. In response, constraints are imposed on culturally extended cognition: artifacts should play their role fluently and automatically, and be available as and when needed (Clark 2005a, p. 3).

Cultural extension arguments and the parity principle may seem to be in tension with another strand of how-externalism, which holds that details of embodiment can be essential to how minds work. The tension isn't deep. Bodily details do contribute to how minds work: the distance between eyes and ears, the range of possible eye and head movements, the left–right symmetry and back–front asymmetry of the body, and so on (see Lakoff and Johnson 1999; Noë 2004). But it doesn't follow that embodied minds cannot be culturally extended. Rather, artifactual extensions of minds are informed and constrained by bodily mind-enabling mechanisms; mind extensions cannot be body-neutral. Tactile visual substitution systems, for example, are not body-neutral—though they capture only some aspects of normal vision's embodiment, and the cognition they enable is correspondingly limited (see Hurley and Noë 2003b). We can recognize the importance of embodiment in enabling minds without relocating the magical membrane accordingly: without assuming that only what's within a boundary around natural bodies could enable mental states. Distortions or deficits at skin level can sometimes be compensated for by external artifacts, restoring an extended content-enabling pattern of brain–body–world interactions.

A prominent critique of cultural extension arguments objects that (1) cognitive states must have "intrinsic" content and (2) it's empirically implausible that cognitive science will find extended states with intrinsic content (Adams and Aizawa 2001). Neither claim should be accepted.

As Clark (2005a, p. 4) argues, the idea of intrinsic content is not very clear. Intrinsic contents supposedly do not ultimately derive from other intrinsic contents. Social practices, conventions, and language may be regarded as having nonintrinsic contents that derive from intrinsic mental contents. Various accounts of intrinsic content appeal to causal, historical, functional, or other relations, excluding social relations that presuppose intentional mental content. But content is no more intrinsic to brains in virtue of their relations to nonsocial environments than their relations to social environments. Underivedness is not the same as intrinsicness. We do better (as Adams and Aizawa now do) to focus on the underivedness rather than the intrinsicness of content.

But there are still problems with treating underived content as the mark of the cognitive. Consider artificially evolved robots; do they have only derived contents? If the artifice of evolvers deprives evolved robots of underived content, would a divine creator's intentions also deprive his creatures of underived content, hence of genuine cognition? Moreover, consider the way language transforms and enhances a child's cognitive capacities. Even if language builds on prior mental contents, so that linguistic contents are derived, further mental contents also build on language, so that their content is presumably also derived. Yet we do not therefore regard all such linguistically derived contents as not genuinely cognitive. Finally, the relations of derivation between mental contents and the content of language and other social practices are not clear; someone of a Vygotskian persuasion, for example, might argue that mental contents derive from linguistic contents and social interactions through a process of internalization (see Menary 2007). An alternative to the view that underived content is the mark of the cognitive is a view motivated by developments in dynamical cognitive science. On this view, the mark of cognitive processes is that, as well as being available online, in direct interaction with the environment, some version of a cognitive process is also available off-line, in simulative mode (see Clark 1997, p. 465; Clark and Grush 1999, pp. 12–13; and see Hurley 2008 on forward models and other simulations). Adams and Aizawa (2001, p. 47) suggest that extended mind advocates largely ignore what's known about the brain and cognitive processes, casting such advocates as neo-behaviorist. But we should be wary of the dated dichotomy between classical computational and behaviorist conceptions of cognition. As van Gelder comments, dynamics is arguably the single most widely used and powerful explanatory framework in all of science; we shouldn't be surprised to find it explaining cognition (van Gelder 1998, sect. 5).

What are the implications of this dynamically motivated "availability off-line" criterion for extended mind hypotheses? This is a further question, about which there is disagreement (see Grush 2003; cf. section 5 below). But Adams and Aizawa (2001) display no recognition that extended

mind views are motivated by boundary-crossing in contemporary dynamicist cognitive science, according to which what enables cognition is not
bare brains but actively embodied and situated brains (van Gelder 1995,
1998, 1999a,b, 1998; Clark 1997). This thriving body of work raises empirical and theoretical issues about whether cognition-enabling processes must
be purely neural, excluding relations to social and natural environments—
or indeed must even be representational.[17]

4.2   Extended dynamics and cognition: A-not-B; acallosal integration   Cultural examples of extended minds should be located within a broader
dynamicist approach to cognition in terms of the dynamic coupling of
brains, bodies, and environments. On this view, content-enabling processes can extend beyond the brain in the absence of cultural artifacts,
although the coupling of brains via bodies to cultural artifacts can extend
cognitive processes in further ways, distinctive of human cognition. Without disputing the importance of cultural extension, I suggest that mind-
extension arguments that appeal to dynamic coupling with natural
environments in general are more fundamental than those that appeal to
cultural artifacts in particular (Keijzer and Schouten [2007] make a similar
claim; thanks for Fred Keijzer for discussion on this point).

Dynamical cognitive science has been well surveyed and referenced by
those cited above; I won't repeat the job here. The general framework is
one of a multidimensional space of possible states, developing over time,
often in complex, nonlinear, and surprising ways. Variables in different
dimensions can be interdependent, each changing in ways that can depend
on values of and relations among other variables. From each point in multidimensional space, a trajectory develops over time in accord with system
parameters, which can themselves change over time. The dynamical system can be expressed as a characteristically structured geometry of possible trajectories through this space, which may converge on certain attractors
or avoid certain repellors in the space, or display other distinctive patterns
of flow. Abrupt changes in flow structure can emerge from continuous
changes in variables or parameters. In coupled dynamical systems, the
variables of one system are the parameters of the other, and vice versa;
they can be viewed as one system. The boundaries of dynamical systems
are not exogenous to explanatory aims. In cognitive applications, the state
space can extend to include dimensions whose variables are bodily and
environmental as well as neural, as brain, body, and environment interact
in mutually shaping patterns. However, there's no ban on purely internal
cognitive dynamics, in cases where it provides the best enabling explana-

tion. In dynamical cognitive science it's debated whether some geometrical features of flow structure should be viewed as representations, or whether dynamic cognitive science can dispense with representations. Cognitive processes, however, are construed as features of the temporal evolution of a multidimensional space, not as static structures.

An example of dynamical cognitive science that contrasts nicely with traditional approaches is Thelen and Smith's account of the much-studied A-not-B error, made by infants of 7 to 12 months of age (Thelen and Smith 1994, chap. 10; van Gelder 1999a). A child faces two bins, bin A and bin B. If you hide an attractive toy in bin A, the child will reach for bin A. If you continue to hide it in bin A, he will continue to reach for bin A. If you then hide it in bin B instead, and responding is delayed a few seconds, the child will still reach for bin A; but he'll reach for bin B if responding is not delayed. Why? Various traditional approaches explain this error in terms of limitations in the child's conception of objects, representation of space, or memory. But they don't explain certain context effects in the experimental data. The error depends on length of delay in a way that changes with age, and the presence of more bins reduces the tendency to make the error. Thelen and Smith's dynamical model explains these wrinkles in terms of ongoing interactions between a "what" system, for seeing toy, bin, and/or hand, and two "where" systems, for looking and for reaching. Changing inclinations to reach in a direction at a time depend on position of the system in various interacting dimensions, including the direction of current reaching inclinations, general and specific features of the environment (such as number of bins present and their markings, and which bin the toy is currently hidden in), and memory-based habit. They find parameters for a complex equation that, when computationally simulated, produces the A-not-B error, including the subtle variations traditional approaches don't explain. Moreover, their model predicts further results that have subsequently been confirmed experimentally. Bodily and environmental features play essential roles in this dynamical account of how early cognition works. Such dynamical models motivate an extended view of cognitive processes, without relying on cultural artifacts to do the extending (assuming the bins could equally well be natural containers).

Another example of embodied, dynamically extended cognition that doesn't rely on cultural coupling is my hypothetical acallosal subject with extended mechanisms of integration via bodily movements (Hurley 1998a, 2003). Although not set in a formal dynamical systems framework, it may be more intuitive. Information normally passes between the brain's two hemispheres via the corpus callosum. In commissurotomy patients this is surgically severed; as a result, information in their two hemispheres is not integrated under various experimental conditions. In acallosal patients, the corpus callosum is congenitally absent; yet they show unified cognition under experimental conditions in which commissurotomy patients do not (Jeeves 1965; Milner and Jeeves 1979; Diamond 1972, pp. 61–66). What enables the integration of information in acallosals? In principle, integration could be enabled by wholly internal processes, partly external processes, or both. It's likely that internal processes, relying on ipsilateral or subcortical neural paths, are at least partly responsible for integration. But, by the parity principle, partly external processes could also enable integrated cognition; these could rely on bodily movements that distribute or transfer information across the hemispheres. Access movements—automatic, habitual side-to-side movements of head or body—could give each hemisphere direct sensory inputs from an object that would otherwise appear in only one hemisphere's visual field. Cross-cuing by automatic facial expressions accessible to both sides could also function to transfer information across hemispheres (Bogen 1990).

The experimental tests of integration that commissurotomy patients fail and acallosal subjects pass are designed to exclude access movements and cross-cuing. That's why it's likely that acallosals actually have internal, neural mechanisms of integration (unless some extended mechanisms of integration are so subtle and automatic that they evade experimental control). Nevertheless, in ordinary, uncontrolled circumstances, access movements and cross-cuing could also contribute to integrating information, along with secondary neural pathways; acallosals might rely exclusively on the latter only when deprived of the former. This could be an efficient, robust developmental solution to enabling acallosal integration. Marcel Kinsbourne (1974) remarks that absence of the corpus callosum is biologically trivial, since minor adjustments in orientation distribute the same information to both sides; there's some evidence of motor habits in acallosal subjects that could serve this purpose (see Hurley 2003 for further discussion). Such extended mechanisms of integration would depend on bodily activity and feedback rather than purely neural factors. If they functioned when needed, reliably and automatically, by parity they would illustrate extended cognition.

4.3 Diagnosing intuitions: Explanatory relations between online and off-line processes in enabling cognition   Why is content-enabling, vehicle externalism less intuitive than familiar philosophical what-content externalism? Adams and Aizawa (2001, this volume), for example, regard the former as a "wild idea," at odds with common sense. Magical membrane assumptions may influence some intuitions, despite the causal congress of brains with bodies and environments (though Adams and Aizawa disavow such assumptions). Moreover, unfamiliarity with boundary-crossing dynamical cognitive science, as opposed to the traditional in-the-head computational variety, may wrongly make extended cognition seem empirically implausible.

But I want to consider a further possibility. The attention given to cultural cases of extended cognition, important and distinctively human as they are, may distract intuitions from a more basic point about the dynamics of extended minds, a point that doesn't depend on cultural artifacts. The more basic point concerns the explanatory relations between online processes and off-line simulations. In cultural extension cases, these relations are complicated by the way online processes involve external representations. We can make the more basic point salient by separating it from issues about relations between external and internal representations in cultural extension cases. In the rest of this section, I'll explain the distracting issues raised by external representations in the cultural cases. In the next section, I'll focus on noncultural cases and the more basic issue about explanatory relations between online processes and off-line simulations.

4.3.1 Explanatory relations between online processes and off-line simulations: Cultural versus noncultural cases of extension   Consider the distinction between online and off-line processes in cultural extension cases. The relevant cultural artifacts are themselves external representations, or work in ways that depend on external representations. External representations stand in for something else, which may not be present for direct interaction. Recall the skilled accountant's fingers and pencil flying over the pages of her notebook; her eyes move to access just the information she needs just when she needs it. Such extended computation is a process of online sensorimotor interaction with an external medium of information storage and external symbols, pencil marks on paper. It involves direct interaction with symbols already at one remove from the items they stand for—such as bank balances and tax owed—not direct interaction with these worldly referents.

However, the same work might be done by taking these online interactions with symbols off-line, using internal computations that simulate finger movements and symbol perception and relying on memory instead of pencil and paper to hold information for further use. Via internal simulation, an analogue of the extended process involving pencil and paper is available off-line. Note that such off-line simulations of interactions with symbols are at a second remove from the items the symbols stand for: they don't rely on direct interaction with external symbols, any more than interaction with the items the symbols stand for. It's been proposed that such availability off-line is a mark of cognitive processes (Clark 1997, p. 465; Clark and Grush 1999, pp. 12–13). It doesn't follow that only the off-line processes are cognitive, of course; the view is rather than online processes are themselves cognitive in virtue of availability off-line.

Issues now arise about relations between processes involving external representations and internal simulations thereof. Arguably, off-line simulations of interactions with external representations lack explanatory independence from the online interactions appealed to in cultural extension cases. For example, the off-line capacity for mental arithmetic arguably derives in normal development from long online practice with pencil and paper, so that the online version is explanatorily prior to the off-line version in an important ontogenetic sense (see Clark this volume for related discussion). More generally, the capacity for much off-line thought arguably continues to depend on online public language to maintain simulations. On the other hand, cultural extension may seem to enable cognition only because it presupposes symbols that can function to represent what's not present. And if this capacity is enabled by contentful internal processes, then the extended, online aspect of cultural cases is a detour (cf. Adams and Aizawa's (2001, this volume) concerns about the derivativeness of content). Cultural extension cases seem to make extended cognition hostage to these issues about whether external representation derives from internal representation, and thus seem not to provide independent leverage for content-enabling externalism.

However, this set of issues about relations between internal and external representations distracts attention from a more basic underlying issue. The tangent develops because of the way cultural extension cases involve direct interactions with external representations but not with what they are about—since external representations are already at one remove from the items they're about, even before they're taken off-line. Even if external representations do *not* derive content from independent internal contents, nevertheless internal off-line simulations of interactions with external representations will inherit independence of the world represented from external representations. For example, even if interactions with external representations of bank balances enable thinking about bank balances, it doesn't follow that interactions with bank balances themselves enable thinking about bank balances. The more basic issue I want to separate out concerns relations between online interactions with the world—not external representations of it—and off-line simulations of such interactions. Can interactions with trees enable experiences of trees, or do only internal simulations of interactions with trees enable experiences of trees?

To address this more basic issue, we should bracket issues about external representation and hence cultural extension cases. What's needed is a focus on explanatory relations between online interactions that *don't* involve external representations and internal simulations of such interactions. That is, we should focus on sensorimotor interactions among brain, body, and natural environment, where the relevant online processes don't presuppose external symbols already at one remove from what they are about. The more basic issue concerns whether, in a Brooksian phrase, the world can be its own best representation—and in particular, whether what the world is like can be part of what enables us to experience what it is like.

I gave two noncultural examples of extended cognition: the A-not-B error and acallosal integration. One involves cognition in infants, the other pathology. The intuitiveness of mind extension would be better served by cases involving normal adults (see Keijzer and Schouten 2007 on change-blindness). The adaptability and neural plasticity found in normal adults provided examples for what-quality explanations in terms of extended sensorimotor dynamics, in section 3 above. I'll return to such cases to bring into sharper relief the issue of whether off-line processes are explanatorily independent of online processes, by separating it from the complications raised by cultural extension and external representation. I'll argue in the next section that online extended sensorimotor dynamics can provide quality-enabling explanations.

5   Phenomenal-Quality-Enabling (Vehicle) Externalism

I now turn from content-enabling externalism to that most unintuitive and radical form of externalism, phenomenal-quality-enabling (vehicle) externalism. Surprisingly, it's in this unpromising territory where extended mind intuitions can be run to ground.

5.1   Preliminaries: What-quality externalism versus quality-enabling externalism, and the middle ground   I'll shortly address explanatory relations between online interactions with the world and off-line simulations thereof, and consider whether the former can provide quality-enabling explanations. But first it will be helpful to make some preliminary points about what-quality explanations and quality-enabling explanations. It

might be thought that even if my argument from variable neural correlates for what-quality externalism succeeds, the further, even more unintuitive step to quality-enabling externalism should be resisted. After all, most what-content externalists are content-enabling internalists. Why not similarly combine what-quality externalism with quality-enabling internalism? That would be a middle ground position that concedes some ground to radical externalism, contrary to initial intuitions, but is not *so* radically unintuitive as quality-enabling externalism. Why depart from this middle ground to countenance extended vehicles of phenomenal qualities? To answer, we need to compare the roles that extended dynamics would have in what-quality explanations and in quality-enabling explanations.

What-quality externalism appeals to characteristic dynamic sensorimotor patterns in explaining the qualities of experiences: of visual versus auditory experience, or specific qualities within one modality. It holds that in some cases qualities of experiences can best be explained in terms of extended dynamics in which brain, body, and world all participate, while in other cases the best explanations may be in purely internal. In particular, I have argued, what-quality explanations may need to appeal to extended dynamics to explain qualities with variable neural correlates. Qualities of experience adapt to follow characteristic extended patterns when their neural portions are reimplemented as a result of, say, normal developmental neural plasticity, or wearing distorting lenses such as those in Kohler's goggles (see Hurley and Noë 2003a for other examples, e.g., TVSS, or the projection of tactile inputs to visual cortex in blind persons). In such cases the quality of experience can defer to extended sensorimotor dynamics despite variable neural correlates. Since they are not counterexamples to neural supervenience, they underscore that externalist what-quality explanation is compatible with neural supervenience. What-quality externalism holds that what predict and explain phenomenal quality in some such cases are extended dynamics, rather than the properties of a particular reimplementation of the neural portion of the dynamics, or an internal functional "shadow" of extended dynamics. That is, when the neural portions of an extended dynamic are reimplemented over development or in response to distorting lenses, what collects the various neural implementations together under a given quality is the extended dynamic in which they participate.

The middle-ground view concedes that *what* qualities we experience can require externalist explanation, in light of variable neural correlates, but insists that vehicles of phenomenal qualities—the enabling processes that explain *how* we are able to experience given qualities—are internal neural processes. For example, a middle-ground view could concede that extended sensorimotor dynamics can explain what quality we experience, and that skills in negotiating such extended dynamics and associated expectancies of the sensory consequences of movement can enable our experiencing of qualities—while still insisting that enabling explanations in terms of skills and expectancies should be understood in terms of internal simulations of such extended dynamics. Can what-quality externalism be held apart from quality-enabling externalism in this middleground way?

Note that this question is *not* analogous to a question about cultural extension cases, about whether what-content externalism can be held apart from a content-enabling externalism that invokes interactions with external representations. A middle-ground view might be supported in cultural extension cases by the purported derivativeness of the content of external representations. But noncultural extension doesn't involve external representations; so noncultural cases remove at least this basis for occupying the middle ground. The disanalogy follows from the way external representations in cultural extension cases are already at one remove from the world represented, discussed in the last section. As a result, the relations of extended dynamics in what- versus how-explanations differ across cultural versus noncultural extension cases.

Table 6.2
Contrast: Relations of extended dynamics in what- vs. how-explanations for cultural vs. noncultural extension

	Externalist What-Explanations	Externalist How-Explanations (Enabling Explanations)	
Content	Direct interactions with world represented. →*Dynamics do not converge in world*	Cultural extension cases, online: Direct interactions with external representations, at one remove from world represented←	Cultural extension cases, off-line: Simulations of interactions with external representations, at two removes from world represented
Quality	Direct interactions with world and its qualities. →*Dynamics converge in world*	Noncultural/natural extension cases, online: Direct interactions with world and its qualities←	Noncultural/natural extension cases, off-line: Simulations of direct interactions with world, at one remove from world

In *cultural extension* cases, externalist what-content explanations and extended content-enabling explanations do not converge in the world represented: what-content explanations typically appeal to direct interactions with the world represented, whereas how-explanations appeal to direct interactions not with the world but with external representations of the world (e.g., notebooks). And off-line internal simulations of interactions with external representations—*cultural simulations*—are at two removes from what is represented, presupposing stable external representations of the world.

By contrast, in noncultural or *natural extension* cases, extended what- and how-explanations would indeed converge in the natural world. Neither type of explanation would appeal to external representations of the world, but rather to extended sensorimotor dynamics, patterns of interaction with the natural world and its qualities. Off-line internal simulations of such dynamics—*natural simulations*—are thus only at one remove from the natural world and presuppose direct interactions with the world to be simulated.

This contrast predicts, for example, that cultural simulations would show greater stability in, say, an isolation tank than would natural simulations. Moreover, we should expect externalist what-explanations and extended how-explanations to constrain one another more directly in natural cases than in cultural cases: in natural cases, it should be harder to keep enabling explanations from leaking into the world along with what-explanations, and thus harder to occupy the middle-ground position.

5.2 Why go radical? Explanatory relations between online extended dynamics and off-line simulations Return to the question: Haven't variable neural correlates and extended dynamics done all the externalist work they can do in arguing for the middle-ground position? Why go further, to radical quality-enabling externalism? My argument concerns explanatory relations between extended online processes and internal off-line simulations thereof. The extended online processes I have in mind aren't interactions with cultural artifacts or external representations, but are more basic: direct sensorimotor couplings with a natural environment, converging with the extended dynamics that feature in externalist what-quality explanations. The corresponding off-line processes are what I called "natural simulations": internal simulations of direct couplings with the natural world, rather than with cultural items that represent the world.

What are the explanatory relations between extended sensorimotor dynamics and simulations thereof? And how does the answer bear on whether extended dynamics as opposed to simulations thereof can provide quality-enabling explanations?

Here's a story about the explanatory relations between extended sensorimotor dynamics and simulations thereof. Consider subpersonal neural expectancies or predictive simulations of sensory feedback from movements. Such "forward models" associated with efference copy are in effect internal feedback loops that mimic external feedback loops. Consider three contexts in which such simulations could play enabling roles. (Keep in mind that all these enabling roles are described at a subpersonal level.)

(1) Online simulations in comparator control systems. Comparator control systems can compare predicted sensory feedback from movement with actual feedback during online environmental interactions. Such predictive simulations have two important online functions:

(A) Permitting smoother, faster movements directed at a certain target, by comparison with movements controlled solely by actual feedback. A thermostat can function more efficiently by predicting room temperature and turning the heat off before reaching target temperature, to avoid overshooting. Similarly, bodily control and instrumental movement can be more efficient when predictive simulations are available during online interactions with the environment.

(B) Distinguishing sensory events deriving from exogenous environmental events from those resulting from endogenous movements. Once correlations are established between actual and simulated feedback from movement, divergence between them can indicate an exogenous rather than endogenous source of sensory input, making a contribution to enabling sensory experience.

Note that it is the extended dynamic, including external and internal feedback loops, that provides improved control and distinguishes exogenous and endogenous events; internal simulations alone would not do this work.

(2) Off-line simulations with monitoring of inhibition. Once internal simulations of the results of movement are available for online functions, they can be exapted for off-line use also, permitting the results of inhibited movement to be simulated. Off-line processes detach predictive simulations from the environmental aspects of the online dynamics with which it was originally coupled. Off-line simulations can enable instrumental cognition such as imagining the likely results of your own alternative acts and assessing which is the best means to a goal, instead of relying on

costly trial-and-error learning. Dennett's "Popperian" animals let simulations die in their stead.[18]

For off-line simulations to do this enabling work, the information must
be available that they are off-line simulations of results of inhibited possible
movements, not online simulations of results of actual movements. Very
different responses are appropriate when simulations predict results of possible as opposed to actual movements. Two capacities thus work together in
this enabling explanation: capacities to simulate off-line while inhibiting
actual movement, and capacities to monitor off-line status or inhibition.

(3) Off-line simulations without monitoring of inhibition. However, these two
capacities might dissociate: off-line simulations might occur without monitoring of their off-line status. This could explain how some illusions or
hallucinations work: if online simulation normally makes an enabling contribution to sensory experience (1B), then when off-line simulation occurs
without inhibition monitoring and thus is not distinguished from online
simulation (2), it can be predicted to have effects on sensory experience.
Resulting illusions would be a natural by-product of cognitive functions
enabled by off-line simulation, which in turn is a by-product of functions
enabled by online simulation.

Put the other way round, in this account the contribution of off-line simulations to enabling illusions presupposes their contribution to enabling instrumental cognition, which in turn presupposes the contribution of online
simulations to enabling effectively controlled movement and to distinguishing endogenous from exogenous sensory events. The account is not obviously biased toward how-externalism; Grush (2003) tells a story similar to
parts of this account in arguing against enabling externalism. So why do I
think something like this account favors enabling externalism?

As I see it, the issue is this. Internal simulations can occur online, as
part of an extended dynamical process (as in context 1 above) or off-line
(as in contexts 2 and 3); in both cases, they can provide at least part of a
quality-enabling process. When internal simulations occur off-line, they
can provide internal enabling explanations of qualities of experience (as
in context 3). But do internal simulations alone provide the best quality-
enabling explanation *when they occur online, embedded in an extended
dynamic?* Or can an extended dynamic that includes internal simulations
provide the best explanation of qualities of online experience? Arguably,
internal simulations are necessary for the enabling of experience; if so, a
creature with no predictive simulations and sensory feedback from movement, but only external feedback control mechanisms, would lack experi-

ence with phenomenal qualities. But it remains open whether enabling explanations must be purely internal in online as well as off-line cases. The internalist holds that the internal simulations that explain how qualities are enabled off-line also explain how they are enabled online; the external portions of the extended dynamics in online cases are not part of the enabling process. The externalist holds that even though internal simulations explain how qualities are enabled off-line, extended dynamics that include internal simulations can explain how qualities are enabled online; in online cases, the external portions of the extended dynamic can be part of the enabling process.

How should this issue be decided? Can the processes that enable a given quality of experience vary? Can they be internal for some instances of the quality, and extended for others? The internalist may argue that if the same qualities of experiences can result off-line (say, in hallucinations) as online, then the external parts of extended dynamics are not needed to explain how experience works, any more than to explain what it's like. But as we've seen in section 3, this type of argument about what-quality explanations doesn't work. The neural correlates of a given quality can vary across illusory and veridical cases, and across veridical cases. On this basis I argued that extended dynamics can in some cases provide what-quality explanations, which explain sameness of quality despite varying neural correlates. For example, an extended dynamic might explain the quality shared by the illusion of movement in the paralyzed eye case and the veridical perception of movement in the sideways earthquake case, despite different neural correlates. It's no objection when explaining quality type that the type-explanatory external factors are absent in illusory cases, any more than it's an objection when explaining content type. The extended dynamic in which an internal simulation normally participates can explain quality type in illusory cases, just as normal causes might explain content-type in cases of mistake, where normal causes are absent (recall Burge 1986 on cracks and shadows; ditto proper functions).

The internalist argument doesn't work for quality-enabling explanations either, for related reasons. We've seen that neural correlates can vary across veridical and illusory instances of the same quality, but still be collected under one extended what-quality explanation. So why not allow that quality-enabling processes can vary so as to be extended in online cases and internal in off-line cases of the same quality, but similarly be collected under the same extended what-quality explanation? Externalists claim that, in some online cases, what enables qualitative experience is ongoing embodied interactions of brain with environment, via probings and samplings and movements with external feedback loops intact—not merely the internal simulative portions of those interactions. If so, the extended what-quality explanation and the corresponding extended quality-enabling explanation in online cases would converge in the natural world.

Support for this externalist claim is provided by the above account of how the off-line enabling roles of internal simulations presuppose their more fundamental roles within extended dynamics. On this account, the enabling roles of internal simulations are explanatorily derivative from, not independent of, their role in online dynamics. Enabling explanations in online cases have explanatory priority, just as what-quality explanations in veridical cases do. By contrast, the internalist view that internal simulations explain how qualities are enabled both online and off-line gives internal simulations explanatory independence from extended online dynamics. This puts the cart before the horse. If the enabling role of internal simulations in off-line cases is derivative from their role in extended dynamics, it provides no reason to hold that only internal processes can do quality-enabling work in the primary, online cases.

So far in this section I've argued that extended online dynamics are explanatorily prior to off-line simulations thereof, and that this supports the externalist view that extended dynamics can provide quality-enabling explanations in online cases, even though internal simulations do so in off-line cases.

5.3   Neural plasticity and development: Avoiding the internal endpoint error   Extended online dynamics provide internal simulations thereof with ongoing tuning and maintenance (see also Clark 1997, p. 479). The way many illusions adapt away, yielding variation in neural correlates of given qualities, illustrates how online processes, with the external loops of their dynamics intact, continually set and reset the parameters of off-line simulations. Illusory experiences can themselves reflect ongoing tuning by online dynamics—for example, illusory aftereffects of adaptation when goggles are removed.

The internalist may regard the tuning and maintenance of internal simulations by extended dynamics as "merely causal, not constitutive": processes of acquisition, over development or learning, of a mature capacity for the internal processes that do the real quality-enabling work. However, if we avoid the "causal–constitutive error" error of assuming that only internalist explanations can be constitutive, we shouldn't assume that extended tuning and maintenance processes cannot be part of the sought-for explanation of how experience works, as well as of what it is like.

In particular, the distinction between acquisition and mature capacity should be treated with empirical caution in this context. Nervous systems, especially human ones, are by nature more plastic than we've tended to suppose. Neural correlates don't vary only in response to distorting goggles and pathologies such as congenital blindness. Over normal childhood and adolescence, the overall shape of the neural correlates of many types of experience changes dramatically, from relatively diffuse and bilateral to more efficiently localized, while the capacity for the relevant experiences is sustained (Huttenlocher 2002). This makes good evolutionary sense, allowing environmental interactions to influence the efficient specification of neural functions. But we shouldn't assume that it is only *after* online processes have finally fixed the parameters of internal simulations that given types of experience can be enabled: this is the *internal endpoint error* (a close relation of the "causal–constitutive error" error). Rather, many neural processes are continually open to and reparameterized by online interactions with the environment, as body and brain grow, and into adulthood. Quality-enabling externalism holds that extended online dynamics needn't be just a way of acquiring a mature capacity for an internal endpoint, but can enable and sustain qualities of experience across normal developmental variation in neural correlates.

Quality-enabling externalism may not be as radical as it first seemed. The view isn't that external factors by themselves enable experience, or that internal factors by themselves cannot enable experience. Rather, it's that *purely* internal processes are not the *only* way experience can be enabled. In online cases, what the world is like can be part of what enables us to experience what it is like. Evolution has no reason of principle to respect the skin in enabling experience, no reason not to enable experience by exploiting both interactions with the world and internal processes. It may be a mystery why evolution should enable experience at all—but that point is a double-edged sword, as the magical membrane problem reveals. If we really have no idea how experience is enabled, why be so sure the explanation must be internal? Perhaps inner–outer interactions are part of the needed gap-antidote.

6 Concluding Summary

Taxonomy I've distinguished what-externalism, about the content or quality of mental states, from how-externalism, about the processes that enable mental states with given contents or qualities. A two-by-two taxonomy of varieties of externalism results: what-content externalism, what-quality externalism, content-enabling externalism, and quality-enabling externalism. The what–how distinction doesn't align cleanly with a constitutive–causal or an internal–external distinction. Many intuitions resist moves from what- to how-externalism or from content to quality externalism, and are most resistant to that most exotic form of externalism, about the processes that enable phenomenal qualities.

Summary Two general principles have animated my discussion under these headings: First, externalism should be understood in both its "what" and "how" varieties as making explanatory rather than metaphysical claims. Second, veridical and online cases are explanatorily prior to cases involving illusions or hallucinations and to off-line cases.

What-content externalism   What-content externalism is usually supported by externalist intuitions in supervenience thought experiments (STEs), which postulate twins who are internal duplicates but embedded in different environments. STEs are controlled thought experiments that seek to separate out the explanatory roles of internal and external factors; they presuppose explanatory separability, which requires that internal factors be unpluggable from external factors. Since the truth of an internal supervenience claim does not require unpluggability, internal supervenience is necessary but not sufficient for the possibility of an STE. Internalist explanation requires explanatory separability and unpluggability; if the relevant STE is not possible, internal supervenience provides no support for internalist explanation. Supervenience claims should aim to draw boundaries that are neither too wide, including explanatorily redundant factors,

Table 6.3

	Content	Quality
What	Supervenience vs. explanation	Magical membrane problem
	Supervenience thought experiments and control	Variable neural correlates
	Unpluggability	Illusions and brains in vats "Causal–constitutive error" error
How	Worries about cultural extension presupposing external representation	Explanatory relations between online extended dynamics and off-line simulations/illusions
	Cf. natural extension: what- and how-explanations converge in world	Carry across from what- to how-explanations that converge in world

nor too narrow, cutting between explanatorily nonseparable factors. Supervenience boundaries should be open to revision in a process of reflective equilibrium between intuitive evidence and theorizing.

What-quality externalism   Intuitions about content in STEs provide authoritative evidence, but intuitions about quality don't. While STEs for phenomenal qualities typically yield strong internalist intuitions, these coexist with metaintuitions to the effect that qualities are ultimately autonomous, that internalist intuitions could just turn out to be wrong. Such autonomy metaintuitions express the explanatory gap separating neural processes and internal functions from phenomenal qualities. The combination of strong internalist intuitions with autonomy metaintuitions presents a puzzle about the explanatory significance of the internal–external boundary, namely, the magical membrane problem: if we have so little understanding of how phenomenal qualities could possibly be explained, why are we so confident that *if* they can be, the explanation must be internalist?

Two internalist responses to the magical membrane problem were considered, both of which attempt to support internalist intuitions in STEs: one on the basis of illusions, the other on the basis of brains in vats. In reply I argued that neural correlates of a given quality can vary, across normal development and perceptual adaptation, as well as between illusory and veridical experiences. Variable neural correlates make trouble for both responses: what explains why they are collected by the same quality type? In some cases, plausible answers can be provided by extended dynamics in which internal and external factors are not explanatorily separable but admit of varying neural implementations. If so, what the world is like can be part of what explains what experience is like.

Externalist what-quality explanations need not provide counterexamples to supervenience claims: without unpluggability and separability, there's no violation of internal supervenience. Failures of internal supervenience are not the touchstone of externalism; rather, externalism competes case by case with internalism to provide the better explanation. There's no shortcut to internalism via the claim that only internalist explanations are constitutive; we should avoid the "causal–constitutive error" error, of assuming a causal–constitutive distinction that coincides with an external–internal distinction.

Content-enabling externalism   Extended conceptions of the processes that enable cognition often appeal to cultural examples, involving interactions with external representations, such as Otto's notebook or the accountant's pencil and paper, plus a principle of parity. One internalist objection to cultural arguments for extended cognition claims that cognitive processes must have underived content, which internal representations have and external representations lack. The underived content criterion itself raises difficulties, and has rivals, such as an availability off-line criterion motivated by dynamical cognitive science. But these issues about relations between the contents of internal and external representations distract attention from a more basic underlying issue, concerning relations between online interactions with the natural world—not external representations of it—and off-line simulations of such interactions.

Quality-enabling externalism   What-quality externalism may seem radical enough already. Why not stop at a middle ground that combines what-quality externalism with quality-enabling internalism, instead of going all the way to the latter? Quality-enabling externalism claims that, in some online cases, what enables qualitative experience is ongoing embodied interactions with the environment, probings and samplings and movements with external feedback loops intact, not merely the internal simulative portions of those interactions. By contrast, internalism claims that the internal simulations that explain how qualities are enabled off-line also explain how they are enabled online. If the same qualities of experiences can result off-line (say, in hallucinations) as online, it may be argued, then the external parts of extended dynamics are not needed to explain how experience works, any more than to explain what it's like. However, I've argued that neural correlates can vary across veridical and illusory instances of the same quality, yet still be collected under one extended what-quality explanation. If so, why not allow that the processes that enable a given quality of experience can be internal in off-line cases and extended in online cases? The explanatory priority of extended online interactions with the natural world to internal simulations thereof supports the externalist view that extended dynamics can provide quality-enabling explanations in online cases, even though internal simulations do so in off-line cases. What the world we are interacting with is like can be part of what enables us to experience what it is like.

Acknowledgments

For discussion and comments, I'm grateful to Fred Adams, Ken Aizawa, Jan Bransen, Ron Chrisley, Andy Clark, Jan Degenaar, Barbara de Ruijter, Hans

Dooremalen, Mark Greenberg, Fred Keijzer, Julian Kiverstein, Menno Lievers, Richard Menary, Alva Noë, Tom Roberts, Don Ross, Mark Rowlands, Rob Rupert, Richard Samuels, Nick Shea, Susanna Siegel, Dave Ward, Mike Wheeler, and an anonymous referee.

Notes

1. Internalism claims to characterize all mental states, and externalism denies that this claim must hold without itself claiming to characterize all mental states. Externalism thus has a lower burden of proof than internalism: externalism is vindicated by providing counterexamples to internalism, but internalism is not vindicated by providing counterexamples to externalism. Externalism can accommodate examples of internalist explanation with equanimity, since it denies that internalism's universal ambitions are justified without adopting comparable universal ambitions of its own. This assumption applies to all the varieties considered.

Externalism also has a lower burden of proof than internalism in a second way. Internalist explanations can appeal only to internal factors. But externalist explanations can appeal to internal as well as external factors; they are typically externalist in virtue of extending the explanans to include external factors that interact with internal factors.

2. It's also referred to as "active externalism" (Clark and Chalmers 1998, reprinted in this volume), "environmentalism" (Rowlands 1999), "locational externalism" (Wilson 2004), and "process externalism" (Keijzer and Schouten 2007; see also Keijzer 2001).

3. Wheeler (2001) argues that the related conditions of arbitrariness and homuncularity are needed for representational explanations, and these may not be met by neural processes where continuous reciprocal causation makes for nontrivial causal spread of enabling explanatory factors. See also Clark 1997.

4. An interesting analogy is that between explanations of what phenotype a gene expresses and how the processes work that enable a gene to express a given phenotype (see Wheeler and Clark 1999; Wheeler 2003).

5. Mark Johnston gives constitutive internalist what-explanations of the "primary objects of hallucination" (Johnston 2004, pp. 166–168) and of the phenomenal qualities that perceptions and hallucinations can share, in terms of "qualitative sensible profiles" that are instantiated in the case of perceptions but not hallucinations (pp. 133, 135, 140). He also asserts that externalist what-explanations for the intentional contents of perceptions (pp. 138–140) are constitutive, as against conjunctivist views that wrongly regard external causal processes as causing rather than partly constituting perceptions. However, his underlying account of the

causal–constitutive distinction, which would explain why he holds that the distinction falls just where it does in these cases, is not clear. Johnston, like many discussants of arguments from illusion, does not explicitly distinguish what-quality issues from quality-enabling issues.

6. See Greenberg 2005 on why STEs are an insufficient basis for externalism.

7. In complex nonlinear dynamical systems, nonseparability is common. Arguably, even though the system's behavior might be explicable as evolving according to certain deterministic dynamical laws, nonseparability may undermine the sense in which certain factors causally explain the system's behavior, while others are merely background conditions. If so, causal explanation is arguably not the general form of explanation but a special case, just as intentional explanation is, and should not be overgeneralized.

8. Though if the laws of nature that govern internal factors differ across worlds, internal factors are arguably not constant across the worlds; see Hurley 1998a, chap. 8, for discussion.

9. As Kim (1993) has emphasized, though for different reasons; see also Greenberg 2005.

10. I've introduced this problem in the context of what-explanations, but it also arises for how-explanations. Intuitions strongly favor internalism about enabling processes, despite the widespread bafflement Maudlin (1989, p. 413) expresses as follows: "How pulses of water in pipes might give rise to toothaches is indeed entirely incomprehensible, but no less so than how electro-chemical impulses along neurons can."

11. See, e.g., Johnston 2004, who argues that "there seems to be no obstacle to supposing that the kind of awareness involved in hallucination," individuated in terms of what he calls sensible profiles, supervenes on brain state, since "none of the familiar models of Externalism" seem relevant (pp. 166–167). He takes the familiar models to include Putnam's arguments for externalism concerning the thoughts of brains in vats, and Burge's arguments for social externalism. One can agree that these are not relevant, but note that Johnston assumes supervenience on brain state to be the default position, and overlooks entirely the dynamic embodied/embedded explanations that I take to motivate what-quality externalism. Since the latter offers an empirical as well as a philosophical explanation, it may be at cross purposes with Johnston's conception of the territory. Johnston takes an example of a "seamless transition" from a local hallucination to veridical perception (p. 122) as his "stalking horse" in explaining what is right and what is wrong about traditional arguments from illusion. In his own positive account, the common explanatory factor in hallucination and veridical sensing (p. 144) is "at the level of experience" (p. 123), rather than a brain state per se, in contrast with the conjunctive view he

describes (pp. 115–116) and rejects. Nevertheless, Johnston takes quality types to supervene on brain state. His reasons for doing so, as above, appear weaker than his arguments for his own positive account and are dissociable from it, if mere supervenience on internal factors is distinguished, as I have urged, from internalist explanation.

12. Or indeed even simply after adaptation: consider Pappert, who wore left–right reversing goggles only half the time, until he could ride a bicycle while taking his goggles on and off, and experienced no visual reversal when doing so; a building on the right looked to be on the right to him, both with goggles on and with goggles off. For discussion and references, see Hurley 1998a, chaps. 8, 9.

13. The interactions of an active agent with her environment generate what I've called a *dynamic singularity* (Hurley 1998a): a tangle of causal and informational feedback loops centered on herself that moves with her and ropes in her brain, body, and elements of her environment. Dynamic singularities are extended in the same sense that phenotypes can be extended (Dawkins 1982); the skin is transparent to the dynamic feedback processes whose character explains what phenotype, or what type of experience, is in question.

14. See O'Regan and Noë 2001a,b for more on the dynamics of color experience.

15. For a somewhat different argument, see also the discussion of El Greco cases in Hurley 1998a, chap. 8; and see Wilson 2004 on the inefficient redundancy of internalizing the extended aspects of some processes. See also Noë 2004, and O'Regan and Noë's (2001 a, b) work on "change-blindness" phenomena, and the way active visual sampling of an environment by means of eye movements determines the contents and quality of visual experience.

16. Parity is named by Clark and Chalmers (1998, this volume); the same principle is independently invoked on behalf of vehicle externalism in Hurley 1998a (e.g., pp. 190–193, 325). More recently discussion in extended mind circles has shifted from the parity to the complementarity of internal and external processes (see Sutton and Menary this volume and Menary 2006, 2007); but this issue cuts across my purposes here, so I don't pursue it.

17. Recall: I assume that processes that explain how minds work can be *cognitive*, whether or not they all turn out to be *representational*. Any nonrepresentational dynamical processes that explain how minds work are not thereby disqualified from counting as cognitive. The point isn't how the label "cognitive" should be used, but that it's an open question whether nonrepresentational dynamical processes can explain how minds work.

18. See Millikan's (2004) squirrel; Hurley (2005) relates predictive simulation to processes that can enable understanding of others' actions.

References

Adams, F., and Aizawa, K. (2001). The bounds of cognition. *Philosophical Psychology*, *14*(1), 43–64.

Bogen, J. (1990). Partial hemispheric independence with the neocommisures intact. In Colwyn Trevarthen (ed.), *Brain Circuits and Functions of the Mind* (pp. 215–230). Cambridge: Cambridge University Press.

Block, N. (2005). Review of Alva Noë, *Action in Perception*. *Journal of Philosophy 102* (5)(May), 259–272.

Brooks, R. (1991). Intelligence without representation. *Artificial Intelligence*, *47*, 139–159.

Brooks, R. (1999). *Cambrian Intelligence*. Cambridge, MA: MIT Press.

Burge, T. (1986). Cartesian error and the objectivity of perception. In P. Pettit and J. McDowell (eds.), *Subject, Thought, and Context* (pp. 117–136). Oxford: Clarendon Press.

Clark, A. (1997). The dynamical challenge. *Cognitive Science*, *21*(4), 461–481.

Clark, A. (2005a). Intrinsic content, active memory, and the extended mind. *Analysis*, *65*(285), 1–11.

Clark, A. (2005b.) Word, niche, and super-niche: How language makes minds matter more. *Theoria 20*(54), 255–268. Special issue on Language and Thought: Empirical and Conceptual Viewpoints, eds. J. Acero and F. Rodriguez.

Clark, A. (2006) Material symbols and the extended mind. *Philosophical Psychology 19*(3) 291–307.

Clark, A. (2008). Pressing the flesh: Exploring a tension in the study of the embodied, embedded mind. *Philosophy and Phenomenological Research*, *76*(1), 37–59.

Clark, A., and Chalmers, D. (1998). The extended mind. *Analysis*, *58*(1), 7–19. Reprinted as chapter 2 of this volume.

Clark, A., and Grush, R. (1999). Towards a cognitive robotics. *Adaptive Behavior*, *7*(1), 5–16.

Dawkins, R. (1982). *The Extended Phenotype*. Oxford: Oxford University Press.

de Gaynesford, M. (2004). *John McDowell*. London: Polity Press.

Dennett, D. C. (1991). *Consciousness Explained*. Boston: Little, Brown.

Diamond, S. (1972). *The Double Brain*. London: Churchill Livingstone.

Dretske, F. (1996) Phenomenal externalism: If meanings ain't in the head, where are qualia? In Enrique Villanueva (ed.), *Philosophical Issues*, vol. 7 (pp. 143–158). Atascadero, CA: Ridgeview.

Grush, R. (2003). In defense of some "Cartesian" assumptions concerning the brain and its operation. *Biology and Philosophy*, *18*, 53–93.

Harman, G. (1990). The intrinsic quality of experience. In James Tomberlin (ed.), *Philosophical Perspectives*, vol. 4: *Action Theory and Philosophy of Mind* (pp. 31–52). Atascadero, CA: Ridgeview.

Hurley, S. (1998a). *Consciousness in Action*. Cambridge, MA: Harvard University Press.

Hurley, S. (1998b). Vehicles, contents, conceptual structure, and externalism. *Analysis*, *58*(1), 1–6.

Hurley, S. (2003). Action, the unity of consciousness, and vehicle externalism. In A. Cleeremans (ed.), *The Unity of Consciousness: Binding, Integration, and Dissociation* (pp. 78–91). Oxford: Oxford University Press.

Hurley, S. (2005). The shared circuits model: How control, mirroring and simulation can enable imitation and mind reading. http://www.interdisciplines.org/mirror/papers/5.

Hurley, S. (2008). The shared circuits model: How control, mirroring and simulation can enable imitation and mind reading. *Behavioral and Brain Sciences*, *31*, 1–58.

Hurley, S., and Noë, A. (2003a). Neural plasticity and consciousness. *Biology and Philosophy*, *18*, 131–168.

Hurley, S., and Noë, A. (2003b). Reply to Block. *Trends in Cognitive Sciences*, *7*(8), 342.

Hurley, S., and Noë, A. (2006). Can hunter-gatherers hear color? In G. Brennan, R. Goodin, F. Jackson, and M. Smith (eds.), *Common Minds: Essays in Honor of Philip Pettit*. Oxford: Oxford University Press.

Huttenlocher, P. R. (2002). *Neural Plasticity: The Effects of Environment on the Development of the Cerebral Cortex*. Cambridge, MA: Harvard University Press.

Jacob, P. (2002). Review of *The Body in Mind*, by Mark Rowlands. *Mind and Language*, *17*(3), 325–331.

Jeeves, M. A. (1965). Agensis of the corpus callosum—physiopathological and clinical aspects. *Proceedings of the Australian Association of Neurologists*, *3*, 41–48.

Johnston, M. (2004). The obscure object of hallucination. *Philosophical Studies*, *120*, (1–3), 113–183.

Keijzer, F. (2001). *Representation and Behavior*. Cambridge, MA: MIT Press.

Keijzer, F., and Schouten, M. (2007). Embedded cognition and mental causation: Setting empirical bounds on metaphysics. *Synthese, 158*(1).

Kim, J. (1993). *Supervenience and Mind.* Cambridge: Cambridge University Press.

Kinsbourne, M. (1974). Mechanisms of hemispheric interaction in man. In M. Kinsbourne and W. L. Smith (eds.), *Hemispheric Disconnection and Cerebral Function* (pp. 260–285). Springfield, Ill.: Charles C. Thomas.

Kohler, I. (1951). Über Aufbau und Wandlungen der Wahrnehmungswelt. *Österreichische Akademie der Wissenschaften. Sitzungsberichte, philosophisch-historische Klasse, 227*, 1–118. Translated as Kohler 1964.

Kohler, I. (1964). *The Formation and Transformation of the Perceptual World.* Published as a monograph in *Psychological Issues*, vol. 3 (monograph 12). New York: New York International University Press.

Lakoff, G., and Johnson, M. (1999). *Philosophy in the Flesh: The Embodied Mind and Its Challenge to Western Thought.* New York: Basic Books.

Maudlin, T. (1989). Computation and consciousness. *Journal of Philosophy, 86*, 407–432.

McDowell, J. (1994). The content of perceptual experience. *Philosophical Quarterly, 44*(175), 190–205.

Menary, R. (2006). Attacking the bounds of cognition. *Philosophical Psychology, 19*(3), 329–344.

Menary, R. (2007). *Cognitive Integration: Mind and Cognition Unbounded.* Basingstoke: Palgrave Macmillan.

Millikan, R. (1984). *Language, Thought, and Other Biological Categories.* Cambridge, MA: MIT Press.

Millikan, R. (1993). *White Queen Psychology and Other Essays for Alice.* Cambridge, MA: MIT Press.

Millikan, R. (2004). *Varieties of Meaning.* Cambridge, MA: MIT Press.

Milner, D., and Jeeves, M. A. (1979). A review of behavioural studies of agensis of the corpus callosum. In I. Steele, M. Russell, W. Van Hof, and B. Berlucchi (eds.), *Structure and Function of Cerebral Commissures.* London: Academic Press.

Noë, A. (2004). *Action in Perception.* Cambridge, MA: MIT Press.

Noë, A., Pessoa, L., and Thompson, E. (2000). Beyond the grand illusion: What change blindness really teaches us about vision. *Visual Cognition, 7*, 93–106.

O'Regan, J. K., and Noë, A. (2001a). A sensorimotor approach to vision and visual consciousness. *Behavioral and Brain Sciences, 24*(5), 939–973.

O'Regan, J. K., and Noë, A. (2001b). What it is like to see: A sensorimotor theory of perceptual experience. *Synthese, 129*, 79–103.

Rowlands, M. (1999). *The Body in Mind*. Cambridge: Cambridge University Press.

Rowlands, M. (2003). *Externalism*. Chesham, Buckinghamshire: Acumen Press.

Thelen, E., and Smith, L. B. (1994). *A Dynamical Systems Approach to the Development of Cognition and Action*. Cambridge, Mass.: MIT Press.

van Gelder, T. (1999a). Revisiting the dynamical hypothesis. Preprint No. 2/99. University of Melbourne, Department of Philosophy.

van Gelder, T. J. (1999b). Dynamic approaches to cognition. In R. Wilson and F. Keil (eds.), *The MIT Encyclopedia of Cognitive Sciences* (pp. 243–246). Cambridge, MA: MIT Press.

van Gelder, T. J. (1995). What might cognition be, if not computation? *Journal of Philosophy, 92*, 345–381.

van Gelder, T. J. (1998). The dynamical hypothesis in cognitive science. *Behavioral and Brain Sciences, 21*, 1–14.

Wheeler, M. (1997). Cognition's coming home: The reunion of life and mind. In P. Husbands and I. Harvey (eds.), *Proceedings of the 4th European Conference on Artificial Life*. Cambridge, MA: MIT Press.

Wheeler, M. (2001). Two threats to representation. *Synthese, 129*, 211–231.

Wheeler, M. (2003). Do genes code for traits? In A. Rojszczak, J. Cachro, and G. Kurczewski (eds.), *Philosophical Dimensions of Logic and Science: Selected Contributed Papers from the 11th International Congress of Logic, Methodology, and Philosophy of Science* (pp. 151–164). Synthese Library, vol. 320. Dordrecht: Kluwer.

Wheeler, M., and Clark, A. (1999). Genic representation: Reconciling content and causal complexity. *British Journal for the Philosophy of Science, 50*(1), 103–135.

Wilson, R. A. (2004). *Boundaries of the Mind*. Cambridge: Cambridge University Press.

7 The Alleged Coupling-Constitution Fallacy and the Mature Sciences

Don Ross and James Ladyman

Leading critics of the thesis that cognition is extended ("outside the head") have increasingly focused their attention on an alleged central equivocation in arguments for the thesis. The equivocation in question is between the banal point that external factors causally influence cognition and the surprising claim that external factors are partly constitutive of cognition (Adams and Aizawa 2001, 2008a,b). On one reading of this criticism, it simply emphasizes how much work can be done in models by allowing for *complex* causal relations (e.g., bidirectional feedback), encouraging questions about whether anything that makes a substantive modeling difference is added by replacing causal relations with set-theoretic relations (e.g., such-and-such manipulation of the abacus is a member of such-and-such a set of cognitive processes that generated such-and-such a solution) or identity relations (e.g., the conjunction of such-and-such neural processes and such-and-such verbal auto-stimulation and such-and-such manipulations of the abacus is identical to the cognitive process that generated output solution X at t). For reasons on which we will elaborate below, we are sympathetic to the criticism on this interpretation. Note that on this reading the criticism does not imply the opposite thesis to the claim that cognition is outside the head, that is, the claim that cognition is "inside the head." One can consider questions about how best to model cognition without thereby taking oneself to be wondering where cognition takes place against a fixed background arrangement of objects.

However, a good deal of Adams and Aizawa's rhetoric, coursing steadily through all of the sources cited above, *does* suggest that they mean to defend internalism. It is not hard to see what might motivate this. In developing cognitive models, one typically must make assumptions about systems. Systems are by definition bounded, and so decisions about boundaries are part of the process of choosing among models. Both the extended mind thesis and its internalist rival can be interpreted as alternative claims about what kind of ontology of systems any cognitive model should presuppose. The idea that there might be a justified *general* such claim about *all* cognitive models, which could rationally be made in advance of tackling specific modeling problems one at a time, would have to be based either on a universal tractability constraint or on metaphysics. Some of Jerry Fodor's earlier defenses of internalism (e.g., Fodor 1980[1]) seem to turn on tractability considerations. However, the basis for the overwhelming majority of the philosophical discussion of the issue is clearly explicit or implicit metaphysics.

The view we will defend here is that metaphysical considerations should play no role in deciding how to model cognition. We do not believe there is any basis for a general fact of the matter about what is and what isn't a cognitive system. Modelers will and should draw system boundaries in whichever ways maximize efficient capture of local phenomena. Of course, as models are aggregated into more general theoretical perspectives, local optima should often be expected to be sacrificed for the sake of more parsimonious and powerful global models. But this is compatible with the suggestion that even a fully general theory of cognition—as information processing by relatively autonomous goal-driven systems—need incorporate no single overarching account of limits on the boundaries of cognitive systems. A cognitive system might simply be anything described by the hypothetical fully general theory, and be open to limitless cross-classification with respect to biological or chemical (etc.) principles for system identification. We think that this attitude is closer to that of many advocates of extended mind perspectives (e.g., Clark 1997, 2004; Hurley this volume) than to that of any internalists we can think of. That said, our view is straightforwardly opposed to any thesis to the effect that minds are, as a matter of fact, partly located outside people's heads. We don't think that there is any such matter of fact, as a special case of there being no fact about where minds are located at all. To talk about the location of the mind is simply to resort to metaphor. We don't object to using metaphors, but we do object to arguing over whose metaphors are literally true.

As is typical of philosophers promoting metaphysical hunches, Adams and Aizawa (2001) explicitly associate the internalist view with "common sense," while at the same time insisting that the evidence for it is furnished by the nature of the most sophisticated generalizations of cognitive science as it progresses toward "scientific maturity." In this chapter, we will not dispute Adams and Aizawa's contention about common sense. However, we will indicate grounds for doubting that common sense and mature sciences should ever be expected to agree with one another. To their credit, Adams and Aizawa (this volume) claim only that concordance of their position with that of common sense is a bonus rather than evidence for their view; they grant that the relevant sciences are decisive on the issue at stake. However, we deny that concordance with conventional folk wisdom is even a bonus for an intended scientific thesis; on the contrary, such concordance has no probative force whatever. More specifically, we argue that: (a) the intuitive distinction between causes and constitution to which Adams and Aizawa appeal tends to be abandoned as sciences converge on robust models of general structure; (b) the metaphysical notion of constitution or composition is an abstraction that does not correspond to any general idea that figures nonmetaphorically in science; and (c) the notion of causation, insofar as it is relevant to science, may not be applicable to fundamental physics, which casts strong doubt on its appropriateness as an explanatory element in any set of restrictions on unification of models.

We begin our assessment of the status of the causal–constitutive distinction in science with the following observations:

(i) As Hurley (this volume) points out, the causal–constitutive distinction is typically deployed by philosophers without being explained or motivated in detail. Instead, philosophers help themselves to the idea that there must be some such distinction and that it must be important to science, and then set about showing that particular types of entities or processes are better candidates for the causal role or the constitutive role as the case may be.

(ii) Constitution is usually discussed in analytic metaphysics under the description "composition." The metaphysical notion of composition has become the subject of much debate recently, but like many metaphysical debates these days, it is not engaged with real, as opposed to stylized, science.

(iii) In contemporary fundamental physics, arguably there are no "little things" out of which matter is ultimately made. Individual substances dissolve into physical structures that are only adequately describable by mathematics and that resist conceptualization in material terms. Of course, the debate over constitution as it arises in this volume concerns the domain of a special science, not fundamental physics. We think it is clear, however, that a conception of physical constitution inherited from early modern atomism is the model for contemporary metaphysicians' applications of constitution and composition to supposedly "higher-level" domains, and that if the model is based on mythical science then its extensions can have no more than metaphorical status.

(iv) Causation is the subject of much debate in the philosophy of the special sciences and the philosophy of physics, and those debates concern, on the one hand, how there can be genuine causation in the macro domains studied by the special sciences given the generalized causal exclusion problem (see, e.g., Elder 2004), and on the other, whether or not there is any causation in physics. (See Price and Corry 2007 for discussion inspired by Russell's claim that causation is not a feature of fundamental science.)

(v) The notion of causation itself is hugely problematic, and where one stands in the debate between Humeans (Lewis), necessitarians (Armstrong, Tooley, Dretske), Aristotelians (Cartwright), and others has implications for the metaphysical weight that can be put on the causal–constitutive distinction.

Let us begin from observation (i) above. Hurley (this volume) says "in philosophy of psychology, explanations tend to be treated as causal or constitutive, in accord with prior assumptions or intuitions about boundaries, which often themselves have no clear basis and do not illuminate the [causal–constitutive] distinction." Faced with this challenge, we imagine a philosopher who relies on the distinction, and who thinks, like Adams and Aizawa, that it is relevant to science, trying to motivate it from consideration of the standard sort of example found in the more general analytic metaphysics literature. There one encounters frequent references to the compositional structure of samples of water. (For critical discussion of such references, see Ponce 2003.) Chemistry explains recurring properties of water samples by reference to underlying properties of hydrogen and oxygen atoms and the way they combine to form molecules of H_2O. For example, the question of what makes water a solvent of common salt is answered, in broadly causal terms, by appealing to the chemical properties of the oxygen and hydrogen molecules. However, the metaphysician insists that the question of what constitutes the water is altogether different. This is held to concern what substance or matter makes up the water, and appeal is to be made only to the existence, rather than the causal powers, of the hydrogen and oxygen atoms. However, this special sort of explanation is foreign to sciences, especially as they mature.

Lakoff[2] and Johnson's (1980) and Lakoff's (1987) pioneering work in uncovering the linguistic basis of habitual metaphysics documents the extent to which the deep metaphors of English, which govern everyday inferences made in that language, are structured according to an implicit doctrine of "containment."[3] On this doctrine, the world is a kind of container bearing objects that change location and properties over time. These objects cause things to happen by interacting directly with one another. Prototypically, they move each other about by banging into one another. At least as important to the general picture, they themselves are containers in turn, and their properties and causal dispositions are to be explained by the properties and dispositions of the objects they contain (and which are often taken to entirely comprise them).

Elsewhere (Ladyman and Ross 2007) we argue against what we call the *metaphysics of domestication*, which consists of attempts to render pieces of contemporary science—and, more often, stylized or mythical interpretations of contemporary science—into terms that can be made sense of by reference to the containment metaphor. Domesticating metaphysicians seek to account for the world as "made of" myriad "little things" in roughly the way that (some) walls are made of bricks. Unlike bricks in walls, however, the little things are often held to be in motion. Their causal powers are usually understood as manifest in the effects they have on each other when they collide. Thus the causal structure of the world is imagined to be based on emergent or reducible consequences of reverberating networks of what we call "microbangings"—the types of ultimate causal relations that prevail among the basic types of little things, whatever exactly those turn out to be. Metaphysicians, especially recently, are heavily preoccupied with the search for "genuine causal oomph," particularly in relation to what they perceive to be the competition between different levels of reality.[4]

This picture, familiar as it is, finds absolutely no corresponding image in contemporary fundamental physics. The types of particles which physical theory describes do not have spatiotemporal boundaries in anything like what common sense takes for granted in conceptualizing everyday objects, and in that respect are not classical individuals—the philosopher's little things (French and Krause 2006). There are nothing like microbangings in fundamental physics; indeed whether there is causation in any sense that doesn't stretch the meaning of the word to the point of obscurantism is often disputed (Norton 2007; Ross and Spurrett 2007; Ladyman and Ross 2007, chap. 5). Michael Redhead expresses a common view among careful students of physics when he says that "to most physicists the old-fashioned idea of cause arises from the idea of our interfering in the natural course of events, pushing and pulling objects to make them move and so on. In modern physics there are just regularities of one sort or another" (Redhead 1990, p. 147). Even among experts who think this claim is too strong, it is not supposed that physical theory features a general model of causation in the sense of a family of processes that flow from the insides of containers to their outsides. The world as described by actual physics is in no interesting ways like a wall made of bricks in motion (that somehow manages not to fall apart), or, in the more sophisticated extension of the metaphor dominant since the rise of modern science, like a chamber enclosing the molecules of a gas. Indeed, it is no longer helpful to conceive of either the world, or particular systems of the world that we study in partial isolation, as "made of" anything at all. The attempt to domesticate twenty-first-century science by reference to homely images of little particles that have much in common with seventeenth- and eighteenth-century mechanistic and materialist metaphysics is forlorn. The basic structure of reality as described by fundamental physics can only be accurately rendered in mathematics; to attempt to translate it into the terms of natural language is at once to resort to metaphor, which no amount of elaboration in a metaphysical tone of voice can render plausible as a literal account.

The causal–constitutive distinction is part of the metaphysics of domestication. On the other hand, composition in real science, as opposed to in metaphysics and stylized science, is usually a dynamic and complex idea that does explanatory work by reference to distinctive features of specific applications rather than the metaphysician's illusory generic properties. To return to the standard example above, water is composed by oxygen and hydrogen in various polymeric forms, such as $(H_2O)_2$, $(H_2O)_3$, and so on, that are constantly forming, dissipating, and reforming over short time periods in such a way as to give rise to the familiar properties of the macroscopic kind water.[5] The usual philosophical identity claim "water is H_2O" ignores a rich and subtle scientific account that is still not complete. What is important in this context is that the causal–constitutive distinction dissolves because the kind water is an emergent feature of a complex dynamical system. It makes no sense to imagine it having its familiar properties synchronically. Rather, the water's wetness, conductivity, and so on all arise because of equilibria in the dynamics of processes happening over short but nonnegligible time scales at the atomic scale. From the point of view of any attempted reductive explanation, the kind water is not held by physicists to be "constituted" as opposed to "caused," because it is not a "substance" in the classical metaphysical sense of that term. Instead, it is a kind of process explained as the result of emergent features of the interaction of atomic properties. As observation (iii) points out (and as is documented by an extensive survey of the relevant physical theory in Ladyman and Ross 2007, chap. 3), the picture of water we have just presented is equally applicable to oxygen and hydrogen atoms in their turn, which are also not little things, but themselves emergent dynamical structures.

The model of the world as structured by commonsense containment metaphors and the model of the world as given by physics are therefore not even approximately isomorphic. Only the latter has any claim to possible (incomplete) viability as an objective description. The former is itself an interesting object of scientific study, for explanation by the combined forces of evolutionary primatology, anthropology, and linguistics. The container model should not be taken seriously by philosophers who purport to contribute to veristic modeling, as Adams and Aizawa do.

Unfortunately, Adams and Aizawa's discussions of constitution appear to be wholly based on naive objectification of everyday containment metaphors. Their leading example appeals to intuitions denying that the processes by which the bimetallic strip of a thermostat expands and contracts in correlation with states of room temperature and the activation of the air conditioning system "extend beyond the limits of the strip and into the room or air conditioner" (Adams and Aizawa 2008a,b). But neither the sentence "The expansion and contraction occur inside the strip" nor "The room is not the smallest container inside which the expansion and contraction are contained" admits of any possible translation into the terms of physical theory; the claims are irreducibly metaphorical. The grip of the containment metaphor on Adams and Aizawa is particularly clear when they claim that the following is an important question *for science*: "What regions of spacetime contain cognitive processing?" Not only is this not a question actually posed by any science, it is not a question that has literal sense in the technical vocabulary of any science. The closest we can get to it is (roughly): "Which set of events have episodes of cognitive processing in their backward light cones?" But this, in contrast to "Which kinds of events are systematically and distinctively caused by cognitive processing?," isn't a question of much or any scientific interest. Another of Adams and Aizawa's recurring sites for exemplifying the causally coupled–constituted distinction is a Watt governor: "The combustion of fuel in the governed engine is tightly coupled to the rotation of the weighted arms, yet the process of combustion does not extend beyond the bounds of the engine" (forthcoming). It is worth noting that with this example, "common sense" seems indeed to be firmly on their side, unlike the previous case where what Adams and Aizawa say surely strikes common sense as weird. We suggest that the basis of the asymmetry between the examples lies here: the ubiquity of the containment metaphor derives from the fact that as tool builders we humans are naturally interested in isolating systems in such a way that we can transport them around without significantly changing the kinds of processes we can use them to effect (Cartwright 1989). But modeling the world in terms of the affordances it offers for human manipulation at the special spacetime scales in which we plan and execute actions is not the way to construct objective accounts of the universe.

The causal–constitutive distinction thus is not drawn in physics. To take another example, many theoretical physicists believe that mass is the result of interaction between established "particles," such as quarks and electrons, and the so-called Higgs boson. A new generation of particle accelerators will shortly begin the search for evidence of these interactions. The account of mass in these terms is dynamical and, at least on first approximation, causal. But it is laughable to imagine a physicist saying, "Well, I understand this account of what causes mass, but I am still puzzled about what constitutes it." Or consider the account given by Batterman (2002) of the way in which light rays as described by ray optics can be mathematically recovered from wave optics and how doing so is necessary to explain certain :emergent" phenomena. Here we have a causal story about the production of raylike effects, but the question of what constitutes the rays is not a genuinely separate question; it is at best an alternative way of (metaphorically) speaking.

A reader might complain that we are trying to get too much mileage out of the differences between physics and the "macro-level" styles of description and explanation found in special sciences such as psychology. "Up there," it might be objected, a good deal of clearly serious scientific activity consists in studying particular kinds of composition characteristic of special-science domains. For example, biologists concern themselves with how cells compose multicellular organisms, economists with how individual markets compose national or international economies, chemists with how oxygen and hydrogen compose water, and so on. The problem with trying to derive metaphysical significance from this set of activities is that there is little reason for thinking that (e.g.) economic composition and chemical or anatomical composition have anything in common except shared resort to the container metaphor. Is the U.S. life insurance market really "in" the U.S. economy in anything objectively resembling the sense in which a person's nucleus accumbens is said to be "in" her brain? Recall that the application of constitution relevant to the debate in this volume is to the question "Is the mind 'in' the brain?" This seems to be yet another *sui generis* extension of the metaphor, but it is a good deal less clear than the other examples just given. We suggest that the reason for this is that cognitive science, unlike economics or neuroscience, remains immature in the sense of having no canonical general modeling framework. As a result, there are no standard procedures for turning applications of the container metaphor in its domain into literal theoretical propositions.

Adams and Aizawa (2008a, p. 101) recognize this point when they consider other views that, like ours, are suspicious of the distinction between causal and constitutive relations in science (Rockwell 2005, Hurley this volume). "There is," they concede, "some reason for their suspicion, namely that it is hard to make out this distinction for the case of cognition. . . . What . . . is the difference between things that merely cause cognitive processes and things that are cognitive processes? The problem lies in the uncertainty about what exactly cognitive processes are." We emphatically agree. Unfortunately, Adams and Aizawa then assert that the distinction is "intuitively clear" on the basis of an example from physics. They claim that there is a clear fact of the matter about the distinction between what "constitutes" nuclear fission and what "causes" it. This may be true enough at the level of everyday description, which helps itself to a specific expression of the container metaphor. But the literal description of nuclear fission is mathematical and incorporates no such simple intuition.

Fortunately, we need not restrict ourselves to comparisons between mature physical theory and immature special sciences. There are (theoretically) mature special sciences, the character of which might be suggestive of some aspects of a mature cognitive science of the future. Consider the way in which compositional notions are interpreted in the (theoretically) mature science of economics. Economic models are typically models of "systems," which are taken to participate in larger such systems. However, the relations between systems and subsystems are not compositional in the philosopher's sense because they are model-relative. A system is distinguished by reference to variables that can be treated as endogenous, that is, as having their values codetermined as a set *given* simultaneous identification of some other set of variables as exogenous, that is, as background to be fixed in advance. Economists freely admit that interesting phenomena typically admit of multiple parsings along different endogenous–exogenous boundaries for varying predictive and explanatory purposes. In general, although economists are mainly concerned to discover which variables are "control levers" for which others, their theoretical structure has no use for the kind of rigid distinction between causal relations and compositional relations that domesticating metaphysicians assume as fundamental. This is reflected in the fact that economists move smoothly back and forth, as practical traction dictates, between two different bases for the endogenous–exogenous distinction, which may cross-classify one and the same set of variables. Context normally tells an economist whether to interpret exogeneity by reference to causal independence (again, *given* and relative to a specified model), or econometrically. On the latter operationalization, we say that a variable x_i is exogenous against a matrix X: $x_i \notin X$ if the expected coefficients of all regressions of x_i against variables in X are 0. Note that neither of these interpretations attempts to *reproduce* the container metaphor; instead, they fully *replace* it by reference to patterns of inferential determination in networks of structural relations.

Induction suggests to us that development of such procedures for replacing—that is, eliminating—traces of anthropomorphic descriptive metaphors is among the main things it means to call a science "mature." Thus the positive lesson we take from the debate in this volume over whether the constituents of the mind are "inside" or "outside" the cranium is that cognitive science is still relatively immature (as we would expect on other grounds). We regard it as entirely unhelpful and regressive to try to assist it to maturity by insisting that it be bound to go on taking the original metaphor seriously; we shudder to consider how far from the insights of contemporary physics or economics we would now be had these sciences been governed in their development by such a stricture. We note that the proponents of the extended mind thesis, when they describe their claim in terms of "pushing" the mind "out into the world" (and so on) encourage precisely the sort of conservative protectionism over the metaphor we have deplored as counterscientific. But we expect that if and when there is a mature cognitive science, then when people render its canonical process descriptions that won't use the container metaphor back into the terms of that metaphor for pedagogical purposes, many appropriate translations will feature containers larger than the skull and many others won't. This difference will be no basis for rational disputation.

Notes

1. His more recent ones go in the opposite direction; see Fodor 2008.

2. This paragraph is drawn from Ladyman and Ross 2007, pp. 3–4.

3. Here are some of their examples of everyday English phrases that encode the implicit metaphysic of containment: There was a lot of good running *in* the race;

Halfway into the race I ran out of energy; How did Jerry *get out of* washing the windows?; *Outside of* washing the windows, what else did you do?; He's *immersed in* washing the windows right now; We're *out of* trouble now; I'm slowly getting *into* shape; He *fell into* a depression (Lakoff and Johnson 1980, pp. 31–32).

4. We take it that "causal oomph" is a synonym of "biff" (Armstrong 2004).

5. See van Brakel 2000.

References

Adams, F., and Aizawa, K. (2001). The bounds of cognition. *Philosophical Psychology*, *14*, 43–64.

Adams, F., and Aizawa, K. (2008a). *The Bounds of Cognition*. Malden, MA: Blackwell.

Adams, F., and Aizawa, K. (2008b). Challenges to active externalism. In P. Robbins and M. Aydede (eds.), *The Cambridge Handbook on Situated Cognition*. Cambridge: Cambridge University Press.

Armstrong, D. (2004). Going through an open door again: Counterfactual versus singularist theories of causation. In J. Collins, N. Hall, and L. A. Paul (eds.), *Causation and Counterfactuals* (pp. 445–458). Cambridge, MA: MIT Press.

Batterman, J. (2002). *The Devil in the Details*. Oxford: Oxford University Press.

Cartwright, N. (1989). *Nature's Capacities and Their Measurement*. Oxford: Oxford University Press.

Clark, A. (1997). *Being There*. Cambridge, MA: MIT Press.

Clark, A. (2004). *Natural Born Cyborgs*. Oxford: Oxford University Press.

Elder, C. (2004). *Real Natures and Familiar Objects*. Cambridge, MA: MIT Press.

Fodor, J. (1980). Methodological solipsism considered as a research strategy in cognitive science. *Behavioral and Brain Sciences*, *3*, 63–73.

Fodor, J. (2008). *LOT 2: The Language of Thought Revisited*. Oxford: Oxford University Press.

French, S., and Krause, D. (2006). *Identity in Physics: A Historical, Philosophical and Formal Account*. Oxford: Oxford University Press.

Ladyman, J., and Ross, D. (2007). *Every Thing Must Go: Metaphysics Naturalised*. Oxford: Oxford University Press.

Lakoff, G. (1987). *Women, Fire, and Dangerous Things*. Chicago: University of Chicago Press.

Lakoff, G., and Johnson, M. (1980). *Metaphors We Live By.* Chicago: University of Chicago Press.

Norton, J. (2007). Causation as folk science. In Price and Corry 2007 (pp. 14–44).

Ponce, V. (2003). Rethinking natural kinds. Doctoral dissertation, Duke University.

Price, H., and Corry, R. (eds.) (2007). *Causation, Physics, and the Constitution of Reality: Russell's Republic Revisited.* Oxford: Oxford University Press.

Redhead, M. (1990). Explanation. In D. Knowles (ed.), *Explanation and Its Limits* (pp. 135–154). Cambridge: Cambridge University Press.

Rockwell, T. (2005). *Neither Brain nor Ghost: A Nondualist Alternative to the Mind–Brain Identity Theory.* Cambridge, MA: MIT Press.

Ross, D., and Spurrett, D. (2007). On notions of cause: Russell's thesis revisited. *British Journal for the Philosophy of Science, 58.*

van Brakel, J. (2000). The nature of chemical substances. In N. Bhushan and S. Rosenfeld (eds.), *Of Minds and Molecules: New Philosophical Perspectives on Chemistry.* Oxford: Oxford University Press.

8 Meaning Making and the Mind of the Externalist

Robert A. Wilson

1 Intentionality and the Mind

During the 1980s, many philosophers of mind, and even the occasional cognitive scientist, were very exercised about something called "the problem of intentionality." The problem was something like this. There are certain things in the world that appear to possess, through their operation and functioning, a special kind of property: intentionality. This is the property of being about something, of having content about that thing, of carrying information about that thing. The problem of intentionality was threefold: to explain what intentionality was; to delineate which things had intentionality (and so which things didn't); and to provide an account of just why they had not only intentionality, but the particular intentionality they had—their *content*. The third of these chores was the core one, the task of specifying in virtue of what certain things in the world were about the particular things they were about.

The problem of intentionality was especially pressing within the naturalistic view of the mind that motivated much of the discussion of the problem. The idea was to view naturalism as a kind of constraint on what could count as an acceptable endeavor to complete the core chore: that one's account of what made for intentionality could not itself rely on unexplicated intentional or semantic notions. An answer to the problem of intentionality must be given solely in terms of "naturalistically acceptable" notions, such as causation, counterfactual dependence, material composition, biological function, or phylogenetic history.

To understand a little more about the problem of intentionality, we need to turn to its second part, the part that divides the world into things with intentionality and things without it. Two of the things that paradigmatically have intentionality are the language that people use to communicate, and the thoughts that people have (often, but not only, while participating in those communicative acts). Of these, it is plausible to hold that the intentionality of language derives from that of thinking. That is because people mean something by making an utterance because that utterance conveys a thought (belief, desire, expectation, fear, memory, etc.) about that very thing. When I say to you that the kangaroo paws in King's Park are flowering, that's in part because I believe that very thing, having ridden by them earlier in the day. But more to the point, the utterance means what it does in part because of the meaning that the mental representations that led me to utter it have. The meaning of an utterance is "derived" from the meaning of an act of thought. Thought, however, has *original* intentionality in that the meaning that its constituent mental representations have does not in turn derive from the intentionality of anything else.

If that is true of the intentionality of spoken language and the mind, then perhaps it is true more generally. There are other things that have some kind of intentionality—road signs, gestures, written language, computer programs—and if the intentionality of speech derives from that of the mental representations that generate it, then it doesn't seem too much of a stretch to think that these too have much the same kind of derived intentionality. In short, underlying all of intentionality, perhaps, is the intentionality of the mind. This, together with the naturalistic constraint, created a certain kind of research program, one that aimed to provide an account of the intentionality of mind in non-intentional terms. Hence the rise of informational semantics (Dretske 1981, 1988), causal theories of representation more generally (Fodor 1984, 1987), and biosemantics (Millikan 1984, 1993)—all primarily accounts of the intentionality of mental representations and minds, and all putatively kosher from a naturalistic point of view.

There are many nuances to the problem of intentionality that this sketch ignores, giving rise to a variety of misgivings that could be expressed about proceeding without further elaboration. My main purpose in beginning with this thumbnail, however, is simply to say that there is one thing that this literature has been right to seize on, and one thing that it presupposed that, in hindsight, is more dubious. First, the Good News.

Whether or not one agrees with the reductive drift underlying the treatment of cognition as asymmetrically primitive when it comes to intentional phenomena, and whether or not one views the naturalistic constraint as, in effect, making the problem of intentionality unsolvable, the mind really is special when it comes to matters meaningful. Mental representation of some kind or other is involved in some way or other in all other cases of intentionality. Language, conventions, social practices, images, causal chains of dependence, information transmission, biofunctions, historical anchoring, resemblance, and systematicity—all of which have been proposed as contributing or critical factors in responses to the problem of intentionality—have to pass the acid test of accounting for mental representation in order to do so. This is sufficient to support the point I am making here. But I also think that the mind is presupposed in the operation or application of each of these to the problem of intentionality.

One might wonder in just what sense mental representation is presupposed in positing, say, that the heart has the (bio)function of pumping blood, or in proposing that there is an informational relation between smoke and fire. Surely, one might think, both of these turn solely on whether the corresponding naturalistic grounding relations exist. In the case of the biofunction of pumping blood, these are historical facts concerning what ancestral hearts did, and in that of smoke and fire, the kind of causal dependence between the two. Yet at best, in the complexities of the actual world, natural selection is not fine-grained enough to distinguish the pumping of blood from myriad properties with which it is entwined (*sensu* Wilson 2003b). And similarly, the robust clustering of properties means that "carries information about" will be, at best, a one–many relation. What is needed, in both cases, is ultimately something mindful—either an individual mind itself, able to select and discriminate among the property clusters, or a convention, habit, or agreed-on practice that, in turn, presupposes individual minds that are able to do so.

In short, the mind is crucially implicated in the making of meaning, both directly (in nearly all cases) and indirectly (in the remainder). That is the Good News about how the problem of intentionality has been construed. By homing in on mental meaning, it has hit Intentionality Central.

The Bad News is that the task of solving the problem of intentionality has been complicated by an innocuous-enough sounding assumption, namely, that mental states are "in the head." In fact, they often are not. To see why, we need to remind ourselves of how the debate between individualists and externalists about cognition has developed over the past thirty years.

2 Externalism about Cognition and the Extended Mind

The predominant view of cognition throughout the short history of cognitive science and the longer history of the philosophy of mind has been *individualistic* in that cognitive processes have been understood by abstracting away from the physical and social environments in which cognition takes place. That is, it is not simply that cognition is a property of individuals (see Zerubavel 1997; cf. Barnier et al. 2008), but that it is construed and investigated as if that individual were the only thing that existed in the world. This "methodological solipsism" (Fodor 1980) about cognition has been defended as a consequence of accepting a computational theory of cognitive processing (Devitt 1990; Egan 1995), and by appealing to broader claims about the nature of scientific taxonomy (Fodor 1987) and the metaphysics of mental causation (Crane 1991). Acceptance of the constraint of individualism has gone hand in hand with a view of the mind as possessing a rich, internal structure, whether that structure be innately hardwired or largely acquired through training or regimentation of some kind; modular or generalist in its functional decomposition; or rules-and-representational or associationist in its operational dynamics.

Those who reject individualism are *externalists* about the mind, and they have both responded to the arguments for individualism (Wilson 1992, 1995, part I) and, more recently, constructed positive visions of the study of cognition based on the rejection of individualism (Clark 2003; Rowlands 1999; Wilson 2003a, 2004). Those visions have taken the idea of externalism in more radical directions in recent years (e.g., Menary 2007; Wilson and Clark 2008; Wilson and Craver 2007; Chemero and Silberstein 2008; Clark 2008). The "radicalness" of these recent directions can perhaps be seen most clearly by reflecting briefly on how externalism began.

Doubts about individualism were first raised in the now classic arguments of Putnam (1975) and Burge (1979), both turning on the question of whether individualistic views of the mind could adequately account for meaning or mental content. These original challenges to individualism were cast in terms of whether psychological states, particularly intentional states, should be individuated or taxonomized in accord with the constraint of individualism. For this reason I have elsewhere (Wilson 2000, 2004) called the resulting forms of externalism *taxonomic externalism*; it has also been called "traditional externalism" and "philosophical externalism." The general idea was to continue to view content-laden mental states as some kind of internal state of the individual, but to argue that, nonetheless, because of their content, they did not supervene on, or were not metaphysically determined by, what fell within the physical boundary of that individual. Hence the debates over whether folk psychology was individualistic (Burge 1979; Fodor 1982; Loar 1988), whether the notion of content used in Marr's celebrated theory of vision was internalist or externalist (Burge 1986a; Egan 1992; Segal 1989; Shapiro 1997), and the issue of the relationship between individualism and the normativity of the mental (Burge 1986b; Ebbs 1998; Pettit 1993).

More radical forms of externalism about the mind—what I (Wilson 2000, 2004) call *locational externalism*, Rowlands (1999) calls *environmentalism*, and, following Clark and Chalmers (1998 and this volume), many call the *extended mind thesis*—hold that the mind and the cognitive pro cesses that constitute it extend beyond the boundary of the skin of the individual agent. The extended mind thesis identifies cognitive systems themselves as reaching beyond individuals into their physical and social environments. The thesis challenges individualism directly by implying that an individualistic psychology could only, at best, tell part of the story about cognitive processing: the inside story. An early gesture at such a view was my *wide computationalism* (Wilson 1994), the view that the computational systems that make up the mind can extend into, and include as a part of themselves, aspects of an organism's environment.

Locational externalism, environmentalism, and the extended mind thesis are radical forms of externalism in at least two ways. First, they do not rest on claims and intuitions about whether the content of a pair of states of two individuals in different environments (or one individual in two such environments over time) is the same or different, about how particular intentional states are taxonomized, or about the role of the physical or social environments in individuating such states. Instead, they appeal to the nature of psychological processing, to the arbitrariness of the head (or the skin) for bounding cognitive systems, and to what happens in real-life, online cognitive activity in the world. Thus, if the extended mind thesis is true, it is true in virtue of something implementationally deep about cognition, rather than some debatable view of mental content. Second, locational externalism is not simply a view of how we "talk about" or view cognition and the mind—about the epistemology of the mind, one might say—but about what cognition and the mind *are*—about the ontology of the mind.

If the mind is not, literally, "in the head" (and for resistance to radical externalism, see Adams and Aizawa 2008, this volume; cf. also Aizawa 2007), then maybe we need to reconceptualize the many issues that turn on the assumption that it is—such as the problem of intentionality. But it will take us some time to return to this point, for we first need to probe the idea of extended cognition, and arguments for accepting that large chunks of cognition are extended, more thoroughly.

3   On Arguments for Extended Cognition

As externalism has articulated and developed its own positive vision for the study of the mind, it has also drawn, often implicitly, on arguments that are not simply of the form "Arguments for my opponent's position are no good." The argument I shall focus on concerns intentionality, although it does not rely on intuitions about Twin Earth kinds of thought experiments, as did the early arguments of Putnam and Burge. It belongs to a family of arguments that I shall call *active cognition* arguments.

Active cognition arguments are so called because they all appeal to the active exercise of cognitive capacities in the real world (see Clark 1997; Haugeland 1998; Hurley 1998, 2001; Rowlands 1999, chaps. 5–8; Wilson 2004, chaps. 8–9). Active cognition arguments have appealed especially to a range of work in perceptual psychology, ranging from Gibsonian approaches (Gibson 1966; see also Rowlands 1999) through to Dana Ballard's animate vision paradigm within computational psychology (Ballard 1991; Ballard et al. 1997; see also Wilson 2004, chap. 7) and the more recent view of visual experience as involving the animated exploration of one's environment and in so doing displaying a sensitivity to sensorimotor contingencies in the environment of the organism (O'Regan and Noë 2001). As one might expect, given the diversity in this work, active cognition arguments for the extended mind have also appealed to other areas of psychology: to problem solving, in cases where this involves exploiting the visual or tactile features of one's environment to complete the problem-solving task (Clark 1997, 2003; Wilson 2004, chap. 8); to actual and possible cases involving sensory inversion (Hurley 1998, 2001); and to the mediational approach to cognitive development pioneered by Vygotsky and Luria, championed in the contemporary literature by Michael Cole (1996) and James Wertsch (1998, 2002).

These arguments all focus on determinate forms of a particular cognitive ability (e.g., memory, attention, problem solving) as they are exercised by individual agents. They view the integration of individuals with both their biological and artificial environments as critical to their status as cognitive agents with these particular capacities. With this focus on actual agents and the abilities they act on, active cognition arguments try to pre-empt the objection that "the extended mind" is merely a conceptual possibility or a *façon de parler*. The chief aim of active cognition arguments has been to show directly that much of cognition as we know it is extended; the real question for their proponents is just which aspects of cognition are extended, and in what ways.

Active cognition arguments contrast, in these respects, with another kind of argument for the extended mind, due chiefly to Andy Clark, which I shall call *cyborg fantasy* arguments. These arguments, like the classic arguments of Putnam and Burge for taxonomic externalism, turn primarily on intuitions about imagined cases ("intuition pumps," as they are called). The best-known of these—from Clark and Chalmers 1998 (this volume, chap. 2), and discussed in several papers in the current volume, the case of Otto and Inga—focuses on a person's (Otto's) reliance on a notebook as a memory-storage device. Otto is a kind of cyborg, even if, in the basic case at least, his cyber-enhancement relies on an old form of technology—the book. Some versions of cyborg fantasy arguments (e.g., many of those in Clark 2003) imagine amplifications of dependencies on existing technologies—on cell phones, electronic implants, and telerobotics, for example—to argue that future cognition will likely be more radically extended than it currently is, with implications for the headier notions of the self, identity, and bodily integrity.

Cyborg fantasy arguments for the extended mind proceed by introducing an imaginative example in which an individual's cognitive performance is mediated by external forms of technology, typically arguing, through a comparison to cases in which the same kind of activity is performed without such mediation, to the conclusion that the boundary between what's inside the head and what is in the environment is irrelevant to whether a given agent has some particular cognitive capacity. The focus in cyborg fantasy arguments is on imagined cases (albeit ones that sometimes are or can seem close to actual cases), and there is an emphasis on techno-facilitation, rather than the individual's integration with her natural environment. The chief aim of cyborg fantasy arguments has been to establish the extended mind as a kind of conceptual default; they do so by shifting the burden of proof to internalists, challenging them to identify why the skin should be a relevant boundary for cognition at all.

Common to both active cognition and cyborg fantasy arguments for extended cognition is the idea that by examining just what is involved in the exercise of some particular cognitive capacity, one finds that it actually does or could well involve causal loops that extend beyond the body of the individual agent. In particular, these causal loops (do or may) pass through objects and other entities in the agent's environment, and it is only the whole, functioning, beyond-the-head causal system that constitutes the matter in motion that realizes the exercise of the capacity. In this system, some of the cognitive resources—what Hurley (1998) and Rowlands

(2003) would call cognitive *vehicles*—lie inside, and others outside the head. Just as not all of the resources used to build an organism's *developmental resources* are genetic, and not all of these nongenetic developmental resources are located inside the organism's existing boundary, so too with cognitive resources: not all of these are neural, and some of those that are not are located beyond the head of the individual.

Both active cognition and cyborg fantasy arguments have recently been attacked by critics of the extended mind thesis, with these critiques drawing broader conclusions about the tenability of radical forms of externalism on the basis of putative failings of particular arguments: Adams and Aizawa (2001) on Clark and Chalmers (1998), Grush (2003) on Haugeland (1998), and, most recently, Rupert (2004) largely on Rowlands (1999). For the most part, these critiques have to reconstruct, sometimes quite imaginatively, the arguments that they critique, leaving one with the feeling that externalists must surely have something more up their sleeves than what their critics draw from the hat. I think there are several explicit, active cognition arguments for externalism that have not thus far been considered in the literature; I shall focus on one of them.

4   The Argument from Meaning Making

Here is a bald statement of the particular argument that I want to explore in more detail, the *argument from meaning making*, together with a brief gloss on each premise:

(a) *Minds are intentional machines or semantic engines.* This is to identify an important and distinctive feature of minds, namely, that they are mechanisms or devices that operate on items that are intentional or semantic in nature, language-like entities such as propositions and propositional attitudes, but also nonlinguistic actions and objects that are imbued with meaning and significance.

(b) *Intentional machines or semantic engines detect and create meaning.* They detect meaning when it preexists in some structure in the world, whether it be a sentence that someone utters or an action they undertake; they likewise create meaning through both linguistic and nonlinguistic means.

(c) *Meaning detection and creation involve the sequestering and integration of internal and external cognitive resources.* Internal cognitive resources include individual mental symbols and rules for their combination, neural networks, categories, and schemas. External cognitive resources include individual spoken and written symbols and rules for their combination, social networks, collective representations, and the bodily activities of oneself and other agents.

(d) *Internal cognitive resources are part of the structure of the intentional machine that detects and creates meaning.* This is a traditional assumption within individualistic cognitive science that contributes to explaining how postulated internal structures generate cognitive behavior.

(e) *External cognitive resources often play the same or similar functional roles in the detection and creation of meaning as do internal cognitive resources, or complement, compensate for, or enhance those roles.* External cognitive resources can replace internal cognitive resources (e.g., external memory) or can create capacities in agents that they would not otherwise have (e.g., Kanzi, the bonobo who has exhibited advanced linguistic capabilities). In either case, they are no less central to cognition than are internal cognitive resources.

Thus:

(f) *External cognitive resources, like internal cognitive resources, are part of the structure of the intentional machine that detects and creates meaning.* This follows from a parity assumption, namely, that things that have the same relevant properties vis-à-vis some cognitive process should have the same status in cognition as one another. Whether one is in the head and one is in the environment is irrelevant.

Therefore:

(g) *The extended mind thesis is true.*

There are analogues to premises (c)–(e) in other arguments for externalism, such as those that appeal to the nature of memory, or consciousness, or to some other aspect or property of cognition. Thus, a more thorough examination of at least these parts of the argument from meaning making will perhaps shed light on those arguments as well.

5   Meaning, External Resources, and Fundamentality

There are at least three points at which the argument from meaning making might be challenged by those working within the cognitive sciences and the philosophy of mind. First, one might claim that the very first pair of premises begs a crucial question by assuming a broad view of the kinds of entities to which intentional machines are sensitive. Traditional cognitive scientists might well balk at the idea that intentional machines process "actions" or entities in the world, or might think that the sense in which they do so is incompatible with the extended mind thesis. Second, the very idea of an external cognitive resource, invoked in the third premise, might be taken to express an oxymoron, in that "cognitive resources," whatever else they might be, must be internal. Third, even those happy to make both of these concessions might well think that the final premise, (e), is indefensible, since there will always remain a crucial asymmetry between internal and external cognitive resources. Roughly speaking, the latter only gain purchase on cognitive activity via the former, and so internal resources remain fundamental to cognition in a way that vitiates the inference to externalism.

Although these objections are closely related, considering each in turn will allow us to discuss a variety of issues to which the debate over the extended mind is important, and to home in on some of those that separate externalists from their opponents. It will also provide some clues about how we might recast the problem of intentionality.

Does the First Premise Beg the Question?
The idea that minds are semantic engines commands relatively widespread assent within the cognitive science community, and there are particular ways of understanding how this idea is to be integrated with the claim that cognition is computational in nature. In traditional, AI-inspired cognitive science, the idea was roughly this: minds are semantic engines in virtue of being syntactic engines, together with the correlation between the syntactic strings that the rules governing such syntactic engines operate on and the meaning that we ascribe to those strings. More precisely, these syntactic strings *encode* meaningful mental representations and are themselves in turn *realized in* physical configurations in the brain. In connectionist cognitive science, matters are more complicated, in part because some connectionists are *eliminativists* about the idea of mental meaning, and so altogether reject the idea that minds are semantic engines, while others view themselves as providing an account of the realization of mental representations that simply dispenses with the correlation thesis. For those connectionists willing to hop on the mental representation bus, representations can be nonpropositional, subsymbolic, or distributed, for example, with the networks underlying representation departing from the traditional rules and representations of traditional cognitive science.

Although both traditional and connectionist forms of representationalism acknowledge that there is causal interaction across the boundary between world and head, both also hold that the intentionality of the mental lies firmly on the head side of this boundary, whether it derives from some kind of syntactic encoding or emerges more holistically from a distributed system of interconnected neural nodes. The world can provide background conditions necessary for representations to have the specific content that they do, but it is not physically constitutive of representational content itself. Meaning is not out there in the world waiting for us to detect it, but created by the mind in its interactions with the world; meaning is *intrinsic* to in-the-head mental representation. If objects in the world are part of the representational content of our mental representations, that is because (let's assume) they are coded for by intrinsic properties of rich in-the-head representations, or because (again, let's assume) they are distributively represented by simple in-the-head representations.

My own view is that these general conceptions of meaning and representation are flawed (see Wilson 2000, 2004, chap. 7), but the question here is whether the argument from meaning making presumes this in a way that begs the question in favor of the extended mind. To see that it does not, we should construe premises (a) and (b) in a way that is neutral between various accounts of how mental representation operates. All that has to be conceded in accepting (a) and (b) is that (i) agents have some kind(s) of mental representation that play causal roles in their perception and behavior; (ii) whatever form(s) these mental representations take, and whether or not they are located exclusively inside the skin, they often causally derive from and in turn causally generate actions, objects, and events that are not so bounded. Both (i) and (ii) concern the phenomena to be explained, and as such should be granted by individualists and externalists alike.

This clarificatory response might be thought to place a heavier burden on premise (c), which now appears to make a substantial claim about how to conceptualize the detection and generation of meaning. If there is, however, something suspect about the very idea of an external cognitive resource, then the argument from meaning making is in trouble.

Is "External Cognitive Resource" an Oxymoron?

In introducing the term "cognitive resource" in section 3 I invoked an analogy between cognitive resources and developmental resources, an analogy that calls for more extensive explication. Within the philosophy of biology over the past two decades the predominant gene-centered view of inheritance and development has been challenged by a number of alternative paradigms. Developmental systems theory (hereafter, DST), deriving from the work of Susan Oyama (1985, 2000), is one of these paradigms. In the past decade DST has shifted from providing a critique of the genocentrism of developmental biology to articulating its own, positive vision of research on inheritance and organismic development. The key idea in the DST paradigm is that the most fundamental units of agency needed to understand these biological phenomena are developmental *systems*, where genes are one among many elements in those systems. These elements are called developmental *resources*, but since such resources always operate within the context of some developmental system or other, they should be viewed as neither ontologically nor epistemically more fundamental than those systems. Although not all forms of DST have embraced the idea that developmental systems, and so cognitive resources, can extend beyond the boundary of the skin of the organism, some proponents of DST have advocated precisely this view, arguing that this is a consequence of the logic behind DST, together with the empirical details that are provided by a consideration of the inheritance and development of particular traits.

As I have suggested elsewhere (Wilson 2005, chap. 7), there is a fairly direct parallel between the relationship between DST and traditional views of inheritance and development, on the one hand, and locational externalism and traditional views of cognition, on the other. Just as (wide) DSTers in biology argue that developmental systems extend beyond the organism's boundaries, including developmental resources from both sides of those boundaries, externalists in psychology argue that cognitive systems extend beyond the head of the individual, including cognitive resources both inside and outside the skin. Indeed, the analogy between the two cases reaches as far as the connotations possessed by the most ubiquitous adjectival terms in each—"genetic" and "mental"—both of which convey the sense of an entity, process, or activity that goes on entirely inside an organism or agent. Hence, the idea of an extended mind sounds just as odd, perhaps, as does that of an extended gene (or even an extended genetic system).

This connotation of "innerness" stems, I suggest, from a common source: from an overarching dominant framework for thinking about both organismic development and cognitive agency that is individualistic. To challenge that framework in either or both areas of inquiry, some less heavily loaded terminology is needed. "System" and "resource" fill this niche in both cases, together with a shift from "mental" and "genetic" to "cognitive" and "developmental" (or "heritable," when moving from ontogeny to intergenerational transmission).

Suppose, then, that we can accept the minimal readings of premises (a) and (b) that remain neutral about the mode of representation through which cognition operates, and that there is some rationale for shifting from semantically loaded terms to those that allow the idea of an external cognitive resource to make no less sense than that of an external developmental resource. The claim in premise (c) is, roughly, that intentionality operates in the mind via the integrated functioning of internal and external cognitive resources. This itself remains compatible with individualism about cognition, provided that there is some way to single out only internal cognitive resources as themselves truly cognitive.

Are Internal Resources More Fundamental to Cognition Than Are External Resources?

One way to express the extended mind thesis is to say that, for at least a variety of cognitive activities, the physical configuration of the brain is not metaphysically sufficient for their performance *qua* cognitive activities. Something more is needed, and that something more involves the physical configuration of the world beyond the head. When locational externalism is expressed in this way, however, pointing to an asymmetry between what's in the head—Brain—and what's outside of it—World—seems easy. For Brain is always involved in cognition, whereas World is only sometimes involved. More to the point, World is only putatively relevant to cognition when it forms part of a causal chain that passes through Brain. But the converse is not true of Brain. In short, since World must be causally connected to Brain in order for World to result in cognition, but not vice versa, cognitive resources are properly all internal, and so restricted to Brain. Thus, the mind is not extended, and what I have been calling "external cognitive resources" are more accurately labeled in their traditional way: they are *inputs to*, not parts of, cognition.

That brain activity is always involved in cognition is not something that I wish to dispute, since I'm happy to stick my neck out and say that it is actually *true*. The significance of this for the debate over the extended mind, however, is what is up for grabs. Consider again the analogy to developmental systems theory in biology. One should grant that gene expression is always causally involved (however minimally or indirectly) in the development of any particular phenotypic trait an organism possesses, whereas other developmental resources sometimes are and sometimes are not causally active. But whether that provides reason to endorse accounts of ontogenetic development exclusively in terms of genes and their immediate expression remains a further issue. (In this case, this is not least of all because other developmental resources are always required for genes not only to be expressed as organism-level phenotypic traits, but for genes to do anything at all.)

To maintain our analogy with the case of cognition, however, we need to consider not simply genes but the full range of internal developmental resources—methyl groups, RNA complexes, mitochondria, cytoskeletal structures (such as actin fibers and microtubules), and so on. And there certainly are developmental systems—the chromatin marking system would be one—whose operation does consist solely of changes within the organism. Such processes are internalist, and though they do not operate in a contextual vacuum, the environment is properly viewed an providing either inputs to these processes or as specifying background conditions necessary for their functioning. The same is true, I think, of some cognitive processes, such as some acts of visual imagining, some kinds of problem solving, and some decision making. Yet this does not establish the requisite asymmetry between internal and external resources, in either the biological or the psychological case, because it is not true for *all* developmental and cognitive processes. Consider two examples that I have discussed previously (Wilson 2004, chap. 8) that differ in an important way.

First, consider the bonobo Kanzi's planning, thinking, and decision making that utilizes a 256-symbol keyboard, which Kanzi has, over the years, learned to use to communicate his beliefs and desires. Bonobos in the wild surely have desires (e.g., for bananas), but just as surely they don't have the kind of sophisticated, cooperative desires that Kanzi expresses, such as the desire to be taken by a particular person to a sequence of locations, or to do one activity first and then another. What the symbol board has done is to reconfigure Kanzi's capacity for belief and desire, much as our using pen and paper reconfigures our mathematical ability by augmenting the in-the-head capacity we have for multiplication. Both are cases in which an external symbol system becomes integrated with preexisting cognitive capacities in ways that significantly modify the nature of those capacities. We can, of course, distinguish between the *parts of* those capacities that are internal and those that are not, but this is already to concede that the overall cognitive process itself is extended.

Second, suppose that you are playing a visual problem-solving game, such as Rush Hour, or completing a jigsaw puzzle. (Rush Hour involves a square board loaded with cars and trucks in various positions, and the object is to move these in a sequence so as to allow a designated car to leave the board through the only exit.) Here the problem solving in part consists of internal mental operations (let us suppose), but also in part it consists of the active physical manipulation of pieces on a board or pieces within the puzzle. One might suppose that these manipulations—rotations of puzzle pieces, or trials of car move sequences—were simply presented to you in a computer simulation, or through an automation of trial moves from which you select the best outcome. I suspect that this would change the problem-solving task in a significant way; but note that even here problem solving requires active engagement with a part of the world beyond the head, namely, the various visual displays from which one must select. In both cases, the problems are solved by utilizing, exploiting, or manipulating a set of resources, some of which are outside of the head. These are not simply inputs to those that are inside the head, because the very process of problem solving involves them as much as it involves resources inside the head. There is nothing bounded by the skull that counts as solving these kind of problems.

In both cases it is not simply environmental structures that somehow magically make for cognition, but the causal integration of these with onboard capacities that organisms already have. In general this causal integration can be ontogenetic or phylogenetic, individual or collective, cultural or biological, and the cognitive abilities such integration generates are often genuinely novel. Some of these compensate for organismic cognitive limitations (say, in short-term memory capacity) through external augmentation; some may actually further diminish such internal capacities (as, for example, the shift from oral to literary traditions has likely done with respect to auditory recall). The point here is that there is a lot of variation in the kinds of transcranial cognitive processes that the extended mind thesis embraces, and a corresponding breadth to the range of cases of which it is true.

This brings me to the chief difference between these two examples that I want to draw explicit attention to. This is that whereas the first involves the causal integration of explicit symbols located in an organism's environment into that organism's cognitive regime, the second appeals to the cognitive incorporation of nonsymbolic aspects of that environment. Much of the discussion of the extended mind has focused exclusively on cases of just the former kind. In combination with the emphasis on cyborg fantasy arguments for the extended mind thesis, this has created (however inadvertently) the impression that the scope of the thesis is narrower than it actually is. It is primarily a view neither about technological enhancement of existing cognitive abilities, nor about the conceptual possibility of the mind being extended. Rather, it is a view of what cognition is for at least as long as it has been a trait of human beings, before we had writing systems (6,000 or so years ago), and before we developed pictorial representation (25,000 or so years ago).

I would hazard a guess that the cognitively most significant forms that our nonsymbolic environment takes are, broadly speaking, *social* in nature. (I also think that these are, in many respects, more fundamental than the technological innovations that have also reshaped our cognitive architecture, but that is not my plaint here). These social features include the interpersonal relations found in human social groups—from dyads through to face-to-face communities; the group-level structures, such as kin groups and social hierarchies, that human agents are sensitive to; and the range of social practices, customs, and rituals—such as song, burial, and marriage—that can be found stretching back various distances through the history of the species. Put roughly, the idea is that it is because we are socially oriented creatures in a fairly rich and deep sense that we have biologically evolved and culturally developed extended minds that incorporate these very aspects of our social world.

This isn't to say that technological development and appropriation is unimportant in thinking about extended cognition, or that it is never a primary shaper of the extended mind. Rather, it is to claim that we need also to take the nonsymbolic environment seriously in articulating the extended mind thesis, and that the most important place to look in doing so is the social realm. The social and the technological are both significant aspects of extended cognition—evolutionarily, historically, biologically, culturally—and I suspect that it is in tandem that they have sculpted human cognition over tens of thousands of years to its present level.

6   Rethinking the Problem of Intentionality

I began by identifying three parts to the problem of intentionality—to say what intentionality is, to delineate things that have intentionality from things that don't, and to provide an account of in virtue of what it is that representations have the particular content that they do. The problem, especially this final part of it, has been subject to a naturalistic constraint, and the intentionality of the mental has been taken to be the core phenomenon to be explained. At the end of section 1 of the chapter I suggested that the problem of intentionality was complicated by internalism; at the end of section 2 I said that externalism would provide us with the means for reconceptualizing that problem. How so? In at least three ways.

First, the extended mind thesis amplifies the number of kinds of mental representations that there are by including at least some external representations as cognitive in nature. One might think that this makes the problem of intentionality worse, in that instead of being faced with a relatively well-circumscribed set of entities to puzzle about—internal mental representations—we now have a hodgepodge comprised of almost anything we make perceptual or cognitive contact with. But I think just the opposite is true. Recognizing the variety of mental representations embraced by the extended mind thesis undermines the very terms in which the problem of intentionality has been formulated. It is not so much that the question "In virtue of what does internal state R represent condition (state, object, property) C?" has been replaced by one that substitutes "internal or external" for "internal," as that this is just the wrong kind of question to ask about representation. It is to ask for something like the *essence* of mental representation, and one of the consequences of the extended mind thesis, I am suggesting, is that this is to ask for something that does not exist.

But what *is* the right question to ask here? Does the promised reconceptualization of the problem of intentionality go beyond this diagnosis of error? This brings me to a second way in which externalism helps: by shifting our focus from representational essences to representation in practice. Although I have distinguished between "active cognition" and "cyborg fantasy" arguments for the extended mind, both arguments take the dynamic aspects to cognition seriously and appeal to how we engage in cognitive practices that make use of representations. The shift is one from a focus on "things," such as representations, to a concern with "activities," such as the act of representing. Such activities are often bodily, and are often world-involving in nature. A version of the problem of intentionality formulated so as to apply to them—"In virtue of what is activity A the representation of C?"—seems hardly pressing at all. Rather, what cries out for discussion is the question of just what forms these activities take, and just how they bring about the effects they do.

And so a third way in which the extended mind thesis allows us to reconceptualize the problem of intentionality is that it suggests a methodological reorientation. We no longer seek the essence of representations, for there is none to be found; we focus instead on activities or acts of representing. But the methodology appropriate here, in the sense of likely being the most fruitful in outcome, is not traditional conceptual analysis but an interdisciplinary, pluralistic motley. The task is to understand a variety of representational practices and wherein they are representational. The means we employ in doing so will be various: historical analysis of their emergence, sociological analysis of the conditions under which they operate, experimental psychological analysis of representational gaps and gluts, anthropological analysis of practices of symbolization, evolutionary analysis of social environments and our sensitivity to them.

This is very much to echo John Sutton's (2004, this volume) call for a more adventuresome interdisciplinary development of the extended mind thesis (see also Chemero and Silberstein 2008; Barnier et al. 2008; MacIver 2009; MacIver and Wilson in progress), one that doesn't simply augment cognitive science with a few snippets from studies of human–computer interaction or speculative tales about the evolution of cognition. When cognition is extended, intentionality is extended and the traditional problem of intentionality transformed. Precisely what that transformation results in will turn largely on how thoroughly the philosophical naturalism driving the work on the extended mind becomes integrated with the kind of interdisciplinary adventures mentioned above. As that integration proceeds, we will gain a deeper sense of what intentionality is and a clearer idea of what things have it and what things don't; and we will be as moved by the final, "in virtue of" part of the problem of intentionality as we are by the question of in virtue of what gravity operates, or in virtue of what matter exists.

Acknowledgments

This chapter was written while on sabbatical leave from the University of Alberta in 2004–05. I thank the university for granting this leave, which was spent anchored in Perth at the University of Western Australia. I would also like to thank Dr. Myra Keep for her hospitality in providing me with office space in her geology lab during this time. Thanks also to Richard Menary for the invitation to contribute to the volume. Comments and correspondence are welcome (rob.wilson@ualberta.ca).

References

Adams, F., and Aizawa, K. (2001). The bounds of cognition. *Philosophical Psychology*, *14*, 43–64.

Adams, F., and Aizawa, K. (2008). *The Bounds of Cognition*. New York: Blackwell.

Adams, F., and Aizawa, K. (2009). Why the mind is still in the head. In P. Robbins and M. Aydede (eds.), *The Cambridge Handbook of Situated Cognition*. New York: Cambridge University Press.

Aizawa, K. (2007). The embodiment of perception. *Journal of Philosophy*, *104*, 5–25.

Ballard, D. H. (1991). Animate vision. *Artificial Intelligence*, *48*, 57–86.

Ballard, D. H., Hayhoe, M. M., Pook, P. K., and Rao, R. P. N. (1997). Deictic codes for the embodiment of cognition. *Behavioral and Brain Sciences*, *20*, 723–742.

Barnier, A., Sutton, J., Harris, C., and Wilson, R. A. (2008). A conceptual and empirical framework for the social distribution of cognition: The case of memory. *Cognitive Systems Research*, *9*(1–2), 33–51.

Burge, T. (1979). Individualism and the mental. In P. French, T. Uehling Jr., and H. Wettstein (eds.), *Midwest Studies in Philosophy*, vol.4: *Metaphysics*. Minneapolis: University of Minnesota Press.

Burge, T. (1986a). Individualism and psychology. *Philosophical Review*, *95*, 3–45.

Burge, T. (1986b). Intellectual norms and foundations of mind. *Journal of Philosophy*, *83*, 697–720.

Chemero, A., and Silberstein, M. (2008). After the philosophy of mind: Replacing scholasticism with science. *Philosophy of Science*, *75*, 1–27.

Clark, A. (1997). *Being There: Putting Brain, Body, and World Together Again*. Cambridge, MA: MIT Press.

Clark, A. (2003). *Natural-Born Cyborgs: Minds, Technologies, and the Future of Human Intelligence*. New York: Oxford University Press.

Clark, A. (2008). *Supersizing the Mind*. New York: Oxford University Press.

Clark, A., and Chalmers, D. (1998). The extended mind. *Analysis*, *58*, 7–19. Reprinted as chapter 2 of this volume.

Cole, M. (1996). *Cultural Psychology: A Once and Future Discipline*. Cambridge, MA: Harvard University Press.

Crane, T. (1991). All the difference in the world. *Philosophical Quarterly*, *41*, 1–25.

Devitt, M. (1990). A narrow representational theory of mind. In W. G. Lycan (ed.), *Mind and Cognition: A Reader*. Cambridge, MA: Blackwell.

Dretske, F. I. (1981). *Knowledge and the Flow of Information*. Cambridge, MA: MIT Press.

Dretske, F. I. (1988). *Explaining Behavior: Reasons in a World of Causes*. Cambridge, MA: MIT Press.

Ebbs, G. (1998). *Rule-Following and Realism*. Cambridge, MA: Harvard University Press.

Egan, F. (1992). Individualism, computation, and perceptual content. *Mind*, *101*, 443–459.

Egan, F. (1995). Computation and content. *Philosophical Review, 104,* 181–203.

Fodor, J. A. (1980). Methodological solipsism considered as a research strategy in cognitive psychology. *Behavioral and Brain Sciences 3*: 63–73. Reprinted in Fodor 1981.

Fodor, J. A. (1981). *Representations.* Sussex: Harvester Press.

Fodor, J. A. (1982). Cognitive science and the Twin-Earth problem. *Notre Dame Journal of Formal Logic, 23,* 98–118.

Fodor, J. A. (1984). Semantics, Wisconsin style. *Synthese, 59,* 231–250.

Fodor, J. A. (1987). *Psychosemantics: The Problem of Meaning in the Philosophy of Mind.* Cambridge, MA: MIT Press.

Gibson, J. J. (1966). *The Senses Considered as Perceptual Systems.* Boston: Houghton-Mifflin.

Grush, R. (2003). In defense of some Cartesian assumptions concerning the brain and its operation. *Biology and Philosophy, 18,* 53–93.

Haugeland, J. (1998). Mind embodied and embedded. In his *Having Thought: Essays in the Metaphysics of Mind.* Cambridge, MA: Harvard University Press.

Hurley, S. (1998). *Consciousness in Action.* Cambridge, MA: Harvard University Press.

Hurley, S. (2001). Perception and action: Alternative views. *Synthese, 129,* 3–40.

Loar, B. (1988). Social content and psychological content. In R. Grimm and D. Merrill (eds.), *Contents of Thought.* Tucson: University of Arizona Press.

MacIver, M. (2009). Neuroethology: From morphological computation to planning. In P. Robbins and M. Aydede (eds.), *The Cambridge Handbook of Situated Cognition.* New York: Cambridge University Press.

MacIver, M., and Wilson, R. A. (in progress). Taking an extended view of embodied cognition: Evolution, control, and computation.

Menary, R. (2007). *Cognitive Integration: Mind and Cognition Unbounded.* London: Palgrave Macmillan.

Millikan, R. G. (1984). *Language, Thought, and Other Biological Categories: New Foundations for Realism.* Cambridge, MA: MIT Press.

Millikan, R. G. (1993). *White Queen Psychology and Other Essays for Alice.* Cambridge, MA: MIT Press.

O'Regan, J. K., and Noë, A. (2001). A sensorimotor account of vision and visual consciousness. *Behavioral and Brain Sciences, 24,* 939–1031.

Oyama, S. (1985). *The Ontogeny of Information* (2nd ed.). Durham, NC: Duke University Press, 2000.

Oyama, S. (2000). *Evolution's Eye: A Systems View of the Biology–Culture Divide*. Durham, NC: Duke University Press.

Pettit, P. (1993). *The Common Mind: An Essay on Psychology, Society, and Politics*. New York: Oxford University Press.

Putnam, H. (1975). The meaning of "meaning." In K. Gunderson (ed.), *Language, Mind, and Knowledge*. Minneapolis: University of Minnesota Press. Reprinted in H. Putnam, *Mind, Language, and Reality: Philosophical Papers* (vol. 2). New York: Cambridge University Press, 1975.

Rowlands, M. (1999). *The Body in Mind: Understanding Cognitive Processes*. New York: Cambridge University Press.

Rowlands, M. (2003). *Externalism: Putting Mind and World Back Together Again*. Chesham: Acumen.

Rupert, R. (2004). Challenges to the hypothesis of extended cognition. *Journal of Philosophy, 101*, 389–429.

Segal, G. (1989). Seeing what is not there. *Philosophical Review, 98*, 189–214.

Shapiro, L. (1997). A clearer vision. *Philosophy of Science, 64*, 131–153.

Sutton, J. (2004). Representation, reduction, and interdisciplinarity in the sciences of memory. In H. Clapin, P. Staines, and P. Slezak (eds.), *Representation in Mind: New Approaches to Mental Representation*. Amsterdam: Elsevier.

Wertsch, J. (1998). *Mind as Action*. New York: Oxford University Press.

Wertsch, J. (2002). *Voices of Collective Remembering*. New York: Cambridge University Press.

Wilson, R. A. (1992). Individualism, causal powers, and explanation. *Philosophical Studies, 68*, 103–139.

Wilson, R. A. (1994). Wide computationalism. *Mind, 103*, 351–372.

Wilson, R. A. (1995). *Cartesian Psychology and Physical Minds: Individualism and the Sciences of the Mind*. New York: Cambridge University Press.

Wilson, R. A. (2000). The mind beyond itself. In D. Sperber (ed.), *Metarepresentations: A Multidisciplinary Perspective* (pp. 31–52). New York: Oxford University Press.

Wilson, R. A. (2003a). Individualism. In S. Stich and T. A. Warfield (eds.), *The Blackwell Companion to Philosophy of Mind* (pp. 256–287). New York: Blackwell.

Wilson, R. A. (2003b). Pluralism, entwinement, and the levels of selection. *Philosophy of Science, 70*, 531–552.

Wilson, R. A. (2004). *Boundaries of the Mind: The Individual in the Fragile Sciences: Cognition*. New York: Cambridge University Press.

Wilson, R. A. (2005). *Genes and the Agents of Life: The Individual in the Fragile Sciences: Biology.* New York: Cambridge University Press.

Wilson, R. A., and Clark, A. (2008). How to situate cognition: Letting nature take its course. In P. Robbins and M. Aydede (eds.), *The Cambridge Handbook of Situated Cognition.* New York: Cambridge University Press.

Wilson, R. A., and Craver, C. (2007). Realization. In P. Thagard (ed.), *Handbook of the Philosophy of Science,* vol. 12: *Philosophy of Psychology and Cognitive Science* (pp. 81–104). Amsterdam: Elsevier.

Zerubavel, E. (1997). *Social Mindscapes: An Invitation to Cognitive Sociology.* Cambridge, MA: Harvard University Press.

9 Exograms and Interdisciplinarity: History, the Extended Mind, and the Civilizing Process

John Sutton

1 Exograms, Interdisciplinarity, and the Cognitive Life of Things

1.1 The Extended Mind Hypothesis

On the extended mind hypothesis (EM),[1] many of our cognitive states and processes are hybrids, unevenly distributed across biological and nonbiological realms (Clark 1997; Clark and Chalmers 1998). In certain circumstances, things—artifacts, media, or technologies—can have a cognitive life, with histories often as idiosyncratic as those of the embodied brains with which they couple (Sutton 2002a, 2008). The realm of the mental can spread across the physical, social, and cultural environments as well as bodies and brains. My independent aims in this chapter are: first, to describe two compatible but distinct movements or "waves" within the EM literature, arguing for the priority of the second wave (and gesturing briefly toward a third); and, second, to defend and illustrate the interdisciplinary implications of EM as best understood, specifically for historical disciplines, by sketching two case studies.

EM, an offshoot of mainstream functionalist information-processing cognitive science, has been focused in particular on our abilities to hook up with what Merlin Donald calls "exograms" or external symbols, by analogy with the brain's memory traces or "engrams" (Donald 1991, pp. 308–333; 2001, pp. 305–315).[2] These abilities allow us to create and support cognitive profiles quite unlike those of creatures restricted to the brain's biological memories or engrams alone. Among other typical features, Donald points out that exograms last longer than engrams, have greater capacity, are more easily transmissible across media and context, and can be retrieved and manipulated by a greater variety of means (1991, pp. 315–316): so our skilled use of such crafted aids changes both the locus of memory in general and the role of our biological memory within the new larger systems (see also Rowlands 1999, pp. 129–147).

As I'll argue, it's important not to overstate the differences between internal and external traces: the version of EM I'm developing here, following in particular in Andy Clark's wake, is aimed precisely at investigating a wide range of possibilities on these and other dimensions of variation. I distinguish two versions or "waves" of EM, differentiated partly by the way these dimensions are characterized. These waves are not ultimately incompatible, but they are distinct strands in the EM literature and within Clark's own work: as we'll see, he acknowledged "a potential tension" between them as long ago as 1998 (Clark 1998, p. 99; see section 4 below). Before introducing the two waves, let me reiterate the key commitment they share, tweaked and applied differently in each case. External symbol systems and other "cognitive artifacts" are not always simply commodities, for the use and profit of the active mind: rather, in certain circumstances, along with the brain and body that interact with them, they *are* (part of) the mind. For Clark, "it is our basic *human* nature to annex, exploit and incorporate nonbiological stuff deep into our mental profiles" (2003a, p. 198). The human mind is "leaky" both because it thus extends beyond the skin to co-opt external devices, technologies, and other people, and because our plastic brains naturally soak up labels, inner objects, and representational schemes, internalizing and incorporating such resources and often redeploying them in novel ways.

1.2 EM and Interdisciplinarity: Historical Cognitive Science
These general claims about the nature of the (extended) mind have been developed through striking examples, such as Otto with his notebook (Clark and Chalmers 1998, this volume). But concentration on the metaphysics of Otto's case, I'll suggest, underplays the ambition of the EM hypothesis, which can be better grasped by examining its far-reaching methodological dimensions. Perhaps, to study even mundane mental states and processes, we will need to look beyond the skin of cognizing organisms (Rowlands 1999, p. 8). Consequently, proponents suggest, EM motivates new perspectives on relations between the cognitive sciences, the social sciences, and the humanities disciplines. In a programmatic statement, Clark pinpoints "the single most important task" for "a science of the biotechnological mind" as the search for better understanding of "the *range and variety* of types of cognitive scaffolding, and the *different* ways in which non-biological scaffoldings can augment (or impair) performance

on a task" (Clark 2002a, p. 29, my emphasis). Elsewhere he clarifies the dramatic implications of this agenda:

Much of what matters about human intelligence is hidden not in the brain, nor in the technology, but in the complex and iterated interactions and collaborations between the two. . . . The study of these interaction spaces is not easy, and depends both on new multidisciplinary alliances and new forms of modelling and analysis. The pay-off, however, could be spectacular: nothing less than a new kind of cognitive scientific collaboration involving neuroscience, physiology, and social, cultural, and technological studies in about equal measure. (Clark 2001a, p. 154)

Such wild and whirling promises are not welcomed by EM's critics: Keith Butler, for example, argues that this kind of anti-individualism is "wrong headed," for

it tries to turn psychology into a kind of anthropology or sociology or ecology; and it just won't fit. There already are sciences whose topic of inquiry is the interpersonal and environmental. . . . There is no room for an expanded psychology, no motivation for it, and no need for it. (Butler 1998, p. 222)

In this chapter I aim to unpack the line of thought which takes us from EM to a methodological recommendation of strong interdisciplinarity[3] for cognitive science. The path here is to display the methodological implications of EM at work in two historical case studies, rejecting any neat disciplinary division of intellectual labor. The EM framework is shown to be more than a mere philosophical injunction: the case studies operate within it, and their contributions to historical debates of independent interest are best understood in its terms. EM thus promises to be a potentially unifying gloss on and stimulus toward a wide array of research in diverse disciplines and subdisciplines which study those "cognitive and computational architectures whose bounds far exceed those of skin and skull," in which we "biotechnological hybrids" are primed to participate (Clark 2001b, p. 138).

But it's worth pointing out immediately that no imperialist agenda is necessary here: the possibility of an "expanded psychology" does not wipe out or negate all psychology's existing frameworks. First, EM is not a claim that cognitive processes are *necessarily* extended. Whole swathes of work on particular internal systems and processes can go on in relative independence of investigation into external processes, and any realistic proposal for active interdisciplinarity in the cognitive sciences is still likely to set mainstream experimental psychology and neuropsychology at the heart of the sciences of the mind.[4] But without more careful, unprejudiced attention to the extraordinarily diverse array of research within psychology—

across developmental, social, and personality psychology as well as cognitive psychology, and social-cognitive and systems neuroscience as well as cellular and molecular neurophysiology—we should not assume that these current cognitive sciences are wholly or primarily committed to a form of individualism that's in any substantial tension with EM.[5]

Yet two misreadings of this disclaimer, about the compatibility of EM with existing cognitive psychology of memory, need to be warded off. First, this doesn't mean that all those lines of research which do focus on internal systems and processes will remain untouched by EM (section 5 below). Second, we should reject the recent characterization of my inclusive and synthetic approach, with its recommendation that the EM-inspired sciences of the interface be seen as *complementing* rather than *replacing* cognitive psychology, as "a non-revolutionary approach to embodied cognition" (Adams and Aizawa 2008, p. 179): this attempt to deflate and assimilate the current version of EM, as I seek to show in the remainder of this chapter, fails to recognize the novelty of a genuinely integrated interdisciplinary approach.

By developing the arguments for EM in the right way, Clark's distinctive and ambitious vision of interdisciplinary interaction can be elucidated, defended, and applied, and also refined and extended. Clark's (1997) own influential synthetic presentation of EM in *Being There* incorporated ideas from developmental psychology, robotics, human–computer interaction, dynamical systems approaches to cognition, complex-systems theories in biology and economics, and post-connectionist computational modeling. As he realized quickly, there was no good reason to stop there, and his inquiries have moved on to wearable, tangible, and ubiquitous computing, to telerobotics and neuroprosthetics, and to the future of software agents (Clark 2003a). But despite Clark's pleasure in novelty, he is also explicit about the fact that EM does not depend on or apply only to our couplings with *new* technologies. We are cyborgs *by nature*, and the human mind has *never* been "bound and restricted by the biological skin-bag . . . the ancient fortress of skin and skull" (Clark 2003a, pp. 4–5). Ambitiously reclaiming the language of human nature from narrower forms of evolutionary psychology, Clark argues that "our technologically enhanced minds are barely, if at all, tethered to the ancestral realm" or "constrained by the limits of the on-board apparatus that once fitted us to the good old Savannah" (2003a, p. 197; 2005b, p. 242; cf. Wheeler and Clark 2008). This opens up the cognitive sciences to history and culture, so that the EM-inspired study of our "extended cognitive physiologies" can (and should) draw on and in turn enrich certain lines of research in historical disciplines as well as in economics, sociology, science studies, and media theory.

It's in this spirit that my complementary studies in EM look backward. Since there's nothing particularly "posthuman" about EM—since, if we are cyborgs now, we always have been—there should be room for what I've called a "historical cognitive science" (Sutton 1998, 2000, 2002a; Richardson 2004, p. 23; Tribble 2006) to sit alongside work in cognitive anthropology (Hutchins 1995) and cognitive archaeology (Renfrew and Scarre 1999; Knappett 2005; Knappett and Malafouris 2008; Renfrew, Frith, and Malafouris 2009) as productive allies for EM. To see what might be gained in practice, I sketch here two examples of such historical work: Evelyn Tribble's study of the extended cognitive system of Shakespearean acting companies (Tribble 2005), and my own account of the 'arts of memory', the strange techniques inherited from the ancients that were popular in the medieval and Renaissance periods for internalizing elaborate architectures to aid recall and cognitive discipline (Sutton 2000). In each case, historical topics of entirely independent scholarly interest can be given a new twist by the EM framework: conversely, quite specific ideas in that framework are further explicated and illuminated in its applications. And as well as exemplifying historical cognitive science, both help me to describe and defend the second of two lines of thought behind the case for EM.

1.3 Two Waves of EM Thinking

Failure to pick up the existence of quite different agendas behind EM has led both critics and proponents into trouble. Most published discussion has focused on first-wave EM, so I start in section 2 by explaining why problems which some have thought apply to EM *in general* in fact apply only to its first wave. (I'm calling these "waves" partly because they don't really qualify as *arguments* for EM, and partly because the second flows from the first.) In this chapter I merely distinguish between first- and second-wave EM, and defend the conceptual priority and fruitfulness of the second wave; then toward the end of the chapter I suggest some ways of stretching the second wave, which might be natural extensions or which might turn out to require a distinct third framework.

First-wave EM is based on the *parity principle* (Clark and Chalmers 1998, reprinted in this volume): cognitive states and processes extend beyond the brain and into the (external) world when the relevant parts of the world function in the same way as do unquestionably cognitive processes in the head. If "exograms" *act* as engrams do, then for explanatory purposes they can be treated as engrams, the difference in their location being entirely superficial. Thus breaking down classical and individualist distinctions between brain, body, and world, we see that the object can be (part of) the subject, and that, as we've noted, things can have a cognitive life.

Second-wave EM is based on a *complementarity principle*: in extended cognitive systems, external states and processes need not mimic or replicate the formats, dynamics, or functions of inner states and processes. Rather, different components of the overall (enduring or temporary) system can play quite different roles and have different properties while coupling in collective and complementary contributions to flexible thinking and acting. So "exograms" can be radically unlike engrams even while co-opted for the same purposes, and these differences will often be the focus of complementarity-oriented explanations in the EM framework. We need both historical and developmental accounts of how our brains have just about managed "to make the world smart so that we can be dumb in peace" (Clark 1997, p. 180).

Although there is clear evidence for both these lines of thought in Clark's own work and in other recent EM literature, most critics have addressed parity alone.[6] The two waves are not incompatible, but second-wave EM offers natural answers to a number of objections to EM which spring from parity considerations. But—although I won't labor the case here—complementarity too, I'll suggest, may have to be stretched considerably to deal with more deterritorialized investigations of shifting networks of heterogeneous components temporarily clustered or clumped together in contingent coalescence.

With these blunt statements of the two waves in place, I go on now to examine first-wave EM thinking. Along with other problems arising from the parity principle, at least as strictly interpreted, it threatens to undermine the methodological recommendations I've mentioned, and to render EM's connection with the search for "new multidisciplinary alliances" entirely mysterious. It will take recourse to the second wave to salvage the interdisciplinary agenda.

2 First-Wave EM: Parity

2.1 The Parity Principle

Clark and Chalmers introduced and defended EM by interpreting their examples in the light of a parity principle:

If, as we confront some task, a part of the world functions as a process which, *were it done in the head*, we would have no hesitation in accepting as part of the cognitive process, then that part of the world *is* . . . part of the cognitive process. (Clark and Chalmers, this volume, p. 29; compare Clark, this volume, chap. 3, sec. 1)

This principle motivates the idea that Otto's notebook is itself playing a cognitive role when he uses it to get to MoMA. When extended from cognitive processes to cognitive states, it also then animates the stronger claim that the *standing* information in the notebook counts as cognitive even when it's not in use, because it functions in relevant respects just as do the standing, non-occurrent beliefs and memories in Inga's brain.

The parity principle stresses the functional isomorphism of inner and outer processes and states. It would be chauvinistic and unfair to treat Otto's notebook and Inga's brain differently *just* because one is external: and, claim Clark and Chalmers, since they play the same functional role in driving behavior in both cases, and when not in use are both still poised and available to play those same roles, there is no good reason at all to treat them differently. In particular, we can take it that Otto's notebook is as accessible, as reliable, and as transparent in use as is Inga's brain: though it can, under certain nonstandard circumstances (like theft and sleep), become inaccessible, the same holds for Inga's biological equipment.

It's this parity principle which gives EM its immediate metaphysical bite, enthusing sympathizers and infuriating critics. Parity is EM in critical mode, rejecting boundaries between brain, body, and world, undermining the easy assumption that the cognitive is inner and the outer is noncognitive. The "parity probe" was intended, Clark comments, "as a means of freeing ourselves from mere bio-chauvinistic prejudices," and "as a kind of veil of metabolic ignorance" which was "specifically meant to *undermine* any tendency to think that the shape of the (present day, human) inner processes sets some bar . . . on what should count as part of a genuinely cognitive process" (2005a, p. 2; 2008, p. 114). In John Haugeland's metaphor, the aim is to get "the whole rug smooth." We shouldn't, argues Haugeland, treat brain and body as clearly separable components joined at a well-defined psychophysical interface, nor can we slide "the hump in the rug" outward by identifying principled interfaces between body or sense organs and the physical world: instead, "we have to make it *all* lie flat" by denying that the mental is "categorically different" in kind from "anything bodily or worldly" (Haugeland 1998, pp. 228–229).

This urge toward parity also derives from considering studies of "densely coupled unfolding" (Clark 2005b, p. 234) in the dynamical and embodied cognitive sciences. Paradigm cases of continuous reciprocal causation show the rich real-time integration of neural, bodily, and worldly processes: the exploitation of continuous perceptual-motor feedback allows us to achieve complex and flexible action in rapidly changing environments (Beer 2000). In such cases, where the world can serve as its own representation, even if (*contra* Haugeland) inner and outer aspects of the coupled system *can* for certain purposes usefully be treated as distinct components (Grush 2003; Clark 2007), nonetheless the relevant dynamical parameters will often span body, brain, and world, rendering less significant any differences in the respective implementing mechanisms.

2.2 Problems with Parity: Active Memory

But exclusive focus on these cases, and on the case of Otto, where parity considerations do naturally apply, can cause trouble. The existing critical literature on EM has gone astray in ways which suggest that this first-wave line of thought at least needs clarification. Clark acknowledges that the original parity principle has been "subject to a persistent misreading" (2008, p. 114): in distinctive treatments which need attention on another occasion, he and Mike Wheeler have sought to restate, revise, and defend it (Wheeler, this volume). In contrast, here I suggest that we can move EM along both faithfully and fruitfully by downplaying parity and focusing instead on an alternative route to EM.

There are two stages to the initial dialectic here as we hone in on the first significant problem for parity. A number of individualists point out, first, as if in criticism of EM, that Otto has to use motor and visual processes which are not required by Inga (Adams and Aizawa 2001, p. 55; cf. Butler 1998, pp. 211–212, and the discussion in Chalmers 2008). This is to push unrealistically hard on the parity principle, as if EM is refuted if there are *any* differences between relevant intracranial and transcranial processes: so, further, discussing different ways of doing long multiplication, Adams and Aizawa think it relevant to point out that someone who does the computation without using any external aids does not use the same visual and motor processing as someone using pencil and paper to do the sum (2001, p. 59). Likewise, Bernecker offers as part of an "objection" to EM the point that "unlike a notebook, biological memory need not be charged, may get wet, and is immune to the Y2K bug" (Bernecker 2010, chap. 6).

Clark rightly responds in "*Memento*'s Revenge" that EM does *not* require "that the processes in Otto and Inga are identical, or even similar, in terms of their detailed implementation" (Clark, this volume, chap. 3, sec. 3). The kinds of functional similarity which, under the parity principle, are to count as relevant are not to do with specific mechanisms, but with the *functional poise* of the information in question: its accessibility, availability, transparency in use, and so on, no matter what other differences there may be in the specific ways in which it enters into ongoing processing. There are, after all, as Clark points out, likely to be radically diverse causal processes involved in different kinds of inner process, too.

As Clark recognizes, however, the initial worry can be restated in more persuasive form (O'Brien 1998; Dartnall, 2004, 2005; Weiskopf, 2008). Even abstracting away from incidental details of mechanism and realization, even looking at functional poise alone, are not the format and the dynamics of biological and nonbiological representations and representational schemes just too different? We start to lose our grip on how to incorporate Merlin Donald's (1991, p. 315) points about typical *differences* between engrams and exograms into the EM story if we focus on parity alone. The storage and organization of information in Otto's notebook is, in Donald's terms, typically exogrammatic. Notably, information is stored there in discrete fashion, and representations in the notebook (linguistic or pictorial representations, for example) have no intrinsic dynamics or activity, are not intrinsically integrated with other stored information, and do no cognitive work in their standing or dispositional form. Representations in Inga's biological memory, in contrast, may well blend and interfere: according to connectionist accounts of memory, for example, non-occurrent standing representations, "stored" superpositionally in a single network's weight matrix, influence processing continually in a holistic fashion and are themselves subtly shaped by this ongoing history (McClelland and Rumelhart 1986). *This* dissimilarity, unlike the other superficial dissimilarity, matters.

But like Donald, Hutchins, Rowlands, and other post-connectionist theorists of the extended mind, Clark is of course well aware of such differences (Clark 1989, chap. 5; 1993, chap. 2). It's true, as he points out, that the existence of these differences is contingent, and that some or all of our biological memory systems might be, or might have been, less dynamic than radical connectionism suggests (Clark 2005a, pp. 5–7). It's also true, conversely, as I'll stress below, that not all external cognitive artifacts are as static and permanent as Donald suggests. So in *some* cases the homogenizing of inner and outer suggested by the parity principle will be salvageable.

Even where inner and outer resources are clearly heterogeneous in functionally relevant ways, where there really are significant differences in format and dynamics between engrams and exograms, application of parity may still be part of an EM-style explanation. In such cases, parity can operate alongside Clark and Chalmers's various criteria for treating objects as genuine parts of a cognitive system. These criteria of "glue and trust" (Clark, this volume, chap. 5) might include the requirements that the external resources should (when needed) be accessible, actually used, more or less automatically endorsed, and more or less reliable. Here I'm not defending any particular set of criteria. Rather, I note first that such criteria are, significantly, matters of degree: it's possible that, though they may clearly be satisfied on some occasions and clearly unmet on others, there will be many uncertain cases in between. This is, I suggest, not a cause for concern, as it might seem if your primary concern is establishing a single clear-cut mark of the mental: rather, the existence of a number of distinct dimensions on which particular cases can differ is the sign of a promising multidimensional space for doing EM-inspired cognitive science, by developing taxonomies or typologies of external resources in use, or of coupled systems (Poirier and Chicoisne 2006; Sutton 2006; Barnier et al. 2008; Wilson and Clark 2009). Second, notice that once any set of such criteria is brought in to adjudicate on particular cases, it's not the parity principle itself doing the real work: we're now seeing the existence of a range of possibilities, on a number of distinct dimensions, and we may rightly suspect that a more general and inclusive framework is needed, within which to locate many different kinds of case.[7]

2.3 Problems with Parity: Individual Differences and Interdisciplinarity

Such a framework—in my terms, a shift to a second-wave EM based on complementarity—is not in formal contradiction with the parity principle, for the relevant functional isomorphism postulated by parity can hold at a very abstract level of task analysis. But although the parity principle is technically loose enough to allow the parts of the world which combine in a particular cognitive process to be wildly heterogeneous, it at least does not encourage attention to the distinct features of the components in particular extended cognitive systems. Because parity downplays—or even collapses—differences between inner and outer resources, it is in some tension with the interdisciplinary dreams with which we started: when certain criteria are met, parity suggests, we shouldn't care if exograms rather than engrams are involved in the production of intelligent behavior. If Inga's brain and Otto's notebook are playing relevantly similar roles in driving what they each do, then there's no special point in studying the peculiar properties either of brains or of notebooks and other external media. There are two aspects to this concern, related to the individuals and the artifacts in question respectively.

First, parity leaves no obvious space for investigating individual differences in relation to EM, because it asks us to focus on generic features of cognitive states and processes, whether in the world or in the head. Yet we often want to understand the specificities of particular embodied subjects: just why and how one system—such as a particular embodied agent of one kind or another—can move between a variety of different artifacts. Moving around in our idiosyncratic and complex sociotechnological worlds, each of us can decouple from and recouple with external resources of quite different kinds on a regular and continuing interactive basis. Mainstream psychology has long studied individual differences in the ways people approach various cognitive tasks *without* significant use of external resources. So, likewise, even in tasks which *can* involve extended looping and coupling cognition, we're all familiar with folk who *aren't* content or able to leave the information out there in the world. Developing Rodney Brooks's antirepresentationist arguments, Haugeland writes that "it would be silly, for most purposes, to try to *keep track of* what shelf everything in the refrigerator is currently on; if and when you want something, just *look*" (Haugeland 1998, p. 219). But we all know people who *do* typically upload such information into their onboard biological memories: such individual differences in the amount and style of reliance on external resources are often glaring in the ways people plan and engage in complex activities, such as writing an academic paper, shopping for a party, or chairing a department meeting. Do I memorize the train timetable in advance, or do I just turn up at the station and see? EM theorists have a great opportunity to work closely with cognitive, social, and personality psychologists to understand such differences, which are often not superficial.

So even if, as Clark (2007) suggests, EM sees embodied agents like ourselves are "essentially incomplete" in that we are deeply sculpted and continually transformed by plugging in to such wider networks, this in no way commits us to treating what we bring to the interface as a blank slate. We often want to understand whatever diachronic stability and continuity particular subjects exhibit. Critics like Keith Butler (1998, pp. 208–210) and Rick Grush (2003, pp. 79–81) have raised this problem against EM in general: but in fact it applies only to first-wave, parity-driven versions of the framework.

On the other side of the coin, parity also threatens to flatten out the important differences between cognitive artifacts. The particular nature of the external resources, it may seem, does not really matter: as long as the resources are appropriately accessible and so on, we wouldn't need media theory, history, or any other "social, cultural, and technological studies" in cognitive science. Further, parity fails to explain or motivate the interest shown by cognitive anthropologists, developmental psychologists, sociologists of science, and historians in the *different* effects which different cognitive artifacts may in turn have on our brains, behavior, affective life, and cognitive structure. The parity principle, in short, fails directly to suggest study of idiosyncratic or peculiar features of particular external symbol systems, or of particular ways of interfacing with them.

For these reasons, then, the parity principle is either wrong or incomplete as a motivation for EM. My suggestion that on its own, parity is in some tension with the interdisciplinary dreams with which we started, is supported by the fact that the critics of EM who focus on parity considerations have been puzzled at the way EM theorists actually do engage in detailed theoretical and empirical consideration of both the nature and the use of extremely specific kinds of exogram in diverse external symbol systems.

Discussing Merlin Donald's "theory of exograms as part of the human cognitive architecture," Adams and Aizawa note that Donald himself gives both rich accounts "of the development of all manner of external representations, including body decorating, grave decorating, sculpture, Stonehenge, hieroglyphics, cuneiform, maps, graphs, and musical scores," and careful analyses of the many "ways in which the processing of exograms differs from the processing of engrams" (Adams and Aizawa 2001, p. 58). They cite approvingly Donald's discussion of the different "properties of engrams and exograms" in relation to (for example) medium-dependence, capacity, and constraints on retrieval path (ibid., pp. 58–59).

But Adams and Aizawa (2001) find it bewildering that Donald still pursues the EM agenda while thus *agreeing* with them that internal and external states and processes differ on important dimensions regarding representational format and dynamics. This shows that Adams and Aizawa have misunderstood the dialectic here, because they see EM as resting on parity considerations alone. Since Donald's framework is in tension with (or at least downplays) parity in stressing various dimensions of *difference* between exograms and engrams, Adams and Aizawa assume that it is thereby in tension with EM, and that Donald should consequently *reject* EM and embrace their conclusion that "there can be no cognitive science of transcorporeal processes" (2001, p. 58).

Yet, as we'll see in the next section, it's precisely this kind of investigation of the *variety* of cognitive interfaces, and the many dimensions on which differing inner and outer resources are *unequal*, which characterizes detailed and sophisticated work across the disciplines by writers who also defend EM and distributed cognition.

But then the humps in Haugeland's rug will multiply, rather than disappear. I noted above that the motivation of the flattening-out urge which drives first-wave EM is primarily critical. Immediately before his rug analogy, Haugeland has told us that "the idea is not to wipe out all distinctions and homogenize everything on general principles, but rather to call certain very familiar divisions into question" (1998, p. 228). The apparent shift in emphasis across these two passages is symptomatic of the more general dual movement I'm identifying in the EM literature, which oscillates between first breaking down confidence in entrenched boundaries and then, once distinctions have been exchanged for networks, reinstating heterogeneity. This dual pull is natural within EM thinking, and not a vitiating tension: rendering it explicit may help move the debates along. And after urging us to "make it *all* lie flat," Haugeland shows that he's aware of the tension by urging us not to read this advice "in a way that washes out all distinctions [between mind, body, and world], rendering the three terms synonymous" (1998, p. 230).[8] Since that's what the parity principle seemed on first reading to suggest, that first reading needs to be clarified or supplemented.

So, despite Adams and Aizawa's puzzlement, there must at least be an alternative motivation—or even justification—for fully interdisciplinary research from within the general EM framework. Before sketching such an alternative—second-wave EM, based on "complementarity"—let's illustrate it with a case study.

3   Cognition in the Globe

Evelyn Tribble's (2005) study "Distributing Cognition in the Globe" applies EM surprisingly directly to an existing historical puzzle. Inspired in particular by Hutchins's (1995) study of navigation, *Cognition in the Wild*, this impressive project is the most successful and intriguing historical application yet of EM—and the form of EM hypothesis which Tribble shows off in strongly interdisciplinary action, I'll suggest, is clearly a second-wave version.

One of many striking differences between modern Western theater and the repertory system of Shakespearean England (in the late Elizabethan and early Jacobean periods, either side of the year 1600) is that, as Tribble puts it, the (exclusively male) actors then performed in the Globe and other theaters "a staggering number of plays . . . with relatively infrequent repetition, and with the additional demands of putting on a new play roughly every fortnight" (2005, pp. 135–136). Between 1594 and 1597, for example, a leading player such as Edward Alleyn "had to secure and retain command of about seventy-one different roles, of which number fifty-two or fifty-three were newly learned" (Beckerman 1962, p. 9). Yet the actors did not have the full texts of these plays. How did the actors cope, and how did the companies rehearse and perform so many different plays under such pressures?

Studies of actors' memory in cognitive psychology (Noice and Noice 1997) can't fully answer these questions, because as Tribble demonstrates their models of acting cognition rely on quite different modern assumptions (about "character" and "subtext") and practices (such as long rehearsal periods, and few new plays). And existing scholarly explanations of early modern theater practices have gone, Tribble shows, in two mistaken directions. Either, it's been suggested, an actor rehearsed privately within a routinized formula, by which he covered every performance by playing roughly the same part, learning in "parrot fashion"; or an authoritative individual (Shakespeare himself?) must have been constantly present at rehearsal, like a modern director, to explain and install every aspect of each performance. Both views neglect the active cognitive role of the larger systems within which actors worked:

the nature of the playing system, and particularly of the mnemonic demands that the repertory system made upon its participants, has been consistently misunderstood because of a tendency to view cognition as individual rather than social and therefore to imagine the workings of complex group systems in mechanistic terms. (Tribble 2005, p. 135)

In contrast, Tribble offers a sustained reinterpretation of the historical evidence to show how diverse tools, practices, and aspects of the social and institutional form of the early modern theatrical system together "form elements of a cognitive structure that, in constraining and limiting, also enables an extraordinary level of achievement" (2005, p. 142). As in the expert navigational cognition described by Hutchins, so in the Globe physical architecture, artifacts, social structure, and the characteristics of the plays themselves combine to support the collective success of the company in performance.

It's not just that the stage space itself operated in conjunction with simple conventions as a cognitive map for sequencing the play's action. The vehicles supporting the actors' memory capacities included a diverse array of distinctive artifacts. Tribble focuses as well on early modern cue-scripts or "sides," and on some large documents called "plots" which were probably hung on walls. Both forms of surviving evidence puzzle scholars because the information they contain seems "impossibly scanty," quite inadequate by our standards. The cue-scripts contained only the barest of cues: instead of having copies of a whole play, actors were given only minimal information in textual form, and had instead to rely on hearing cues wrapped into the structure of the plays in performance. The cryptic "plots," in turn, which have seemed "maddeningly incomplete" to modern scholars, were concerned primarily with only entrances (but not exits) and scene division: if considered as compressed encodings of entire performances, they are failures. But Tribble, inspired by Hutchins, sees them instead as computational devices within extended cognitive systems, taking these two-dimensional renderings of the complex spatiotemporal paths of a performance to work in their immediate action-guiding context just *because* of the paucity and resulting clarity of the explicit information they held. As with the models and representations used in children's play, or in the complex design cognition of modern adults, the success of these various tools in supporting the actors' fluent performance may have depended, "to a certain extent, on actively keeping the level of nonessential detail quite low" (Clark 2005b, p. 237). Roughly, the Globe's artifacts worked to get the actors to the right place at the right time for further local environmental alterations (such as a particular line or event on stage) to call forth spontaneously the required specific behavior (cf. Clark 1997, p. 76, on Hutchins).

So before we even consider the mnemonic and action-guiding nature of the plays themselves, or the broader hierarchical social system of the playing companies, we can see that a wide array of factors conspire to solve the various coordination and memory problems facing the company. Contrary to any default assumption that the overall play is controlled by a single plan in the mind of Shakespeare as writer or Shakespeare as director, or by a single authoritative script, in fact the sequences of actions and interactions which collectively constitute the performance "need not be explicitly represented anywhere" (Clark 1997, p. 77, on Hutchins).

Though this isn't yet meant as a full explanation of the historical phenomena, Tribble's work dramatically remolds the issues so that they no longer look like problems about the capacity and limits of the individuals' memories. The actors' skill was not only in semantic memory for their lines or characters but also in their procedural memory or know-how, in their mastery of the cognitive resources of their highly structured dramatic environment. We want now to ask more about the interface between actors, props, plots, stage space, verse, and so on. We can follow Hutchins again (for example) in simultaneously examining the computational and social embedding of novices within the overall system: in the case of the Globe, apprentices initially played minor (theatrical and computational) parts in a smoothly functioning whole, and then might understand and internalize the appropriate actions and skills only after they were already performing them (Tribble 2005, pp. 153–155; Hutchins 1995, p. 224).

Tribble's careful analysis of cognition in the Globe demonstrates the practical value of the extended mind framework for offering new perspectives on cross-disciplinary topics of independent importance. It helps us to identify and undermine the temptation, common in cognitive-scientific investigation of complex collective action in specific cultural contexts, to think that some single or determinate component of the overall system (such as the cue-scripts, the plots, or the individual actors) must have fully encoded "the play" in order for a successful performance to emerge in practice. Further, it thus exemplifies the shift from first- to second-wave EM. Like the process of navigation described by Hutchins, the case of early modern acting differs from the case of Otto in an important respect: whereas Otto's notebook acts directly as an equal substitute for his brain, the cue-scripts and plots which (like Hutchins's nautical slide rules, charts, and so on) were elements in an extraordinary complex system of distributed social cognition are nothing like the internal resources brought to bear by the individual actors (or navigators). There's no sense in which the various nonhuman artifacts which scaffold successful performance have to be doing the same thing as the individual participants are, or even storing the same information as might have been stored in their individual brains: to quote Clark's apt account of Hutchins's case study again, "the computational power and expertise is spread across a *heterogeneous* assembly of brains, bodies, artifacts, and other external structures" (Clark 1997, p. 77, my emphasis).

4   Second-Wave EM: Complementarity

In addition to the parity principle, Clark has also stressed a different aspect of the case for EM, one which is more sensitive to the "essential causal dynamics" (Adams and Aizawa 2001, p. 44) of inner and outer processes, respectively. In his response to Gerard O'Brien's (1998) critique, Clark defends this second line of argument for EM, noting that although it is formally compatible with parity, there is indeed "a potential tension" between them (Clark 1998, p. 99). This "more interesting and plausible argument" for EM turns on "the way external elements may play a role different from, but complementary to, the inner ones": in thus stressing "complementarity," we should see the functional isomorphism required by the parity principle as "at most part of a sufficient condition for cognitive extension, rather than a necessary feature" (Clark 1998, p. 99).

The parity principle, then, is better seen as "an informal test" (Clark, this volume, chap. 3, sec. 3) or temporary indicator of cognitive extension, a place-holder for fuller, more inclusive sciences of the interface. Biological and nonbiological resources, in certain circumstances, work together, coalescing into integrated larger cognitive systems. As Clark writes in a key passage, the external resources on which cognition sometimes leans are best seen as alien but *complementary* to the brain's style of storage and computation.

The brain need not waste its time *replicating* such capacities. Rather, it must learn to interface with the external media in ways that maximally exploit their particular virtues. (Clark 1997, p. 220)

With this complementarity principle, as we might call it,[9] we return connectionism to the heart of the case for EM. It's just *because* isolated items aren't stored atomically in the brain that our relatively vulnerable biological memories are supplemented by more stable external scaffolding. Brains like ours need media, objects, and other people to function fully as minds. Seeing the brain as a leaky associative engine, its contents flickering and unstable rather than mirroring the world in full, forces attention to our reliance on external representations in the technological and cultural wild. The classical search for the engram (as an enduring discrete item stored at a fixed address) fell foul of the holistic and dynamic nature of representation in the brain: biological traces are typically integrative, active, and reconstructive, but in using them we hook up with more enduring and transmissible exograms, mostly of our own making, which supplement and extend our powers. According to this second-wave EM,

The argument for the extended mind thus turns primarily on the way disparate inner and outer components may co-operate so as to yield integrated larger systems capable of supporting various (often quite advanced) forms of adaptive success. (Clark 1998, p. 99)

The complementarity principle explains why, to the critics' dismay (section 2 above), an EM theorist would catalog differences between the properties of engrams and exograms: "unlike the constantly-moving contents of biological working memory, the products of thinking, when reformatted exogrammatically, could be frozen in time, held up to scrutiny at some future date, altered and re-entered into storage" (Donald 1991, p. 316). The EM perspective offers a typology or framework in which many different relations (and kinds of relations) between inner and outer resources can be understood. Cases like Otto with his notebook, which are transparent examples of parity in that a single external resource is doing just what could otherwise be done in the head, can be seen as special cases of complementarity.

If complementarity thus subsumes and takes precedence over parity, it's clear that EM as a general thesis need say nothing about exactly what kinds of formats and dynamics there must be inside and outside the skin. Different kinds will permit and encourage quite different kinds of interaction and coupling and thus different kinds and degrees of extendedness. EM, thus understood, is more an invitation to give detailed attention to these differences in specific contexts and case studies than a fixed new metaphysics of mind. So its second wave both encourages and makes sense of the interdisciplinary agenda I described in section 1 and exemplified with Tribble's case study. Such an agenda, of course, may bring problems of its own. In section 6, after we've looked at another historical example, I'll briefly consider problems about the nature of explanation in this form of EM. But I want to close this section with two different challenges for second-wave, complementarity-based EM, without here needing to decide whether they will turn out to be manageable within its framework, or will require sufficient amendment to justify thinking in terms of a third wave.

First, it's important to resist a tendency within second-wave EM still to treat the inside and the outside as distinct realms with fixed properties. Merlin Donald's tabulation of the different characteristics of engrams and exograms does deal successfully with the problem critics raised for parity, about the active, reconstructive, and context-dependent nature of biological memory, in contrast with the passive, stable, medium- and context-independent nature of external symbol systems. But, to repeat, not all exograms are as discrete and as fixed as is the information about the museum recorded in Otto's notebook: external representational systems need not be permanent, of unlimited capacity, translatable across media, or endlessly reformattable as Donald's typology suggests (see also Sutton 2008, 2009). The words and sentences in Otto's notebook, for example, might be replaced by some much more dynamic new-media system incorporating a range of sensory modalities, which is continually updating or appropriately reconfiguring in ways which (we could imagine) still met the criteria of accessibility, direct availability, and automatic trusting endorsement; in a further extension, such a system might come to high-light information or options aligned with Otto's moods or emotions. Think of the various ways in which other people enter our external memory fields, with their dynamic engrams potentially our exograms (Wegner 1987; Wegner, Erber, and Raymond 1991). Another as yet merely fictional example is the personalized book *A Young Lady's Illustrated Primer* in Neal Stephenson's (1995) novel *The Diamond Age*, which bonds and couples with a particular little girl, initially through simple imprinting but soon through a brilliantly imagined range of interactive technologies, which include both dynamic databases and live actors-at-a-distance. More generally, not all systems of exograms are meant to be permanent or endlessly transmissible: and not all such systems which are intended to endure actually do so (Kwint 1999). Whether by design or not, medium and message are often not as independent as in Donald's scheme: the degree of context-dependence itself depends on the context. In relation to permanence, medium-dependence, ease of reformatting, and all the other dimensions of Donald's picture, nothing intrinsic to the second-wave complementarity framework imposes such stark gaps between the natural and the artificial: so genuine interdisciplinary inquiry should not assume them.

Second and conversely, we need to see just how naturally complementarity can make sense of a further strand of EM-inspired research: the investigation into ways in which integration into larger cognitive systems may alter even the inner parts of those larger systems. As Clark has long argued, "cognitive technologies" don't have to be external: among the many resources we use to think about (for example) the past, the abstract, and the absent are a range of internalized representations and symbol systems, which we learn (historically and developmentally) to manage with both idiosyncratic and culturally specified techniques. The first step in this line of thought, taking us into a second historical case study, is to recognize that it's not that the same basic inner resources are brought to the interface with all these different media and symbolic technologies and left untouched. If that were the case, then cognitive science could remain the study of individuals, interacting variously with different external artifacts. Instead, in turn, such interfacing is often inherently transformative. Consider Clark's account of language (Clark 1997, 2005c; see also Millikan 2001; Sutton 2002b; Wheeler 2004): drawing on developmental studies of inner speech and representational redescription, Clark sees language as not primarily a tool for the communication of fully formed thoughts, but as providing us with a code which "minimizes contextuality" and is itself the ultimate cognitive artifact.

By "freezing" our own thoughts in the memorable, context-resistant, modality-transcending format of a sentence, we thus create a special kind of mental object—an object that is amenable to scrutiny from multiple cognitive angles, is not doomed to alter or change every time we are exposed to new inputs or information, and fixes the ideas at a high level of abstraction from the idiosyncratic details of their proximal origins in sensory input. (Clark 1997, p. 210)

Like other internalized schemes, language here is itself a kind of prosthesis, an imported aid which allows for higher-order dynamics of self-control and mind control that can, as we'll see, be cognitive and affective at once. To continue pushing at the edges of this second-wave, complementarity-inspired form of EM, we can move on to our second case study in historical cognitive science, EM-style.

5 The Arts of Memory and the Civilizing Process

The remarkable medieval and Renaissance memory practices have been richly described by such wonderfully interdisciplinary modern scholars as Frances Yates and Mary Carruthers, whose works should be consulted for historical detail of specific mnemonic practices and writings (Yates 1966; Carruthers 1990). Although the broad techniques in question have survived from the ancient world to the present and are still studied in contemporary applied cognitive psychology (Moè and de Beni 2005), we can find in their heyday an intriguing case study in how cognitive artifacts were internalized in an alien moral, social, and theoretical context.

The historical distance afforded by this kind of exercise is vital, because it's often harder to see the mutual entanglings and contaminations operating between brains, technologies, and culture in the present. Among other things, this work is a first step toward answering John Haugeland's challenge to EM theorists to care more for the public norms, communal practices, and moral dimensions of our relations with artifacts (Haugeland 2002). Haugeland complains that Clark's approach is impoverished because it draws so much on work involving robots, infants, and other animals, none of which is a full member of a human community, with the full-blown histories and traditions which attach to complex public norms. So any help which EM offers in understanding such culturally embedded practices as these old methods of managing memory and imposing cognitive discipline might help us to see some of the "roots of norm-hungriness" (Clark 2002b) in our ability to interiorize relatively stable forms of culturally sanctioned scaffolding in the quest for self-mastery.[10]

Each adept gradually constructed an artificial memory, a set of locations or places (in a memory palace or theater, an ark or an alphabet or an angel, a grid or a bestiary). This permanent set of locations could then be used to hold the images or other items to be remembered. Each representation encoded must be independent of all others, with each content mapping individually on to its place: that's why strict division of material was required, to keep items distinct. This atomistic storage system then allowed the remembering subject to move around the memory locations at will, extracting or manipulating items from their arbitrary addresses. Despite the apparent doubling of effort required to remember both the locations and then the specific items to be remembered, the system was both economical and flexible, for once the virtual architecture was securely internalized, it could be used and reused at will. The adept's mind had become a random access memory (Carruthers 1990, p. 7, 1998, p. 16).

The key, then, was the static nature of the items, whether they were bizarre images placed on memory plinths or verbal cues written onto memory tablets. Mistakes were due not to distortion in recall, but to failure to render images distinct enough at the time of encoding. After successful encoding, items are context independent, to be inspected, recombined, and transformed again only under deliberate executive control. So the system has no intrinsic dynamics, and semantic stability is maintained across contexts.

What does this have to do with the extended mind hypothesis? These Renaissance scholars were not hooking up with any literally external technologies: they were specifically refusing to use the world as its best model, instead laboriously soaking up whole baroque memory edifices. Of course there's a complicated narrative to trace here about the history of books and the spread of print media, which would address changing historical relations between these cognitive practices and the available external artifacts for recording and transmitting information. But taking EM seriously, I suggest, means that we treat such architectures, systems, and practices as both cognitive and extended whether or not they happen to be outside the skin. They are cognitive even though they are not, in a straightforwardly ancestral way, natural and biological; and they are extended even though they are not literally external. The cognitive skills which individuals roam round with, more or less successfully, have histories which are just as much cultural and developmental as biological.

In particular, this example shows starkly how cognitive practices can be tangled in with communal norms and moral requirements. These techniques were explicitly driven by awareness that what scholars called "natural memory" had built-in tendencies to confusion. Artifice was needed because of the corrupt nature of embodied humanity, where one effect of the Fall was loss of control over the personal past. Especially by the Renaissance period, the eclectic default humoralist physiology offered little room for unaided inner stability.[11] So the natural dynamics, the "disorderly floating" of ordinary memory had to be suppressed. Even the use of strikingly affective images, bloody and violent, in the memory palaces, was aimed at neutralizing indiscipline, containing emotional items in their places. These schemes thus operated on a picture of the relations between the natural and the artificial, the biological and the virtual, which is very like the post-connectionist account of the profound differences between engrams and exograms through which I characterized second-wave EM thinking, based on complementarity, above: and this perspective guided my own earlier take on the arts of memory, which I now think needs some amendment.

In that earlier work, I saw the localist style of representation in the memory arts, with its built-in fantasy of totally voluntary memory, as a wishful stabilizing of confusion from above. The techniques were meant to supplement and strengthen, or more often to supplant and bypass entirely, the mixture and blending which was natural to the roving animal spirits as they ceaselessly constructed their overlapping patterns of flow in the spongy brain. Cognitive discipline was an achievement, to be carefully worked at and guaranteed by the interiorizing of these sanctioned supplements. Escaping the murky forests of natural memory, the adept resists the crowding and interfering of traces in the brain, and traps all intensity in his memory rooms.

I still think it clear that the arts of memory were a moral quest, to ward off the intrusion of unwanted thoughts, to undertake the disciplined purging of what Saint Bernard called "filthy traces" from the past (Coleman 1992, pp. 182–191). But now I think this analysis was taken in by the rigidity of the historical practitioners' own dichotomy between natural and artificial memory. I saw the quest for control over items in memory, guaranteed by separating data from process, memory from executive self, as the external and artificial imposition of order by reason or will on the true and naturally confused memory system of fleeting animal spirits. So—in rather primitivist fashion—I saw the arts of memory as the cognitive wing of a heavily moralized civilizing process: by freezing the contents of memory, and locking them into separate rooms for later extraction, monks and scholars sought to tame and recalibrate their minds, in a retreat from multiplicity, disturbance, and embodiment. In a similar vein, in his recent reading of the same techniques Paul Ricoeur describes the *ars memoriae* as "an outrageous denial of forgetfulness and . . . of the weaknesses inherent in both the preservation of traces and their evocation" (2004, p. 66).

But now I want to develop further themes from Clark to question this kind of reading. In recent work on "self-scaffolding," Clark surveys various forms of "virtuoso artificial self-manipulation" available to symbol-users like us. By finding tags, labels, or images for higher-order patterns in our own thought and action, we create "a kind of affect-dampening layer of insulation," which allows us "to productively dampen and control (but not counter-productively destroy altogether) the fluidity and context-sensitivity of biologically basic forms of neural representation" (Clark 2005c, pp. 263–264). These abilities "to vehicle our thoughts" in language and in other representational formats (Clark 2003b) are entirely continuous with the other, more direct ways in which we actively restructure our external environment (cf. Dennett 2000). Clark describes a general need for "anchoring" in terms highly reminiscent of the medieval and Renaissance monks and scholars: we collectively and individually devise "cognitive strategies (which may be more or less indirect and baroque)" to address "the problem of stabilization," the need to discipline our "mental spaces in ways that tame (though never eradicate) those biologically more 'natural' processes of merging and change" (Clark 2005c, p. 264). The memory artists' active training in memory and meditation, from this perspective, starts to look more like a particularly explicit attempt to develop the ongoing capacity to treat memories and other items as themselves objects for thought, to buffer or influence their affective impact, and (again in Clark's terms) to "drive, sculpt and discipline the internal representational regime" (ibid.).

I don't want to deny the historical excesses of inebriated rationalism in the Renaissance memory arts, as noted in my prior analysis and by Ricoeur: but Clark's take on cognitive discipline might also help us to see even such ostentatious strategies of memory control as natural for human cyborgs like us. Despite the ease with which both Clark and I have contrasted, in our different contexts, the fluid biological memory with the more rigid artificial system, we shouldn't take this profound dichotomy between engrams and exograms as the end of the story. It's not quite right to treat the true, or natural memory as that given by the brain alone, whether by humoral nervous fluids or by post-connectionist neural networks. Why should we treat the internal prosthesis provided by the memory palaces and their internalized exograms as genuinely external to the mind? Are culture, artifice, and moral practice optional extras, merely dispensable surrogates which ride on top of the brain's own unchanged tendencies? Or are they instead in one form or another inevitable, structuring supplements which construct and maintain the biological processes that they simultaneously and deeply transform?

In contrast to later moral physiologists who simply denied the productive cognitive role of mixture and blending in the brain, these earlier memory practitioners took it very seriously.[12] That's why they were so sensitive to the need for artifices and prostheses—in this case, internalized prostheses—creating secure locations, virtual nooks and clear unswampy corners of the memory, secret angles of the mind in which they hoped to find what and only what they had deliberately put there. Of course the quest is imperfect: as Hamlet discovered, despite his promise to the ghost, "baser matter" doesn't just disappear, and the personal past doesn't always flatten out. But it's not as if we can avoid leaning on artificial systems. Recalibration is ongoing, as we alter our own cognitive machinery by exploiting and importing whatever tools and labels we can. The memory artists' skillful use of a manageable and reliable set of cognitive artifacts was an unusually developed, culturally anchored way to deal with contextuality. The civilizing process, thus understood, includes the tidying of our own brains as well as of our behavior, and it isn't really optional.

This slightly shifted picture of these weird old practices should also have some historical benefit: in particular, it allows us better to incorporate Mary Carruthers's rich and persuasive work on the meditative aspects of mnemotechnics as a skillful "craft of thought" (Carruthers 1990, 1998). Where previously we might have seen a "deadly infatuation" with the exercise of sovereign choice after an "original denial" of "the constraints of traces" (Ricoeur 2004, p. 66), by putting Carruthers's revisionary history together with Clark's version of EM we can reinstate a sense of the practical cognitive and emotional labor, and the riskiness of the quest for wisdom in the "things" and the "devices" of this "architecture for thinking" (Carruthers 1998, pp. 7–35).[13] Just as in offloading both information and procedures into external technologies and social systems we thereby reconfigure our cognitive tasks and profiles, so in constructing elaborate inner machines for sedimenting and working with affectively laden images and thoughts, the memory artists gradually developed different cognitive skills. Discussing the basis of composition and digression in the memory-based arts of rhetoric, Carruthers and Ziolkowski describe—in terms which might put us in mind both of Hutchins and of Tribble—the memory expert's ability spontaneously to shuffle and reorder, to gather up materials and then find the way again: once the inner architecture is securely founded and its navigational principles well practiced, then "I can always be sure of 'where I am' in the composition—not in the manner of a parrot (which, reciting mindlessly, never knows 'where' it is) but in the manner of an experienced harbor pilot recalling landmarks" (Carruthers and Ziolkowski 2002, p. 5).

Many "high-level," "representation-hungry," and "decoupled" cognitive processes—whether thinking about intimate aspects of the long-gone personal past, or predicting the effects of a shift in foreign policy, or recollecting the ways to salvation through the gospels—occur in the absence of actual or possible immediate external stimulation. But, as Clark (2005b) argues, this does not mean that they are decontextualized and disembodied. For just as in other cases we create "surrogate situations" in the external world so as to amplify cognition and "direct and distribute attention in new ways," so—like the dead adepts of the memory arts—we can also use culturally sculpted internalized surrogates.

Like Clark's treatment of language (section 4), this is starting to push the second wave's nice dichotomy between fluid inner engrams and stable outer exograms pretty far: as Hutchins argues, "it is not that some content is copied from the outside world into some internal storage medium . . . what used to look like internalization now appears as a gradual propagation of organized functional properties across a set of malleable media" (1995, p. 312).[14] If there is to be a distinct third wave of EM, it might be a deterritorialized cognitive science which deals with the propagation of deformed and reformatted representations, and which dissolves individuals into peculiar loci of coordination and coalescence among multiple structured media (Hutchins 1995, p. 316; Sperber 1996, pp. 57–63; Suchman 1998; Johnston 2002, pp. 481–482; Clark 2003a, pp. 130–142, 2004b, pp. 177–180; Mackenzie 2004). Without assuming distinct inner and outer realms of engrams and exograms, the natural and the artificial, each with its own proprietary characteristics, this third wave would analyze these boundaries as hard-won and fragile developmental and cultural achievements, always open to renegotiation.

6 Conclusion: A Note on Explanation

Even the basic second-wave complementary route to EM, of course, has its costs. As critics and friends of EM alike have realized, the extended cognitive architectures it would encompass include a daunting array of the social and technological systems with which embodied brains can couple. What would cognitive science be like, how could it continue, if its objects include notebooks, sketchpads, and tattoos as well as embodied brains? Systems of brains coupled with cognitive tools, computing devices, or memory aids, complain Adams and Aizawa, "would seem to form such a motley collection that they will not form the basis for any significant scientific theorizing" (2001, p. 63). EM thus threatens to thwart cognitive science's connected quests for natural kinds and for disciplinary identity. If—to sample the relevant literature—other people, scrabble tiles, theater architecture, cocktail glasses, slide rules, incised sticks, shells, languages, moral norms, knots, codes, maps, diagrams, fingers, monuments, software devices, rituals, rhythms and rhymes, and roads can count as part of the legitimate subject matter of the sciences of mind, isn't EM obviously absurd? The fear is that EM would leave cognitive science paralyzed, in the same way—and for the same reason—that Tooby and Cosmides mock "mainstream sociocultural anthropology" for being in "a situation resembling some nightmarish story Borges might have written, where scientists are condemned by their unexamined assumptions to study the nature of mirrors only by cataloguing and investigating everything that mirrors can reflect" (Tooby and Cosmides 1992, p. 42).

In conclusion, I want to underline the two responses to this worry that Clark offers in section 3 of "*Memento*'s Revenge" (this volume, chap. 3). First, we shouldn't work with an overly restricted or puritanical notion of scientific explanation: nonpredictive narrative explanations are common enough in the natural and social sciences of many complex systems, including branches of history, geography, geology, evolutionary biology, and meteorology.[15] This doesn't inevitably diminish these frameworks' rigor, whereas premature quests for lawlike regularities might: more particularized illustrative studies may just be the best way for us to get what Paul Churchland has called "objective knowledge of a highly idiosyncratic reality" (1996, p. 306). Of course, it will sometimes be fruitful artificially to simplify the hopeless multiplicity we're faced with in studying remembering, acting, thinking, interacting, feeling, talking, imagining, perceiving, planning and so on. But as I've argued before, amid the Kuhnian "normal science" of the modern cognitive sciences and neurosciences, with their vast apparatus and institutions, it might also be rational sometimes for some to indulge an "untidy preference for proliferation over prudence in difficult domains" (Sutton 1998, p. 3, 2004, p. 190).

And, second, we shouldn't rule out in advance the possibility that in fact there may be higher-level accounts which do find commonalities or patterns across the alleged "unscientific motley of capacities" (Adams and Aizawa 2001, p. 62) exhibited by extended hybrid minds. On this point we'll just have to wait and see.[16] Just as Clark has been advancing his own optimistic vision of sciences of the interface, investigating "varied, multiplex, interlocking, and criss-crossing causal mechanisms" over "a wide variety of mechanistic bases" (this volume, chap. 3, sec. 7) by exploring new cognitive technologies, so I hope the reverse-angle case studies sketched in this chapter have hinted at the patterns and possibilities which might emerge in historical cognitive sciences. At the very least, second-wave EM can thus tap and in turn influence the enormous and diverse scholarship on memory, perception, emotion, and so on in humanities disciplines, to see what might happen if we try to study cognition scientifically and culturally at once.

Acknowledgments

Special thanks to Richard Menary for his work as editor, and for organizing wonderful conferences on the extended mind at the University of Hertfordshire, where I first tried out some of these ideas. Later versions were presented at the annual conference of the Australasian Association for History, Philosophy, and Social Studies of Science in 2002, at the joint International/Australasian Cognitive Science conference in Sydney in 2003, and at a reading group and workshop on memory and embodied cognition at Macquarie University in 2004. Many thanks to these audiences, to Andy Clark and Lyn Tribble for their enthusiasm and help, and for various contributions and support to Samir Chopra, Hugh Clapin, Stephen Cowley, Tom Evans, Adam Holland, Eve Keller, Doris McIlwain, Andrew Murphie, Gerard O'Brien, Mark Rowlands, David Spurrett, Tony Stone, Maria Trochatos, Mike Wheeler, and Carl Windhorst. I'm particularly grateful to Tim Bayne and the late Terry Dartnall, who both wrote detailed comments on an earlier draft: I've tried to respond to all their queries and suggestions. For discussion on the arts of memory over the years, thanks in particular to Ed Cooke, Jim Franklin, Jamie Kassler, Doris McIlwain, and Gail Kern Paster.

Notes

1. I use the label "EM" for brevity throughout, as if this family of ideas were unified. This chapter is an exposition and development specifically of Andy Clark's version, although it hones in on distinct strands of his account of EM. But I treat

the following labels from the philosophical literature as closely related: active externalism (Clark and Chalmers 1998, reprinted in this volume), vehicle externalism (Hurley 1998; Rowlands 2003), locational externalism (Wilson 2004), environmentalism (Rowlands 1999), systemic anti-individualism (Butler 1998), and transcranialism (Adams and Aizawa 2001). My take on EM, based on the "complementarity" rather than the "parity" of inner and outer resources, brings it closer to the related theory of "distributed cognition" (Hutchins 1995; Kirsh 2006; Rogers 2006), which arose independently in cognitive anthropology.

2. Despite its relevance and promise, I don't in this essay consider the "nonsymbolic environment," which some proponents of EM include (Haugeland 1998; Wilson 2004, pp. 192–196). So readers who come to EM from science studies and actor–network theory, or HCI (human–computer interaction) and CSCW (computer-supported cooperative work), or whose interest is in material agency and posthuman technics, will likely find (on this point as on others) that the underlaboring, ground-clearing work I attempt in this chapter is disappointingly slow, as I'm still talking with cognitivists and trying to convert individualists: but for some initial suggestions see Sutton 2008. One aim of a third-wave EM might be to incorporate the best work of such theorists from outside the cognitive sciences, who often, as Clark notes (this volume, chap. 3, conclusion) regard EM "as patently true": see my brief remarks at the end of section 5.

3. For present purposes we can understand "interdisciplinarity" by thinking of a spectrum from the easier mere juxtaposition of disconnected theoretical and empirical frameworks, toward more integrated novel projects and approaches which genuinely fuse disciplines and methods. Rogers, Scaife, and Rizzo (2005), in an important consideration of relevant methodological questions in the context of EM-related research, call the former "multidisciplinarity" and the latter "interdisciplinarity": cf. von Eckardt (2001). I outline a position toward the stronger end of such a spectrum in relation to memory research in Sutton 2004.

4. This makes some objections to the project look misplaced. Rick Grush, in a fine critique of John Haugeland's version of EM, worries that, if Haugeland is right, then "cognitive neuroscience as a discipline would be somewhat ill-formed, for it presumes to be studying perception, cognition, and the like, by focusing on neurophysiology. But if it does not make sense to treat the brain as a conceptually autonomous component, then cognitive neuroscience is something like an ill-formed art history sub-discipline that, rather than studying paintings from this or that historical period, studies the bottom third of paintings from all periods" (Grush 2003, p. 64). But this is not an apt analogy. Even the strongly interdisciplinary agenda I defend in this chapter can allow that in many contexts many of the brain's operations can still be relatively shielded from contextual influence: the extent of context-dependence, I argue, itself varies dramatically across contexts. The kinds of coordination, mediation, and reformatting of representations in

which brains are involved, for example, offer more interesting patterns to study than would the geometrically defined subject matter of Grush's "ill-formed art history." Indeed, second-wave complementarity-based EM should specifically encourage attention to the *unique* roles played by brains in heterogeneous larger systems. See also Clark 2008, chapter 7, and my brief remarks in section 6 of this chapter on explanation in EM.

5. Although a detailed defense of this claim will have to await another occasion, I'd suggest that the interpretations of work in the cognitive psychology of memory, for example, offered by recent critics of EM (Rupert 2004; Adams and Aizawa 2008, pp. 63–68, pp. 137–139) do not fully and accurately characterize the whole diverse field. Not all research in the field treats intracranial processes as the only cognitive explananda; and not all research which does focus on intracranial processes does so to the exclusion of transcranial cognitive processes. For initial discussions of these issues in the case of memory see Wilson 2005; Tollefsen 2006; Barnier et al. 2008; Sutton 2009.

6. Adams and Aizawa (2008, chaps. 7–8) have, however, now discussed the complementarity argument: quoting my statement above of the complementarity principle, they note that they "agree with this completely," but deny that it supports EM (2008, p. 145). Since their discussion relies on an earlier draft of this current chapter, which has also been put to work in that earlier form by others, including defenders of EM like Menary (2006, 2007), Rowlands (2009), and Wilson (2005), I've thought it best to leave this first attempt at a systematic statement and defense of complementarity intact, postponing a full reply to Adams and Aizawa's deflationary reading to another occasion.

7. As this and other criticisms leveled at EM—such as those based on intrinsic content—reveal, the parity principle can also unhelpfully be read as leaving the inner as the standard of the cognitive, treating engrams in an individual brain as the unmarked case of the mental against which exograms must be judged. It's for this reason that Richard Menary rejects parity, because it seems to treat Otto's notebook as part of his cognitive system only due to its being coupled to him: "this is a residual form of internalism, because it assumes a discrete, already formed cognitive agent" (Menary 2006, p. 333). Clearly this isn't part of Clark's application of the parity principle: even so, it's notable that, responding to the kind of criticisms discussed in the text, Clark rightly resorts to considering "Otto-and-the-notebook" as "a single, integrated system" (2005a, p. 7). This, in my terms, is to shift from parity toward complementarity, from first- to second-wave EM.

8. Compare Bruno Latour's similar disclaimer: "in abandoning dualism our intent is not to throw everything into the same pot, to efface the distinct features of the various parts within the collective. We want analytical clarity, too, but following different lines than the one drawn for the polemical tug of war between subjects and objects" (Latour 1999, pp. 193–194).

9. Richard Menary (2006, 2007, this volume) calls this take on EM "cognitive integration," characterizing it as "the view that internal vehicles and processes are integrated with external vehicles and processes."

10. Here I'm drawing on, but also significantly revising, my own previous account of the memory arts (Sutton 2000). That paper has much more detail on this interpretation, with full reference to primary and secondary sources. My reading of the historical material there was particularly influenced by Stephen Greenblatt (1980) and Elaine Scarry (1988). The summary here for my current purposes is at a very general level, ideally to be filled out with studies of more specific contexts. In Sutton 2007 I have aligned this revised treatment of the arts of memory with a broader picture of the array of characteristic memory artifacts available in early modern Europe.

11. Gail Kern Paster characterizes humoralism as "a way of thinking about bodily behavior that . . . finds it much easier to account for a subject's moment-to-moment fluctuations in mood and action than to account for emotional steadiness and a high degree of psychological self-sameness. . . . Psychological self-sameness presupposes disembodied consciousness, not the humoral subject's full immersion in and continuous interaction with a constantly changing natural and cultural environment" (Paster 2004, p. 60). I survey psychological aspects of the holistic physiology of humors and fleeting animal spirits in Sutton 1998, chapter 2.

12. The story of the gradual rejection of animal spirits and of the reconstructive nature of memory in later seventeenth- and eighteenth-century philosophy and moral physiology is told in chapters 4–10 of my *Philosophy and Memory Traces* (Sutton 1998). A fuller prehistory of (and for) EM would incorporate that story into a larger narrative of the modern "invention of autonomy" (Schneewind 1997, pp. 3–11) and the correlative purifying "depsychologizing" of artifacts (Latour 1993; Jones and Stallybrass 2000; Sutton 2007).

13. In a footnote added to the second (2008) edition of her classic *The Book of Memory*, Carruthers acknowledges the relevance of Clark's work, suggesting that some of the medieval ideas she discusses are "in keeping with the extended-mind hypothesis of mental 'scaffolding,' exploited for the craft of thinking" (2008, p. 380). This is a neat demonstration of the two-way benefits which can flow from historical cognitive science, especially of the EM variety.

14. The second half of this quotation is highlighted in Bruno Latour's important celebratory review of Hutchins's "theory of computation by propagation of representational state" (Hutchins 1995, p. 230): Latour comments that "this means that there is nothing below the skin except the continuation of the same processes that go on outside" (Latour 1996, p. 58).

15. These points were powerfully made in some pre-EM philosophical engagements with the new dynamical approaches to cognition, for example by Jeff Foss

(1992) and James Garson (1996). Dan Sperber's "epidemiology of representations" also embraces "a rather heterogeneous ontology, in that psychological and ecological phenomena are mixed together" (Sperber 1996, p. 26).

16. But note an interesting extremism in Adams and Aizawa's more recent treatment of this point. They question not only the "broad range of phenomena" which EM would address by studying (for example) "humans and computers, humans and books, humans and personal digital assistants, and who knows what else," but also the unity of a class which includes "human memory, canine memory, [and] mollusk memory" (Adams and Aizawa 2008, p. 141). This complaint is in tension with their wish elsewhere to rely firmly on scientific practice in the cognitive and neurosciences of memory, where carefully applied animal studies are entirely mainstream, providing vital evidence for key points of scientific consensus.

References

Adams, F., and Aizawa, K. (2001). The bounds of cognition. *Philosophical Psychology*, *14*, 43–64.

Adams, F., and Aizawa, K. (2008). *The Bounds of Cognition*. Oxford: Blackwell.

Barnier, A. J., Sutton, J., Harris, C. B., and Wilson, R. A. (2008). A conceptual and empirical framework for the social distribution of cognition: The case of memory. *Cognitive Systems Research, 9*, 33–51.

Beckerman, B. (1962). *Shakespeare at the Globe*. New York: Macmillan.

Beer, R. (2000). Dynamical approaches to cognitive science. *Trends in Cognitive Sciences, 4*, 91–99.

Bernecker, S. (2010). *Memory: A Philosophical Study*. Oxford: Oxford University Press.

Butler, K. (1998). *Internal Affairs: Making Room for Psychosemantic Internalism*. Dordrecht: Kluwer.

Carruthers, M. (1990). *The Book of Memory*. Cambridge: Cambridge University Press (2nd edition, 2008).

Carruthers, M. (1998). *The Craft of Thought*. Cambridge: Cambridge University Press.

Carruthers, M., and Ziolkowski, J. (eds.) (2002). General introduction. In *The Medieval Craft of Memory: An Anthology of Texts and Pictures* (pp. 1–31). Philadelphia: Pennsylvania University Press.

Chalmers, D. (2008). Foreword to Clark, *Supersizing the Mind*. Oxford: Oxford University Press.

Churchland, P. M. (1996). Flanagan on moral knowledge. In R. McCauley (ed.), *The Churchlands and Their Critics*. Oxford: Blackwell.

Clark, A. (1989). *Microcognition: Philosophy, Cognitive Science, and Parallel Distributed Processing*. Cambridge, MA: MIT Press.

Clark, A. (1993). *Associative Engines: Connectionism, Concepts, and Representational Change*. Cambridge, MA: MIT Press.

Clark, A. (1997). *Being There: Putting Brain, Body, and World Together Again*. Cambridge, MA: MIT Press.

Clark, A. (1998). Author's response: Review symposium on *Being There*. *Metascience*, *7*, 95–103.

Clark, A. (2001a). *Mindware: An Introduction to the Philosophy of Cognitive Science*. Oxford: Oxford University Press.

Clark, A. (2001b). Reasons, robots, and the extended mind. *Mind and Language*, *16*, 121–145.

Clark, A. (2002a). Towards a science of the bio-technological mind. *International Journal of Cognitive Technology*, *1*, 21–33.

Clark, A. (2002b). The roots of "norm-hungriness." In H. Clapin (ed.), *Philosophy of Mental Representation* (pp. 37–43). Oxford: Oxford University Press.

Clark, A. (2003a). *Natural-Born Cyborgs: Minds, Technologies, and the Future of Human Intelligence*. Oxford: Oxford University Press.

Clark, A. (2003b). Forces, fields, and the role of knowledge in action: Commentary on Randall Beer. *Adaptive Behavior*, *11*, 270–272.

Clark, A. (2004a). Is language special? Some remarks on control, coding, and co-ordination. *Language Sciences*, *26*, 717–726.

Clark, A. (2004b). Author's response: Review symposium on *Natural-Born Cyborgs*. *Metascience*, *13*, 169–181.

Clark, A. (2005a). Intrinsic content, active memory, and the extended mind. *Analysis*, *65*, 1–11.

Clark, A. (2005b). Beyond the flesh: Some lessons from a mole cricket. *Artificial Life*, *11*.

Clark, A. (2005c). Word, niche, and super-niche: How language makes minds matter more. *Theoria*, *20*, 255–268.

Clark, A. (2007). Reinventing ourselves: The plasticity of embodiment, sensing, and mind. *Journal of Medicine and Philosophy*, *32*, 263–282.

Clark, A. (2008). *Supersizing the Mind: Embodiment, Action, and Cognitive Extension.* Oxford: Oxford University Press.

Clark, A., and Chalmers, D. (1998). The extended mind. *Analysis, 58,* 7–19. Reprinted as chapter 2 of this volume.

Coleman, J. (1992). *Ancient and Medieval Memories.* Cambridge: Cambridge University Press.

Dartnall, T. (2004). "We have always been . . . cyborgs," review symposium on Clark, *Natural-Born Cyborgs. Metascience, 13,* 139–148.

Dartnall, T. (2005). Does the world leak into the mind? Active externalism, internalism, and epistemology. *Cognitive Science, 29,* 135–143.

Dennett, D. C. (2000). Making tools for thinking. In D. Sperber (ed.), *Metarepresentations: A Multidisciplinary Perspective* (pp. 17–29). Oxford: Oxford University Press.

Donald, M. (1991). *Origins of the Modern Mind.* Cambridge, MA: Harvard University Press.

Donald, M. (2001). *A Mind So Rare: The Evolution of Human Consciousness.* New York: W. W. Norton.

Foss, J. (1992). Introduction to the epistemology of the brain: Indeterminacy, micro-specificity, chaos, and openness. *Topoi, 11,* 45–57.

Garson, J. (1996). Cognition poised at the edge of chaos: A complex alternative to a symbolic mind. *Philosophical Psychology, 9,* 301–322.

Greenblatt, S. (1980). *Renaissance Self-Fashioning.* Chicago: Chicago University Press.

Grush, R. (2003). In defense of some "Cartesian" assumptions concerning the brain and its operation. *Biology and Philosophy, 18,* 53–93.

Haugeland, J. (1998). Mind embodied and embedded. In his *Having Thought: Essays in the Metaphysics of Mind* (pp. 207–237). Cambridge, MA: Harvard University Press.

Haugeland, J. (2002). Andy Clark on cognition and representation. In H. Clapin (ed.), *Philosophy of Mental Representation* (pp. 24–36). Oxford: Oxford University Press.

Hurley, S. (1998). *Consciousness in Action.* Cambridge, MA: Harvard University Press.

Hutchins, E. (1995). *Cognition in the Wild.* Cambridge, MA: MIT Press.

Johnston, J. (2002). A future for autonomous agents: Machinic *Merkwelten* and artificial evolution. *Configurations, 10,* 473–516.

Jones, A. R., and Stallybrass, P. (2000). *Renaissance Clothing and the Materials of Memory.* Cambridge: Cambridge University Press.

Kirsh, D. (2006). Distributed cognition: A methodological note. *Pragmatics and Cognition, 14*, 249–262.

Knappett, C. (2005). *Thinking through Material Culture: An Interdisciplinary Approach.* Philadelphia: University of Pennsylvania Press.

Knappett, C., and Malafouris, L. (eds.) (2008). *Material Agency: Towards a Nonanthropocentric Approach.* Berlin: Springer.

Kwint, M. (1999). Introduction: The physical past. In M. Kwint, C. Breward, and J. Aynsley (eds.), *Material Memories* (pp. 1–16). Oxford: Berg.

Latour, B. (1993). *We Have Never Been Modern.* Cambridge, MA: Harvard University Press.

Latour, B. (1996). Cogito ergo sumus! Or, Psychology swept inside out by the fresh air of the upper deck: Review of Hutchins 1995. *Mind, Culture, and Activity, 3*, 54–63.

Latour, B. (1999). A collective of humans and nonhumans. In *Pandora's Hope: Essays on the Reality of Science Studies* (pp. 174–215). Cambridge, MA: Harvard University Press..

Mackenzie, A. (2004). "We have always been . . . cyborgs," review symposium on Clark, *Natural-Born Cyborgs. Metascience, 13*, 153–163.

McClelland, J. L., and Rumelhart, D. E. (1986). A distributed model of human learning and memory. In J. L. McClelland and D. E. Rumelhart (eds.), *Parallel Distributed Processing: Explorations in the Microstructure of Cognition*, volume 2 (pp. 170–215). Cambridge, MA: MIT Press.

Menary, R. (2006). Attacking the bounds of cognition. *Philosophical Psychology, 19*, 329–344.

Menary, R. (2007). *Cognitive Integration: Mind and Cognition Unbounded.* Basingstoke: Palgrave Macmillan.

Millikan, R. (2001). The language-thought partnership: A bird's eye view. *Language and Communication, 21*, 157–166.

Moè, A., and de Beni, R. (2005). Stressing the efficacy of the loci method: Oral presentation and the subject-generation of the loci pathway with expository passages. *Applied Cognitive Psychology, 19*, 95–106.

Noice, T., and Noice, H. (1997). *The Nature of Expertise in Professional Acting: A Cognitive View.* Mahwah, NJ: Lawrence Erlbaum.

O'Brien, G. (1998). Review symposium: *Being There. Metascience, 7*, 78–83.

Paster, G. K. (2004). *Humoring the Body: Emotions and the Shakespearean Stage.* Chicago: Chicago University Press.

Poirier, P., and Chicoisne, G. (2006). A framework for thinking about distributed cognition. *Pragmatics and Cognition*, *14*, 215–234.

Renfrew, C., Frith, C., and Malafouris, L. (eds.) (2009). *The Sapient Mind: Archaeology meets Neuroscience.* Oxford: Oxford University Press.

Renfrew, C., and Scarre, C. (eds.) (1999). *Cognition and Material Culture: The Archaeology of Symbolic Storage.* Cambridge: MacDonald Institute for Archaeological Research.

Richardson, A. (2004). Studies in literature and cognition: A field map. In A. Richardson and E. Spolsky (eds.), *Cognition, Culture, and Complexity* (pp. 1–30). Aldershot: Ashgate.

Ricoeur, P. (2004). *Memory, History, Forgetting.* Chicago: Chicago University Press.

Rogers, Y. (2006). Distributed cognition and communication. In K. Brown (ed.), *Encyclopedia of Language and Linguistics*, 2nd ed. (pp. 731–733). Amsterdam: Elsevier.

Rogers, Y., Scaife, M., and Rizzo, A. (2005). Interdisciplinarity: An emergent or engineered process? In S. J. Derry, M. A. Gernsbacher, and C. D. Schunn (eds.), *Toward A Cognitive Science of Interdisciplinary Collaboration.* Mahwah, NJ: Lawrence Erlbaum.

Rowlands, M. (1999). *The Body in Mind: Understanding Cognitive Processes.* Cambridge: Cambridge University Press.

Rowlands, M. (2003). *Externalism: Putting Mind and World Back Together Again.* Chesham: Acumen.

Rowlands, M. (2009). Extended cognition and the mark of the cognitive. *Philosophical Psychology*, *22*, 1–19.

Rupert, R. (2004). Challenges to the hypothesis of extended cognition. *Journal of Philosophy*, *101*, 389–428.

Scarry, E. (1988). Donne: "But yet the body is his booke." In E. Scarry (ed.), *Literature and the Body* (pp. 70–105). Baltimore: Johns Hopkins University Press.

Schneewind, J. B. (1997). *The Invention of Autonomy.* Cambridge: Cambridge University Press.

Sperber, D. (1996). *Explaining Culture: A Naturalistic Approach.* Oxford: Blackwell.

Stephenson, N. (1995). *The Diamond Age.* New York: Bantam Spectra.

Suchman, L. (1998). Human/machine reconsidered. *Cognitive Studies*, *5*, 5–13.

Sutton, J. (1998). *Philosophy and Memory Traces: Descartes to Connectionism.* Cambridge: Cambridge University Press.

Sutton, J. (2000). Body, mind, and order: Local memory and the control of mental representations in medieval and Renaissance sciences of self. In G. Freeland and

A. Corones (eds.), *1543 and All That: Word and Image in the Proto-Scientific Revolution* (pp. 117–150). Dordrecht: Kluwer.

Sutton, J. (2002a). Porous memory and the cognitive life of things. In D. Tofts, A. Jonson, and A. Cavallaro (eds.), *Prefiguring Cyberculture: An Intellectual History* (pp. 130–141). Cambridge, MA, and Sydney: MIT Press and Power Publications.

Sutton, J. (2002b). Cognitive conceptions of language and the development of autobiographical memory. *Language and Communication, 22,* 375–390.

Sutton, J. (2004). Representation, reduction, and interdisciplinarity in the sciences of memory. In H. Clapin, P. Staines, and P. Slezak (eds.), *Representation in Mind: New Approaches to Mental Representation* (pp. 187–216). Amsterdam: Elsevier.

Sutton, J. (2006). Distributed cognition: Domains and dimensions. *Pragmatics and Cognition, 14,* 235–247.

Sutton, J. (2007). Spongy brains and material nemories. In M. Floyd-Wilson and G. Sullivan (eds.), *Embodiment and Environment in Early Modern Europe* (pp. 14–34). London: Palgrave.

Sutton, J. (2008). Material agency, skills, and history: Distributed cognition and the archaeology of memory. In L. Malafouris and C. Knappett (eds.), *Material Agency: Towards a Non-anthropocentric Approach* (pp. 37–55). Berlin: Springer.

Sutton, J. (2009). Remembering. In P. Robbins and M. Aydede (eds.), *The Cambridge Handbook of Situated Cognition* (pp. 217–235). Cambridge: Cambridge University Press.

Tollefsen, D. P. (2006). From extended mind to collective mind. *Cognitive Systems Research, 7,* 140–150.

Tooby, J., and Cosmides, L. (1992). The psychological foundations of culture. In J. H. Barkow, L. Cosmides, and J. Tooby (eds.), *The Adapted Mind* (pp. 19–136). Oxford: Oxford University Press.

Tribble, E. (2005). Distributing cognition in the globe. *Shakespeare Quarterly, 56,* 135–155.

Tribble, E. (2006). "The dark backward and abysm of time": *The Tempest* and memory. *College Literature, 33,* 151–168.

von Eckardt, B. (2001). Multidisciplinarity and cognitive science. *Cognitive Science, 21,* 453–470.

Wegner, D. M. (1987). Transactive memory: A contemporary analysis of group mind. In B. Mullen and G. R. Goethals (eds.), *Theories of Group Behavior* (pp. 185–208). New York: Springer-Verlag.

Wegner, D. M., Erber, R., and Raymond, P. (1991). Transactive memory in close relationships. *Journal of Personality and Social Psychology, 61,* 923–929.

Weiskopf, Daniel A. (2008). Patrolling the mind's boundaries. *Erkenntnis, 68*(2), 265–276.

Wheeler, M. (2004). Is language the ultimate artefact? *Language Sciences, 26,* 693–715.

Wheeler, M., and Clark, A. (2008). Culture, embodiment, and genes: Unravelling the triple helix. *Philosophical Transactions of the Royal Society Series B, 363,* 3563–3575

Wilson, R. A. (2004). *Boundaries of the Mind: The Individual in the Fragile Sciences—Cognition.* Cambridge: Cambridge University Press.

Wilson, R. A. (2005). Collective memory, group minds, and the extended mind thesis. *Cognitive Processing, 6,* 227–236.

Wilson, R. A., and Clark, A. (2009). How to situate cognition: Letting nature take its course. In P. Robbins and M. Aydede (eds.), *The Cambridge Handbook of Situated Cognition.* Cambridge: Cambridge University Press.

Yates, F. (1966). *The Art of Memory.* London: Routledge and Kegan Paul.

10 Cognitive Integration and the Extended Mind

Richard Menary

1 Introduction: First-Wave Extended Mind

The first wave of arguments[1] for the extended mind focuses on questions of functional parity between internal and external processes and especially the functional role of causal coupling between internal vehicles and external vehicles. The arguments and examples of Clark and Chalmers (1998, reprinted in this volume) have come under pressure from internalist critics such as Adams and Aizawa (2001, this volume) and Rupert (2004, this volume), who have targeted the arguments from functional parity and causal coupling.

However, there is also a second wave of arguments for the extended mind, which focuses on questions of the complementarity of internal and external vehicles (Sutton this volume) and their consequent integration into a cognitive whole (Menary 2007, this chapter). This second wave of arguments also takes a more enactive approach to cognition, seeing it as constituted by our bodily activities in the world in conjunction with neural processes and vehicles (Rowlands 1999, this volume; Wilson 2004, this volume).

I will call the first-wave arguments *extended-mind-style* arguments. Allied to extended-mind-style arguments are those of distributed and embodied cognition (Hutchins 1995; Gallagher 2005), with their emphasis on social situation and embodiment. When we bring together the arguments and evidence in support of extended, distributed, and embodied cognition we form the view that cognizers are embodied and located in a situation which has both physical and social aspects, and that some bodily interactions with the environment constitute cognitive processing.

Extended-mind-style arguments present cases of extended cognition as involving a tight causal interaction between internal neural processes and external environmental processes. This two-way causal interaction is often called *causal coupling* or *continuous reciprocal coupling*.[2] A different way of arguing for extended cognition has been proposed by Rowlands (1999), in terms of what he calls the *manipulation thesis*:

Cognitive processes are not located exclusively in the skin of cognising organisms because such processes are, in part, made up of physical or bodily *manipulation* of structures in the environments of such organisms. (Rowlands 1999, p. 23)

Hence, extended-mind-style arguments aim at establishing that some cognition is, in part, externally located. However, simply to think of this emerging view of cognition as externalist is misleading. This is because the payoff from extended-mind-style arguments is the *integration* of the bodily "internal" and "external" aspects of cognition into a whole. This is to think of a cognitive process as hybrid, straddling both brain and bodily manipulation of environmental vehicles. There is, of course, a continuous looping causal interaction between neural processes and bodily manipulations of external vehicles; but the focus shifts from this to the nature of the bodily manipulations themselves and how they are integrated with neural processes such that they form a hybrid cognitive process.

Therefore, I will refer to the second wave of arguments as *cognitive-integration-style arguments* (or *integration-style arguments* for short), because they have the aim of beginning the job of explaining how the bodily internal and external aspects of cognition are integrated into a whole, where this integration is to be understood in terms of the manipulation of environmental vehicles (Wilson 2004, this volume; Sutton, this volume; Menary 2007).

My main line of argument is to show that the upshot of extended-mind-style arguments leads us to understand cognition (and the mind) as hybrid—involving both internal and external processes—and integration-style arguments show us how the bodily internal and external processes coordinate with one another in the completion of cognitive tasks. A second, crucial role of integration-style arguments is to show that we cannot make good on the manipulation thesis without understanding the normativity of the bodily manipulations of external vehicles of cognition.

Therefore, the primary motivation for cognitive integration is not that we are causally coupled to external vehicles; nor is the primary motivation the view that the mind is first in the head and then gets extended out into the world (into the vehicles themselves). Adams and Aizawa's caricature of the extended mind is, therefore, an attack on a straw man (Adams and Aizawa 2001, this volume). The primary motivation for cognitive integration is the brute fact of our embodiment, especially our bodily manipulation of environmental vehicles. Our primary engagements with the world are embodied, and, unsurprisingly, our initial cognitive engagements with the world are embodied engagements; they are primarily sensorimotor engagements (see Menary 2007, chapter 4). At least some of our mature cognition retains the structure of these embodied engagements in the form of manipulations of the environment; hence some cognitive processes are hybrid processes, that is, they comprise neural processes and vehicles and bodily processes on environmental vehicles.

This is what I take extended cognition/cognitive integration to be about: it is the attempt to understand the nature of the integration between these elements of a hybrid process. One way to do so, suggested in the introduction to this volume, is to think of hybrid cognitive processes as enacted skills or capacities for manipulating the environment. However, we should not forget that the embodied cognizer is embedded in a physical and social environment, and that environment contains norms which determine the content of environmental vehicles and how we manipulate them. In the rest of this chapter I shall outline the central features of cognitive integration.

2   What Is Cognitive Integration?

Integrationists argue that cognition is not bounded by the brain. Internalist critics of the extended mind, such as Adams and Aizawa and Rupert, believe that cognition has a natural boundary: it is contained in the brain. They argue that if you want to study cognition and the mind, then you need to study the cognitive and mental phenomena implemented in the brain, and only those phenomena implemented in the brain can count as members of a cognitive or mental kind. The critics assume that the "bounded by the brain" view is quite intuitive; the mind is "in the head"— where else would it be?

Perhaps if we begin by defining, or at least sketching, the nature of cognitive phenomena themselves we will be able to determine whether there is more to the brain-bound view than a philosophically "intuitive" position. Most philosophers and cognitive scientists take cognition to be a clump of mental acts or processes that come under broad headings such as: remembering, perceiving, learning, and reasoning. Identifying what makes a process cognitive, as opposed to strictly physiological, is more difficult. Take the humble neuron: everyone thinks that neural nets in the hippocampus are involved in the cognitive processes responsible for remembering; however, presumably no one thinks that the migration of sodium and potassium ions along the nerve fiber of a neuron is responsible for remembering. Yet, of course, it is the depolarization and polarization of millions of neurons in the hippocampus that is supposed to implement the cognitive process of remembering. When we look at the process itself, it doesn't look cognitive at all, certainly not from any position we might call "intuitive."

In their continuing critique of the extended mind, Adams and Aizawa (2001, this volume), stipulate that processes that exhibit the mark of the cognitive are identified as those that involve representations with non-derived (intrinsic) content. However, it is not only notoriously difficult to specify just what intrinsic content is supposed to be (Hutto 1999; Dennett 1990; Mendola 2003), but also the definition looks to be unduly restrictive (Menary 2006). It makes even brain-bound processes noncognitive; where, for example, is the intrinsic content in the physiological processes taking place in the neuron?

In general, there is no real agreement in the cognitive science community on a definition of what a cognitive process is, nor of what the vehicles of cognition are. For example, classical computationalists take the vehicles of cognition to be symbols that have formal, or syntactic, properties in virtue of which they are processed (Fodor and Pylyshyn 1988). Connectionists deny that the vehicles of cognition are symbols in the classical sense; instead they are patterns of activation distributed across nodes in a network. Connectionists understand cognitive processes to be algorithms for the spread of activation across the network (Smolensky 1995a,b). It is quite natural to be pluralistic about cognitive processes and vehicles; as such, there is no single genuine "cognitive kind." The classical–connectionist debate demonstrates that there is a plurality of types of manipulations and vehicles employed by empirical theories of cognition. However, what we do have is a sense of the cognitive task as defined by Rowlands (2003, p. 161):

it does seem fairly clear that the notion of a cognitive process is defined, in part, in terms of the notion of a cognitive task. A cognitive process is one that plays a fairly central role in allowing a subject to accomplish a cognitive task.

Quite generally this amounts to perceiving the world, remembering things about the world, and employing things remembered in making inferences, problem solving, and the like (Rowlands 2003).[3] The task-based definition of a cognitive process allows cognitive scientists to fill in the details of what cognitive processes are as they are empirically discovered. It does not begin with an a priori definition of cognitive process that all empirical theories must conform to.

What general reasons do integrationists have for thinking that cognitive internalism is wrong to suppose that all cognitive processes, vehicles, and systems supervene exclusively on the brain? Humans spend a lot of time and effort creating linguistic and representational surrounds and then maintaining and manipulating them. The exercising of the capacities to create external linguistic and representational vehicles is, of course, fleeting, although the long-standing disposition is not (see the introduction to this volume). We often, for example, write out mathematical problems, rather than completing them "in the head." Often humans directly manipulate the environment to complete cognitive tasks. For example, expert players of the game Tetris prefer to rotate the shapes on the screen using buttons, rather than rotating images of them "in the head." If cognition is bounded by the brain, why do we not complete all these cognitive tasks, and many others like them, "in the head"?

Cognitive integration provides an answer to this question. Its cash value is that the coordination of bodily processes of the organism with salient features of the environment, often created or maintained by the organism, allows it to perform cognitive functions that it otherwise would be unable to; or it allows it to perform functions in a way that is distinctively different and is an improvement on how the organism performs those functions via neural processes alone. These are some of the motivations for adopting the integrationist position on cognition.

Developing the integrationist position begins with the fact of our embodiment. Embodied approaches to the mind and cognition are supposed to reveal to us something profound about the *embodiedness* of our minds, that we ought to understand the mind as *shaped* by the body. However, there seems to be a bifurcation of approach in the embodied mind community. There is on the one hand the phenomenologically inspired approach of Gallagher (2005), with a detailed account of how bodily activity in the environment constrains what we perceive and of what we are consciously aware. This approach takes seriously the detailed description of embodiment with regard to cognitive and mental capacities such as perception and social cognition. Then there is the distributed/extended approach to cognition and mind of the likes of Hutchins (1995), Clark (1997), and Rowlands (1999), who begin with the assumption that cognition is embodied but then concentrate on the ways in which we interact, bodily, with the environment. They take seriously detailed descriptions of manipulations of external representational vehicles such as diagrams, mathematical notations, or written sentences with regard to mental and cognitive capacities such as memory and belief. Theories of extended cognition do not give a detailed account of the way in which the body shapes cognition in these cases; rather they tend to focus on how external vehicles (artifacts, representations) shape and transform cognitive capacities.

The difference in approach does not constitute a profound difference. Rather, we are approaching the same phenomenon from different directions. Therefore, we need to reconceive the mind on both bodily and environmental grounds. For example, integrationists take the manipulation of external vehicles to be a prerequisite for higher cognition and embodied engagement to be a precondition for these manipulative abilities. Therefore, it would be a mistake not only to disengage the body from its environment, but also to ignore the contribution of external representational systems to our cognitive capacities. A straightforward way of understanding the position of cognitive integration is in terms of bodily engagement with vehicles in the extrabodily environment, in such a way that they are integrated into a whole.

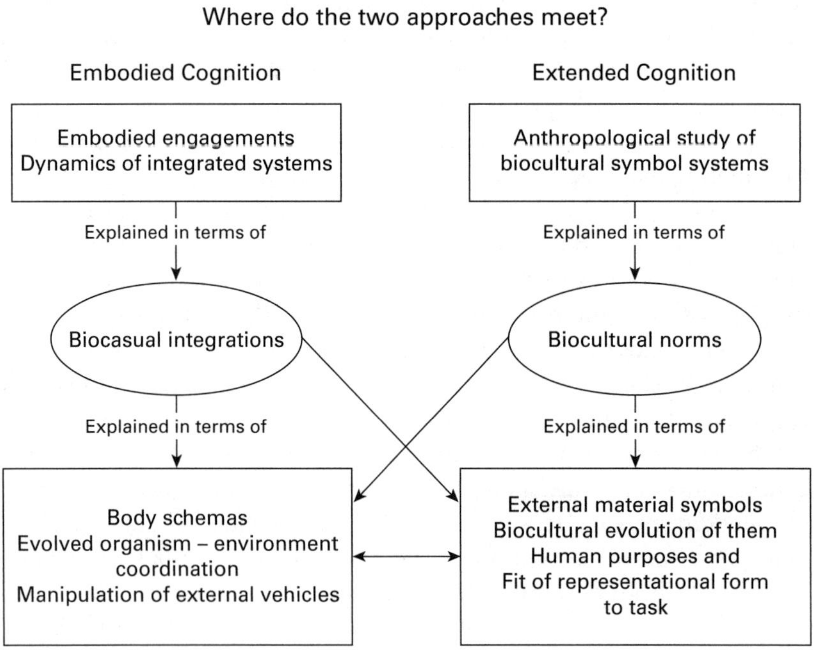

Where do the two approaches meet?

Figure 10.1

The study of biocultural representational systems is reliant on a clear understanding of those systems as structured by biocausal coordinations/integrations and on an understanding that the functioning of the system requires the stability and availability of extrabodily vehicles and the bodily manipulation of those vehicles. This is certainly true, but these explanatory projects lack the resources to fully explain how and why we manipulate extrabodily vehicles in the way that we do. To do this satisfactorily we need to place the dynamics of the system in a wider cultural and normative setting.

Our abilities to manipulate the extrabodily environment are normative and are largely dependent on our learning and training histories. Hence, explanations of the dynamics of integrated cognitive systems will only be one, important, explanatory factor among others.

There are three complementary ways in which we can understand integration:

1. *Biocausal coordinations/integrations*: The dynamical approach analyzes the reciprocal coupling between systems that are part of a larger system. They have causal influence over each other for as long as they are coupled. This is a symmetrical relation; the two systems are mutually constraining of each other's behavior.

2. *Embodied engagements*: The body is integrated with the environment through its body schemas, which are unconscious sensorimotor programs for action. These programs often integrate with the environment in two ways, first by training (or evolutionary adaptation) and second by norms governing practices such as driving, playing a sport such as tennis, or writing, and so on.

3. *The manipulation thesis*: Humans manipulate their local environment with their bodies. They might directly manipulate the physical structure of the environment, and they might use tools to do this. They create artifacts, such as tools and representational vehicles. Humans very often create and manipulate external representational vehicles to complete a cognitive task. In doing so they are carrying out a cognitive practice which is governed by its own norms—which I call *cognitive norms*.

Unlike first-wave arguments for the extended mind, cognitive integration does not rely on the parity principle; the motivation is found in the brute fact of our embodiedness and our bodily manipulation of environmental vehicles. The parity principle is apt to confuse and mislead (see the introduction to this volume) as a motivation for the extended mind.

I elaborate on this in the next section. In the final two sections, I outline and explain the manipulation thesis and cognitive practices.

3   Cognitive Integration and the Parity Principle

As I explained in the introduction to this volume, external processes/ vehicles do not get to have cognitive status conferred on them because they are relevantly *similar* to (supposedly) uncontroversial cases of cognitive processes and vehicles that are internal (see also Sutton this volume). Nor do they get to be relevantly similar because external processes/vehicles are causally coupled to internal processes/vehicles. Parity will not necessarily come from the direct similarity of the external with the internal. Internal process X may have properties a, b, c, and external process Y may have properties d, e, and f. Internalists latch on to these differences and use them to deny parity and, therefore, deny that there are any external cognitive processes and vehicles.[4]

This version of the parity principle that most critics assume is endorsed by the extended mind is fatally flawed, because it assumes the very position it is meant to displace. Extended-mind-style arguments based on the parity principle have encouraged critics to think in terms of an internal cognitive system that is extended outward into the world. Hence, on one interpretation, it implicitly endorses a picture of a discrete cognitive agent some of whose cognitive processes get extended out into the world. It also argues for the cognitive role of the environment by claiming that such roles are functionally similar to (or the same as) the functions of neural processes.[5] The main question of the extended mind would then be: "How do processes in the world get to function like processes in the brain?"

A major difference between extended-mind-style arguments and cognitive integration is that the latter does not depend on the parity principle. It cannot be misinterpreted as claiming that cognition is extended from inside the head out into the world, or that external processes are cognitive because they are similar (weak version) or isomorphic (strong version) to internal processes. Cognitive integration differs from first-wave extended-mind-style arguments because it takes the manipulation thesis to be its starting point, not the parity principle.

The parity-based formulation of the extended mind is a functionalist thesis; this is easily illustrated by the Otto example. Clark and Chalmers say that in the case of Otto and Inga there is a sufficient *functional similarity* between Otto's use of his notebook and Inga's recall from biological memory that we are inclined to say that Otto has beliefs. Otto's retrieval of information about the location of MoMA causes him to go to 53rd street, and the pattern of activation in a part of Inga's brain causes her to go to 53rd street. Otto's information retrieval and Inga's neural activations play the *same kind* of causal role in producing actions. As such, the physical implementation of the causal role is irrelevant to the *functional* level of description—Otto's deployment of his notebook and Inga's pattern of activation in her brain. Otto receives input from the environment: there is an exhibition on at the MoMA; he then retrieves the location of MoMA from his extended memory system, which causes him, as behavioral output, to go to 53rd street.

Only at the grossest level of functional description can this be said to be true. Otto and his notebook do not really function in the same kind of way that Inga does when she has immediate recall from biological memory. There are genuine and important differences in the way that memories are stored internally and externally, and these differences matter to how the memories are processed. John Sutton has pointed out that biological memories stored in neural networks are open to effects such as blending and interference (see Sutton, this volume). The vehicles in Otto's notebook, by contrast, are static and do no work in their dispositional form (Sutton, this volume).

This is, of course, no problem for cognitive integration, which does not work from the assumption that internal and external vehicles and processes need to be functionally equivalent. They may function in very different ways, as Sutton points out. However, this is the point: it is because the external vehicles provide a different kind of functionality and because they can coordinate with internal processes that they are integral parts of our cognitive systems. Again, putting this complementary integration in the wider context of cognitive tasks and practices highlights the cognitive roles that external vehicles can play; but this is not a matter of functional similarity. It is in the details of the integration between neural processes and vehicles and environmental vehicles via bodily manipulations that we will understand the hybrid nature of cognition. I spend the rest of this chapter outlining what the integrationist thinks about this.

4   The Manipulation Thesis

Extended-mind-style arguments recognize the importance of the manipulation thesis:

In all these cases the individual brain performs some operations, while others are delegated to manipulations of external media. Had our brains been different, this distribution of tasks would doubtless have varied. (Clark and Chalmers, this volume, p. 28)

Clark (1997, 2001, this volume, chaps. 3, 5) explains the manipulation thesis by causal interaction between organism and environment, often referred to as causal coupling. Rowlands (1999, 2003) explains the manipulation thesis in terms of the bodily manipulation of external vehicles, or information-bearing structures. There is a clearer version of the parity principle at work here which also deals with Adams and Aizawa's admonition that the extended mind does not provide a clear mark of the cognitive. The mark of the cognitive is that cognitive processes involve the manipulation of information-bearing vehicles in completing a cognitive task. Hybrid cognitive processes involve the integration of neural manipulations of vehicles and bodily manipulations of environmental vehicles:

there seems to be no great theoretical divide between manipulating *internal* information bearing structures and manipulating *external* information bearing structures to make available to oneself, or to one's cognitive operations, the information that results. To claim that only the former constitutes genuine information processing seems little more than an internalist prejudice. (Rowlands 2006, p. 39)

There is a great variety of external vehicles that are talked about in the literature. Sometimes external vehicles are talked of as affordances (Hurley 1998; Rowlands 1999), and sometimes as external representations such as written sentences, diagrams, and other notations (Clark and Chalmers 1998, this volume).

In the extended mind, Clark and Chalmers take external vehicles to play the role of cognitive vehicles, and they take the external manipulations of those vehicles to play the role of cognitive processes. When Otto accesses his notebook to recall the address of the Museum of Modern Art, he is manipulating an external vehicle as part of his act of remembering where the museum is located.

The external vehicles in Otto's notebook are integrated with internal vehicles and are thereby constituents of the same cognitive process. We can see this integration at work in the coordination of internal manipulations and external manipulations, which allows the cognitive agent to complete the cognitive task. In this case the cognitive agent, Otto, manipulates the vehicles in his notebook to retrieve the desired information concerning the location of MoMA. Therefore, the cognitive integrationist claims that for any cognitive system, some cognitive vehicles and cognitive processes are externally located. Nevertheless, the overall cognitive system is integrated because "internal" and "external" coordinate with one another in completing cognitive tasks. I cannot give a full account here of how these coordinations are established.[6] However, I will give an outline in the next section of how we can think of them in the case of the manipulation of external representational vehicles.

Now we need to give an account of the different kinds of manipulations of external vehicles. We can group bodily manipulations into four general classes:

• *Biological coupling*: such as extended phenotypes (Dawkins 1982), animate vision (Ballard 1991), and sensory motor contingencies (O'Regan and Noë 2001).

• *Epistemic actions*: using the environment as its own representation, obviating the need for internal representations—as in Tetris (Kirsh and Maglio 1994).

• *Self-correcting actions*: The use of language and external props to direct and structure practical actions in completing tasks.

• *Cognitive practices*: the manipulation of external representational and notational systems according to certain normative practices—as in mathematics (Vygotsky 1978; Karmiloff-Smith 1992; Menary 2007).

Examples of biological coupling run from cases such as phonotaxis in crickets (Webb 1994) and bee dances (Millikan 1993, 2004) to sensorimotor contingencies (O'Regan and Noë 2001) and animate vision (Ballard 1991).

Kirsh and Maglio (1994) have dubbed the second class of manipulations epistemic actions. An epistemic action involves directly manipulating the environment to bring about a better state in a problem-solving/planning task, rather than constructing an internal representation and manipulating that.

An example of a self-correcting action is the role of spoken language in structuring activity, such as reminding oneself of the order in which one must conduct a sequence of actions. In these kinds of cases we use speech as a corrective tool.

The classic example of a cognitive practice is Rumelhart and McClelland's (1986) example of using pen and paper to complete a mathematical algorithm. Performing long multiplication involves mastery over a notational system, which involves cognitive norms for manipulating those notations when completing cognitive tasks.

In the final section I look in more detail at the nature of cognitive practices.

5 Cognitive Practices

I shall call manipulations of an external representation to complete a cognitive task a *cognitive practice*. We are able to manipulate external vehicles because we gain manipulative abilities that are governed by cognitive norms. These are norms that govern manipulations of external representations, which aim at completing cognitive tasks. This is obvious given that external vehicles, such as written language and mathematical symbols, are tokens of representational systems. Such systems have their own norms governing manipulations of token representational vehicles. Hence, they are cognitive norms, as opposed to moral or social norms. Otto's cognitive practice involves writing things in his notebook and then accessing them later. Otto's practice falls under the definition of a cognitive process given in the previous section—that cognition is equivalent to the manipulation of information bearing structures.

Therefore, manipulations of internal and external vehicles are causally integrated, but we should place this within a wider cultural and normative context. This is what is missing from the first wave of extended-mind-style arguments, which fall prey to some of the internalist worries about parity I outlined above.

However, cognitive integration does benefit from the central insight of the extended mind hypothesis—some cognitive vehicles are bodily external, and manipulations of these vehicles are part of the overall cognitive process, which includes manipulations of bodily internal vehicles.

If we focus on manipulations of classical representations that are external, such as mathematical symbols, we can see the importance of these two points. Classical representations are best understood as representational schemes that can be physically embodied, on paper or on a computer monitor, for example. What extended-mind-style arguments have not explained, and what their claims of causal coupling do not show, is how we are able to manipulate a variety of notational and representational types. There is a great variety of representational systems,[7] which mirrors the great variety of tasks to which we put them. Examples of such tasks include: solving problems, making inferences, planning, working out answers to questions, and so on (these are cognitive tasks).

A manipulation of an external representation is normative, in the sense that we learn or acquire a practice that is an established method of manipulating representations to produce an end. For example, we write down the intermediate stages in problem solving, which can function as part of the working memory space, making information available for further manipulation. Therefore, we might directly manipulate the world as part of the problem-solving process, rather than only manipulating internal representations. Plans are often written down and then transformed, updated, and shared. Lists and diaries allow us to retrieve information that requires long-term storage and is easily and conveniently accessible. The representational properties of maps enable easy and shared navigation, allowing for the kind of detailed representations and orientations that internal representations alone cannot provide.

In each case, there is a cognitive task that must be completed and the cognitive practice allows us to complete the task by manipulating the representation. The implementation of a cognitive practice depends on cognitive norms that guide that practice. So, for example, there are:

1. *Purposive norms*: The activity is engaged in for a purpose, or end.
2. *Corrective norms*: These are norms for using representations to correct activity in pursuit of an end.
3. *Manipulative norms*: These are norms for manipulating inscriptions of a representational system.
4. *Interpretative norms*: These are norms for interpreting inscriptions of a representational system as having some wider significance, not just within the representational system itself but also with regard to the wider world and interests of others.

Manipulations of representations are embedded in a practice, which has a normative, as well as a physical/causal dimension, such as the practice of manipulating mathematical notations. The practice of manipulating a representation is normative because we learn how to manipulate the representations correctly and because of the cognitive purpose of the practice. The purpose is to achieve a particular kind of goal, such as solving a problem, planning, or making inferences, which I have been calling the cognitive task. It follows that we will need an account of how we learn cognitive practices.

This will, in part, involve the acquisition of capacities to manipulate representations and thereby transform our cognitive abilities. However, acquiring these capacities should be understood in the context of the cognitive practices required to complete cognitive tasks. As such, the practice of manipulating representations, a cognitive practice, is essentially the embodying of norms in an activity.

We have already seen that writing is such an activity; therefore, I shall finish this section by giving an analysis of writing as a cognitive practice. The crucial elements of writing, or typing, are the ability to manipulate tools to create external vehicles, words, sentences, and paragraphs. The pen and paper or the CPU, keyboard, and monitor are not themselves cognitive (nor are the sodium ions traversing nerve fibers in the brain), but the creation and manipulation of the external vehicles and the coordination of internal and external vehicles is.

For example, my reading and rereading what I have written gives me new ideas about what I should write next. Though it is true that tools such as keyboards and pens enable me to write, it is manipulating the written vehicles themselves that partly constitutes my cognitive processes. The sentences are, of course, what can be rewritten, erased, moved to another paragraph, and so on. It is, moreover, precisely these kinds of manipulations that are not easily, if ever, achieved in the head. Therefore, writing as an active and creative process is enabled by tools such as pen and paper or word processors, but it is the bodily manipulation of the external vehicles themselves that is where the cognitive work gets done.

Once written, the vehicles are then available for further manipulations such as restructuring, revising, and redrafting. Manipulating written vehicles is a kind of problem solving where a particular cognitive task must be completed: for example, "how do I make this piece of writing clearer?" Completing these kinds of goals without external media would be made more difficult by their absence. Without them, behavioral competence will drop and the completion of the cognitive task be made exasperatingly difficult. Hence, cognitive integrationists are inclined to think that those external manipulations play an important enabling role in the processing of the task, one different from the enabling role of tools.

What kinds of processes do external manipulations afford that purely internal manipulations will not? If, for example, I tried to compose an essay in my head, the likelihood of retaining much of the argument and structure would become very limited. Making revisions and corrections would be almost impossible. Stable and enduring external written sentences allow for manipulations, transformations, reorderings, comparisons, and deletions of text that are not available to neural processes. This is the upshot of second-wave cognitive-integration-style arguments: bodily manipulations of external vehicles are different from, but complementary to, internal processes (Sutton, this volume). The coordination of internal and external processes in one extended dynamic process enables the completion of complex cognitive tasks such as composition.

6 Conclusion

Cognitive integration takes the first wave of extended mind arguments to establish that cognition is hybrid. However, it is not motivated by the parity principle, but rather takes embodied engagement with the world as its starting point. The manipulation thesis provides a further motivation and a definition of integrated cognition. It is then the job of the integrationist to provide a taxonomy of the different kinds of manipulation and to provide empirical examples of them (see the chapters in this volume by Clark, Wilson, Sutton, Hurley, Cowley, and Spurrett, for examples). The manipulations must also be understood in terms of cognitive norms as well as causal explanations of the manipulation of external vehicles. This explanatory project is very different from the straw man version of the extended mind criticized by Adams and Aizawa in this volume.

Notes

1. I follow John Sutton's distinction between first- and second-wave arguments for the extended mind (Sutton, this volume).

2. See, e.g., Clark and Chalmers 1998, this volume; Hurley 1998, this volume.

3. A general definition of a cognitive task can easily end up being unhelpfully vacuous. If we define the cognitive task as any task for the completion of which cognition is required, then almost every task will be a cognitive one. I think it is more helpful if we think of cognitive tasks as involving the exercise of particular cognitive capacities such as remembering a date, solving a problem, learning to do something, and so on. These are tasks where the exercising of cognitive capacities is directly tied to their successful completion.

4. See Adams and Aizawa's chapter in this volume.

5. See Wheeler's chapter in this volume.

6. I can point the reader in the direction of Menary 2007, where over chapters 4 through 7 I outline just how we are to think of the coordination of internal and external vehicles for completing cognitive tasks across a range of cases, from the biological to the cultural.

7. I take all classical notations to be representational. Hence, when I speak of a notation it should be taken to be a representation.

References

Adams, F., and Aizawa, K. (2001). The bounds of cognition. *Philosophical Psychology*, *14*, 43–64.

Ballard, D. (1991). Animate vision. *Artificial Intelligence, 48*, 57–86.

Clark, A. (1997). *Being There: Philosophy, Cognitive Science, and Parallel Distributed Processing*. Cambridge, MA: MIT Press.

Clark, A., and Chalmers, D. (1998). The extended mind. *Analysis, 58*, 7–19. Reprinted as chapter 2 of this volume.

Dawkins, R. (1982). *The Extended Phenotype*. Oxford: Oxford University Press.

Fodor, J., and Pylyshyn, Z. (1988). Connectionism and cognitive architecture. *Cognition, 28*(1–2), 3–71.

Gallagher, S. (2005). *How the Body Shapes the Mind*. Oxford: Oxford University Press.

Hurley, S. (1998). *Consciousness in Action*. Cambridge, MA: Harvard Press.

Hutchins, E. (1995). *Cognition in the Wild*. Cambridge, MA: MIT Press.

Hutto, D. (1999). *The Presence of Mind*. Amsterdam: John Benjamins.

Karmiloff-Smith, A. (1992). *Beyond Modularity: A Developmental Perspective on Cognitive Science*. Cambridge, MA: MIT Press.

Kirsh, D., and Maglio, P. (1994). On distinguishing epistemic from pragmatic actions. *Cognitive Science, 18*, 513–549.

Menary, R. (2006). Attacking the bounds of cognition. *Philosophical Psychology, 19*(3), 329–344.

Menary, R. (2007). *Cognitive Integration: Mind and Cognition Unbounded*. Basingstoke: Palgrave Macmillan.

Mendola, J. (2003). A Dilemma for Asymmetric Dependence. *Noûs, 37*(2), 232–257.

Millikan, R. (1993). *White Queen Psychology and Other Essays for Alice*. Cambridge, MA: MIT Press.

Millikan, R. (2004). *The Varieties of Meaning: The Jean-Nicod Lectures*. Cambridge, MA: MIT Press.

O'Regan, J. K., and Noë, A. (2001). A sensorimotor account of vision and visual consciousness. *Behavioral and Brain Sciences, 24*, 939–1031.

Rowlands, M. (1999). *The Body in Mind: Understanding Cognitive Processes*. Cambridge: Cambridge University Press.

Rowlands, M. (2003). *Externalism: Putting Mind and World Together Again*. Chesham: Acumen.

Rowlands, M. (2006). *Body Language: Representation in Action*. Cambridge, MA: MIT Press.

Rumelhart, D., Smolensky, P., Hinton, G. E. (1986). Schemata and sequential thought processes in PDP models. Chap. 14 in J. McClelland, D. Rumelhart, and the PDP Research Group, *Parallel Distributed Processing: Explorations in the Microstructure of Cognition*, vol. 2 (pp. 7–58). Cambridge, MA: MIT Press.

Rupert, R. (2004). Challenges to the hypothesis of extended cognition. *Journal of Philosophy, 101*, 389–428.

Smolensky, P. (1995a). On the proper treatment of connectionism. In C. Macdonald and G. Macdonald (eds.), *Connectionism: Debates on Psychological Explanation* (pp. 28–89). Oxford: Blackwell.

Smolensky, P. (1995b). Constituent structure and explanation in an integrated connectionist/symbolic cognitive architecture. In C. Macdonald and G. Macdonald (eds.), *Connectionism: Debates on Psychological Explanation* (pp. 223–290). Oxford: Blackwell.

Vygotsky, L. (1978). *Mind in Society*. Cambridge, MA: Harvard University Press.

Webb, B. (1994). Robotic Experiments in Cricket Phonotaxis. In David Cliff, Philip Husbands, Jean-Arcady Meyer, and Stewart W. Wilson (eds.), *From Animals to Animats 3: Proceedings of the Third International Conference on the Simulation of Adaptive Behavior* (pp. 45–54). Cambridge, MA: MIT Press.

Wilson, R. A. (2004). *Boundaries of the Mind: The Individual in the Fragile Sciences—Cognition*. Cambridge: Cambridge University Press.

11   In Defense of Extended Functionalism

Michael Wheeler

1   The Dynamic Duo

According to the extended cognition hypothesis (henceforth ExC), there are conditions under which thinking and thoughts (or more precisely, the material vehicles that realize thinking and thoughts) are spatially distributed over brain, body, and world, in such a way that the external (beyond-the-skin) factors concerned are rightly accorded fully paid-up cognitive status.[1] According to functionalism in the philosophy of mind, "what makes something a mental state of a particular type does not depend on its internal constitution, but rather on the way it functions, or the role it plays, in the system of which it is a part" (Levin 2008). The respective fates of these two positions may not be independent of each other. The claim that ExC is in some way a form of, dependent on, entailed by, or at least commonly played out in terms of functionalism is now pretty much part of the received view of things (see, e.g., Adams and Aizawa 2008; Clark and Chalmers 1998 [reprinted in this volume]; Clark 2005, 2008a,b, this volume, chaps. 3, 5; Menary 2007; Rupert 2004; Sprevak forthcoming; Wheeler forthcoming). Thus ExC might be mandated by the existence of functionally specified cognitive systems whose boundaries are located partly outside the skin. This is the position that Andy Clark has recently dubbed *extended functionalism* (Clark 2008a,b; see also Wheeler forthcoming).

Against this background, the present chapter has two main goals. The first (sections 2 and 3) is to clarify and amplify the relationship between ExC and functionalism, and thereby to plot the path to extended functionalism. The second (sections 4, 5, and 7) is to defend extended functionalism against three potentially damaging critical assaults. Section 6 is an interlude that highlights a key aspect of the extended functionalist picture. The chapter ends (section 8) with a brief (and I mean brief) remark on extended functionalism and phenomenal consciousness.

2   The Extended Cognition Hypothesis

ExC is a view about the whereabouts of thinking and thoughts that is distinct not only from the position adopted by orthodox (classical or connectionist) cognitive science, but also from the position adopted by any merely embodied–embedded account of mind. That is why my opening characterization of ExC included the qualification that the target phenomena must be distributed over brain, body, and world, *in such a way* that the external (beyond-the-skin) factors concerned are themselves rightly accorded fully paid-up cognitive status. In other words, as Adams and Aizawa (e.g., 2008, this volume) have repeatedly emphasized, it is not sufficient for genuine cognitive extension that thinking be spatially distributed over brain, body, and world solely in the weak sense that applies when some instance of intelligent behavior is discovered to be causally dependent, perhaps in previously unexpected ways, on the bodily exploitation of certain external props or scaffolds. We may even introduce the additional feature that the cognitive task in question could not have been achieved by brains like ours without the causal contribution of the external elements in question. Still the shortfall remains. Bare causal dependence of mentality on external factors—even when that causal dependence is of the "necessary" kind just highlighted—is simply not enough for genuine cognitive extension. What is needed is the *constitutive* dependence of mentality on external factors, the sort of dependence indicated by talk of the beyond-the-skin factors themselves rightly being accorded fully paid-up cognitive status. Only this latter kind of distribution—we might call it *ontological distribution*—will do.

In order to illustrate this crucial point, we can adapt an analysis due originally to Rumelhart et al. (1986) that has since become something of a stock example in the embodied–embedded–extended mind literature. Most of us solve difficult multiplication problems using pen and paper.[2] The pen-and-paper resource is a beyond-the-skin factor that helps to transform a difficult cognitive problem into a set of simpler ones and acts as a temporary store for the results of intermediate calculations. For orthodox cognitive scientists *and for supporters of the merely embodied–embedded view of mind*, the pen-and-paper system is to be conceived as a noncognitive environmental prop. It is an external tool that aids certain cognitive processes via embodied interaction, but is not itself a proper part of those processes.

Of course, orthodox cognitive scientists and embodied–embedded theorists differ on how best to characterize the interactive arrangement of skin-side cognitive processes and external prop. In particular, the embodied–embedded theorist is likely to count the bodily activity involved as itself a cognitive process, as opposed to a mere output of neurally located cognition, and to trace rather less of the source of the manifest complexity of the observed behavior to the brain, and rather more to the structured embodied interactions with the external pen-and-paper system. For all that, however, both of these camps ultimately think of cognition as a resolutely skin-side phenomenon. By contrast, the ExC theorist considers the coupled combination of pen-and-paper resource, appropriate bodily manipulations, and in-the-head processing to be a cognitive system in its own right, a system in which although the differently located elements make different causal contributions to the production of the observed intelligent activity, nevertheless each of those contributions enjoys a *fully cognitive* status. In my view, the supporting case for the hypothesis of embodied–embedded cognition has been successfully made over and over again.[3] If that's right, then the key issue facing ExC theorists right now is not how to argue against the received (if that's what it still is) orthodox view in cognitive science, but rather how to justify the transition from a "merely" embodied–embedded mind to an extended one.[4]

3   From Functionalism to Extended Functionalism

Some of the conceptual machinery required to effect the transition just identified plausibly comes in the form of a familiar philosophical theory of mind, namely *functionalism*. According to the traditional formulation of this view, the canonical statement of which is arguably due to Putnam (1967), a mental state counts as the mental state it does because of the causal relations it bears to sensory inputs, behavioral outputs, and other mental states. Who gets to decide what the psychologically relevant causal relations are (e.g., philosophers performing conceptual analyses of folk-psychological terms, psychologists performing scientific experiments) is a matter of intellectual debate. For the present the key point is this. As every undergraduate who has ever taken a class in philosophy of mind knows, traditional functionalism triumphantly frees us from a kind of neural or carbon chauvinism about the mind. In so doing it bolsters the intellectual credentials of *Doctor Who, Star Wars, Ben 10*, and every other science fiction adventure predicated on encounters with alien intelligence. It also keeps the good people of SETI in their jobs. In other words, traditional functionalism provides a principled basis for concluding that creatures whose brains happen to be built out of physical stuff different from our own may still be cognizers. It achieves this heady feat because it bequeaths to the mind the chauvinism-busting property of *multiple realizability*. To explain: if psychological phenomena are constituted by their causal-functional roles, then our terms for mental states, mental processes, and so on pick out equivalence classes of different material substrates, any one of which might in principle realize the type-identified state or process in question. But of course that means that robots, Martians, and the Ood and may all join us in having mental states, just so long as the physical stuff out of which they are made is capable of being organized so as to implement the right functional profiles.

What has this brief excursion into the history of philosophy got to do with ExC? The answer, I suggest, is that one of the standard considerations used in pro-ExC arguments, namely *the parity principle*, forges a strong connection between functionalism and ExC. To remind us of the parity principle, here is a much-quoted passage from Clark and Chalmers (1998; in this volume, p. 29): "If, as we confront some task, a part of the world functions as a process which, *were it done in the head*, we would have no hesitation in recognizing as part of the cognitive process, then that part of the world is (so we claim) part of the cognitive process. Cognitive processes ain't (all) in the head." In broad terms, then, the parity principle states that if there is functional equality with respect to governing behavior, between the causal contribution of certain internal elements and the causal contribution of certain external elements, and if the internal elements concerned qualify as the proper parts of a cognitive trait, then there is no good reason to deny equivalent status—that is, cognitive status—to the relevant external elements. Parity of causal contribution mandates parity of status with respect to inclusion in the domain of the cognitive.[5]

So what? The parity principle is based on the thought that it is possible for the very same type-identified cognitive state or process to be available in two different generic formats—one non-extended and one extended. Thus, in principle at least, that state or process must be realizable in either a purely organic medium or in one that involves an integrated combination of organic and non-organic structures. In other words, it must be multiply realizable. So, if we are to argue for cognitive extension *by way of parity considerations*, the idea that cognitive states and processes are multiply realizable must make sense. Now, as we have seen, functionalism provides one well-established platform for securing multiple realizability. That said, we don't quite have a case of plug-and-play philosophy here.

Functionalism—or rather, how we formulate it—needs to be tweaked a little before current needs are met. To see why, recall that, according to the traditional formulation of the position as given earlier, a mental state is constituted by the causal relations that it bears to sensory inputs, behavioral outputs, and other mental states. But depending on how one hears terms like "sensory inputs" and "behavioral outputs," this statement of the view may harbor a bias toward the inner that isn't, at root, a feature of its defining commitments. Fundamentally, the functionalist holds that what makes a systemic state a mental state is the set of causal relations that it bears to systemic inputs, systemic outputs, and other systemic states (cf. the formulation given by Levin 2008, as quoted near the beginning of this chapter). Once we give this more general characterization of the functionalist line, we can allow the borders of the cognitive system to fall somewhere other than the sensorimotor interface of the organic body. And that opens the door to a cognitive system whose boundaries are located partly outside the skin. It is in this way that we arrive straightforwardly at the position that, following Clark, I shall call *extended functionalism* (Clark 2008a,b; see also Wheeler forthcoming). I think that extended functionalism is an attractive position with good philosophical and cognitive-scientific credentials. Not everyone agrees.

4   Troubles for Extended Functionalism, Part I: The Adams–Aizawa Distinctiveness Principle

As part of their sustained critical treatment of ExC, Adams and Aizawa (2008) argue that we should expect the vehicles of cognition to be exclusively neuronal in character, because we should expect processes as distinctive as cognitive processes to be realized by correspondingly distinctive lower-level processes. The latter expectation is allegedly justified by the general principle that "roughly speaking, lower-level processes should be as distinctive as the higher-level processes they realize" (ibid., p. 68). Call this the *Adams–Aizawa distinctiveness principle.* As evidence for the way in which this principle plausibly identifies neuronal states and processes as the only vehicles of cognition, Adams and Aizawa point to the differences between two sets of lower-level vision-related processes that are instantiated on either side of a transduction interface positioned at the retina. Thus, in the eye, prior to the retina (e.g., in the cornea and the lens), we find optical processes essentially similar to those present in non-organic optical machinery. When light enters the retina, however, there is a shift to molecular processes that, among other things, result in the color-sensitive,

orientation-sensitive, and motion-sensitive selective release of neurotransmitters. According to Adams and Aizawa, this transition in lower-level
processes also marks a transition from the noncognitive to the cognitive.

It is at this point that a critical engagement with functionalism ensues.
Adams and Aizawa write: "Functionalists about cognition might . . .
observe that, in principle, anything could be organized in such a way as to
give rise to cognitive processing. But our point is that, even though many
things *could*, in principle, be organized to form a cognitive processor, it is
reasonable to conjecture that only neuronal processes are in fact so organized" (ibid., p. 69). As far as I can tell, the specific language of "processes"
is not essential to Adams and Aizawa's point, which ultimately concerns
the distinctiveness of a range of relevant phenomena (including, for example, states and mechanisms, as well as processes) at the different levels.
With that clarification in place, we can see that Adams and Aizawa's argument implies a rejection of the general claim that human cognitive traits
are sometimes multiply realized. To be clear: Adams and Aizawa do not
reject the *in-principle* possibility of cognition-realizing substrates that
involve (wholly or partly) nonneuronal elements. What they reject is the
idea that minds like ours are *in fact* ever realized by such substrates. Understood as part of their general critique of cognitive extension, now interpreted in terms of extended functionalism, their argument is thus leveled
not against the in-principle possibility of cognitive extension, but against
the idea that minds like ours are in fact ever extended. In view of all this,
one defensive strategy open to the ExC theorist would be to find examples
of scientifically well-established cases which show that the Adams–Aizawa
distinctiveness principle is false. If there are extant distinctive higher-level
phenomena, such that each of those phenomena is, *in fact*, multiply realized by more than one kind of lower-level phenomenon, then we would
have no *general* reason to expect each distinctive higher-level phenomenon to be realized exclusively in a single material substrate, and thus no
general reason to expect cognition in particular to be realized exclusively
in a neuronal substrate.

As it happens, it seems that the evidence needed by the ExC theorist is
plentiful, in examples of what is known in biology as *functional convergence in evolution*. Convergent evolution is a widespread phenomenon in
which a particular biological trait evolves independently in more than one
lineage, from different ancestors. One kind of convergent evolution involves
functional convergence (Doolittle 1994), a process in which two or more
biological entities perform the same function, but do so by way of entirely
different underlying structures and mechanisms. Here is an example of

functional convergence in molecular evolution. Alcohol dehydrogenases are enzymes that, in humans and many other animals, break down alcohols that might otherwise be dangerous. They figure in the molecular economies of vertebrates and fruit flies, and perform functionally equivalent roles in each of these biological contexts, but the vertebrate enzymes and the fruit-fly enzymes display no sequence similarity with each other, have fundamentally different tertiary structures, and catalyze alcohol into acetaldehyde using different chemical reactions (Doolittle 1994). This is just one example of a distinctive higher-level phenomenon (relatively speaking) that is multiply realized. The Adams–Aizawa distinctiveness principle is false. Extended functionalist minds may yet be actual.

5   Troubles for Extended Functionalism, Part II: The Rowlands Deadlock

A second analysis that, in a different way, questions the ability of extended functionalism to deliver cognitive extension hails from Mark Rowlands (unpublished ms). According to Rowlands, if one reflects on the interplay between (i) an argument against parity-driven ExC developed by Rob Rupert (2004; for related considerations see Adams and Aizawa 2008) and (ii) a way of responding to Rupert's argument that I have been known to pursue (Wheeler forthcoming), what emerges is a deadlock between the two sides, the paralyzing character of which may be traced to the functionalist terms of the debate. In what follows I shall lay down a path that leads to this stalemate, a path that adds detail to Rowlands' own analysis, but which ends up at the same unfortunate (for ExC) point. Let's begin, then, by revisiting Rupert's argument against ExC and what might be wrong with it.

Rupert calls on empirical psychological data which, he argues, may be used to indicate significant differences between the profile of internal memory and the profile of certain external resources, as such external resources might plausibly figure in the process of remembering. According to Rupert, such differences tell against any attempt to see the latter phenomena as being of the same explanatory kind as the former. For example, there are psychological experiments which show that internal memory is sensitive to what is called the *generation effect*. Where this effect is in evidence, subjects gain a mnemonic advantage by generating their own meaningful connections between paired associate items be learned. Rupert argues that the generation effect will simply not occur in some extended "memory" systems (e.g., in a system according to which, during recall, the subject refers to a notebook in which the paired associates are accompanied by connection sentences produced by those subjects during learning, but which were entered into the notebook by the experimenter). He concedes that it might occur in others (e.g., in a system according to which, during recall, the subject refers to a notebook in which the paired associates to be learned are accompanied by connection sentences produced and entered by the subjects during learning). In the latter case, however, he suggests that the effect is an accidental feature, rather than an essential or definitional dimension, of the memory system. Rupert concludes that the processes involved in putative cases of extended memory differ in such fundamental ways from those involved in cases of ordinary internal memory that the extended cases cannot count as cognitive.

The final step is to generalize from this conclusion about memory to a conclusion about all cognitive traits. As Rupert points out, this step is plausibly justified by the fact that memory is a core cognitive trait, suggesting that what goes for memory goes for cognition in general.[6]

Rupert's argument has the following form: first we identify certain features of some core cognitive trait as standardly (internally) conceived that are not shared (or not shared in the "right" way) by any extended arrangement that might be thought to perform the same cognitive task; then we conclude that since the parity principle is not satisfied, ExC is false. But once this two-part structure is exposed, the parity-driven ExC theorist will want to lodge a complaint (Wheeler forthcoming). For although in general that theorist must concede the existence of the kinds of functional differences identified by Rupert, she will want to object to the further claim that such differences result in a breakdown of parity. What allows the ExC theorist to block this further claim is the fact that it depends on a seemingly contestable assumption that the benchmark for parity (in effect, what counts as cognitive) should be set by the extant fine-grained details of what is internal to the human—the human inner. It is only because these details are being allowed to call the cognitive shots that the divergent functional profiles exhibited by the extended systems in question mandate the judgment that those systems should be denied cognitive status. However, when properly understood, the parity principle does not privilege the organization and processing of the actual human inner in the way that Rupert's argument suggests. Full discussion of this issue would take us too far afield (for a longer treatment, see Wheeler unpublished ms). But, in somewhat sketchy and general terms, here is a way of unpacking the appeal to parity so that ExC is insulated against Rupert's concerns. First we give an account of what it is to be a proper part of a cognitive system that is fundamentally independent of where any candidate element happens to be spatially located. Then we look to see where cognition falls—in the brain, in the nonneural body, in the environment, or, as the ExC theorist predicts may sometimes be the case, in a system that extends across all of these aspects of the world. On this model, parity is conceived not as parity with the inner simpliciter, but rather as parity with the inner *with respect to a locationally uncommitted account of the cognitive.* Although I am no legal philosopher, it seems to me that this way of understanding the notion of parity in cognitive theory has a recognizable and illuminating (although arguably slightly strained) analogue in the way that two citizens of a democratic state may be understood as having the right to equality of treatment under the law. Ignoring cases of precedence, what counts as the correct treatment under the law is presumably not fixed by the case of one of the parity-enjoying citizens. Rather, each of the two citizens enjoys parity with the other with respect to an independently fixed standard of correct legal treatment.[7]

At this point one might wonder what remains of Clark and Chalmers's original idea that, in applying the parity principle, we should ask of some external process that plays a part in governing behavior, *"Were this process done in the head,* would we have any hesitation in recognizing it as part of a cognitive process?"* The first thing to note here is that the appeal to the inner contained in this method for reaching a judgment regarding parity is not an appeal to the fine-grained profile of the extant human inner. All that happens in the thought experiment is this: certain external processes get shifted spatially, across the boundary of the skin, in an inwardly moving direction. Of course, we are not supposed to imagine that the relevant externally located physical elements themselves are grafted onto the brain. Rather, we imagine that exactly the same functional states and processes that are realized in the actual world by those externally located physical elements are now realized by certain internally located physical elements. Having done this, if we then judge that the now-internal but previously external processes count as part of a genuinely cognitive system, we are driven to conclude that they did so in the extended case too. After all, by hypothesis, nothing about the functional contribution of those processes to intelligent behavior has changed. All that has been varied is their spatial location. And if one were to claim that that spatial shift alone is sufficient to result in a transition in the status of the external elements in question, from noncognitive to cognitive, one would, it seems, be guilty of begging the question against the ExC theorist. Now notice that at no point in this explanation of how the appeal to the inner contained in the parity principle works have we been forced to use the fine-grained profile of the extant human inner in order to determine what counts as cognitive. In other words, the application of the parity principle does not itself set the benchmark for parity (fix what counts as cognitive). Instead it acts as a heuristic device designed to free us from what Clark (2007a, p. 167) has called "the pervasive distractions of skin and skull."

Of course, given the stress that the foregoing analysis places on functional role in judgments of cognitive status, one thing that this initial response to Rupert does is reemphasize the connection between functionalism and ExC, at least where the latter is played out by way of parity considerations. Indeed, if the critic of ExC refused to endorse a broadly functionalist theory of mind, the aforementioned charge of question-begging would arguably lose some of its force. Without functionalism to sustain the multiple realizability of the mental, conceptual space would remain for the claim that cognitive states and processes are somehow intrinsically related to the materiality of the target system in such a way that multiple realizability fails. Given a failure of multiple realizability, the imagined inward shift across the boundary of the skin would presumably have an impact on whether the processes in question were cognitive or noncognitive in character, even if the external factors in the extended case and the relevant inner factors in the wholly inner case enjoyed functional equivalence with respect to governing intelligent behavior. This observation points to an underappreciated and underexplored tension between extended functionalism and any embodied cognition view which holds that human thought and experience are tied inextricably to the details of human bodily form. Given the goals of the present analysis, however, this particular conflict will not detain us here. (For preliminary investigations of the issue, see Clark 2008a,b; Wheeler forthcoming.) Our concern is with a deadlock that, as we are about to see, emerges *within* a broadly functionalist framework, *between* extended and non-extended versions of that view.

What the Rupert-style critic of ExC needs to unearth is independent support for the key assumption that the benchmark for parity should be set by the extant fine-grained details of the human inner. It might be thought that Rupert himself has the resources to marshal such support, given that his appeal to the inner is supposed to be founded not on some pro-inner prejudice or some unwarranted theoretical conservatism, but rather on a healthy and entirely defensible respect for the methods and results of contemporary cognitive science. Thus he writes: "as cognitive science currently describes its explanatory kinds, they are not likely to have realizations with external components. If, for example, cognitive science is to characterize functionally the causal role of memories, this characterization must be tailored to accommodate the generation-effect, various forms of interference, the power laws of learning and forgetting and the rest" (Rupert 2004, pp. 423–424; for similar reasoning, see Adams and Aizawa 2008, pp. 140–141). Two aspects of this short quotation are crucial. The first is that Rupert takes current cognitive science to be a broadly *functionalist* enterprise (its job being to "characterize functionally" psychological phenomena). The second is that, by "cognitive science," Rupert means *conventional human-oriented and inner-oriented cognitive psychology* (note the list of psychological phenomena that Rupert gives at the end of his quotation). What this tells us is that the justification for the assumption that the benchmark for parity should be set by the extant fine-grained details of the inner comes from the idea that what counts as cognitive should be fixed by the details of the functional organization of human cognition, as identified by conventional human-oriented and inner-oriented cognitive psychology. In effect, then, Rupert is arguing for a *chauvinistic* form of functionalism that privileges the scientifically identified human-specific inner. But the extended functionalist is unlikely to be moved by this extra consideration. Why, she will ask, should we privilege conventional human-oriented and inner-oriented cognitive psychology in this way? Indeed, it seems that Rupert's more developed argument continues to beg the question against extended functionalism. For, as we have seen, extended functionalism looks to be predicated on the more liberal form of functionalism that generates a locationally uncommitted account of the cognitive.

It is at this point in the exchange of argument and counterargument that the problem highlighted by Rowlands emerges. Here it is, in Rowlands's own words:

This charge [that Rupert's objections are question-begging] has been leveled by Wheeler ([forthcoming]). However, this charge seems to cut both ways. If Rupert's arguments against the extended mind are question-begging because they presuppose a chauvinistic form of functionalism, it is difficult to see why arguments for the extended mind are not question-begging given their predication on a liberal form of functionalism. Adjudicating between the extended mind and its critics, therefore, seems to require adjudicating between liberal and chauvinistic forms of functionalism. But this is a dispute that has been ongoing almost since functionalism's inception. In the absence of any satisfactory resolution of this dispute, the clear danger for the extended mind is one of stalemate. (Rowlands, unpublished ms, pp. 6–7)

If this problem is genuine, it spells bad news for extended functionalism. For if Rowlands is right, then to the extent that ExC is allied to functionalism, the best it can achieve against its critics is a stalemate. This is what I shall call the *Rowlands deadlock*.

Is there a way out of the impasse—one that ultimately finds in favor of ExC? Perhaps there is. Imagine we came across a human being whose purely inner memory system didn't exhibit the generation effect, but who nevertheless continued to achieve the context-sensitive selective storage and retrieval of information. I for one have no doubt at all that conventional human-oriented cognitive psychologists would find the functional difference between this generation-effect-free subject and normal human subjects extremely interesting, and that those same psychologists would use their well-honed experimental protocols to probe and explain that difference. But I cannot conceive of any cognitive psychologist concluding that the latter subject lacks the cognitive trait of memory. So why think that exhibiting the generation effect is a defining feature of (human) memory, rather than an accidental feature? And if that's right, then what is the justification (aside from pro-inner prejudice and unwarranted conservatism) for refusing to apply the notion of memory to an extended system with a similar profile to our generation-effect-free subject? The fact that the answers to these questions are "one shouldn't" and "there isn't one" gives us good reason to think that the difference between exhibiting or failing to exhibit the generation effect (in the right sort of way) doesn't mark the boundary between having a memory and not having one, which further suggests that there must be an explanatorily useful, generic account of memory that is broad enough to cover generation-effect and non-generation-effect cases. That account will be apt to encompass, within the category of memory, extended mechanisms for context-sensitive information storage and retrieval that don't exhibit the generation effect. So although Rupert may conceivably be right that for two creatures to realize the cognitive trait of *exhibiting the generation effect in memory*, they will need to share a fine-grained inner profile which resists any extended realization, that fact, if it is one, poses no real threat to ExC. Extended systems of context-sensitive information storage and retrieval that fail to exhibit the generation effect might still count as memory, and thus as cognitive.

It is clear enough that this result is not restricted to memory. Similar arguments could be developed for prediction systems that don't fall for the gambler's fallacy, inference systems that don't exhibit the patterns characteristically revealed by the Wason selection task, and so on. What our reflections suggest, then, is a general principle: just because some specified mode of functional organization happens to be of interest to cognitive psychologists, one cannot infer that the difference between exhibiting that mode of organization and not exhibiting it must in some way play a decisive role in marking off the cognitive from the noncognitive. As the case of the generation-effect-free subject indicates, such functional differences—differences that cognitive psychologists will surely want to investigate—may well be differences *within* the domain of the cognitive. The message here is not, of course, that no mode of functional organization that ever interested a cognitive psychologist could ever be relevant to the issue of how to determine membership of the cognitive. A mechanism that failed to implement the context-sensitive storage and retrieval of information simply wouldn't be memory, wherever it happened to be located. The message, rather, is that working out whether or not a particular mode of functional organization matters to this issue will not be decided by the fact that orthodox cognitive psychologists have studied systems that exhibit it.

If we place the preceding analysis in the explicitly functionalist context that apparently generates the Rowlands deadlock, its lesson is that the difference between exhibiting or failing to exhibit *fine-grained functional traits* (like the generation effect) doesn't mark the boundary between being a cognizer and not being one. Rather, the level of functional grain that matters for the presence or absence of cognition must be set high enough so that, other things being equal, a system that exhibits some fine-grained functional trait and one that doesn't both count as cognitive. (For additional considerations which point in the same direction, see Sprevak forthcoming, esp. p. 11. More from Sprevak in a moment.) In the end, then, it looks as if the Rowlands deadlock may be broken, on the grounds that we have ExC-independent reasons for rejecting the fine-grained, chauvinistic form of functionalism assumed by Rupert, in favor of a higher-level, liberal grain of functional analysis. Such a state of affairs paves the way for extended functionalism.

At this juncture it might seem that the Rowlands deadlock is lurking just out of sight, waiting impatiently to reappear. For although I have just offered reasons, independent of ExC, for rejecting chauvinistic functionalism in favor of liberal functionalism, so the critic of ExC might offer reasons, independent of any case against ExC, for rejecting liberal functionalism in favor of chauvinistic functionalism. For example, the critic might claim that any attempt to fix a generic functional notion of, for example, memory, one that would subsume all the relevant internal and extended systems (those that don't exhibit the generation effect, those that do, those that don't exhibit negative transfer interference effects [see note 6], those that do, and so on) would need to be so devoid of detail (in order to subsume all the different functional profiles) that it would fail to earn its explanatory keep (for this sort of argument, see, e.g., Rupert 2004). In short, the charge is that our more liberal form of functionalism is pitched at such a stratospheric level of generality that it fails to support useful psychological theorizing. And that provides a reason to favor chauvinistic functionalism. But now if there are not only appropriate and defensible reasons for adopting ExC-friendly liberal functionalism, but also equally appropriate and equally defensible reasons for adopting ExC-unfriendly chauvinistic functionalism, then the Rowlands deadlock is restored.

Once again, however, I think the stalemate can be broken. Recall yet again our hypothetical subject whose inner mechanisms of context-sensitive information storage and retrieval do not exhibit the generation effect. As we have seen, the fact that neither common sense nor cognitive psychology balks at the thought that this subject's feats should count as genuine cases of remembering gives us good reason to think that there must be a generic notion of what memory is that is broad enough to cover generation-effect and non-generation-effect cases. Now we can add a further observation. The fact that our subject's abilities would undoubtedly be investigated by cognitive psychologists as one possible form of the psychological phenomenon of memory surely indicates that the generic notion of memory that underwrites this way of proceeding is doing important work in organizing and shaping the project of cognitive-scientific explanation. Thus, on the strength of this example, it seems that the explanatory credentials of that generic notion of memory are in perfectly good order. And that is good news for the liberal version of functionalism that provides the theoretical backdrop against which that generic notion of memory makes sense. For it surely suggests, *pace* the critic of ExC, that that liberal, ExC-friendly version of functionalism is not stymied by explanatory impotence. If this is right, then the restored form of the Rowlands deadlock is ultimately unsustainable.

6   Interlude: Extended Microfunctionalism

So far I have been running with the thought that extended functionalism is naturally predicated on a liberal version of functionalism. Part of the supporting argument has involved the claim that the cognitive–noncognitive boundary does not coincide with the sorts of fine-grained functional differences exemplified by the difference between exhibiting or not exhibiting the generation effect. But this is not the whole story. For in spite of what I have argued so far, the fact is that the cognitive–noncognitive boundary may *sometimes* (although not in the generation-effect case) be determined by fine-grained functional differences. Here is some evidence for this conclusion. It is at least arguable that any architecture deserving of the title "cognitive" will need to display capacities such as flexible (i.e., context-sensitive) generalization and the graceful degradation of performance in the face of restricted damage or noisy or inaccurate input information. Such capacities are plausibly at work in the entire suite of cognitive activities, from online perceptually guided action to off-line reflection and reason. So how do we explain them? To reveal *part of* the answer to this question, recall that one major impetus to the rebirth of connectionist artificial intelligence (AI) in the 1980s was that whereas capacities such as flexible generalization and graceful degradation are often missing from, or difficult to achieve in, classical AI systems, connectionist networks seem to exhibit them as "natural" by-products of their basic mode of organization. So what explains this propensity? It has frequently been noted (perhaps most famously by Smolensky 1988) that the cognitively relevant functions implemented by connectionist networks will often be specified in terms of mathematical relations (between units) that do not respect the boundaries of linguistic or conceptual thought. Given the tendency (it is far from a universal commitment) of classical AI theorizing to adopt functional specifications that do respect the boundaries of linguistic or conceptual thought, one might gloss this point by saying that the salient functional roles that matter for connectionist theorizing are typically pitched at a finer level of grain than those performed by classical computational systems. That's part of the reason why Clark (1989, 2007b) has described connectionist theory as a kind of *microfunctionalism*. Moreover, it is highly plausible that cognitively critical properties such as flexible generalization and graceful degradation may be emergent properties of connectionist networks in part precisely because those networks are functionally organized in a fine-grained way. As Clark (1989, pp. 35–36) puts it:

[Microfunctionalism] would describe at least the *internal* functional profile of the system (the internal state transitions) in terms far removed from . . . contentful purposive characterizations. It would delineate formal (probably mathematical) relations between processing units in a way that when those mathematical relations obtain, the system will be capable of vast, flexible structural variability and will have the attendant emergent properties. By keeping the formal characterization . . . at this fine-grained level we may hope to guarantee that any instantiation of such a description provides at least potentially the right kind of substructure to support the kind of flexible, rich behavior patterns required for true understanding.

This provides evidence for the following claim: for some properties that, one might argue, would need to be displayed by any system worthy of the label "cognitive," the fact that the system realizes a certain fine-grained functional profile may well be crucial to the possession of that property.

Of course, if it were the case that the sorts of fine-grained functional roles just highlighted could *only* be implemented internally, then this would present a serious barrier to extended functionalism. The good news for the extended functionalist, however, is that microfunctionalism is not antithetical to the possibility of extended realizations. Significantly, as Clark (2007b, p. 40) notes, microfunctionalist connectionism "specifies a system only in terms of input–output profiles for individual units and thus is not crucially dependent on any particular biological substrate." This preservation of the functionalist commitment to multiple realizability clears the way not only to nonstandard organic implementations of the microfunctions in question, as Clark's text here directly suggests, but also to extended implementations. In this context, notice that, in the longer quotation from Clark reproduced just above, he states that "*at least* the *internal* functional profile of the system would be described in microfunctionalist terms" (first emphasis mine). In my view this way of putting the point is too conservative. There is every reason to believe that at least some microfunctions will be apt for realization in extended substrates. Thus imagine that I possess a mobile computing device armed with connectionist software capable of the sort of flexible generalization and graceful degradation characteristic of such systems. And let's assume, just for the sake of argument, that the computing device contributes to my behavior in such a way that, on the strength of parity-principle reasoning, we are happy to include it as part of my cognitive systems. In this case, the microfunctions that underlie the key properties of flexible generalization and graceful degradation are at least partly realized beyond the skin.

What this indicates is that, in the end, the question of the grain at which functional analysis should be performed is pretty much orthogonal to the issue of cognitive extension. In other words, the situation is not that for ExC to be true, *all* cognitive traits would need to be specified at a high level of grain, meaning that the ExC theorist assumes a liberal form of functionalism, whereas for ExC to be false, *all* cognitive traits would need to be specified at a fine level of grain, meaning that the opponent of ExC assumes a chauvinistic form of functionalism. Indeed, it is entirely possi-

ble that *some* of the functional roles that will be identified by a locationally uncommitted cognitive science as determinative of cognition will be
fixed at a fine level of grain. The implication—one that enriches our vision
of ExC—is that extended functionalism has a robustly microfunctionalist
dimension.

7   Troubles for Extended Functionalism, Part III: The Sprevak Dilemma

Our third argument against extended functionalism is due to Mark Sprevak (forthcoming). Although this argument shares certain features with
the considerations that generate the Rowlands deadlock, it demands attention in its own right. At its heart is an independently plausible principle
that Sprevak calls the *Martian intuition*:

The Martian intuition is that it is possible for a creature with mental states to exist
even if such a creature has a different physical and biological makeup from ourselves. An intelligent organism might have green slime instead of neurons, and it
might have different kinds of connections in its "nervous" system. The Martian
intuition applies to fine-grained psychology as well as physiology: there is no reason why a Martian should have exactly the same fine-grained psychology as ours.
A Martian's pain response may not decay in exactly the same way as ours; its learning profiles and reaction times may not exactly match ours; the typical causes and
effects of its mental states may not be exactly the same as ours; even the large-scale
functional relationships between the Martian's cognitive systems (e.g. between its
memory and perception) may not exactly match ours. (Sprevak forthcoming, pp.
5–6)

As indicated by our previous discussion of the place of functionalism in
the history of philosophy of mind, one of the key properties of that thesis
(as traditionally conceived) is that it gives us the conceptual resources to
save the Martian intuition. However, Sprevak argues that it can achieve
this only if the level of functional grain is set at a sufficiently coarse level.
If the level of functional grain is set too finely, Martians whose pain
responses decayed differently from ours or whose learning profiles and
reaction times did not exactly match ours would be illegitimately excluded
from being cognizers, and the Martian intuition would be violated. So
how does the Martian intuition bear on the case for cognitive extension?
Sprevak's claim (ibid., p. 8) is that "if the grain parameter is set at least
coarse enough to allow for intelligent Martians, then it also allows
many cases of extended cognition." Why think this? As Sprevak explains
(partially echoing an argument from Clark, this volume, chap. 3), if we
take some putative case of extended cognition, we can always imagine a

functionally equivalent system that is located entirely inside the head of a Martian. On the strength of the Martian intuition, we would count that Martian-internal system as cognitive, so when, as functionalists, we fix the level of grain for our analysis, it must be set coarsely enough to generate that result. But if it is that coarse, then the (by hypothesis) functionally identical extended system too will count as cognitive. Or at least it will do so, if we accept the parity principle. For of course it would be inner chauvinism to exclude the extended system simply because it involves external factors, when in all other relevant respects it is equivalent.

It is at this point that the trouble for extended functionalism starts. For Sprevak argues that once the level of functional grain is set coarsely enough to save the Martian intuition, what is entailed is a radical form of ExC that is wildly overpermissive, because it will welcome in to the domain of the cognitive certain unwanted interlopers. For example, Sprevak argues that, according to this form of ExC, if I have a desktop computer which contains a program for calculating the dates of the Mayan calendar 5,000 years into the future, then, even if I never run this program, I possess an extended cognitive process that is capable of calculating the dates of the Mayan calendar. Why? Because one could imagine a Martian with an *internal* process that is capable of calculating the dates of the Mayan calendar *using the same algorithm as my desktop computer*. Even if the Martian never has cause to use this process, nevertheless it seems right to say that it is part of that creature's cognitive architecture. Now we simply apply the parity principle: there is functional equality between the dispositional contribution of the Martian's inner process to the Martian's behavioral repertoire and the dispositional contribution of the external desktop process to my behavioral repertoire. Since the Martian's inner process counts as cognitive, equal treatment demands that the same status be granted to the process in my desktop computer. And intuitively that seems wrong. Surely the desktop process is a potential aid to cognition, but is not itself part of my cognitive architecture.

This is bad news for extended functionalism, since if Sprevak is right, functionalism entails a wildly overpermissive form of ExC that looks to be false. But it is also bad news for functionalism as a theory of mind, since if functionalism entails a false theory, then functionalism too is false. Of course, the critical argument could be blocked if we gave up on the Martian intuition, since then, to return to Sprevak's Mayan calendar example, the Martian inner process wouldn't count as cognitive. But that is ruled out because the Martian intuition is independently plausible. Alternatively, the critical argument could be blocked if we gave up on the parity principle, since then we could count the Martian inner process as cognitive, while denying that status to the desktop process. But that is ruled out because the parity principle is one of the keystones of the case for ExC (Sprevak forthcoming, p. 16). So it seems that Sprevak has created a serious dilemma for the extended functionalist who favors a parity-driven case for ExC.

Or has he? Let's look again at the structure of Sprevak's argument. The conceptual backdrop against which it operates involves three factors: a functionalist understanding of ExC, the independent plausibility of the Martian intuition, and the centrality of the parity principle to the positive case for ExC. The path to the apparently troublesome dilemma then has four steps. At step 1 Sprevak describes an example of distributed (over brain, body, and world) problem-solving that intuitively looks to be a wildly unlikely candidate for a case of extended cognition, so unlikely in fact that any theory according to which the external parts of that system counted as cognitive would, by virtue of that fact, look to be false. At step 2 he imagines a functionally identical system located entirely inside the head of a Martian, and concludes, on the grounds of a functionalism committed to the Martian intuition, that we would grant that system cognitive status and thus that the level of functional grain should be set coarsely enough to deliver that result. At step 3 he argues, on the strength of the parity principle, that the entire distributed system described at step 1 must also count as cognitive. At step 4 he draws the anti-ExC and antifunctionalist conclusions. It's compelling stuff. So what has gone wrong?

It seems that step 2 of Sprevak's argument depends on a form of the Martian intuition that is *significantly more radical* than the one he explicitly formulates as part of his conceptual backdrop. And whereas the latter intuition does indeed command considerable plausibility, the former doesn't. To explain: What Sprevak does at step 2 is take what he assumes to be the noncognitive, externally located elements in a distributed process, place them inside the head of a Martian, and conclude that they now deserve to be rewarded with cognitive status. But where is the justification for suddenly counting these elements as themselves cognitive? Apart from their spatial location, nothing about them has changed from when they were judged to be noncognitive. The only new factor is their recently acquired in-the-head-ness. So it certainly looks as if an external element that we took to be noncognitive has since become cognitive, *purely in virtue of being moved inside the head.* Now, the core of the Martian intuition, as explicitly formulated by Sprevak, is that "it is possible for a creature with mental states to exist even if such a creature has a different physical and biological makeup from ourselves." But it certainly doesn't follow from this highly plausible principle that any state or process that happens to be found inside the head of an intelligent Martian must, simply because of its in-the-head-ness, count as a cognitive state or process. The latter claim, which is what Sprevak seems to need for his anti-ExC argument, would constitute a significantly more radical form of the Martian intuition. Moreover, it is one that clashes unhelpfully with the parity principle that Sprevak assumes at step 3 of his argument. Indeed, it is a corollary of the parity principle that the smuggled-in, more radical form of the Martian intuition cannot be right. After all, the parity principle implies that an in-the-head element that we take to be cognitive doesn't become noncognitive purely in virtue of being moved outside the skin. And the direction of travel here is irrelevant. The more general slogan is *equal treatment regardless of location*. Thus the parity principle also implies that an external element that we take to be noncognitive doesn't become cognitive *purely in virtue of being shifted inside the head*.

What this suggests is that the extended functionalist can avoid the Sprevak dilemma by refusing to endorse the more radical form of the Martian intuition. This is something that the fan of the parity-driven case for cognitive extension ought to do anyway, given that the parity principle is inconsistent with that version of the intuition. The orthodox version, the one explicitly stated by Sprevak, remains in force, of course. But that is consistent with the claim that the class of Martian in-the-head elements (indeed, the class of in-the-head elements in general) may contain some noncognitive members. Thus it does not entail that where the causal contribution to intelligent behavior of certain in-the-head elements is functionally identical to that of certain noncognitive external elements, the former elements attain cognitive status purely in virtue of being intracranial. The orthodox version of the Martian intuition is also fully compatible with the parity principle. The path to the Sprevak dilemma is thus blocked, at step 2.

It is worth noting that the missing piece of the jigsaw here is some sort of locationally independent account of the cognitive that fixes the benchmark for parity (see section 5 above). Once such an account is part of our conceptual picture, there is no reason at all to think that any old process will count as cognitive, just because it has been rammed inside the head of a Martian. The resulting benchmark for parity does sterling theoretical work in weeding out unwanted interlopers into the domain of the cognitive, wherever they happen to be spatially located.[8]

8   A Loose Ending

In this chapter, I have argued that it is possible to defend the thesis of extended functionalism against some seemingly powerful objections. But perhaps this result, as encouraging as it is for the prospects of extended cognition, provides no grounds for a triumphant concluding flourish. It is common knowledge that functionalism *as a general theory of mind* faces some demoralizing philosophical challenges (for a nice review, see Levin 2008). Perhaps the more daunting of these challenges are connected with phenomenal consciousness—the "what-it's-like-ness" of experience. Who can forget evergreen thought experiments such as the single system comprising the entire Chinese nation, organized so as to satisfy the functional definition of a mind (Block 1980), or the functionally-identical-to-one-of-us zombie (Chalmers 1996)? In such cases the message is supposed to be that since we enjoy phenomenal consciousness, yet certain systems functionally identical to us plausibly don't, no purely functional characterization can explain phenomenal consciousness. Given the thought that phenomenal consciousness is central to mindedness, or at least to any mindedness interestingly similar to human mindedness, this looks like a serious limitation on any functionalist theory of mind, *including of course extended functionalism*. Extended functionalism inherits the disadvantages, as well as the advantages, of its parent theory.

A proper treatment of this issue must wait for another day. I simply want to bring the present discussion to a close by pointing out one thing. It is of course true that, to the extent that there exists a gap between functionalist explanation and an understanding of phenomenal consciousness, that gap is in force whether the realizing vehicles are wholly neural, a combination of neural and nonneural bodily factors, or an extended matrix of elements in the brain, the nonneural body, and the beyond-the-skin environment. But now notice that *it's the functional basis of the explanation that causes the alleged difficulty here, not where the realizing elements happen to be spatially located*. So although functionalism may indeed struggle in the face of phenomenal consciousness, extending one's functionalism certainly doesn't make things worse than they already were. When the topic at hand is the perplexing and recalcitrant question of how to account for phenomenal consciousness naturalistically, not making things worse is perhaps the best for which one can hope.

Acknowledgments

This chapter was prepared thanks to support from the AHRC, under its Research Leave scheme, as part of project AH/F002963/1. Many thanks to Andy Clark and Peter Sullivan for useful discussions, and to Mark Rowlands for permission to include a quotation from an unpublished manuscript.

Notes

1. What I am calling the extended cognition hypothesis (ExC) trades under a number of different names, including the *extended mind hypothesis* (Clark and Chalmers 1998, this volume), *active externalism* (ibid.), *vehicle externalism* (Hurley 1998; Rowlands 2003), *environmentalism* (Rowlands 1999), and *locational externalism* (Wilson 2004).

2. I am sensitive to the fact that the introduction of readily available electronic calculators and related software applications threatens to render this empirical observation about the use of pen and paper false. However, no one need worry about that here, since it is arguable that, with minor local variations to reflect how the different items of equipment are used, the points I go on to make in the main text apply straightforwardly to our relationship with the newer kind of technology.

3. For my own contribution to this process, see Wheeler 2005. See also, among many others, Varela, Thompson, and Rosch 1991; Clark 1997; Noë 2004; Thompson 2007.

4. I have set things up by treating ExC as a kind of radicalization of the embodied–embedded view (cf. Wheeler and Clark 2008). This is good enough for present purposes, but, as suggested in section 5 below, the relationship between the two sets of positions is a complex issue that has yet to be explored fully in the literature. For discussion of a number of apparent tensions between (certain versions of) the embodied–embedded view and ExC, see Clark 2008a,b; Wheeler forthcoming.

5. Of course, not all ExC theorists think that extended cognition should be justified by way of the parity principle. Arguments in support of ExC that don't exploit (and sometimes explicitly shun) the parity principle, are developed and defended by, e.g., Rowlands (1999), Sutton (2006), and Menary (2007).

6. Results from other psychological experiments on memory have been used in a similar way. For example, Rupert (2004) also appeals also to negative transfer interference effects (data which indicate that past learning interferes with the learning and recall of new paired associations), while Adams and Aizawa (2008) appeal to recency and primacy effects (data which indicate that we are better at recalling the elements at the beginning and end of a list than we are at recalling the elements in the middle). In both cases the claim is that extended systems will fail to exhibit the

highlighted effect (or will fail to do so in the right way) and so are different in explanatory kind from the familiar human internal systems studied by cognitive psychologists.

7. Equal treatment interpretations of parity based on (what I am calling) locationally uncommitted accounts of the cognitive are defended by Clark (2007a, 2008b) and Wheeler (forthcoming, unpublished ms). Within the scope of this general approach, there is a further and crucial question concerning how to unpack the key notion of a locationally uncommitted account of the cognitive. Clark (this volume, chap. 3, 2008b) suggests that the domain of the cognitive should be determined by our intuitive folk-judgments of what counts as cognitive. His supporting argument is (roughly) that our intuitive understanding of the cognitive is essentially locationally uncommitted, whereas the range of mechanisms identified by cognitive science is in truth too much of a motley to be a scientific kind, and so will thwart any attempt to provide a scientifically driven, theory-loaded account of the cognitive—locationally uncommitted or otherwise. I disagree with this assessment. I hold out for a locationally uncommitted account of the cognitive that is scientifically driven and theory-loaded, on the grounds (roughly) that our intuitive picture of the cognitive has a deep-seated inner bias, while Clark's argument for the claim that there is a fundamental mechanistic disunity in cognitive science is far from compelling (Wheeler, unpublished ms).

8. In effect, I have argued that the Mayan calendar program may be denied cognitive status, even when it is located inside a Martian head. This allows us to preserve the intuition that the Mayan desktop calendar program *as described* is the sort of element that ought to be excluded from the domain of the cognitive, an intuition with which of course Sprevak agrees. However, it is interesting to note just how sensitive our judgments are to the way the scenario is set up. For example, let's say we begin not, as Sprevak does, with the desktop program, but by imagining a Martian who has an inner program capable of calculating the dates of the Mayan calendar 5,000 years into the future. Even though, by hypothesis, this piece of inner machinery is never actually used, it might seem that we should have no misgivings about awarding it cognitive status. This appears to be at odds with the conclusion drawn previously. Yet it seems all we have done is reverse the order in which the cases are considered. What is going on?

When we begin our reflections on the issues, as Sprevak does, by focusing on an example of a desktop program, our natural tendency is to think of an isolated and easily removable software application, sitting on a machine that sometimes achieves fancy feats of text editing, graphics, and information storage, but which, in the end, is no more than a sophisticated tool for work or play. This encourages us to find it wildly unlikely that the program in question could ever count as cognitive, even if it were to be transported inside a Martian head. On the other hand, when we begin our consideration of the issues by imagining the Martian inner program, our natural tendency is to think of that mechanism as being already

functionally integrated into (although not yet activated within) an organized economy of states and processes. Those states and processes are intimately embedded in
subtle and complex perceptual, memory, and reasoning systems that have been
evolved or developed in relation to each other, and that already meet whatever the
criteria are for cognitive status. If the desktop program for calculating the Mayan
calendar were a functionally integrated element in this kind of economy, then it
may seem far less crazy to conclude that it could be a cognitive mechanism, or at
least part of one, even though it is spatially located outside the head. Various factors might pump our intuitions in this direction. Perhaps the program is config-
ured to reflect a particular individual's favored kind of interface, and has been
made remotely accessible through real-time mobile computing technology, or will,
in the future, be made available at the firing of a neuron through a brain implant
that connects the mechanism to a wireless network. Never mind the cyborg imag-
ery. However we develop the basic idea, the resulting image is a long way from the
one suggested by the scenario as described by Sprevak. In other words, the apparently fickle nature of our intuitions may be explained in terms of subtle changes to
the details of the hypothetical example, changes that have been surreptitiously
introduced by the variation in setup.

References

Adams, F., and Aizawa, K. (2008). *The Bounds of Cognition*. Malden, MA: Blackwell.

Block, N. (1980). Troubles with functionalism. In C. W. Savage (ed.), *Minnesota Studies in the Philosophy of Science* (vol. 9). Minneapolis: University of Minnesota Press.

Chalmers, D. (1996). *The Conscious Mind*. Oxford: Oxford University Press.

Churchland, P. M. (2005). Functionalism at forty: A critical retrospective. *Journal of
Philosophy, 102*(1), 33–50.

Clark, A. (1989). *Microcognition: Philosophy, Cognitive Science, and Parallel Distributed
Processing*. Cambridge, MA: MIT Press.

Clark, A. (1997). *Being There: Putting Brain, Body, and World Together Again*. Cambridge, Mass.: MIT Press.

Clark, A. (2005). Intrinsic content, active memory, and the extended mind. *Analysis, 65*(285), 1–11.

Clark, A. (2007a). Curing cognitive hiccups: A defense of the extended mind. *Journal of Philosophy, 104*, 163–192.

Clark, A. (2007a). Microfunctionalism: Connectionism and the scientific explanation
of mental states. This is an amended version of material that first appeared in A.
Clark, *Microcognition: Philosophy, Cognitive Science, and Parallel Distributed Processing* (Cambridge, Mass.: MIT Press, 1989), chs. 1, 2, and 6. It appears in German

translation as "Mikrofunktionalismus: Konnektionismus und die wissenschaftliche Erklärung mentaler Zustände," in T. Metzinger (ed.) (2007). *Grundkurs Philosophie des Geistes, Band 2—Das Leib-Seele-Problem* (pp. 392–426). Paderborn: mentis.

Clark, A. (2008a). Pressing the flesh: A tension in the study of the embodied, embedded mind? *Philosophy and Phenomenological Research, 76*(1), 37–59.

Clark, A. (2008b). *Supersizing the Mind: Embodiment, Action, and Cognitive Extension.* New York: Oxford University Press.

Clark, A., and Chalmers, D. (1998). The extended mind. *Analysis, 58*(1), 7–19. Reprinted as chapter 2 of this volume.

Doolittle, R. F. (1994). Convergent evolution: The need to be explicit. *Trends in Biochemical Sciences, 19,* 15–18.

Hurley, S. L. (1998). *Consciousness in Action.* Cambridge, MA: Harvard University Press.

Levin, J. (2008). Functionalism. In E. N. Zalta (ed.), *The Stanford Encyclopedia of Philosophy* (fall 2008 edition), http://plato.stanford.edu/archives/fall2008/entries/functionalism/.

Menary, R. (2007). *Cognitive Integration: Mind and Cognition Unbounded.* Basingstoke: Palgrave Macmillan.

Noë, A. (2004). *Action in Perception.* Cambridge, MA: MIT Press.

Putnam, H. (1967). Psychological predicates. In W. H. Capitan and D. D. Merrill (eds.), *Art, Mind, and Religion.* Pittsburgh: University of Pittsburgh Press.

Rowlands, M. (1999). *The Body in Mind.* Cambridge: Cambridge University Press.

Rowlands, M. (2003). *Externalism: Putting Mind and World Back Together Again.* Chesham, Bucks: Acumen.

Rowlands, M. (unpublished ms). Perception: From extended mind to embodied phenomenology. Unpublished paper given at a symposium on Embodied Perception held at the spring 2008 meeting of the Pacific Division of the American Philosophical Association, March 18–23, 2008, Pasadena, California.

Rumelhart, D. E., Smolensky, P., McClelland, J. L., and Hinton, G. (1986). Schemata and sequential thought processes in PDP models. In J. L. McClelland and D. Rumelhart (eds.), *Parallel Distributed Processing: Explorations in the Microstructure of Cognition,* vol. 2: *Psychological and Biological Models* (pp. 7–57). Cambridge, Mass.: MIT Press.

Rupert, R. (2004). Challenges to the hypothesis of extended cognition. *Journal of Philosophy, 101*(8), 389–428.

Smolensky, P. (1988). On the proper treatment of connectionism. *Behavioral and Brain Sciences, 11,* 1–74.

Sprevak, M. (forthcoming). Extended cognition and functionalism. *Journal of Philosophy*.

Sutton, J. (2006). Distributed cognition: Domains and dimensions. *Pragmatics and Cognition, 14*(2), 235–247.

Thompson, E. (2007). *Mind in Life: Biology, Phenomenology, and the Sciences of Mind*. Cambridge, MA: Harvard University Press.

Varela, F. J., Thompson, E., and Rosch, E. (1991). *The Embodied Mind: Cognitive Science and Human Experience*. Cambridge, MA: MIT Press.

Wheeler, M. (2005). *Reconstructing the Cognitive World: The Next Step*. Cambridge, MA: MIT Press.

Wheeler, M. (forthcoming). Minds, things, and materiality. In C. Renfrew and L. Malafouris (eds.), *The Cognitive Life of Things: Recasting the Boundaries of the Mind*. Cambridge: McDonald Institute for Archaeological Research Publications.

Wheeler, M. (unpublished ms). Draft chapters from an "in preparation" book, *Extended X: Recarving the Biological and Cognitive Joints of Nature*, available online (as of September 11, 2008) at http://www.philosophy.stir.ac.uk/staff/m-wheeler/ExtendedX.php.

Wheeler, M., and Clark, A. (2008). Culture, embodiment, and genes: Unravelling the triple helix. *Philosophical Transactions of the Royal Society of London, Series B, Biological Sciences, 363*, 3563–3575.

Wilson, R. A. (2004). *Boundaries of the Mind: The Individual in the Fragile Sciences*. Cambridge: Cambridge University Press.

12 Consciousness, Broadly Construed

Mark Rowlands

1 Introduction

In this chapter, I argue for an extended account of states that are both conscious and intentional (i.e., experiences but not sensations).[1] The argument turns on two claims: (a) the intentional directedness of experiences consists in a form of revealing or disclosing activity, and (b) disclosing activity typically straddles neural processes, bodily processes, and things we do in and to the world. The chapter has three parts. In the first, I examine and undermine the widespread tendency to suppose that whatever else is true of conscious experience, it must be something exclusively constituted by what is going on inside the heads of subjects. The second part develops the idea of the intentional directedness of conscious experience as revealing or disclosing activity. The third part uses this account of intentional directedness to argue for an extended model of conscious experience.

I Fregean Consciousness

2 Two Senses of Sense

I shall begin with what, I hope to show, is a constructive misreading of Frege's ruminations on the concept of sense. It is a misreading, because it attributes to Frege a concern with the psychological that he did not have, and so veers in the direction of a *psychologism* that he eschewed. It is constructive, because the primary concern of this chapter is the psychological: specifically, conscious experiences defined by there being something it is like to have them. The thesis I shall defend is that the advertised Fregean ruminations on sense translate almost exactly into contemporary discussions of consciousness. And this reveals an important way in which those discussions are incomplete.

As many commentators have noted, there is a pronounced tension in Frege's account of *sense (Sinn)*. Frege wants to attribute two distinct types of feature or function to *senses* or *thoughts (Gedanken)*. On the one hand, Frege claims that senses can be objects of mental acts in a way akin— although not identical—to that in which physical objects can be the objects of mental acts (Harnish 2000). Physical objects can be perceived; senses or thoughts (i.e., the sense of a declarative sentence) can be *apprehended*. Moreover, when a thought is apprehended, Frege claims, "something in [the thinker's] consciousness must be *aimed at* the thought" (Frege 1918, pp. 34–35). In one of its guises, therefore, a sense is an intentional object of an act of apprehension.

However, according to Frege senses also have the role of fixing reference. Although senses can be objects of reference, that is not their only, or even typical, role. In its second guise, the function of sense is to direct the speaker's or hearer's thinking not to the sense itself but to the object picked out by that sense.[2] In this case, senses do not figure as intentional objects of mental acts, but as items in virtue of which a mental act can have an object. In their customary role, senses are *determinants* of reference: they are what fix reference rather than objects of reference.

It is clear that there is a tension between these two ways of understanding sense. It is not simply that these characterizations are distinct. More importantly, when sense is playing the role described in the first characterization, it cannot also play the role described in the second, and vice versa. This inability to play both roles simultaneously shows itself in a certain *non-eliminability* that attaches to sense in its reference-determining role. In its first guise, a sense is an object of apprehension: an intentional object of a mental act. But the second characterization of sense tells us that whenever there is an intentional object of a mental act, there is also a sense that fixes reference to this object. If we combine these characterizations, therefore, it seems we must conclude that whenever sense exists as an intentional object of a mental act of apprehension, there must, in that act, be another sense that allows it to exist in this way. And if this latter sense were also to exist as an intentional object of a mental act, there would have to be yet another sense that allowed it to do so. Sense in its reference-determining guise, therefore, has a non-eliminable status within any intentional act. In any intentional act, there is always a sense that is not, and in that act cannot be, an intentional object.[3]

It is the second way of thinking about sense, sense as determinant of reference, which underwrites the familiar idea that Fregean sense is *inexpressible*: as something that can be *shown* but not *said*. Dummett states the initial worry: "even when Frege is purporting to give the sense of a word or symbol, what he actually *states* is what its reference is" (1973, p. 227). Some have tried to upgrade this worry to a charge of outright incoherence. Consider an analogy employed by Searle (1957). There is a collection of tubes through which marbles pass to drop into holes below; in some cases different tubes may lead to the same hole. We cannot succeed in getting a marble to lodge in a tube; it always passes through the tube to the hole beneath. Senses, it might be thought, are like this. And, if so, they are not the sorts of thing that can be grasped. Thus, sense in its reference-determining role undermines the possibility of its figuring as an object of apprehension.

This conclusion would, however, be premature. Searle's analogy invites us to think of sense as a *route* to a referent. This sits comfortably with Frege's idea that different senses can determine one and the same reference: there can, similarly, be many routes to one and the same location. However, the analogy introduces too much of a gap between sense and reference. One might imagine, for example, someone switching around the tubes so that they now pass into entirely different holes. A better way of thinking about reference is not as route to a referent, but as a *way or manner of presenting* a referent (Dummett 1981). If the sense of an expression is the manner in which we determine its referent, then should we want to convey the sense of an expression, all we can do is choose a means of stating the referent where this means displays the sense we wish to convey. Thus, we *say* what the referent of an expression is, and in choosing the particular means for saying this, we thereby *show* what the sense of the expression is (Dummett 1981, p. 131).[4]

Three ideas emerging from the foregoing discussion are particularly pertinent to the concerns of this chapter:

(1) The notion of Fregean sense functions in two different ways: (a) as an intentional object of a mental act of apprehension, and (b) as that which determines reference.
(2) As a determinant of reference, sense has a non-eliminable role within any intentional act.
(3) This combination of 1(a) and 1(b) is not incoherent as long as we are willing to accept that sense is simply a manner of determining a referent, and therefore is something that can be shown but not said.

I shall argue that clearly identifiable counterparts of these principles can be found in recent attempts to understand phenomenal consciousness: what it is like to have or undergo an experience. However, almost all recent discussions have been oriented around a conception of consciousness along the lines of Frege's first conception of sense: the idea of sense as an object of an act of apprehension. What it is like to have an experience is thought of as something of which we are aware in the having of that experience. What it is like to have an experience is an object of experiential *apprehension*. However, just as Fregean sense is more than an object of apprehension, I shall argue that what it is like to have an experience is more than an object of apprehension. Just as Fregean sense is that which determines reference, what it is like to have an experience is, in part, that which determines the objects of experiential acts. Its role in this regard is non-eliminable in any such act.

The rest of this chapter comes in three parts. In the rest of part I, I shall examine the default conception of consciousness presupposed in most recent discussions, and exhibit the similarities between this conception of consciousness and the understanding of Fregean sense as an object of apprehension. In the part II, I shall develop an argument for understanding what it is like to have an experience more along the lines of the other conception of Fregean sense: sense as a determinant of reference rather than an object of apprehension. Like the corresponding interpretations of sense, these two ways of understanding what it is like to have an experience are not incompatible. Both are legitimate, and therefore each, taken in isolation, is incomplete. In the part III of the chapter, I shall argue that thinking of consciousness along the lines of a Fregean determinant of reference has one consequence that many will find surprising: What it is like to have an experience does not supervene on what is going on inside the head of a conscious subject. Many, perhaps most, will find this conclusion objectionable. Nevertheless, I think it is correct and I shall defend it.

3   The Default Conception: Consciousness as Empirical

Most, in fact almost all, recent treatments of experience presuppose—sometimes implicitly but usually explicitly—that experiences are *objects* of some sort. By this, I do not mean, of course, that they think of experiences as objects as opposed to some other category of existent—events, states, processes, properties, facts, and so on. Rather, I mean that they conceive of experiences as items *of* which we are, or can be, aware. Let us call this the *empirical* conception of experience, where this term has a roughly Kantian sense. To say that an item is empirical is simply to claim that it is an actual or potential object of consciousness: it is the sort of thing of which I might become aware if my awareness is suitably engaged.

Not only experiences but also their *properties* or *aspects* can be empirical in this sense. I can attend both to my experience of a bright red apple and to, as Locke might put it, the forcefulness and vivacity of this experience. Moreover, among these properties is a particularly important—arguably definitive—one: *what it is like* to have or undergo the experience. This too, is one of the things of which we can be aware in the having of the experience. What distinguishes me from my zombie twin, so the idea goes, is that when we have an experience of a given type, I am, but he is not, aware of what it is like to have the experience. It is my awareness of the *phenomenal character* of my experiences that distinguishes me from my zombie twin.

The precise nature of the relation between a subject and her experiences required for her to be aware of these experiences and/or their properties is a matter of debate. The following categories—not necessarily mutually exclusive ones—have proved influential:

(1) Experiences and what it is like to have them are objects of *knowledge.*
(2) Experiences and what it is like to have them are objects of *introspection.*
(3) Experiences and what it is like to have them are items to which we have *access.*

Each of these claims can be subdivided further, depending on one's favored model of how each of these relations is implemented.[5]

Frank Jackson's (1982, 1986) *knowledge argument* is explicitly predicated on claim (1). The knowledge argument is based on the assumption that what it is like to have an experience can be an object of knowledge—a peculiarly factive attitude, but nonetheless a form of awareness in the general sense employed in this chapter. Mary, despite the impediment of being locked away in a monochromatic environment for her entire life, becomes the world's leading authority on the neurology of color vision. In fact she knows everything there is to know about the neural processes involved in seeing colors. However:

It seems . . . that Mary does not know all there is to know. For when she is let out of the black-and-white room, she will learn what it is like to see something red, say. This is rightly described as learning—she will not say "ho, hum." Hence physicalism is false. (Jackson 1986, p. 292)

Before her release, she does not know what it is like to see red. After her release, she does. What it is like to see red, therefore, becomes an object of her knowledge. I am presupposing only a very minimal sense of "object of knowledge": if *s* knows that *p*, then *p* is an object of knowledge for *s*. This claim is distinct from, and does not entail, more sanguine claims concerning the nature of this knowledge or the object. For example, to claim that p is an object of knowledge for s does not entail that p is some sort of peculiar "mental object"—a particular with irreducible and intrinsic phenomenal qualities on which the mind can direct its knowledge-acquiring gaze. I doubt that there are any such objects, and I am using the term "knowledge" in such a way that it entails no such thing. The sense of the term is so broad that it is compatible with any proposal concerning what a subject knows when they know what it is like to have an experience. If there is a presupposition here, it is a tautology.

Colin McGinn's (1991, 2004) defense of his transcendental naturalist position explicitly requires claim (2). His arguments presuppose that what it is like to have an experience is an object of introspection—in the broad sense of "object" presupposed in this chapter. Thus:

Our acquaintance with consciousness could hardly be more direct; phenomenological description thus comes (relatively) easily. "Introspection" is the name of the faculty through which we catch consciousness in all its vivid nakedness. By virtue of possessing this cognitive faculty we ascribe concepts of consciousness to ourselves; we thus have "immediate access" to the properties of consciousness. (McGinn 1991, p. 8)

Through introspection, we become aware, introspectively, of what it is like to have a conscious experience; or, as McGinn puts it: it is through introspection that we catch consciousness in "all its vivid nakedness." What it is like is, thus, an object of our introspection: something given to us by a form of "immediate access." Again, given the broad conception of object presupposed in this chapter—one that is entirely neutral with regard to the nature of the object (and, indeed, the nature of introspection), this is a tautology. If you can introspect what it is like to have or undergo an experience, then what it is like is an object of introspection.

I have been emphasizing the entirely unremarkable character of the idea that what it is like to have an experience is an object—in the sense required by this chapter—of awareness. If the claim that what it is like to have an experience is an object of awareness is tautological then it can hardly be false. Nonetheless, it is disingenuous because it is incomplete. The very ordinariness of the idea that consciousness is an object of awareness masks something deeply significant about consciousness. What this is begins to emerge if we turn our attention to (3). On this point, Thomas Nagel's (1974, 1986) position is particularly instructive, because here we find an implicit commitment to (3), and this, in the work of the arch-

champion of subjectivity, brings out just how widespread and tenacious—
utterly unremarkable—is the empirical conception of experience. We also
begin to see just what this conception hides.

In his seminal paper "What Is It Like to Be a Bat?" Nagel argued that (1)
"Fundamentally, an organism has conscious mental states if and only if
there is something that it is like to be that organism—something that it is
like *for* the organism" (1974, p. 166). However, (2) "If physicalism is to be
defended, the phenomenological features of experience must themselves
be given a physical account" (ibid., p. 167). But (3) "When we examine
their subjective character it seems that such a result is impossible. The reason is that every subjective phenomenon is essentially connected with a
single point of view, and it seems inevitable that an objective physical
theory will abandon that point of view" (ibid.).

What is important for our purposes is not the success or otherwise of
Nagel's argument, but a particular conception of subjectivity embodied in
it. Nagel begins with a certain common understanding of objectivity. An
"objective fact *par excellence*" is "the kind that can be observed and understood from many points of view" (ibid., p. 172). Objective facts are ones to
which there exist many *routes of epistemic access*. It is the existence of such
many and varied routes, capable of being adopted by many and varied
individuals, that constitutes an item as objective. In short, objective items
are ones to which epistemic access is *generalized*. Taking this concept of
objectivity as primary, Nagel then constructs a concept of subjectivity
based on the guiding metaphor of a route of access. Subjective phenomena
are ones to which our routes of access are reduced to one: they are items to
which our access is *idiosyncratic*. To think of subjective phenomena in this
way is to think of them as part of a region of reality that *in itself* is just like
any other. This region of reality differs from other regions not in any of
its intrinsic features: the only difference lies in our mode of access to it.
Our port of epistemic entry to this region of reality is unusually small.
Classically objective phenomena are like objects on a savannah, and can
be approached from many different directions. Conscious phenomena
are locked up in a remote canyon whose only route of access is a narrow
tunnel.

This way of thinking about consciousness is, I think, part of the pull of
the idea that all reality is intrinsically objective. Objectivity is taken as
primary, and subjectivity is understood as a derivative and truncated form
of objectivity. And the notion of a mode or route of access lies at the heart
of both concepts. Thus, it is our having idiosyncratic (i.e., truncated)
access to an item that constitutes that item as subjective. If only our routes

of access could somehow be *beefed up*; if only they could be suitably generalized, then the very same item would become objective.[6] The idea that
reality is intrinsically objective is the idea that this generalizing of routes
of access could, in principle, take place without any change in the intrinsic nature of the object toward which this access is directed.

To see the significance of this way of understanding the subjective–
objective distinction, consider Nagel's tendency to slide from claims
such as:

Every subjective phenomenon is essentially *connected* with a single point of view.
(Nagel 1974, p. 167, emphasis mine)

to claims such as:

For if the facts of experience—facts about what it is like *for* the experiencing
organism—are *accessible* only from one point of view, then it is a mystery how the
true character of experiences could be revealed in the physical operation of that
organism. (Ibid., p. 172)

The claim that a subjective phenomenon is one essentially *connected* with
a single point of view mutates into the claim that a subjective phenomenon is one that is essentially *accessible* from only a single point of view.
Here we find, in effect, the decisive movement in the conjuring trick.
These claims are not equivalent, and to suppose that they are is a symp-
tom of the grip exerted on us by the empirical conception of experience.
To see why this is so, however, we must outline the alternative. In doing
so, the dual nature of Fregean sense is to be our guide.

II The Intentional Core of Experience

4 Extended Consciousness: The Argument from Intentionality

In its second guise, Fregean sense is a determinant of reference. As such, it
is not typically an object of an act of apprehension, and can be such an
object only if there is another sense functioning in reference-determining
mode. As a determinant of reference, therefore, sense has a non-eliminable
role within any intentional act. In the case of conscious experience, the
counterpart to this conception of sense would be that aspect of the experience in virtue of which the experience has or takes an object. I shall argue
that any experience must contain an intentional core—a non-eliminable
component of the experience in virtue of which the experience is an experience *of* something.

I shall be working with a model of intentionality that has become sufficiently widely accepted to be referred to as the *standard model*. According to this, intentionality has a tripartite structure, comprising: (i) act, (ii) object, and (iii) mode of presentation of that object. Widespread acceptance is, of course, not universal acceptance. The claim that all forms of intentional directedness must conform to this model has come under attack in recent decades, largely due to the groundbreaking work of Kripke (1980). The argument I shall develop in this chapter does not dispute the possibility of forms of intentionality that do not conform to the traditional model. However, it assumes that at least some forms of intentional directedness do thus conform. It applies only to states that exhibit this form of intentional directedness. Happily, the claim that perceptual experiences—the primary focus of this chapter—exhibit this form of intentional directedness is commonplace (see, e.g., Martin 2002).

The key to the argument I am going to develop lies in a proper understanding of the concept of a mode of presentation. I shall argue that this apparently univocal concept masks a systematic ambiguity—one that precisely parallels the dual nature of Fregean sense.

According to the standard model, the mode of presentation is what connects intentional act to intentional object. Employing a terminology made famous by Kaplan (1980), we can say that the intentional act has a *character*, and the *content* of this act can be expressed in the form of a description. The intentional *object* of the act is the object that satisfies this description. The *mode of presentation* of the object, then, consists in the content expressed in the relevant description.

If an object satisfies the content-specifying description, however, this will be because the object possesses certain *aspects*: aspects that are picked out by the content-specifying description. Aspects are not to be identified with objective *properties* of objects. Aspects are objects of awareness in an intentional rather than objective sense. Aspects are the ways in which objects are presented, the ways in which they appear, to subjects. And to the aspect there may or may not correspond an objective property of the object. A necessary condition of an object having aspects is the intentional activity of a subject. Therefore, aspects are not identical with objective properties.

Since the *aspects* of the object are that in virtue of which it satisfies the content-specifying description, and since the mode of presentation of the object is the content expressed in that description, this invites the almost irresistible identification: we identify the *mode of presentation* of the object with that object's *aspects*. This identification, however, is problematic: it can be both true and false, depending on how we understand the concept of a mode of presentation. And this reveals a crucial ambiguity in this concept.

Aspects are intentional objects of awareness. I can attend not only to the tomato, but to its size, color, and luster. Indeed, typically I attend to the tomato in virtue of attending to these sorts of aspects. Thus, if we identify modes of presentation with aspects, and if we adhere to the standard model of intentionality as a relation whereby an object of awareness is determined only by way of a mode of presentation, it follows that whenever there is a mode of presentation—an aspect—there must be another mode of presentation to fix reference to it. Intentional directedness toward objects is mediated by way of a mode of presentation. Therefore, if aspects are intentional objects of experience, there must be a mode of presentation in virtue of which the intentional activity of a subject is directed toward these aspects.

In short, intentional objects require modes of presentation. If aspects of objects are themselves intentional objects, then there must be a mode of presentation that allows them to be as such. So if modes of presentation are aspects, then any experience that contains them as intentional objects must contain another mode of presentation—one that is not, in that experience, an intentional object. And if we were to make this second mode of presentation into an object of awareness—an *aspect* of our experience of which we are aware—there must be another mode of presentation that enables us to do this.

This is an issue of *non-eliminability* rather than *regress*. It is not that any experience must contain an infinite number of modes of presentation. That regress is stopped as soon as we stop trying to make modes of presentation into objects of our awareness. For example, if we identify a mode of presentation of a tomato with an aspect of that tomato, and so think of it as an intentional object of my experience, then it follows from the traditional model of intentionality that there must be another mode of presentation that allows it to be such. However, as long as I do not attempt to make this further mode of presentation into an intentional object, there is no need for an additional mode of presentation to fix reference to it. Therefore, in any given experience, there must be a mode of presentation that cannot, in that experience, be made into an intentional object. In the experience, this mode of presentation is not something *of* which we are aware (as we might, for example, be aware of aspects) but something *in virtue of which* we are aware of the intentional object of our experience.

The concept of a mode of presentation, in other words, admits of two interpretations. The first is *empirical* in the roughly Kantian sense introduced in section 2. An item is empirical, in this sense, if it is the sort of thing that can be an intentional object, an actual or potential object of consciousness: it is the sort of thing *of* which I might become aware if my awareness is suitably engaged. Aspects of objects are empirical in this sense. Let us say, again in at least roughly Kantian mode, that an item is *transcendental* if and only if it is not and cannot be an intentional object—at least not in its transcendental role—because it is that which permits objects to appear under aspects. In its transcendental role, a mode of presentation is a *condition of possibility* of intentional objects. An empirical mode of presentation is an aspect of objects. A transcendental mode of presentation is what makes a given empirical mode of presentation *possible*. That is, it is what permits an object to appear under a given aspect. This, ultimately, is what justifies the rubric *transcendental*.

If we assume that the identification of modes of presentation with aspects is a legitimate way of understanding this concept—and it is certainly common to understand a mode of presentation in this way—then the standard model of intentionality has this clear entailment: any given experience must contain not only an empirical but also a transcendental mode of presentation. It is the transcendental mode of presentation that corresponds to Frege's second concept of sense—sense as determinant of reference rather than object of apprehension. It is in this transcendental mode of presentation that we find the *non-eliminable intentional core* of the experience. If intentionality is understood as directedness toward objects, then it is in the transcendental mode of presentation that this directedness is to be found. Empirical modes of presentation—aspects—are simply objects upon which consciousness is directed. They are not the sorts of thing that could constitute the directedness of consciousness toward its objects. The point is, ultimately, a straightforward one: any intentional object—mundane object, aspect, empirical mode of presentation—is something toward which consciousness or intentional activity is directed. Therefore, if we want to understand intentional directedness itself, we will have to look elsewhere: we will not find intentional directedness in the objects of that directedness.

The transcendental mode of presentation, on the other hand, is not an intentional object of the experience, and in its transcendental role it cannot be an object of any experience. In its transcendental role, it is that which allows mundane worldly objects to be presented to subjects by way of aspects and, thus, that which allows the intentional states of subjects to be directed toward the world. If intentionality is understood as the *directedness* of consciousness toward its objects, it is in this non-eliminable intentional core of experience that this directedness resides. This has one implication that is crucial for the purpose of the argument of part III of this paper: intentional directedness toward the world consists in a form of *revealing* or *disclosing activity*.

Suppose I have a visual experience as of a shiny, red tomato. The empirical mode of presentation of the tomato consists in the way it is presented to me—in this case shiny and red. The transcendental mode of presentation of the experience, however, is that which allows the tomato to be presented to me as shiny and red. This characterization is intended to be neutral with regard to what it is that gets presented—and this neutrality is reflected in my use of the expression "as of." Historically, the candidates have been (i) the thing-in-itself conceived of something lying behind the presentation, or (ii) a structured series of presentations. For our purposes, we need not adjudicate. I shall frame the discussion as if there is something lying behind the presentation—something that gets presented—but this discussion could just as easily be framed in terms of option (ii). If there is no tomato there, of course—if the experience is an illusion—then it is still true that some part of the world—that which is erroneously taken to be a tomato—is presented as shiny and red. In the case of a hallucination, there is no *object* that is taken to be shiny and red—erroneously or otherwise—but, nevertheless, there is a *region* of the world that is taken to be shiny and red. This localization to a region is what makes the hallucination a specifically *visual* hallucination.

In each case, it is the transcendental mode of presentation of the experience that allows the world—object or region—to be presented in this way. The transcendental mode of presentation of my experience is that in virtue of which the tomato, or relevant part of the world, is *disclosed* or *revealed* to me as shiny and red. The non-eliminable core of intentional experience, therefore, consists in a *disclosure* or *revelation* of the world. The fundamental sense in which intentional acts are directed toward the objects, therefore, is that they reveal or disclose them as having certain *aspects* or *empirical modes of presentation*.

5 Causal versus Constitutive Disclosure

The idea of disclosing or revealing activity perhaps lends itself most naturally to a causal or mechanistic interpretation. To study the revealing activity responsible for the tomato being presented to me as shiny and red is to study the causal mechanisms of the visual apparatus and the processes implemented in these mechanisms. However, in fact, the idea of disclosure is not unambiguous, and it is important to distinguish two distinct forms. The distinction tracks that between an experience and its material realizations. Such a distinction will prove important for those who think there is an irreducible explanatory gap between consciousness and the brain. In the remainder of this chapter, I am going to be working primarily with the causal or mechanistic sense of disclosure. However, if you think there is an *explanatory gap* between conscious experience and its material bases, then you will also be forced to accept that the way an experience discloses its objects is quite different from the way the material realizations of experience disclose objects.

Suppose, again, that I have a visual experience as of a shiny, red tomato. The tomato is disclosed to me as shiny and red because, roughly, there is *something that it is like* to see the tomato. At the level of an experience which is essentially characterized by there being something that it is like to have it, this "what it is like" is the transcendental mode of presentation of that experience. Thus, the transcendental mode of presentation of the tomato given to me in my experience of it consists in what it is like to see the tomato: what it is like to see the tomato is that in virtue of which the tomato is revealed to the subject as shiny and red (Rowlands 2001, 2002, 2003b). The expression "in virtue of" should be understood as expressing a *logically sufficient* condition: what it is like to see the tomato, in its concrete phenomenal particularity, is, in this case, a logically sufficient condition for the tomato to be revealed to the subject as shiny and red. If a subject has an experience with the requisite what-it's-like-ness, then there is no logically possible way in which the tomato (or region, etc.) cannot be revealed to him as shiny and red. Transcendentally, what it is like to have or undergo an experience is that in virtue of which the world is revealed to us as being a certain way: that is, as falling under a given aspect or empirical mode of presentation. It reveals the world in this way by providing a logically sufficient condition for the world to be presented in this way.[7]

Let us shift focus, now, from the visual experience as of a shiny, red tomato to the material realization of this experience. By "material realization," I simply mean a *supervenience* or *realizing* base of the experience, where the idea of supervenience is understood in the usual way: as a one-way relation of determination with modal status. The material realizations of experience also reveal or disclose the world, but they do so in a quite different way: the revealing activity performed by the material realization of an experience has a quite different status from that of the experience itself. This, ultimately, is why there is an explanatory gap between consciousness and its material realizations.

Consider, for example, the mechanisms whereby, it is thought, my retinal image of a red tomato is progressively transformed into a visual representation of a tomato. Let us, for now, work with a paradigmatically internalist model of this process: Marr's (1982) account. The retinal image is transformed into a 3-D object representation by way of its progressive transformation through raw primal sketch, full primal sketch, and 2.5-D sketch. To identify these mechanisms responsible for these transformations, if Marr's account is correct, would be to identify the mechanisms that are *causally* responsible for my visual experience of the tomato and its specific aspects.

The successive transformations that collectively produce the visual experience of the red tomato are a form of disclosing activity. However, this is quite different from the form of disclosure exhibited by transcendental modes of presentation. In no part of the Marrian story—or in any story like it—do we find *logically* sufficient conditions for the disclosure of the world as being, for example, shiny and red. This disclosure undoubtedly has physically sufficient conditions in certain psychophysical events, occurring, perhaps, both inside and outside the body. But these *physically* sufficient conditions do not add up to *logically* sufficient conditions. Indeed, this is one way—a simple translation into the language of disclosure—of understanding the force of the various explanatory gap intuitions.

The shift from *physically* to *logically* sufficient conditions is, in effect, a move from what *produces* a given item to what a given item *consists in*. A transcendental item is that in which the appearance of an item as empirical consists. Understood transcendentally, the phenomenal character of my visual experience—what it is like to see a red tomato—does not (causally) *produce* the revealing of the tomato as red. Rather, it is what the revealing of the tomato as red consists in. We can use the ambiguous expression "in virtue of" to express this idea—the phenomenal character of my experience is that in virtue of which the object of the experience is revealed in the way that it is—but only if we are clear that this is a *constitutive* rather than *causal* sense of that expression.

Part III   Extended Consciousness

6   Intentionality as a "Living-Through"

I have argued that (i) any perceptual experience will contain a non-eliminable intentional core, and (ii) this intentional core consists in disclosing or revealing activity, that is, the disclosing of an item in the world as falling under certain aspects or empirical modes of presentation. I have also (iii) distinguished causal from constitutive disclosure. These three claims nicely set up the central thesis of this chapter: conscious experience does not, in general, supervene on intracranial occurrences. The reason is, I shall argue, *pace* Marr, that causal disclosure of the world does not in general take place purely inside the head of a subject. The essence of intentionality is disclosing activity. The sort of disclosing activity occasioned by the vehicles of intentional states and processes—the sorts of vehicles pertinent to the theses of embodied and extended cognition—is causal disclosure. Causal disclosure can be constituted by states and processes occurring in the brain of subjects of intentional states. But, in general, it is not restricted to neural states and processes. There are many ways of causally disclosing the world—many vehicles through which the world may be causally disclosed to subjects—and brain-based ways are only a subset of these. In general, the vehicles of causal disclosure do not stop at the boundaries of the brain, but extend out into the activity we perform in the world, activity that is both bodily and incorporates wider environmental performances.

If the arguments developed in the preceding sections are correct, then the fundamental sense in which intentional acts are directed toward the objects, therefore, is that they reveal or disclose them as having certain *aspects* or *empirical modes of presentation*. This has a crucial, but largely overlooked, implication: as directedness toward objects, intentional acts are also, necessarily, a *living-* or *passing-through* of their material realizations.

This idea can perhaps best be clarified, in the first instance, by way of a well-known example; indeed, by now, possibly a hackneyed example: Merleau-Ponty's (1962) discussion of the perceptual role played by a blind person's cane (cf. Polanyi 1958). As Merleau-Ponty notes, it is possible to tell two quite different stories about this role. The first story treats the cane as an empirical—in the roughly Kantian sense employed in this chapter— object: in this case, an object of theoretical scrutiny and explanation. The resulting empirical story is a familiar one. Tactile and kinesthetic sensors in the blind person's hands send messages to the brain. Various events then occur in the person's sensory cortex, and these are interpreted as the result of ambient objects standing in certain relations to the person's location. When suitably filled out, there is nothing wrong with this story. However, it only describes the blind person's consciousness from the outside; as an empirical phenomenon. The story from the inside—the transcendental story in the sense introduced earlier—is quite different. The cane—in conjunction, of course, with the requisite neural and other biological machinery—*discloses* or *reveals* objects as possessing or falling under certain *aspects* or *empirical modes of presentation*. Thus, an object may be disclosed to the blind person as being "in front" or him or her, as "near," "further away," "to the left," "to the right," and so on.

Merleau-Ponty is at pains to emphasize—quite correctly—the phenomenology of the resulting perception of the world. The blind person does not experience aspects of the objects he encounters as occurring in the cane, even though this is (part of) the material basis of his perception of these aspects. Still less does he experience them as occurring in the fingers that grip the cane; and less again in the sensory cortex that systematizes the experiential input. The cane can be both an *object* of awareness and a *vehicle* of awareness. But when the blind person uses the cane, it functions as a vehicle, not an object, of awareness. As such, the consciousness of the blind person passes all the way through the cane to the world. When the blind person uses the cane, his consciousness, in this sense, *lives through* it.

The notion of living-through requires some clarification. One might say, for example, that consciousness *lives through* the brain. Utterances of this sort typically advert to a one-way relation of dependence that can be characterized in terms of the concept of supervenience or realization. In this sense, consciousness lives through the brain to the extent that the brain is *responsible* for consciousness—that without the requisite neural activity there would be no consciousness. This is not what I mean by "living-through." Rather, "living-through," as I shall use this locution, means something akin to "passing-through." Suppose you are utterly engrossed in a novel. Your consciousness passes through the words on the page—these are not objects of your awareness—through to the characters and plot lines these words communicate. When I talk of consciousness living through its material realizations, I intend this in something akin to the way in which consciousness passes through the words of a book to the characters that these words describe.

However, this clarification is not complete. There are two further ways in which this notion of living- or passing-through might be understood. The first, and most obvious, pertains to the phenomenology of experience. This is the sort of interpretation promoted by Merleau-Ponty's discussion of the blind person's cane. Phenomenologically, from the point of view of what it is like to have or undergo the relevant experiences, the blind person experiences the objects around him as objects in the world rather than modifications of the cane. Phenomenologically, we might say, his consciousness does not stop short of the world. Similarly, in reading the novel, my consciousness stops not at the words on the page but passes all the way through to the characters those words describe.

These points concerning the phenomenology of absorbed coping experience can, I think, scarcely be contested. However, my claim is not one about the phenomenology of experience, but about the underlying structure of consciousness. The claim about phenomenology is, in effect, a consequence of this deeper point concerning structure. Intentional acts are directed toward the world in the sense that they are disclosing or revealing activity. But where does the blind person's revealing activity occur? When the person discloses an object as being in front of him, for example, where does this disclosing activity occur? It occurs, in part, in the brain. But it also occurs in the body, and also, crucially, in the cane and the cane's interaction with the world. Revealing activity, by its nature, *does not stop short of the world*: it *passes through* its material realizations out to the world itself.

The role of the cane, fundamentally, is one not of *object* of disclosure but *vehicle* of disclosure. The blind person does not experience the object as "on the end of the cane," nor does he experience it as a blocking or resistance to the cane. Rather it is *in virtue of* the object of being on the end of the cane, and *in virtue of* the resistance it provides to the cane, that the blind person experiences the object as spatially located in the world. In employing the cane, the blind person ceases to experience the cane. The cane becomes a vehicle of his experience not an object of it. As revealing activity, his experience passes all the way through the cane to the object itself. That is why his experience can be a disclosing of the aspects of those objects.

7   The Vehicles of Perceptual Disclosure

Consider the disclosing activities of a visually unimpaired subject. It is tempting, indeed it is typical, to think of these activities as restricted to processes occurring in the eyes themselves, and subsequent neural-processing operations. Such processes are, of course, vehicles of disclosure, not objects of disclosure. I am not aware *of* these processes; they are processes *with* or *in virtue of* which I am aware of other things. Relative to those things *of* which I am aware—the *empirical* objects of my awareness—the status of these processes is *transcendental*. These processes form part of my causal disclosure of the world.

However, my causal disclosure of the world is not restricted to these inner processes. In addition to the various neural processes occurring in my eyes and brain we can also identify various activities that I perform in the world: and these activities also form part of my causal disclosure of the world. There are many different categories of activity that might be involved, and these categories are not always entirely distinct. But three obvious, partially overlapping, categories stand out: (i) saccadic eye movements, (ii) probing and exploratory activities involved in the identification of sensorimotor contingencies, and (iii) the manipulation and exploitation of the optic array.

Saccadic eye movements

When I perform visual tasks, my eyes engage in various movements—*saccades*. Yarbus (1967) has demonstrated that (i) different tasks resulted in quite different scan paths, and (ii) the pattern of saccadic eye movement is systematically related to the nature of the visual task. In a famous series of experiments, Yarbus (1967) asked subjects, prior to their viewing of a painting, to perform certain tasks. The painting showed six women and the arrival of a male visitor. Subjects were asked to either:

1. View the picture at will.
2. Judge the age of the people in the painting.
3. Guess what the people had been doing prior to the arrival of the visitor.
4. Remember the clothing worn.
5. Remember the position of objects in the room.
6. Estimate how long it had been since the visitor was seen by the people in the painting.

Yarbus demonstrated that the required task had a significant impact on the visual scan path that the subject took: different tasks resulted in quite different visual scan paths. Subjects who were asked questions concerning the appearance of people in the painting—for example, questions about their ages—focused on the area around the face. Subjects who were asked questions concerning the theme of the painting focused on various points throughout the picture. And different themes also resulted in different scan paths. For example, subjects who were asked what the people doing before the visitor arrived employed a different scan path from those who were asked to estimate how long it had been since the visitor was last seen by the family. In general, Yarbus showed, the scan varies systematically with the nature of the task.

Saccadic eye movements, and the more general patterns of search in which such movements are situated, are part of the vehicles of perceptual disclosure. They are part of the means with or in virtue of which the world is disclosed as containing, for example, a collection of people who have not seen the visitor for many years rather than a collection of people who saw him last week. Saccadic scan paths are, of course, not objects of awareness—typically we have little or no idea what our eyes are doing when we extract information from a visual scene. Phenomenologically, we are typically not aware of the eye movements, but of what these movements help us reveal. And, if the arguments of this chapter are correct, this phenomenological point is grounded in the deeper point pertaining to the structure of consciousness: consciousness lives through or passes through saccadic movements and scan paths out to the world itself.

Sensorimotor activity

Sensorimotor or *enactive* accounts of visual experience (e.g., Noë 2004) accord a central role to a certain sort of activity: the probing or exploratory activity required to identify the sensorimotor contingencies pertinent to a given visual scene. Visual perception is essentially hybrid, made up of internal processes (extraction and activation of the laws of sensorimotor contingency) plus external processes (the probing or exploration of information-bearing structures in the environment). Visually perceiving is a process whereby the world—understood as an external store of information—is probed or explored by acts of perception, and the results of this exploration are mediated through the laws of sensorimotor contingency.

Suppose, to use an example of Dennett (1991), you are looking at a wall of photographs of Marilyn Monroe à la Andy Warhol. Your foveal vision subtends no more than three or four of these photographs, and your para-foveal vision is insufficiently precise to discriminate Marilyns from squiggly shapes. Nevertheless, it seems to you as if you are confronted with a wall of Marilyns, and not three or four Marilyns surrounded by a sea of squiggly shapes. The wall of Marilyns, in its entirety, is phenomenologically present to you.

The explanation supplied by the enactive account of this sense of phenomenological presence is simple and elegant. First, the impression we have of seeing everything—the wall of Marilyns in its entirety—derives from the fact that the slightest flick of the eye allows any part of the wall to be processed at will. This gives us the impression that the whole wall is immediately available (O'Regan and Noë 2001, p. 946). Second, the visual system is particularly sensitive to *visual transients*. When a visual transient occurs, a low-level "attention-grabbing" mechanism appears to automatically direct processing to the location of the transient. This means that should anything happen in the environment, we will generally consciously see it, since processing will be directed toward it. This gives us the impression of having tabs on everything that might change, and so of consciously seeing everything.

Casting one's attention at will to any part of the visual scene, or having one's attention drawn by a visual transient to a part of the scene: these are both examples of the sort of probing or exploratory activities that lie at the heart of the enactive approach. Like saccadic scan paths, these sorts of activities are vehicles of perceptual disclosure: they are that with or in virtue of which, in part, the visual world is disclosed in the way that it is. Our visual consciousness lives through or passes through these activities no less than it does through processes occurring in our eyes and brain.

Manipulation of the optic array   Consider, now, Gibson's (1966, 1979) account of visual perception. Light from the sun fills the air—the terrestrial medium—so that it is in a "steady state" of reverberation. The environment is, in this way, filled with rays of light traveling between the surfaces of objects. At any point, light will converge from all directions. Therefore, at each physical point in the environment, there exists a densely nested set of solid visual angles composed of inhomogeneities in the intensity of light. Thus, we can imagine an observer, at least for the present, as a point surrounded by a sphere which is divided into tiny solid angles. The intensity of light and the mixture of wavelengths vary from one solid angle to another. This spatial pattern of light is the *optic array*. Light carries information because the structure of the optic array is determined by the nature and position of the surfaces from which it has been reflected.

A key component of Gibson's account is the idea that by acting on the optic array, and thus transforming it, the perceiving organism is able to make available to itself information that was, prior to this action, present— at least conditionally—but not immediately available. When an observer moves, the entire optic array is transformed, and such transformations contain information about the layout, shapes, and orientations of objects in the world. The transformation of the array makes available to the organism information that was, prior to the movement, there in only a conditional or dispositional form. More specifically, by effecting transformations in the ambient optic array—by transforming one array into another systematically related array—perceiving organisms can identify and appropriate what Gibson calls the *invariant* information contained in the optic array: information contained not in any one static optic array as such but in the transformation of one array into another. In the absence of such transformations, invariant information is present, but only in conditional form: conditionally upon certain types of transformation being systematically related to certain changes in sensory input.

What is crucial here is that (i) the optic array, a structure external to the perceiving organism, is a locus of information for suitably equipped creatures, and (ii) a creature can appropriate or make this information available to itself through acting on the array, and thus effecting transformations in it. What the perceiving organism does, in effect, is *manipulate* a structure external to it—the optic array—in order to make available to itself information that it can then use to navigate its way around the environment.

The manipulation of the optic array, manipulation that is carried out by movement on the part of the perceiving organism, is another vehicle of perceptual disclosure. The perceiving organism is typically not aware of its manipulative activities: these activities are vehicles of disclosure, not objects of disclosure. That is, the activities are ones *with* or *in virtue of* which the perceiving organism becomes aware of certain features of its environment; they are not, typically, activities *of* which the organism is perceptually aware. Phenomenologically, the perceptual awareness of the organism passes through the activities to the world which those activities, in part, disclose to it. Crucially, where does the organism's perceptual disclosure of the environment take place? It takes place, in part, wherever the activities take place. And these activities do not stop short of the optic array. One cannot manipulate an external structure unless one's manipulation reaches out to that structure.

8   Conclusion

The intuition that whatever else is true of phenomenal consciousness it must supervene on intracranial goings-on relies, I have argued, on a lopsided way of thinking about consciousness. This way, in effect, thinks of consciousness as importantly akin to Fregean sense in only one of its incarnations: as an intentional object of an act of apprehension. If we think of consciousness as being like this, we will be irresistibly drawn to the idea that consciousness is one of the things we encounter when our awareness is inwardly engaged. Consciousness is like this; but it is also more than this. If we think of consciousness more along the lines of the second version of Fregean sense—as a determinant of reference rather than an object of apprehension—then the grip of this way of thinking about consciousness is broken. Thought of in this way, consciousness is that in virtue of which objects in the word are revealed as falling under aspects or empirical modes of presentation. And, as this sort of revealing activity, consciousness extends into the world.

Notes

1. As such, this chapter builds on the arguments of Rowlands 2002 and 2003a,b.

2. When the sense is that of a declarative sentence, of course, the object in question is, according to Frege, a truth-value.

3. Indeed, this is one way—a translation into the language of sense—of the commonplace idea that intentionality consists in *directedness-toward* objects. If intentionality is indeed, directedness-toward objects, and if this directedness-toward objects is distinct from the objects thus directed-toward, then we will look in vain at those intentional objects if we want to understand intentionality itself.

4. This commits me to aligning myself with Evans (1982) and McDowell (1977) in attacking Frege's claim that empty proper names—proper names that have no bearer—should be regarded as having sense but no reference. Evans and McDowell insist that empty proper names should be regarded as devoid of sense. I am happy to side with Evans and McDowell on this.

5. It is here, for example, that the debate between first-order and higher-order models of consciousness becomes relevant. The discussion to be developed in this chapter, however, proceeds at this more abstract level represented by (1)–(3).

6. It is this idea that seems to underlie Nagel's rather puzzling remarks about the possibility of an objective phenomenology delivered at the end of the paper.

7. Whether it also provides a logically necessary condition is an interesting question, but not one that needs to be addressed here—although, for what it's worth, I suspect that it does not.

References

Dennett, D. (1991). *Consciousness Explained*. New York: Little, Brown.

Dummett, M. (1973). *Frege: Philosophy of Language*. London: Duckworth.

Dummett, M. (1981). *The Interpretation of Frege's Philosophy*. London: Duckworth.

Evans, G. (1982). *The Varieties of Reference*. Oxford: Oxford University Press.

Frege, G. (1892). *On Sense and Reference*. (Reprinted in P. Geach and M. Black [trans. and eds.], *Translations from the Philosophical Writings of Gottlob Frege*, Oxford: Blackwell, 1960.)

Frege, G. (1918). The thought: A logical inquiry. (Reprinted in R. Harnish [ed.], *Basic Topics in the Philosophy of Language*, Englewood Cliffs, NJ: Prentice Hall, 1994. All page references are to the latter.)

Gibson, J. (1966). *The Senses Considered as Perceptual Systems.* Boston: Houghton-Mifflin.

Gibson, J. (1979). *The Ecological Approach to Visual Perception.* Boston: Houghton-Mifflin.

Harnish, R. (2000). Grasping modes of presentation: Frege vs. Fodor and Schweizer. *Acta Analytica, 15,* 19–46.

Jackson, F. (1982). Epiphenomenal qualia. *Philosophical Quarterly, 32,* 127–132.

Jackson, F. (1986). What Mary didn't know. *Journal of Philosophy, 83,* 291–295.

Kaplan, D. (1980). *Demonstratives.* The John Locke Lectures. Oxford: Oxford University Press.

Kripke, S. (1980). *Naming and Necessity.* Cambridge, MA: Harvard University Press.

Marr, D. (1982). *Vision.* San Francisco: W. H. Freeman.

Martin, M. (2002). The transparency of experience. *Mind and Language, 17*(4), 376–425.

McDowell, J. (1977). On the sense and reference of a proper name. *Mind, 86,* 159–185.

McGinn, C. (1991). *The Problem of Consciousness.* Oxford: Blackwell.

McGinn, C. (2004). *Consciousness and Its Objects.* Oxford: Oxford University Press.

Merleau-Ponty, M. (1962). *The Phenomenology of Perception.* Trans. C. Smith. New York: Humanities Press.

Nagel, T. (1974). What is it like to be a bat? *Philosophical Review, 83,* 435–450. (Reprinted in Nagel, *Mortal Questions,* New York: Cambridge University Press, 1979. All page references are to the latter.)

Nagel, T. (1986). *The View from Nowhere.* Oxford: Oxford University Press.

Noë, A. (2004). *Action in Perception.* Cambridge, MA: MIT Press.

O'Regan, K., and Noë, A. (2001). A sensorimotor account of vision and visual consciousness. *Behavioral and Brain Sciences, 23,* 939–973.

Polanyi, M. (1958). *Personal Knowledge: Towards a Post-Critical Philosophy.* Chicago: University of Chicago Press.

Rowlands, M. (2001). *The Nature of Consciousness.* Cambridge: Cambridge University Press.

Rowlands, M. (2002). Two dogmas of consciousness. In A. Noë (ed.), *Is the Visual World a Grand Illusion?* Special edition of *Journal of Consciousness Studies 9*(5–6), 158–180.

Rowlands, M. (2003a). *Externalism: Putting Mind and World Back Together Again.* London: Acumen.

Rowlands, M. (2003b). Consciousness: The transcendentalist manifesto. In A. Thomas (ed.), *Consciousness in Historical Perspective*, special edition of *Phenomenology and the Cognitive Sciences*, 2, 3, 205–221.

Rowlands, M. (2006). *Body Language: Representation in Action.* Cambridge, MA: MIT Press.

Searle, J. (1958). Proper names. *Mind, 67* (April).

Yarbus, A. (1967). *Eye Movements and Vision.* New York: Plenum Press.

13   The Extended Infant: Utterance-Activity and Distributed Cognition

David Spurrett and Stephen Cowley

Introduction

In "The Extended Mind" Clark and Chalmers (1998, reprinted in this volume) argue for "active externalism"—the view that the mind, or what realizes it, need not be confined within either the brain or body of the minded individual. Among the things outside the brain and body of any particular individual are, of course, other bodies and their brains. This paper is a preliminary and self-consciously speculative sketch of what might happen when the systems implementing minds extend into, and get tangled up with, one another. (Such exercises are not unprecedented in the history of philosophy and psychology.) Unlike Clark and Chalmers, our primary focus is not paradigmatically mental states, as understood by philosophers, such as beliefs and desires. Rather, we're quite generally interested in the control of behavior, whether or not we think of the control systems as operating on beliefs or desires. Our argument here is thus intended as an application of the *parity principle*, Clark and Chalmers's maxim to the effect (roughly) that any process that we'd have no hesitation in regarding as part of the cognitive process if it went on inside the head, is indeed part of the cognitive process no matter where we end up finding it implemented. Our chapter is in two parts—the first establishes some points of reference regarding language and cognition, the second is both more descriptive and more speculative. Finally, we attempt to connect the issues by discussing the parity principle directly.

1   Utterance-Activity and Language

"Utterance-activity" is a term of art (due to Cowley) used here to refer to the full range of kinetic, vocal, and prosodic features of the behavior of interacting humans. Utterance-activity can include, but is not restricted to, what are usually regarded as words and strings of words. We propose that utterance-activity should be regarded as at least as good an object of scientific interest in its own right as "language" traditionally conceived in mainstream linguistics. Further, we regard it as in crucial ways continuous with, and inextricable from, (nonwritten) language. We combine this continuity thesis with the developmental claim that language as usually understood develops out of, or is to some extent an elaboration of aspects of, utterance-activity. For present purposes these claims can be understood as methodological precepts—claims that useful things might be found out by supposing them—rather than as asserting anything stronger. Even so, this is an unorthodox position because, on a standard conception, anything deserving the name of (spoken) *language* is different "in principle" from the rest of behavior.

One argument *for* the standard conception might point out that to do justice to our intuition (if we have one) that written and spoken language are in some fundamental sense the same, we should regard the textlike, or digital, aspects of utterance-activity as language *proper*, and the remaining twitches, whoops, smiles, wavings, and so forth as something else.

This is not our view. We maintain that utterance-activity is the arena in which what is standardly regarded as language gets started, and that both the development and ongoing functioning of word-based language are made needlessly mysterious if utterance-activity is sidelined (Cowley, Moodley, and Fiori-Cowley 2004; Cowley in press).

We expect at least two serious objections to our continuity proposal. Briefly, the first points out that powerful and sophisticated models of language treat language as digital and importantly autonomous, and that the most likely reason these approaches are so powerful is that language is *in fact* digital and autonomous. If this is correct, we are putting apparently secure results needlessly in question. The second objection points out that since we define utterance-activity to include affective display, it includes signals that aren't arbitrary (see, e.g., Ekman 1972 on universality in facial expression of emotion), whereas we all "know" that language consists of tokens that *are* conventionally, arbitrarily, connected up to each other and the world. Both objections assert that we are ignoring important partitions in the data.

We won't offer full arguments against either objection. Both are serious, but we'll restrict ourselves to offering one suggestion about how to make a start in replying to each.

The first objection derives some of its force from the poverty of the stimulus argument.[1] Some explanation is certainly required for the fact that human children typically acquire facility with verbal language within a few years and with little evidence of effort. Debates over the correct explanation are partly organized around a fault line between "empiricists" defending some version of the view that general learning can account for language acquisition, and "nativists" insisting that some language-specific innate capacities are essential. Perhaps the most powerful weapon available to the nativists is the poverty of the stimulus argument, which we gloss as follows:

It is clearly the case that a wide range of sets of organizing principles are consistent with the "stimulus" or primary data available to human children, and further that the subset of "correct" principles are not preferable by the standards of generic criteria for theory choice, such as simplicity. It consequently seems extraordinarily unlikely that any human child would ever come to behave in ways counted as grammatical for their mother tongue (or tongues) in the event that human children were broadly empiricist learners. Since children do come to be regarded as behaving grammatically with such striking reliability, we can conclude that they are not empiricist learners, but rather that they have language-specific innate cognitive endowments

Interesting debates between empiricists and nativists about language acquisition concern, *inter alia*, questions about the real nature of the "stimulus," what mixture of innate and learned capacities is required to explain the phenomena, when particular types of learning start, the extent to which humans and particular nonhuman animals are cognitively alike, and the strengths and limitations of different types of learning.

Although the present chapter is not directly concerned with grammar, we note that neither of us is a Chomskian nativist.[2] Our wariness is fueled by two major considerations. On the one hand, work by figures such Elman (e.g., Elman 1991) and Chater and Christiansen (1999) suggest ways of reevaluating the properties of the learning involved in coming to behave "grammatically." Elman's work seeks to establish what particular connectionist systems are capable of learning, given variations in their architecture, properties of the training data, and the influence of varying general cognitive capacities. An example of this is manipulating the capacity of short-term "memory" discussed by Elman (1991, discussed in Clark 1993), showing that a plausible type of general cognitive maturation could have some of the same effects as the kinds of "hyper-benevolent" structuring of training data otherwise often required to enable a network to converge on efficient generalizations. (Since inputs in the wild are very unlikely to be so structured, any approach requiring such benevolence is vulnerable to the objection that it is unrealistic.) Chater and Christiansen, for their part, urge a kind of Copernican revolution, in which the vastly greater rate of change of languages as compared to genotypes is used in claiming that, to a significant extent, it is languages that are adapted to *our* cognitive peculiarities and limitations, rather than our cognitive abilities that are specifically and genetically optimized for language.

On the other hand, a range of empirical results concerning the cognitive capacities of nonhuman animals indicates that many abilities we might otherwise regard as language-specific adaptations are found in species without language. Chinchillas (Kuhl and Miller 1978) and cotton-top tamarins (Ramus et al. 2000), for example, perform surprisingly well at tasks requiring different (familiar and unfamiliar) language groups to be distinguished from one another—at least as well as human infants of certain ages.[3] To the extent that monkeys can do this, though, it seems reasonable to suppose that the powers of discrimination in question come for free as a consequence of capacities not specifically selected "for" (digital) language. Ramus et al. (2000, p. 351) conclude that since "tamarins have not evolved to process speech, we in turn infer that at least some aspects of human speech perception may have built upon pre-existing sensitivities of the primate auditory system."

Equally important, although in different ways, are some of the results from ape language research (ALR), in particular Savage-Rumbaugh's Sherman, Austin, and Kanzi (Savage-Rumbaugh 1986; Savage-Rumbaugh, Shanker, and Taylor 1998). Kanzi's comprehension is roughly equivalent to that of a two-and-a-half-year-old human child. His skill at production, is more difficult to quantify, partly because it is not clear to what extent it is facilitated or impeded by the constraints of the "lexigram boards." It clearly does not match the level of his comprehension, although Benson et al. (2004) engage in painstaking analysis to suggest that it is more impressive than might have been thought, and that it includes identifiable attempts at vocalization despite inappropriate anatomy. The point we're after here doesn't depend on how much exactly is achieved. It is simply that every increase in nonhuman ape performance is a blow against the view that to make *any headway at all* with language requires specifically human biological endowments.[4] For our present purposes what is especially notable about Sherman, Austin, and Kanzi is the lexigram-board technology used for the research and training, and, especially in Kanzi's case, an unusual biography and learning history.

First, regarding the lexigram boards, recall that chimpanzees and bonobos have, compared to humans, very limited control over their own vocalizations. Where much other ape language research used manual sign-languages, Savage-Rumbaugh's team uses physical arrays of "lexigram" symbols, in the form of fixed keyboards that triggered sound recordings of the relevant spoken term, and as folding boards that could be used on the move as well as privately by her subjects (who manifestly *did* engage in self-directed lexigram activity, and resented others' attempts to get a view of what symbols they were pressing during these episodes). These external, mostly publicly accessible resources allow both memory and other demands of symbolic processing to be handled by nonneural resources, perhaps significantly augmenting the cognitive powers of their users (Cowley and Spurrett 2003).

Second, and just as importantly, Kanzi's learning biography was unusual. Reared by Matata, a foster mother, he was present during, and apparently uninterested in, her own laborious trials with lexigram boards. Matata managed to show facility with only six different lexigrams, given 30,000 trials over a period of two years (Savage-Rumbaugh, Shanker, and Taylor 1998, p. 17). When she was taken away for a period, though, Kanzi began making use of the lexigram boards to communicate with human laboratory workers, showing abilities concealed by his indifferent progress in prior trials with the boards. On the day before Matata's departure, he used the lexigram board on 21 occasions, asking for three different foods. On the following day, he produced 120 lexigram-acts exploiting 12 different symbols (ibid., p. 22), twice what Matata had mastered in two years. Savage-Rumbaugh et al. claim that the sudden change suggested that what had changed was not "his knowledge but . . . his motivation" (ibid.). Consequently, ongoing study of Kanzi focused less on repeated trials, and more on his interactions with human laboratory workers. An aspect of this shift which we regard as especially important is that in the resulting environment Kanzi could gain much from working out how better to manipulate his generally attentive, cooperative, and often downright indulgent human companions. Kanzi, then, lived more like the infants of well-off humans than most ALR subjects.

Both of the features of Savage-Rumbaugh's research just highlighted (the lexigram boards as candidate part of an extended mind, and Kanzi's own biography) suggest that debates over the poverty of the stimulus could stand in need of some reevaluation. Some of these debates often seem to presuppose that the infant learner is a solitary epistemologist, attempting to make sense of external data on the basis of internal processing, and that it does so with a strikingly scholarly disinterest, even a bare appetite for generalizations. This undervalues or ignores both the ways in which non-neural resources can augment and transform cognitive capacities, and those in which social interaction provides both powerful incentives and mediating structures that support the learning process.

In the case of the objection that we needlessly conflate arbitrary and other aspects of activity, we can be briefer. We think that what counts as arbitrary partly depends on where one sets an explanatory frame. We, now, *can't* do much about the association between smiling and feeling happy and/or friendly. Plausibly, though, natural selection *could* have latched onto some different patterns of facial motion and gone on to build connections between *those* and particular social and affective states (see Ross 2007). So the import of smiling could be non-arbitrary *to us*, but arbitrary from the perspective of one interested in the evolution of patterns of affective signaling in humans.

Insisting on viewing language as a formal system of arbitrary elements involves emphasizing its "abstraction-amenable" aspects at the expense of others. One particularly famous instance of this tendency to focus on the abstraction-amenable aspects of language is, of course, Turing's (1950) proposal for an empirical reformulation of the question "can machines think?" Turing said of his approach that it had "the advantage of drawing a fairly sharp line between the physical and the intellectual capacities of a man." We regard it as a compelling virtue of a focus on utterance-activity, in the spirit of much contemporary research in cognitive science, that it attends to bodies and their lives in environments. By making utterance-activity central, we are not eschewing abstraction and theory at all. Rather we are suspending, for the purposes of investigation, commitment to the view that there is a theoretically well-motivated gulf separating language "proper" from behavior. How good an idea this is depends on what the research produces.

2   The "How" Question

We call the question we want to put at center stage the "how" question: *How can anything come to count as a symbol?*[5] We don't say *be* a symbol because, like Clark (e.g., Clark 1993), we are wary of many of the associations carried by the notion of symbols in debates about cognition and language. Any reference to a symbol is too likely, on our view, to suggest some kind of token with fairly precise individuation criteria, determinate intrinsic syntactic properties, and capacities for being more or less literally moved around, operated on, and combined with other symbols, often in the head. Of course, *whatever* is in (and around) the head, what goes on with people can usually be *described* in terms of symbols, and structured arrangements of symbols, as well as rules for operating on and with symbols. We want to remain tactically agnostic about what actually goes on under the cognitive hood, so as to focus more directly on a particular set of phenomena.[6]

Although utterance-activity embraces both analog (or non-textlike) and non-arbitrary elements, we are interested in its symbol-like aspects. In order to say something about symbols, for present purposes, we use an "off-the-shelf" solution. Accordingly, we use the distinctions between iconic, indexical, and symbolic reference due to Peirce (1955). Rather than directly defend these distinctions, recently appropriated by Deacon (1997), we simply take them on board as a taxonomy. By so doing, we leave aside philosophical questions about whether all of the specified categories are occupied, or whether the taxonomic analysis can be defended independently of how it is used here.

Iconic reference involves some kind of perceived resemblance, perhaps even to the extent of failure to distinguish, between two features of the world. Deacon (1997, p. 75) uses a camouflaged moth as an example, where the camouflage is only successfully iconic of tree bark to the extent that it is *not* perceptually distinguished from the bark on which the moth rests. The iconic relationship is, given the range of ways in which two things might be said to resemble one another and the variety of capacities of different perceiving systems, a relatively weak one.

Indexical reference on the other hand requires some degree of correlation between two reidentifiable types. Again there is a wide range of possible types of correlation, including spatial adjacency and temporal succession (that latter especially important for learning about outcomes of actions). In order for there to be an indexical relationship, a perceiver must be able to identify phenomena as instances of the two types (smoke and fire, say), and note a relationship between them so that, for example, identification of the first can lead to anticipation (or production) of the second.

With *symbolic* reference, the idea is that (mostly but not necessarily conventional) symbols stand in a distributed network of relationships with one another, where the "positive" reference of any symbol is partly understood in terms of indexically determined equivalence classes. Symbolic reference is, because of the importance of "horizontal" relationships to other symbols, much less hostage to vagaries of correlation than indexical reference. For this reason, the boy who cried "wolf!" undermined the utterance's indexical force without changing the symbolic reference of "wolf" (Deacon 1997, p. 82). Symbolic representation also permits the construction of higher-order types not directly grounded in experience ("unicorn") but which do nonetheless partly fix experiential criteria ("looking like a unicorn [would]"), and others ("imaginary number") which would be impossible, or nearly so, to fix in indexical terms.

Deacon's view is that symbolic referential relationships are constructed out of indexical ones, which in turn are constructed out of iconic ones, so he envisages a pair of "thresholds" with characteristic cognitive demands and developmental problems in crossing them.[7] We are less confident that the "icon, index, symbol" taxonomy need be aligned with a developmental timetable, partly because we're convinced that dispositions to track at least some iconic and indexical relations are innate.[8]

It is important to bear in mind (Deacon 1997, p. 72) that the question whether some mark is iconic, indexical, or symbolic depends not on the intrinsic properties of the mark, but on the system by which it is consumed. So a kiss might be a part of some person's being affectionate (iconic) or an indicator of affiliation (indexical), or deployed as a conventionalized signal against the grain of "normal" indexical use (as in Judas's signal at the Last Supper to the Romans). While agreeing with Deacon's general point, we note that each type of reference has its own peculiar constraints which, to an extent, make a difference to what can count as a mark. The word "hound" cannot be iconic of dogs as we find them, because it cannot be relied on to be a part of dog-related experiences in the way that hairiness and pointed teeth can. Further, wracking sobs are iconic or indexical of misery in ways that conventional labels like "sad" can't be (Frank 1988, but see also Ross and Dumouchel 2004), because we don't generally think anyone can just *decide* to burst into tears, even though we do think that anyone can *profess* deep sadness.

Note also that on Deacon's view the distinction between three types of reference implies a distinction between (at least) three degrees of competence (Deacon 1997, p. 74). An entity that can make use of iconic reference to deal with its environment (e.g., by climbing some kinds of concentration gradients) may not be able to learn from indexical relations around it, any more than one that masters some indexical relations need be capable of dealing with symbolic ones. The transitions from iconic to indexical, and from indexical to symbolic, are *learning* problems, with their own distinctive demands. Our primary interest here is in these transitions, and the implied learning problems.

We note that Clark himself has relatively little to say about such transitions. This is so even though parts of his work are clearly relevant to them, and highlight aspects of them considered from the perspective of concept formation and "representational redescription" (Clark and Karmiloff-Smith 1994; Clark 1993, esp. chap. 4). As we hope to show, though, other parts of his work concerned not specifically with language, but with the demands of robust real-time embodied responsiveness, help us make more headway with approaching the "how" question.

3   How to Do Things without Words

Human infants are extraordinarily dependent on others. They are only able to support their own heads at around three months, cannot reach until around four months, crawl until nine, or walk until thirteen. Unlike other young primates, they are unable to cling to their parents in order to be moved around; even though they have the clinging reflexes, their parents aren't hairy enough. Almost anything which takes place in accordance with their needs, or, later, their goals, has to be done *for* them. For a being in such a situation there are clearly advantages to be gained from being socially legible—that is, from being manifestly hungry, distressed, uncomfortable, happy, and so forth, when nourishment, comfort, concerned attention, play, and so on, are required and possibly available. Equally, they have much to gain if they are able to use caregiver preferences in regulating events. Not only do infants need social relationships; those who take care of them—typically kin and paradigmatically mothers—also need relationships to manage their own energy and resource allocations.

The relationships in question are, and have to be, more than simply affiliative. While close mutual interest is undeniably crucial, caregivers have other demands on their attention, especially when an infant has siblings, or under conditions of severe scarcity. Even without competing siblings, there are times when no matter what a child seems to want, it is more important to make it keep quiet, or wait for some other more urgent goal to be pursued.[9] Infants and caregivers, that is, share an interest in making sense of and to one another, and, although only partly and contingently, share interests in the outcome of their relationship.[10] But they cannot interact in symbolic language, since only one of them is capable of doing so. Symbolic language is an *outcome* of their communication-hungry interaction, rather than a resource available to it from the outset.

Other resources are, though, available. These include facial expressions, direction of gaze, gestures, body orientation, and prosodic properties of speech, all of which are powerful media of affective signaling. Caregivers are directly affected and motivated by displays of infant affect, especially when the infant is their own offspring (e.g., Wiesenfeld and Klorman 1978). From birth, or very soon after, infants show interest in faces (e.g., Maurer and Young 1983), preference for smiling faces (Easterbrook and Barry 2000), and evidence of imitation of facial expression and gesture (e.g., Meltzoff and Moore 1977). By the time of birth they attend to, and prefer, rhythmic properties like those they heard in the muffled world of the womb, and show a preference for the voice of their mother, which they reliably identify and prefer to other voices following birth (e.g., DeCasper and Fifer 1980). Some prosodic features of infant-directed utterances are indicators of approval, disapproval, and so on, in their own way just as universal as facial expressions are indicators of affective state (e.g., Ekman 1972). Infants across cultures show early preferences for approval vocalizations over ones whose prosodic character is associated with disapproval. Neither parent nor infant need, then, *learn* how to get started with affective interaction. In the terms adopted above, we can say that these capacities for affective response form and make possible a set of innate indexical associations. Fernald (1992) documents, *inter alia*, prosodic patterns (found across multiple cultures) indicating approval, prohibition, comfort-giving, and engaging attention. Our approach departs from hers, as in the final example ("Oeu!"), since we give attention to not only an utterance's "internal" prosodic properties but also to the *relational* properties that link them (see Cowley 1998, in press).

By the middle of the second month of life, infants begin to engage with their caregivers in interactions in ways showing both some universality, and also evidence, as we shortly explain, of cultural particularity. Trevarthen (1977) refers to such episodes in Britain as manifesting "spontaneity, vivacity and delight," while Bateson (1979) describes interactions in Iran as involving "delighted, ritualized courtesy." We might add that our own data concerning Zulu mothers and infants (see below) include periods of "delighted musical chorusing" (Cowley 2003). Around the third month, interaction between infants and caregivers becomes intensely dialogical, involving the production of protoconversation (Bateson 1979) and manifesting what Trevarthen (1979, 1998) calls intersubjective communication. At this stage culturally or individually specific expectations about appropriate infant behavior begin to play a more serious role in shaping the interactions. This poses a variety of learning problems for both, especially as caregivers attempt to develop ways of guiding and controlling infants' exploiting but transcending the innate indexical relations they start with.

While there are distinctive, repeated elements in many of these episodes, it is important to note that significant portions of the interaction consist in "intersubjective downtime" where levels of joint coordination are low (including for reasons of fatigue), and that the interactive "game" being played is characterized by extreme flexibility, manifest in the availability of different routes to a number of acceptable (to the mother) goal states. There are no simple regularities here where infant distress invariably leads to comforting vocalizations, in turn leading to reduced distress. Rather one often sees a rapid shifting of strategies—for example, offers of feeding, comfortings, calls for attention, expressions of disapproval, with, usually, an overall convergence on a parental goal state in which the infant is content and quiet. As Stern (1977) noted, boxing provides an appropriate comparison for mother–infant interaction. Boxers spend a lot of time feinting and otherwise exploring different possible lines of attack, at the same time detecting and closing off their opponent's explorations. Actual punches thrown, or landed, are rare compared to candidate blows that never develop beyond a slight shifting of weight and gaze, or reorientation of the body.

It is also clear enough that infants occupy what one might call "culturally saturated" environments, in which, for example, the likelihood of an adult allowing an infant's direction of attention to initiate and fix the focus of an interaction is variable. Further areas of variation include patterns of response to infant distress, where in some settings attempts to distract the infant by drawing attention to a salient visible object are likely, but in others attempts to comfort or subdue by holding or rocking occur more often. What is not at all clear to us yet is when infants themselves begin to show evidence of enculturation—of behavior partly shaped by the contingent patterns of interaction prevalent in their own culturally saturated environment. (The contingent patterns need not all be cultural. Levels of maternal depression, for example, make measurable differences to patterns of affective display and behavior in their infants and children [Lundy, Field, and Pickens 1997].) Our example comes from our own observational data[11] concerning Zulu infants of between three and four months of age interacting with their mothers, and suggests that infants *may* show signs of enculturation (inherited but not genetically encoded and not species-universal patterns of behavior) surprisingly early.

Thula! (or Shhhhh)

As noted above, there are times when a caregiver will want an infant to stop being distressed or agitated and fall silent, or in isiZulu to "thula." Zulu children, especially in rural settings, are traditionally expected to be less socially active than most contemporary European or North American children, to initiate fewer interactions, and, crucially, to show a respectful attitude toward adults.[12] An early manifestation of this is in behaviors where a mother attempts to make an infant keep quiet, sometimes saying "thula" ("quiet"), "njega" ("no"), while simultaneously gesturing, moving toward or away from the infant, and reacting to details of the infants' own behavior[13] (see Cowley, Moodley, and Fiori-Cowley 2004).

During these episodes the mother regularly leans forward, so that her face and palms take up more of the infant's visual field. When this happens, new vocalizations and movements or reorientations of gaze by the infant are often "nipped in the bud" by dominating vocalizations (sometimes showing prosodic properties indicative of disapproval or comforting) from the mother, sometimes accompanied by increasingly emphatic hand-waving and even closer crowding of the infant's visual field.

At this age, before the onset of what linguists call "babbling," let alone recognizable speech production, there is no reason to think that the infant knows what "thula" or "njega" means, or even that it could reliably reidentify the words (let alone produce or contemplate them). It is extremely unlikely, then, that the word-based aspects of utterance-activity provide labels for the infant. It is not even necessary to suppose that the infant "knows" that it is supposed to be quiet when it behaves as we have described. *We* know that the mother wants the child to be quiet, and not only because she says so, expresses her wish in her behavior, and confirms this in her response to the infant's falling silent (or failing to do so).

Even without knowing what "thula" means, one can make sense of the mother's behavior. She makes it difficult for the infant to attend to distractions by moving forward and filling more of its visual field. She rejects repeated or new undesirable behaviors on its part by cutting off its vocalizations and movements with dominating signals that are timed to coincide with infant behaviors. She largely restricts her own approval signals, including relaxing the crowding, and reducing the magnitude of her gesturing, as well as expressing comfort through vocalization, facial signaling (including smiling), and touch, to moments when the infant begins to quiet down. She continues them when it remains quiet, rewarding signs of calm and happiness. It's not surprising, then, that it often does quiet down.

The mother's behavior includes salient (sometimes exaggerated), repeated features, including but not limited to innate indexical relations that are apt for reidentification and then learning. The patterns of hand gesturing, in some of our examples, could at the outset be iconic of the whole episode, including her behavior and the infant's becoming quiet. When repetition allows the gesture to be individuated and recognized in its own right, it could go on to become an indexical cue that quietness *should* follow, that whatever the infant just did was worth doing again because it led to reinforcement. The infant's responses can then become usefully indexical *for the mother* of the degree to which the child is cooperative, well behaved, or, more plainly, "good." Caregiver descriptions of infant behavior at these times, manifest either in their explicit vocalizations to the child, including references to "good" behavior and disciplinary sanc tions like "kuza baba manje" ("where's your father now?"). Further interviews following the videotaping show that infant behavior even at this age is classified in line with culturally specific expectations of good and bad behavior. Part of being "good" here is sometimes doing what you're supposed to, *before* learning any words, and early ascriptions of "obedience," "cooperativeness," and so forth are often based in episodes of attempted control.

Such parental ascriptions of "goodness" and so forth are almost certainly overinterpretations, if taken to identify explicit infant policies. They are, though, helpful and perhaps necessary overinterpretations, insofar as they motivate caregivers to behave with regularity and thus structure the interaction in ways that become familiar to the infant. A further episode from our data, in this case concerning a child of around four months,[14] illustrates this point about overinterpretation. In it an infant repeatedly vocalizes in ways which to its mother, although not to us, are suggestive of its saying "up." After several responses along the lines of "up?" or "you want to go up?" the mother lifts the child. Prior to this, to the detached observer, there is little evidence that the child actually wants to be lifted, or that its attention is focused on anything at all. When it *is* lifted, though, it beams widely. Whatever it did want, if anything, it is now, we suggest, one step closer to figuring out how to behave in ways that lead to its being lifted up.[15]

Still on the subject of lifting, consider the gesture often made around the eighth month by infants who want to be picked up (that is, who subsequently smile or otherwise show approval when they are picked up following such a gesture): a simultaneous raising, or flapping, of both arms (see Lock 1991). This gesture is not *copied* from common adult behaviors (who do not generally flap their arms prior to lifting anything, and for practical purposes are never in a position to raise their arms to enable something considerably larger than they are to get a grip on their torsos). In the terms we are using here it is partly *iconic*, in virtue of being a common posture of infants while they are in fact being held up, and partly indexical, in virtue of being able to stand on its own as an indicator of "being up," as well as being symbolically interpretable as an *invitation* to lift, or a *request* to be lifted.[16] Such gestures are, importantly, serviceable label candidates, in virtue of being amenable to disembedding from the behavior they might have been part of, and eventually coming under deliberate control. An infant need not want to be lifted the first few times it makes such a gesture; even though getting into a "being lifted" pose could be part of wanting to be lifted, it has only to be able to notice that the gesture tends to be followed by liftings and learn from this.

If and when such learning takes place, it does so in the affectively charged environment we have briefly described. We want to bring discussion of the current example to a close by suggesting a way in which these interactions should be regarded as a further example of how minds can be extended through action. Clark and Chalmers's suggestion is that paradigmatically mental states and processes can be realized by structures and resources external to the brain. The world beyond the skull of any individual includes, as we noted, the skulls and brains of others. If active externalism motivates the recognition of a cognitive prosthesis such as a Filofax as "part" of what realizes a mind, we don't see why (although see the discussion of the parity principle below) the embodied brain of another couldn't also play that role. Here, then, is our suggestion: at times interacting caregiver–infant dyads are neither one individual nor two, but somewhere in between. At the risk of sounding sensational and un-politically correct at the same time, infant minds can be intermittently colonized by caregivers so as to accelerate learning processes.

If this colonization does happen, it is made possible by a mixture of affective coupling through interaction and mechanisms such as gaze-following that are used in coordinating attention (see, e.g., Baron-Cohen 1995 for an attempt to specify the various mechanisms involved). There is ample evidence, some canvassed above, that the affective state of either mother or infant has an immediate impact, and especially direct in very early life, on the affective state of the other, and that affective state itself generally makes a difference to the ways in which features of the world are observed and remembered (Zajonc 1980, 1984; Bargh 1990, 1992),[17] as well as shaping communicative behavior (e.g., Dimberg, Thunberg, and Elmehed 2000; Tartter 1980).[18] It is not possible directly to "install" some piece of know-how in an infant, but it is sometimes possible to direct its attention, to modulate its attention and arousal. Equally, caregivers act to ensure that it is looking in the right direction, at the right time, and in the right way, to pick up on a pattern which is there to be learned. Some of the available patterns are culturally specific indexical relationships which caregivers take as symptomatic of how "good" a particular child is, and which, by structuring caregiver behavior, open the infant to a new world of social opportunities.

The instances of indexical learning we describe also permit the beginning of a kind of signaling arms race (to the extent that their interests sometimes conflict) between infants and caregivers. Once an infant has learned, for example, that the arms-up gesture can lead to being lifted, it is possible for "requests" (i.e., behaviors taken as requests by others, no matter how they are to the infant) to be lifted to be acted on, or to be refused. Prior to the construction and learning of the indexical relationship, this was impossible—a parent would lift a child when the parent wanted to, or thought it would serve some end. Once it has been learned, "requests" will be differentially responded to, depending on their situation in patterns of interaction that extend through time. Personal and cultural contingencies about infants and parents will codetermine what patterns are formed, and whether, for example, requested lifting is more likely after relatively quick acquiescence to silencing behavior, or less likely in the period following failure to attend to objects or events in which a caregiver attempted to arouse interest.

A major shift in the character of this arms race comes with the onset of more deliberate and fine vocal control on the part of the infant, at about the same time as infants begin to engage the world in a triadic fashion, combining interest in things with joint behavior with persons. A striking example is given by the linguist Halliday (1975), who describes how at ten months his son Nigel came to exploit his father by means of vocal behavior.

Nigel produced two distinctive vocal utterances, which Halliday records as [bø] and [nã], and interpreted as, respectively, a request for a favorite toy bird, and a general "give me that" demand. To respond cooperatively to [nã], then, Halliday had to use pragmatic clues to infer what Nigel wanted. As a linguist Halliday may have brought additional (and charitable) interpretive resources to bear on the question whether Nigel, on any two separate occasions, was making the "same" sound again. Although the younger child taken as "asking to be picked up" in the episode described above undoubtedly had less vocal control than Nigel, both cases have in common a movement toward more modality-focused behavior (in one case, gestural; in the other, syllabic). This, we think, is crucial in coming to produce behavior that can be interpreted around disembedded labels.

In the "thula" case the behaviors we described are likely to be seen as too far from language to count as relevantly related to it. In the present case we need to guard against the opposite tendency, that is, to regard Nigel's various [nã]s and [bø]s as *too much* like mature language. Halliday himself regards the vocalizations as uses of "protowords,"[19] and treats them as expressions of relatively well-formed intentions, perhaps even propositional attitudes. Thibault (2000) uses the data as evidence that Nigel has crossed the threshold to indexical reference. On a more deflationary view Nigel need not *initially* "want" the bird, any more than the child described above need "want" to be lifted. A child *does* need to be capable of learning the correlation between some aspect of its behavior and the regularities produced by attentive adult responses. So Nigel's protowords can be a *product* of ongoing interaction that is scaffolded by Halliday's production of regularities in the environment. Given their relationship and familiarity with each other's affective signaling, we lack reason to think that what Nigel does is motivated any such "desire."

Oeu!

The discussion of the childhood examples above is consistent with an interpretation of what we are saying that we wish to dispel. On that view what we are describing is a developmental phase during which motor-centric aspects of utterance-activity play an important role *because* abstraction-amenable ones are relatively underdeveloped. Rather, we maintain that the full range of aspects of utterance-activity remain in play in all live human interaction.[20] By way of illustration we take a single example involving interacting adults.

The episode (for more detail, see Cowley 1998) occurred in Italy, and involved a mother, a father, and their adult daughter. In this case, everything begins with Rosa, the mother, evidently seeking sympathy by claiming to Monica, her (adult) daughter, that a "certain person" had been too lazy to cut some pea-poles she had wanted. This tactic does not succeed in winning Monica's sympathy, and in any event it soon emerges that the husband/father, Aldo, had in fact cut fifteen poles. Rosa changes tack, and instead asserts that the problem is that the pea-poles were unsatisfactory, because they were too long. Still seeking Monica's sympathy, Rosa now ridicules Aldo by claiming that the pea-poles were "even longer than this room, if not longer" ("son più lunghe di questa camera se non più"). At this point words fail Aldo, and he gives a cry not identifiable with any word, but amenable to being glossed as "come on!" in the context clearly legible as an act of good-natured mocking. The vocal gesture in this case is a simple vowel ("Oeu") the duration of which can be stretched to that of a short sentence. What is most striking, though, is not the internal prosodic properties of Aldo's "Oeu" but its relational properties in the context of the interaction, and the shared history of the three people present. To see these features, consider figure 13.1.

Notice that Aldo's "oeu" begins in between Rosa's "non" and "più" ("not" and "longer"),[21] following her assertion that the poles were as long as the room, rather than waiting for the "end" of her utterance where she adds "if not longer." This violates standard notions of turn taking while being in keeping with analogies with either dance or boxing. The beginning of Aldo's vocalization is at an unusually high pitch for him (about an octave above his usual range), and as he stretches the sound out, he raises his pitch to the same level as the end of Rosa's "più," indexing her utterance. A little less than half way through Aldo's "oeu" Monica joins in with an "oeu" of her own, starting with her pitch a little higher than Aldo's, but joining his in harmony and continuing after he has stopped. Soon after he stops, perhaps having run out of breath, Monica drops her pitch uncharacteristically low, and to the top of *his* usual range, and gives a short laugh ("ha!") at that pitch.

Even without understanding of Italian, the sound recording of this episode makes sense as a brief period during which two people good naturedly mock a third one, and do so *together*. The prosodic details just identified

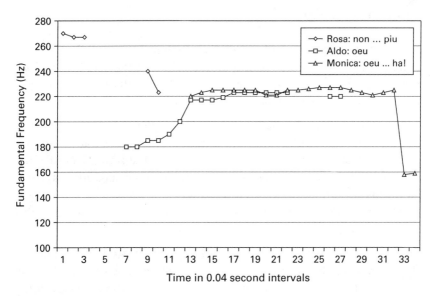

Figure 13.1
Oeu!

help make sense of why this interpretation is so easy. Aldo and Monica are identifiably "together" because their utterances harmonize, showing a brief allegiance in the same way as bodily orientation shows acceptance or rejection. Their vocalizations are identifiably "about" Rosa's partly because the pitch on which they converge is indexical of the end of her last utterance, and because Aldo's unusual starting pitch is also indexical of *her* typical range, rather than his own. Monica's laugh in turn indexes Aldo, again by being pitched into his normal range. While these latter two coordinating properties may be below any noticeable threshold, they provide good evidence of how prosodic patterns between people with histories of shared intimacy are modulated by that history, as they can also be by shared cultural experience. In this case, crucially for our purposes, the gentle mocking that is accomplished doesn't involve a single standard "word." While the literature on prosodic and visible expression describes many incidents that resemble this one, our focus on relational functions is novel. As with boxing, we stress that *inter alia*, accent, timing, and loudness and various kinds of visible movement that allow adults to regulate one another's speaking. While the "oeu" example just discussed is striking, prosodic detail of the same type is ubiquitous in utterance-activity at all ages, and occurs in word-based speech as well as cries like Aldo's (see Cowley 1998, in press).

4   The Parity Principle

In the opening paragraph of this chapter we suggested that what we were arguing was an application of Clark and Chalmers's parity principle. Consider the specific criteria that Clark and Chalmers offer for something to count as part of an individual's cognitive system:

1. That the resource be reliably available and typically invoked.

2. That any information thus retrieved be more or less automatically endorsed. It should not usually be subject to critical scrutiny (unlike the opinions of other people, for example). It should be deemed about as trustworthy as something retrieved clearly from biological memory.

3. That information contained in the resource should be easily accessible as and when required (Clark, this volume, p. 46).

Scrutiny of the above might suggest that processes we have pinpointed during some kinds of coordinated behavior fail, in some way, on all three. As Clark (this volume) notes with reference to the three criteria, other people "typically would not (but could in rare cases)" meet them. What sort of problem is this for our proposal?

With reference to the second and third criteria, we think that their formulation in terms of "information" that is "retrieved" or "contained" merits revision. Those sorts of images are relatively appropriate where the external resource is taking on cognitive functions related to *memory*, but less so for other capacities. Our examples have more in common with what Kirsh and Maglio (1994) report of how Tetris is played. Human players of the game are not best thought of as *storing* and retrieving information. Though there is a sense in which this is what they get the computer to do, they must also trust the machine to perform the rotations and translations they initiate, and not to cheat by modifying the contour at the bottom of the playing area, and so on.[22] Similarly, the various components between keyboard and screen that handle rotations and translations must be "easily accessible as and when required," but, rather than storing information, they perform various manipulations. The "as and when required" part of the third condition and the "reliable availability" requirement of the first must, therefore, be interpreted carefully. It is hardly an objection to the view that experienced Tetris players use external resources to do cognitive work that suitable computers aren't there whenever one might want to play. Similarly, the fact that interaction partners are not always present counts for little if, *when they are there*, interesting cognitive possibilities arise. (Why, after all, should the boundaries of extended minds be relatively stable, when what the minds *do* and the resources available are so variable?)

Although a tweaked set of criteria fleshing out the parity principle might allow the sorts of case we're suggesting to count as examples of extended minds, we can imagine other difficulties. Clark (this volume) notes an objection to Clark and Chalmers (1998, this volume) from Sterelny (2004) to the effect that external resources occupy a "common and often contested" space. To his thinking, this suggests an important disanalogy with paradigmatic biological cognitive systems, selected for reliability. If this is correct, then it's bad for our own cases, which often explicitly involve some degree of conflict and attempted control. Far from thinking that this is so, however, the extended infant helps overthrow this case.

First, we are not convinced that the world within an individual's skull is sufficiently harmonious and cooperative to sustain the suggested contrast. Conflict—crucially including various internal battles over how to interpret and remember events and actions—is a regular part of our internal lives. The behavior of a would-be nonsmoker who takes steps now to limit access of her future self (tomorrow morning, say) to cigarettes and thus bring it about that she smoked a few less would be mysterious if we were agents with consistent sets of preferences (to smoke or not, on balance). The same applies to internal debates over whether *this* situation is special enough, in a good or bad way, for a cigarette smoked *now* to be an exceptional moment of celebration or commiseration or, rather, a lapse that trumpets another failed attempt to quit. Such conflicts arise because our default discount function for determining the present value of future rewards is not the exponential curve that alone keeps preference ranking constant over time. It seems, instead, as though our default discount function is hyperbolic, so that our preferences can be unstable, and consequently we can anticipate actions that we now would prefer not to make. (Ainslie 2001 provides an excellent account of this research and its implications.) This is not a specifically human phenomenon: even pigeons can work *now* to prevent future selves from having opportunities to be impulsive (Ainslie 1974).

As well as not being suitably harmonious *ourselves*, the contrast comes under pressure from the other direction. Competition isn't only a source of instability, although Sterelny is right that it can be that. It is also a spur for innovations intended to enhance stability. Further, gadgets that can function as cognitive prostheses are subject to extensive (not always successful) testing for reliability and cognitive fit, not to mention ongoing refinement in the area of security. Those of us who trust records kept behind various walls of encryption and access control over our memories are not obviously making a mistake. And those of us who trust the outputs of the various daemons we set up to filter and otherwise operate on incoming information aren't always wrong either. (One of us has a mobile telephone that rings with a unique melody when the call is from his wife's mobile phone. It has *never* played that melody for calls from any other number, not even [as humans embarrassingly can] confusing it with, say, the number of a previous partner.)

Second, we observe that one of the flagship examples of research into distributed cognition concerns multiple agents in a "common" and at least sometimes "contested" space. This is Hutchins's (1995) work on navigation in large ships, frequently cited with approval by Clark. Hutchins shows that it is exactly by means of key parts of the navigational process being public, that different agents can monitor and correct aspects of one another's performance, that is, that joint action in a sometimes contested space can be *more* effective at handling particular information-processing demands.

These brief remarks don't entirely dispose of Sterelny's worry, but they do give reason for thinking that at least some of the time our dealings with others are more like our dealings with ourselves than the worry seems to suppose. (The personal is indeed political.) They also suggest that sometimes external resources might have just the reliability (born partly of the sorts of competition Sterelny takes to distinguish on-board biological systems) that Sterelny takes to be the hallmark of internal ones.

Perhaps, though, we have provided no more than an instance of "causal spread" (in which the direct antecedents of some actions lie partly outside the brain, in our case including systems within the bodies and brains of interaction partners), which is what Wheeler and Clark (1999) regard as a "trivial" example. We don't think so. Some of these extraneural systems do indeed turn out to be at the root of *distinctive target features of the phenomenon of interest*, which is the criterion for being nontrivial.

Here is a speculative suggestion as to how this might be. In a provocative paper, Ross and Dumouchel (2004) argue that emotions should be understood as strategic signals, having the particular effect of encoding preference intensities (which are more difficult to infer than preference orderings). This is because, unlike standard commitment devices, they do not have to be explicitly constructed before strategic interaction. By having preference intensities thus (even if roughly) publicly represented, otherwise intractable strategic problems can be negotiated, and mutually uncongenial prisoners' dilemma situations, sometimes, avoided. Focusing on the first of these possibilities, the idea is that negotiations between agents who are mutually affectively legible involve lower computational demands for each agent's individual strategic decision making. As they say:

Thus most games are embedded in meta-games, and there are few restrictions on the possible complexities in this recursion; embedding relationships may stack infinitely, may loop, and so on. This circular dependency implies uncertainty concerning the objects of analysis for which equilibria should be forecast. Reciprocal affective expression can then be seen as a means of reducing this uncertainty. Through such things as bodily posture, muscle tone, pitch of voice and facial expression, we *negotiate* reciprocal intentions into tolerably stable sets of expectations within which our base-level games are well defined. At the meta-game level(s) we do not so much exchange information concerning already formed intentions as *dynamically influence and determine* each others' intentions though exchanges of affective expression. (Ross and Dumouchel 2004, p. 271)

Our suggestion is that a related function is served by emotional signaling in both interactions between infants and their caregivers, and adult conversation. Thus [bø] may serve Halliday's infant as a strategic signal in negotiating social events (his father may well give him a toy). Equally,

Aldo may find himself signaling strategically and thus avoid the unfortunate dilemmas that arise in overtly contradicting his wife. Unlike many accounts of linguistic and some of strategic phenomena, playing down turn-taking, we emphasize the roughly simultaneous coordination of prosodic and affective display. We have, moreover, argued that coordinated display itself constitutes significant information about relationships. Affective display functions like this in social animals without language and, we contend, it continues to do so in humans. If this speculation isn't obviously wrong, then it suggests two lines of development of the notion of the extended mind.

First, especially considering the "Oeu!" example, it is likely that sources of feedback relevant to both Aldo's and Monica's control of their own vocal production, during the period in which they are so strikingly coordinated, include both their own vocal production, and that of the other. More generally, all of the types of affective coordination we have described involve roughly simultaneous integration of inputs from each participant's own behavior and that of others. Since these regulate behavior they are striking examples of distributed control of precisely the kind Clark refers to in reviewing much of his work on "robots." We hope to have suggested something of how this type of embodied control contributes to the functioning of utterance-activity, and why it merits further empirical investigation.

Second, considering the epistemic payoffs of the types of embodied coordination we have described, it is clear that the model of the solitary infant epistemologist, on which much of the poverty of the stimulus debate rests, is seriously in need of revision. In virtue of affective coordination, infants are able to function as a kind of cognitive extension of their own caregivers. They can use other people to focus their attention, regulate their levels of arousal, reinforce and retard patterns in behavior, and provide many sources of environmental regularity that invite infant exploitation. This interactional environment permits the construction of socially indexical relationships, and the gradual disembedding of labels from their social contexts. Within close relationships, adults treat infant behavior as symbolic long before such a description is warranted. The types of embodied coordination noted above thus permit a particular type of extended mind, in which infants' cognitive powers are augmented by those of people with whom they interact. When Clark and Chalmers explicitly consider whether other people might form part of one person's extended mind, they suggest that, after all, it *could* happen in an "unusually interdependent couple." Quite so.

Acknowledgments

Earlier versions of this chapter were presented to the "Mind and World" working group at the University of Natal, Durban, and (under the title "Minded Apes, Talking Infants, and the Distribution of Language") at "The Extended Mind" conference in Hertfordshire. We are grateful to the audiences on both occasions, and especially to Andy Clark, Anita Craig, Andrew Dellis, Dan Hutto, Denis McManus, Richard Menary, Mark Row lands, Fran Saunders, Leslie Stephenson, Susan Stuart, and Michael Wheeler for comments and critical discussion.

Notes

1. See, e.g., Chomsky 1965, 1967. Laurence and Margolis 2001 is a useful recent review of the argument.

2. One of us (Spurrett) is more sympathetic than the other, and we're aware of more recent and more naturalist work such as Hauser, Chomsky, and Fitch 2002.

3. Results in this area (see also Nazzi, Bertoncini, and Mehler 1998) indicate that rather than distinguishing individual languages, infants at least initially distinguish between stress-timed, syllable-timed, and mora-timed patterns.

4. Savage-Rumbaugh herself accepts the poverty of the stimulus argument and then argues that the genetic similarity between chimpanzees and humans suggests that chimpanzees are likely to have at least some of the same adaptations "for" language. We prefer the line suggested here, and in Cowley and Spurrett 2003.

5. A more general form of our question, without the developmental spin of the version in the main text, is: *How do the apparently symbolic aspects of talk relate to wider utterance-activity?*

6. Ross (2007) gives reasons, in the context of a discussion of distributed cognition, for thinking better of symbols, or digitally encoded signals, than our remarks here allow.

7. Deacon's broad proposal regarding the role of the prefrontal cortex (PFC) in constructing symbolic relationships is certainly neurally plausible. The PFC includes areas connected with almost all sensory and motor systems, and has extensive back-projections to "lower" systems. Unlike many other brain areas, PFC subregions are specialized for multimodal convergence, and show remarkable experience-dependent plasticity. See Miller 2000 for a review.

8. Garcia and Koelling (1966) studied aversion responses to different stimuli, showing that rats readily learned to associate (a) a noise and light signal with an

electric shock, and (b) a distinctive flavor with (radiation-induced) nausea. The reversed combinations (light and sound followed by nausea, and distinctive taste followed by a shock) were more difficult to learn. Similarly, we suspect it would be difficult for most humans to learn that smiles predicted hostility or sadness.

9. Falk (2004) considers some questions relating to the evolution of language from motherese with reference to the distinctive challenges faced by apes that walked upright and had unusually dependent infants. See also Spurrett and Dellis 2004.

10. A parent may have other children, or may bet on the chances of success with future offspring, whereas the developing infant has no such options. Haig (1993) documents some of the ways in which, during pregnancy, the fetus (which has less interest than the mother in her own other [including possible future] offspring than it does in its own life) can operate more like a parasite than an ally, competing, *inter alia*, over blood supply, and levels of blood sugar.

11. A quantitative analysis of the data from which we select some episodes has yet to be performed.

12. We have collected, for a variety of purposes, video data of mother–infant naturalistic, and sometimes more structured, interaction at various ages, and with subjects from a variety of socioeconomic, geographical and ethnic/cultural backgrounds.

13. We are describing a *type* of interaction here, but including specific details from one particularly striking example.

14. This infant lived in a non-Zulu sociocultural setting in which mothers tend to go to greater lengths to discern (and satisfy) infants' wishes.

15. Papousek (1969) showed, by creating environments in which specific movements by an infant could make things happen in those environments, that the infants smiled when they did "work out" how to exercise control.

16. Kano (1992, p. 164, quoted by Falk 2004) describes a behavior in which chimpanzee mothers walk a few paces and then pause but remain in a walking posture, as a cue for her infant to come and climb onto her back.

17. Zajonc (1980, 1984) showed that subjects subsequently preferred images that were "primed" with brief (subconscious) images of smiles to those primed with frowns. Bargh's striking research showed, *inter alia*, that subjects exposed to sentences containing words suggestive of age tended to walk more slowly after exposure.

18. Dimberg, Thunberg, and Elmehed (2000) found that observation of, e.g., smiling faces led to neural and muscular activity associated with smiling, even when the images were not consciously perceived. Tartter (1980) showed that smiling changes the shape of the human vocal tract, in ways that raise the mean frequency of vocalizations. Vocalizations with high mean frequencies are generally characteristic of approval (see Fernald 1992).

19. As is often the case (see Bates and Begnini 1979), these have imperative uses (e.g., "up," "more"). It is of interest that while laboratory-trained apes act similarly, even encultured chimpanzees relatively rarely move to declarative forms of expression (e.g., "dadda," "gone").

20. We would be inclined to argue that this holds, albeit in different ways, in the production and consumption of written texts, even typed ones, as well. Although we don't make this argument here, we draw some inspiration from Dennett's remark: "*Le Penseur's* frown and chin-holding, and the head-scratchings, mutterings, pacings and doodlings that we idiosyncratically favor, could turn out to be not just random by-products of conscious thinking, but functional contributors (or the vestigial traces of earlier, cruder functional contributors) to the laborious disciplining of the brain that has to be accomplished to turn it into a mature mind" (Dennett 1991, p. 225).

21. Strictly, it begins during the silent bilabial stop or the [p] of "più." For reasons of emphasis, the sound's duration (perhaps integrated with a gesture) is much extended.

22. It could be interesting to know how players responded to an occasionally "nasty" implementation of Tetris that did such things, and in particular what would happen to the rate at which players engaged in epistemic actions.

References

Ainslie, G. (1974). Impulse control in pigeons. *Journal of the Experimental Analysis of Behavior, 21*, 485–489.

Ainslie, G. (2001). *Breakdown of Will*. Cambridge: Cambridge University Press.

Bargh, J. (1990). Auto-motives: Preconscious determinants of social interaction. In T. Higgins and R. Sorrentino (eds.), *Handbook of Motivation and Cognition*. New York: Guilford.

Bargh, J. (1992). Being unaware of the stimulus vs. unaware of its interpretation: Why subliminality per se does matter to social psychology. In R. Bornstein and T. Pittman (eds.), *Perception without Awareness*. New York: Guilford.

Baron-Cohen, S. (1995). *Mindblindness*. Cambridge, MA: MIT Press.

Bates, E., and Begnini, L. (1979). *The Emergence of Symbols: Cognition and Communication in Infancy*. New York: Academic Press.

Bateson, M. C. (1979). The epigenesis of conversational interaction: A personal account of research development. In M. Bullowa (ed.), *Before Speech: The Beginning of Interpersonal Communication* (pp. 63–77). Cambridge: Cambridge University Press.

Benson, J. D., Debashish, M., Greaves, W. S., Lukas, J., Savage-Rumbaugh, S., and Taglialatela, J. (2004). Mind and brain in apes: A methodology for phonemic analysis of vocalizations of language competent bonobos. *Language Sciences, 26*, 643–660.

Chater, N., and Christiansen, M. H. (1999). Connectionism and natural language processing. In S. Garrod and M. Pickering (eds.), *Language Processing* (pp. 233–279). London: Psychology Press.

Chomsky, N. (1965). *Aspects of the Theory of Syntax*. Cambridge, MA: MIT Press.

Chomsky, N. (1967). Recent contributions to the theory of innate ideas. *Synthese, 17*, 2–11.

Clark, A. (1993). *Associative Engines*. Cambridge, MA: MIT Press.

Clark, A., and Chalmers, D. (1998). The extended mind. *Analysis* 58(1), 7–19. Reprinted as chapter 2 of this volume.

Cowley, S. J. (in press). Beyond symbols: How interaction enslaves distributed cognition. In P. Thibault and C. Prevignano (eds.), *Interaction Analysis and Language: State of the Art.*

Cowley, S. J. (1998). Of timing, turn-taking, and conversations. *Journal of Psycholinguistic Research, 27*, 541–571.

Cowley, S. J. (2002). Why brains matter: An integrational view. *Language Sciences, 24*(1), 73–95.

Cowley, S. J. (2003). Distributed cognition at three months: Mother–infant dyads in kwaZulu Natal. *Alternation, 10*(2), 229–257.

Cowley, S. J., Moodley, S., and Fiori-Cowley, A. (2004). Grounding signs of culture: Primary intersubjectivity in social semiosis. *Mind, Culture, and Activity, 11*(2), 109–132.

Cowley, S. J., and Spurrett, D. (2003). Putting apes (body and language) together again. *Language Sciences, 25*(3), 289–318.

DeCasper, A. J., and Fifer, W. P. (1980). Of human bonding: Newborns prefer their mothers' voices. *Science, 208*, 1174–1176.

Deacon, T. (1997). *The Symbolic Species*. New York: Norton.

Dennett, D. (1991). *Consciousness Explained*. Boston: Little, Brown.

Dimberg, U., Thunberg, M., and Elmehed, K. (2000). Unconscious facial reactions to emotional facial expressions. *Psychological Science, 11*, 86–89.

Easterbrook, M. A., and Barry, L. A. (2000). Newborns respond differently to smiling and frowning faces. Poster presented at the International Society on Infant Studies conference, Brighton, Colorado.

Ekman, P. (1972). Universals and cultural differences in facial expressions of emotion. In J. Cole (ed.), *Nebraska Symposium on Motivation* (pp. 207–283). Lincoln: University of Nebraska Press.

Elman, J. (1991). Incremental learning, or The importance of starting small. Technical Report 9101, Center for Research in Language, University of California, San Diego.

Falk, D. (2004). Prelinguistic evolution in early hominins: Whence motherese? *Behavioral and Brain Sciences, 27*, 491–503.

Fernald, A. (1992). Maternal vocalizations to infants as biologically relevant signals: An evolutionary perspective. In J. H. Barkow, L. Cosmides, and J. Tooby (eds.), *The Adapted Mind* (pp. 367–390). Oxford: Oxford University Press.

Frank, R. (1988). *Passions within Reason.* New York: Norton.

Garcia, J., and Koelling, R. A. (1966). Relation of cue to consequence in avoidance learning. *Psychosomatic Science, 4*, 123–124.

Haig, D. (1993). Genetic conflicts in human pregnancy. *Quarterly Review of Biology, 68*, 495–532.

Halliday, M. A. K. (1975). *Learning How to Mean: Explorations in the Development of Language.* New York: Elsevier.

Hauser, M. D., Chomsky, N., and Fitch, W. T. (2002). The faculty of language: What is it, who has it, and how did it evolve? *Science, 298*, 1569–1579.

Hutchins, E. (1995). *Cognition in the Wild.* Cambridge, MA: MIT Press.

Kano, T. (1992). *The Last Ape: Pygmy Chimpanzee Behavior and Ecology.* Stanford: Stanford University Press.

Kirsh, D., and Maglio, P. (1994). On distinguishing epistemic from pragmatic actions. *Cognitive Science, 18*, 513–549.

Kuhl, P. K., and Miller, J. D. (1978). Speech perception by the chinchilla: Identification functions for synthetic VOT stimuli. *Journal of the Acoustical Society of America, 63*, 905–917.

Laurence, S., and Margolis, E. (2001). The poverty of the stimulus argument. *British Journal for the Philosophy of Science, 52*, 217–276.

Lock, A. (1991). The role of social interaction in early language development. In N. A. Krasnegor, D. M. Rumbaugh, R. L. Schiefelbusch, and M. Studdert-Kennedy (eds.), *Biological and Behavioral Determinants of Language Development.* Hillsdale, NJ: Erlbaum.

Lundy, B., Field, T., and Pickens, J. (1997). Newborns of mothers with depressive symptoms are less expressive. *Infant Behavior and Development, 19*, 419–424.

Maurer, D., and Young, R. (1983). Newborns' following of natural and distorted arrangements of facial features. *Infant Behavior and Development, 6*, 127–131.

Meltzoff, A. N., and Moore, M. K. (1977). Imitation of facial and manual gestures by human neonates. *Science, 198*, 75–78.

Miller, E. K. (2000). The prefrontal cortex and cognitive control. *Nature Reviews Neuroscience, 1*, 59–65.

Nazzi, T., Bertoncini, J., and Mehler, J. (1998). Language discrimination by newborns: Towards an understanding of the role of rhythm. *Journal of Experimental Psychology: Human Perception and Performance, 24*, 756–766.

Papousek, H. (1969). Individual variability in learned responses in human infants. In R. J. Robinson (ed.), *Brain and Early Behavior*. London: Academic Press.

Peirce, C. S. (1955). Logic as semiotic: The theory of signs. In J. Buchler (ed.), *Philosophical Writings of Peirce* (pp. 98–119). New York: Dover Publications.

Ramus, F., Hauser, M. D., Miller, C., Morris, D., and Mehler, J. (2000). Language discrimination by human newborns and by cotton-top tamarin monkeys. *Science, 288*, 349–351.

Ross, D. (2007). *H. sapiens* as ecologically special: What does language contribute? *Language Sciences, 29*, 710–731.

Ross, D., and Dumouchel, P. (2004). Emotions as strategic signals. *Rationality and Society, 16*(3), 251–286.

Savage-Rumbaugh, S. (1986). *Ape Language*. New York: Columbia University Press.

Savage-Rumbaugh, S., Shanker, S., and Taylor, T. J. (1998). *Apes, Language, and the Human Mind*. Oxford: Oxford University Press.

Spurrett, D., and Dellis, A. (2004). Putting infants in their place (commentary on Falk). *Behavioral and Brain Sciences, 27*, 524–525.

Sterelny, K. (2004). Externalism, epistemic artefacts, and the extended mind. In R. Schantz (ed.), *The Externalist Challenge: New Studies on Cognition and Intentionality*. Berlin: de Gruyter.

Stern, D. (1977). *The First Relationship*. London: Fontana.

Tartter, V. C. (1980). Happy talk: Perceptual and acoustic effects of smiling on speech. *Perception and Psychophysics, 27*, 24–27.

Thibault, P. (2000). The dialogical integration of the brain in social semiosis: Edelman and the case for downward causation. *Mind, Culture, and Activity, 7*(4), 291–311.

Trevarthen, C. (1977). Descriptive analyses of infant communicative behaviour. In H. R. Schaffer (ed.), *Studies in Mother–Infant Interaction* (pp. 227–270). London: Academic Press.

Trevarthen, C. (1979). Communication and co-operation in early infancy: A description of primary intersubjectivity. In M. Bullowa (ed.), *Before Speech* (pp. 321–347). Cambridge: Cambridge University Press.

Trevarthen, C. (1998). The concept and foundations of infant intersubjectivity. In S. Bråten (ed.), *Intersubjective Communication in Early Ontogeny* (pp. 15–46). Cambridge: Cambridge University Press.

Turing, A. M. (1950). Computing machinery and intelligence. *Mind, 49*, 433–460.

Wheeler, M., and Clark, A. (1999). Genic representation: Reconciling content and causal complexity. *British Journal for the Philosophy of Science, 50*(1), 103–135.

Wiesenfeld, A. R., and Klorman, R. (1978). The mother's psychophysiological reactions to contrasting affective expressions by her own and an unfamiliar infant. *Developmental Psychology, 14*, 294–304.

Zajonc, R. (1980). Feeling and thinking: Preferences need no inferences. *American Psychologist, 35*, 151–175.

Zajonc, R. (1984). On the primacy of affect. *American Psychologist, 39*, 117–123.

14 Representation in Extended Cognitive Systems: Does the Scaffolding of Language Extend the Mind?

Robert D. Rupert

How might it be established that the human mind extends into the environment surrounding the human organism? The most promising route runs through the scientific investigation of humans' cognitive skills and capacities—through cognitive science. Some authors (Dennett 1991, 1996; Clark 1997, 1998, 2004, 2006) claim that consideration of language use, clearly one of humans' central cognitive skills, is particularly revealing: the use of language, as a system of extraorganismic marks and sounds, creates minds that extend beyond the boundaries of the human organism. This essay examines a number of ways in which such extension might occur, concluding that no compelling case exists for language's mind-expanding effects. Language profoundly influences our thoughts and greatly affects the development of the human cognitive system. Nevertheless, if we understand "cognitive system" in such a way that the location of a cognitive system bears on the mind's location,[1] external bits of language do not become part of that system.

Herein I do not examine detailed models of language acquisition and use. Instead, I set out and criticize what I take to be the most promising general lines of argument that move from empirical observations about language and cognition to the conclusion that the mind is extended—an argument strategy henceforth referred to as the *language-based inference*. Operating at this level of abstraction moves the discussion toward overarching questions about the *explananda* of cognitive science and about what counts as a cognitive system the capacities and states of which stand in need of explanation by cognitive science. From this discussion emerge two substantive concerns, which I now preview.

First, consider that the persisting nature of the capacities investigated by cognitive science cannot be squared with the often fleeting nature of extended systems composed of human organisms and external linguistic resources (Wilson 2002, pp. 630–631); the latter do not have the longevity or integrity to support the capacities of interest in cognitive science, for example, the capacity to use or to respond to language systematically across a wide variety of contexts. Although some might hope to reinterpret the *explananda* and methods of cognitive science in keeping with the extended view, I argue that such reinterpretation is unnecessarily complex and ultimately unmotivated; it succeeds only by reproducing the distinctions and explanatory patterns typical of the orthodox approach. At the same time, the standard framework accommodates in a natural way the results of interest to those outside the mainstream, and thus considerations of conservatism and simplicity speak in favor of the orthodox approach.

Second, we should be concerned that arguments for the extended mind frequently rely on a version of what I will call *dependence-reasoning*: if thought (or mental activity, or cognition) depends on factor X in some especially strong or clear way, then X is literally part of the thinker's cognitive system.[2] Dependence-reasoning is not, in general, a reliable form of inference. There is simply too much dependence in the world for it to ground the individuation of systems, cognitive or otherwise. Thus, some special consideration must drive its use in the language-based case. I argue that, appearances to the contrary notwithstanding, most such considerations fall flat. Even where they seem to support the language-based inference, the concerns raised above, about the methods and *explananda* of cognitive science, tip the scales against the extended view.

1   Causal Spread, Coupled Systems, and Dependence Reasoning

How might external language become wedded tightly enough to human thought to warrant the language-based inference? Begin with the idea that in at least some cases, the human organism and external linguistic resources constitute a coupled system, exhibiting nontrivial causal spread (Wheeler 2004).[3] The concept of a coupled system is rooted in dynamical systems theory (Port and van Gelder 1995). Two distinct systems become coupled, thus becoming a single, coupled system, when their courses of evolution are mutually interdependent: changes in some important aspect of the behavior of each of the systems is affected by the changing state of some aspect of the other. A formal representation of this mutual interdependence is typically effected by differential (or difference) equations in which the value of a collective variable in one equation acts as a parameter value in the other, and vice versa (see Kelso 1995). For present purposes, the relevant form of a coupled system involves the human organism (or one of its subsystems) and some system (using the term loosely) of linguistic resources external to the human organism.

As a sufficient condition for the existence of an extended cognitive system, the criterion of coupling alone is too liberal. In many cases, the human organism is coupled to some external aspect of its environment, yet that external factor plays only a trivial role in accounting for the cognitive process in question. Thus the nontriviality clause (Wheeler and Clark 1999, p. 110; Wheeler 2004, p. 703): if an organism is coupled to an external subsystem that contributes in a nontrivial way to the production of some significant, cognitive aspect of a cognitive process, then that cognitive process is extended. Such cases exhibit nontrivial causal spread because some of the factors determining distinctively cognitive aspects of the process in question lie beyond the boundary of the organism.

Many proponents of the extended view take their position to constitute a major reorientation in cognitive science, a paradigm shift of sorts (Wheeler 2005; Gibbs 2006). Thus, even if language use sometimes involves such coupling, we might wonder whether this fact will play a central role in cognitive science. After all, humans frequently exercise their cognitive skills "off-line," as it were: humans reason, categorize, and remember even though no spoken or written words are actively affecting the human organism (see Wheeler's discussion of off-line language-use—Wheeler 2004, pp. 707ff.; cf. Carruthers and Boucher 1998a, p. 15). This alone does not provide a counterexample to the sufficiency claim (i.e., that coupling with nontrivial causal spread is sufficient for an extended cognitive process), but it does limit the power of a language-based inference to establish extended cognition as the new, reigning outlook in cognitive science.

We might increase the scope of the coupling argument by weakening the coupling requirement, so as to demand a relation between human cognition and current or historical coupling. The second disjunct allows that genuine coupling at some past point in the process by which language affected thought suffices for the current existence of an extended cognitive system. This weakening does not clearly advance the case for the language-based inference. In the case of language *learning*, which one would expect to be home turf for a historical clause, the organism is often passive (Bloom 2000, pp. 8–9, pp. 26ff.), that is, not part of a mutual dependence relation. The child's environment contains external linguistic resources and they affect the child, but the child and the resources do not become a coupled system *at any point in such learning processes*, for the child exerts no active causal control over the external resources. This sort of one-way dependence is a general phenomenon. In many cases, features of the environment drive the activity of the organism in such a way that the organism's behavior or cognitive processes depend in an especially sensitive way on the continuing effects of some environmental features, but not vice versa: the subject watches the airplane move across the sky, but her watching does not affect the plane.[4]

Perhaps, then, we should try an even weaker formulation of the coupling criterion, one that treats merely one-way dependence during historical inter-action as sufficient: if the states of one subsystem depend, or at a previous time depended, on the changes in the states of another (e.g., states of the organism having depended on states of the world) in a way that contrib-utes nontrivially to the production of some current cognitive phenome-non, then an extended cognitive system currently exists. In section 2, I argue that, as a sufficient condition for the existence of extended cogni-tive systems, the criterion in question should be rejected. In section 3, I consider attempts to salvage aspects of this criterion in the language-specific case by considering ways in which the *content* of human thoughts might depend on interactions (including historical ones) with linguistic resources. Section 4 takes a similar approach to cognitive processing, rather than the content of cognitive states.

2 Cognitive Systems

In this section I argue that, given some plausible ancillary assumptions, the weakened condition entails an unnecessary and inelegant prolifera-tion of cognitive systems. Cognitive processing frequently depends on external features in a nontrivial way, but in many of these cases, it is sim-ply beyond credulity that we should treat the resulting systems as cogni-tive systems of the sort that would justify the language-based inference. Every act of visual perception in natural light involves the sun, and it does so in a nontrivial way. As the intensity of light from the sun changes, so change the states of the visual system. There is not perfect stability in the visual image, and large changes make significant differences in the cogni-tive results. The fact that the sun is present and in its current state explains why the resulting perceptual state has many of its cognitively relevant features; take away the sun and the content of the perceptual state changes, as do the opportunities for further processing. Yet, anyone who claims that the proper system of study in cognitive science is an organism-star system provides a *reductio* of the extended approach to cognitive science—at least if the notion of a cognitive system is meant to admit of inference to the location or constitution of a mind (after all, no part of my mind is 91 million miles from Earth).

Some readers might, however, reason in the opposite direction: cognitive systems are extended, even as far as the sun; the cognitive system realizes the mind; an object individuated by its causal-functional role, as the mind is, is located wherever its realizer is located; therefore, the mind is extended, sometimes as far out as the sun! This form of argument deserves consideration, but its first premise requires support, presumably from a principle of cognitive-systems demarcation: some fact must determine what is a *genuine part* of a cognitive system. Furthermore, our principle must plausibly entail something about *minds*. What might do the trick?

In his discussion of cognitive systems and their realizations, Robert Wilson (2004, p. 132) rightly exhorts his readers to defer to nature to determine what is and what is not a genuine cognitive system. Humans do not simply get to stipulate that, for example, a table one sees is part of the total realization of a cognitive process and that the sun illuminating the table is mere background condition. Wilson goes on to claim that, as a matter of empirical fact, the individuals instantiating mental properties are subjects traditionally conceived of, that is, human organisms. He rests this claim partly on the observation that "Individuals—and here, as always, our paradigms are individual people and individual organisms—are spatio-temporally bounded, relatively cohesive, unified entities that are continuous across space and time" (2004, p. 142). He also emphasizes the view's intuitive appeal (ibid., pp. 142–143). Given some of Wilson's other views, it is not clear why he settles on the individualist position; there seems to be a mismatch between his views about the location of cognitive systems and the location of minds.[5] Nevertheless, I think his emphasis on the coherence and persistence of systems is on the right track and should be applied equally to cognitive systems (Rupert 2004, pp. 425–428).

Generally speaking, we estimate which systems exist objectively by combining some intuitive starting point (e.g., that human organisms are the seats of cognition), methodological principles (e.g., simplicity, conservatism, explanatory power), and empirical results to date. Inquiry must initially be driven by defensible judgments regarding the proprietary subject matter of that discipline—among these, judgments about which systems are at all likely to exhibit the properties investigated by that science. As work proceeds, these judgments are refined and sometimes altered in radical ways. At issue, then, are questions about the sorts of properties that cognitive science sets out to investigate, what systems are taken to

instantiate those properties, and to what extent the inquiry in question
has been successful; furthermore, the answers to these questions must be
evaluated through the lens of established methodological principles such
as simplicity and conservatism.

Taken together, these considerations favor a non-extended view of
human cognitive systems. Of great importance is the way cognitive science characterizes its *explananda*. Humans categorize, perceive, remember,
use language, reason, make sense of the actions of others—these and more
are all persisting abilities of persisting systems; they do not consist in the
activities of relatively short-lived coupled systems (or short-lived systems
that exhibit one-way dependence; let this be understood for the remainder of the discussion).[6] The importance of systems that persist and cohere,
even through change, is especially clear in developmental psychology: we
want to know how *that* system—that single developing human—came to
be the way it is and how a similar course of development happens, on average, for the relatively homogeneous multitude of such persisting human
systems. We want to understand how and why the capacities and abilities
of individual persisting systems change over time, eventually taking a
stable form. If the systems to be investigated were relatively short-lived
coupled systems, developmental inquiry would seem incoherent. We want
to be able to explain why, for example, the child categorizes on the basis of
appearance at age two but pays more attention to insides at age five. How
can this question be sensibly posed—and in such a way that it might motivate a research program—if all that exists are relatively short-lived coupled
systems, some behaving in one way and others exhibiting different behavior at a different time? If there is only a multitude of significantly differing
systems, thousands of systems consisting of different *cognitive* components, there seems little reason to catalog differences among them. The
extended approach seems to offer developmental psychologists no more
reason to be interested in, for example, the series of temporal segments we
normally associate with Sally from ages two to six rather than to be interested in, say, Sally, aged two, together with a ball she was bouncing on
some particular day, Johnny, aged five, together with the book he was reading on some particular afternoon, and Terry, aged seven, plus the stimulus
item he has just been shown by the experimenter. It is simply not clear
how one should proceed after giving up the traditional method. It is difficult even to describe the behavior to be explained if one takes coupled
systems to be cognitive systems whose presence constitutes the location of
a mind. How might we describe, for example, appearance-based categorization within a framework of thousands of fleeting coupled systems? Do

we say that there are lots of coupled systems (organisms-plus-stimulus-items), some of them having parts with, say, a certain shape (the stimuli), and that these coupled systems make judgments different from those made by other systems having older organisms put in place of the younger ones, while the other parts (the stimuli) remain the same?

My concern does not depend specifically on the success of developmental psychology. Investigations of adult capacities, for example, for memory and language use, normally presuppose that researchers investigate particular persisting systems. Some such studies are explicitly longitudinal (Bahrick 1979, 1984), and thus much like developmental psychology in the relevant respects. Beyond these cases, however, psychologists and linguists have been interested in a great many contextual effects, some of these perceptual. It is striking that the same person behaves in one way in one context—say, when not primed—and behaves differently in a slightly different context—when, in contrast, she has been primed. There is a large body of literature filled with experiments interpreted in just this way, their *explananda* taken to be persisting individuals having various capacities or abilities that they exercise in different ways in different contexts.

This emphasis on a persisting individual is also evident in research on perception, where coupling, or at least one-way dependence, seems common. We would like to know why, for example, the subject perceives certain features under some conditions—say, against a particular backdrop—but does not perceive those same features under other conditions (see, e.g., results discussed in Treisman 1998). The experimenter asks a single system to perform various visual tasks, and the outcome sheds light on the process by which that system sees. Perhaps, as has been recently emphasized, the subject *does* something as a way of getting information visually. Still, such results seem to reveal something about the ability of a single persisting system; it tells how *that* system gets visual information.[7] The attempt to make sense of these data, and of the explanatory project more generally, faces a dilemma analogous to the one discussed above in the case of developmental psychology.

The preceding discussion might seem to ignore an important aspect of standard methodology: researchers frequently assign experimental subjects to different groups; in a typical experiment, these consist of a control group and an experimental group. In such experiments, researchers do not appear to be investigating the capacities of individually persisting systems as they change over time or as they exercise their capacities in varying circumstances.

This reaction misinterprets standard methodology, however. Research-ers assign subjects to different groups on the assumption that the set of members of each group represents a standard distribution of skills and reactions across an otherwise homogeneous population. That is, by statis-tical analysis of the results, we think we discover something about the way the *standard persisting human system* reacts under different conditions. Of course, data are sometimes analyzed by condition or by question, but even here the role of such analyses in the larger projects in which they are typi-cally set is unclear if the researchers are not taking each of the data points relative to that analysis to be attached to a persisting cognitive system. Analysis by condition or question is meant to reveal something about how organismically bounded cognitive systems are affected by a suspected causal factor introduced by that condition or question.

In response, the proponent of the extended view might recommend that we reconceptualize developmental psychology. In fact, the literature on extended cognition, and situated cognition more generally, contains much talk of reconceptualization, revolution, and paradigm shifts (Varela, Thompson, and Rosch 1991; van Gelder 1991, 1995; Thelen and Smith 1994; Clark 1997; Brooks 1999; Lakoff and Johnson 1999; Wheeler 2005; Gibbs 2006; Spivey, Richardson, and Zednik forthcoming). Reconceptual-ization at what cost, though? Standard cognitive interaction involves an at least one-way causal dependence of organismic processing on environ-mental structures. Thus, if we individuate systems by their functionally important components (relative to the production of the phenomena of interest), then every time the human organism engages with, or disen-gages from, such external components, a new cognitive system is created (Wilson 2002). As a result, much statistical analysis of the data will be lost. Thousands of experiments have yielded interesting results by assuming that the system of interest persists in various conditions in which it is engaged with the external world. Think of the multitude of within-subject analyses of results on short series of experiment—all data lost.

It would seem, then, that the extended theorist can preserve the success of the standard method only by embracing what is, from the extended standpoint, an ad hoc principle of systems individuation. There are a num-ber of possibilities in this vicinity, but they all appear to come down to this: the extended approach accounts for the success of orthodox cognitive psychology by aping the structure of the standard approach to systems-individuation and, correlatively, to mind–world interaction.

Consider one possibility, recently suggested by Andy Clark (2007), that the proponent of the extended view account for the success of mainstream psychological research by focusing on the organism (by studying, as Clark calls it, "Organism-Centered Cognition"—ibid., p. 192). Organisms contribute in important ways to the construction of various short-lived cognitive systems, many of which are extended. Thus, it is natural to study the persisting organism's contribution to the various extended cognitive systems it helps to create, and it is no surprise that such study produces solid results.

The organism-centered view forfeits the distinctive vision of the extended approach. What is the enduring structure that possesses cognitive capacities that develop over time and explain various forms of behavior? This structure is the organism—and it now holds a fundamentally privileged position, at least relative to the research in question. Other bits can be included in what we call cognitive systems, but only because of these bits' causal interaction with the organismic systems—that is, only because the organism, via its cognitive capacities, recruits various materials for use in the production of cognitive phenomena. One might insist on an extended gloss of the situation, but the vision offered is much more in the spirit of an embedded view (cf. Rupert 2004): the organism is the seat of cognition and locus of control (Butler 1998, pp. 180–181, 212; Wilson 2004, pp. 197–198).

Consider, too, how recruitment is supposed to occur. Organismic mechanisms interact with the environment and, as a result, change states in such a way as to create extended cognitive systems. Yet, in a host of cases that clearly do not involve extended cognition—even, I would guess, by the lights of proponents of the extended view—human organisms exercise many of the same mechanisms (e.g., those involved in perception of far distant objects). Such cases include the experimental paradigms used in connection with successful orthodox research programs. Absent a convincing principle of demarcation that assigns cognitive status to external materials brought into play during the recruitment process but not to materials interacted with during the garden-variety activation of the same internal mechanisms, the more conservative, embedded view wins out. The garden-variety processes do not extend cognition; the advocate of the extended view has no principled basis for distinguishing them in kind from those involved in the recruitment process; therefore, the recruitment processes do not extend cognition.

The theoretical virtues also cut against the organism-centered-yet-extended view. The discussion of traditional research programs in cognitive psychology establishes the utility of some kind of organismic cognitive system. Much of the interesting work in cognitive science does explore, and should explore further, the ways in which that persisting organismic system interacts with the extraorganismic factors during garden-variety as well as supposedly extension-creating interactions with the environment. To call some of the external factors "cognitive" seems to be an exercise in relabeling. Both sides in the debate are committed to the existence of organisms with a distinctive role. Both sides must explain how the organism's cognitive states interact with external materials to produce cognitive phenomena. The organism-centered-yet-extended-view adds the label "cognitive" to some of the external materials, to no apparent end. (Or, depending on how the extended view is articulated, it might add otiose systems, the supposedly extended ones.)

We should not pronounce in advance what a completed cognitive psychology will bring. Nevertheless, insofar as we can make out an extended-systems-based alternative to existing methodology, it introduces an inflated set of distinct cognitive systems, then partitions them into useful sets—each set including all systems created by the participation of one component human organism. This merely reproduces the structure of orthodox cognitive science. On measures of simplicity and conservatism, then, the revisionary strategy clearly loses out to the traditional taxonomy. Of course, costly revisions in theoretical frameworks can sometimes be justified when they offer substantial gains in other respects, for example, in explanatory power or accuracy. The shift under consideration does not, however, do so. The significant results in contemporary cognitive science can be cast in terms of organismically bounded cognitive systems that interact with their environments and frequently become coupled to them. (It might be that the visual system relies more heavily on demonstratives than was previously thought—there are lots of deictic pointers; see Ballard et al. 1997.) Perhaps, though, language use offers a distinctive route to the extended mind, something that involves either a special form of content-dependence or processing-dependence. It is to these issues I turn for the remainder of this chapter.

3 Linguistic Content and Thought Content

There is widespread, although not unanimous, agreement that the notion of representation continues to be of use in the study of cognition. Parties to this prevailing view include many philosophers and cognitive scientists who at least sometimes work outside the orthodox tradition in cognitive science (Clark 2004, p. 719; Churchland 1998, p. 31; Elman 1995, pp. 221–222; Wheeler 2001; Clark and Toribio 1994; Wheeler and Clark 1999; Grush 1997, 2003).[8] This suggests a version of the language-based inference pertaining specifically to the content of cognitive structures. On this approach, the content of organismically internal representations depends in some specially strong way on the content or structure of external, linguistic materials.

In this section, I examine three appeals to content-dependence: (1) it might be that, in an important range of cases, external representations carry the contents of our thoughts (Houghton 1997); or (2) it could be that, in some cases, thoughts inherit the contents of external representations after which those thoughts are in some sense patterned; or weaker still, (3) it might be that thought content is determined by the structure of internal cognitive processes where the structure in question is shaped by the causal or temporal structure of external linguistic resources (even though content is not directly inherited from external, linguistic structures).

Consider cases of the first sort, in which an external linguistic representation carries the content of a person's mental state. Persons frequently make lists, write down ideas in personal journals and professional papers, and so on. In such cases, one might think that the content-bearing external resources play a sufficiently integral role in the subject's cognitive life as to warrant the language-based inference: the external resources seem to be part of the realization of the subject's thought; and since a thought is wherever its realization is, and a mind is at least partly wherever its thoughts are, we might conclude that the subject's mind is extended to the external matter that carries her thought's content.

A natural question to ask here concerns the source of externally represented content. In virtue of what do the external markings (or auditory forms) have content? In many cases, the content clearly originates with the subject of the mental states in question (Segal 1997, p. 153; Adams and Aizawa 2001). The examples given above generally fall into this category: the subject first thinks he needs some milk, then writes it on his shopping list. In such cases the subject's thought content is prior to the content of the relevant external linguistic tokens; thus, these cases do not seem to implicate language, in any particularly strong way, in the determination of thought content.

Perhaps, though, once content is off-loaded—that is, encoded in the external linguistic tokens—the content takes on a life of its own. The subject no longer tokens any persisting, internal representation carrying the content of the state, but instantiates only a memory that there is, say, a shopping list (even this might be missing in some cases; the subject might not remember the list until he sees it lying on the table).

Given the systems-based arguments of the preceding section, we should not assume too quickly that, in the cases in question, subjects' thoughts extend into the environment. The individual *is* the cognitive system in the relevant sense, the sense pertaining to the location of minds. If an individual has the relevant belief (say, that he needs milk) at a given time, yet not because he tokens persisting internal representations carrying the content of that belief, it is most likely in virtue of the appearance of internal representations that take fleeting values relative to the task being performed (Ballard et al. 1997); such pointers can carry the contents represented on the list by deferring to the content of what appears on the list, which, in turn, has its content in virtue of the subject's past investment. In this case, although the subject's internal demonstrative-like representations have whatever content the external structures have, the content is attached to organismically internal structures—to the pointers themselves. This picture seems especially compelling when we consider the causal efficacy of the mental states in question. The external resources have the kind of causal efficacy we expect a subject's thoughts to have only insofar as the external resources have intervening effects on the subject, which effects are then causes of further actions.

Now consider a different way of understanding (1): the content of thought has its source not in the subject but in the external linguistic units themselves. The idea here is that the linguistic content appears in the linguistic token prior to the subject's use of it or internalization of it. If it could be added that the subject's thought content is somehow constituted by the content of the linguistic tokens, this would support the language-based inference.

There are two ways to interpret this suggestion, the first strictly in keeping with (1) and the second amounting to alternative (2) listed above (according to which thought content is inherited from the external linguistic resources after which the internal mental representations are patterned). According to the first interpretation, the subject proceeds absent a thought with the content *P*. The subject comes upon external linguistic units having the content *P*; she picks up a book, for example. She then "docks up" to those external resources, coupling to them in a way that creates an occurrent mental state in the subject, for example, a belief that *P*, without there being an internal vehicle with the content that *P* (Hurley 1998); in which case the *content* of the external resources seems to *constitute* the content of the subject's mental state.

Two considerations recommend against this version of the language-based inference. First, we should bear in mind methodological and empirical considerations concerning systems-individuation discussed above. These considerations speak in favor of a general understanding of the human cognitive system as organismically bounded. If reading constitutes an unusual case, one in which we are not sure whether to posit internal representations that carry thought contents, then it might well be considered "spoils to the victor," that is, a borderline case to be decided in favor of whichever theory is better supported by independent considerations. Second, return to my earlier worry about mental causation. What do the mental states of a subject who is reading cause? One possibility, commonly explored in research on reading comprehension,[9] is that these states cause the subject to give particular answers to questions asked after the reading material has been put away. This, however, presupposes that the subject, at some point prior to questioning, forms internal representations (whatever form these take) of the text or its meanings. Presumably, the internal representations are not formed after the reading material was taken away. Thus, during reading, the subject forms internal representations of either the text or its meanings. Therefore, we have independent reason to think that when a subject engages with text, she forms internal representations that carry the content of the text being read. Thus, although the view in question occupies its own bit of logical space, it can claim little empirical support.

This leads us to view (2) from our earlier enumeration of content-related theses. According to (2), there are internal, mental representations active in the relevant cases, but those representations inherit their content from the content of external linguistic units. A significant amount of thought is, on this view, the use of internalized language. This picture obviates concern about systems-identification by claiming a privileged role for linguistic content vis-à-vis thought content, without requiring that external linguistic resources be present at the time the subject employs the relevant internal resources.

Presumably, neural, syntactic, and architectural facts determine whether the same mental representation is active on two different occasions; and the origin of at least some neurally or syntactically individuated mental representations can be traced back to the external linguistic units that originally caused the appearance or formation of these mental representations. The proponent of content-dependence might claim, then, that a significant portion of the internal units of cognition is made up of, even when processing takes place in the absence of external linguistic resources, the same internal structures that are activated when a subject is affected by external linguistic resources. Furthermore, it might be claimed that the content of those internal units is copied, in a straightforward way, from the content of the linguistic units that caused the formation of the internal ones. If correct, this picture appears to support the language-based inference because it identifies a robust sense in which thought is no more than an aping use of external linguistic resources.

As the argument stands, it seems wanting, for a number of reasons. To begin with, the basic logic of the argument does not lead very neatly to an extended mind, at least not without reliance on a dependency premise of the sort criticized above. We simply should not be moved by arguments that proceed from a premise of the form "Condition c is (given certain background assumptions) necessary for individual i to be in state b" to a conclusion of the form "c is a proper part of i (or of b)." Being surrounded by air is a necessary condition for my continued survival; we should not conclude on this basis that the surrounding air is a proper part of me or a proper part of my continued existence.[10] Exposure to language might be a necessary condition for having certain thoughts (Carruthers 2002, p. 659; Carruthers and Boucher 1998a, pp. 2, 10), but we should not conclude on this basis that external language is literally part of the resulting system. As Carruthers notes, the relation here is merely diachronic (2002, p. 660). These concerns would hold even if a fairly strong version of the Sapir–Whorf hypothesis were correct:[11] even if the range of thoughts available to a subject is limited to those expressible in her natural language and even if she cannot think those thoughts until she has had sufficient interaction with that language, thought proceeds absent actual tokens of that language (visual images and subjectively heard sounds are *not* part of any external natural language).

Furthermore, (2) does not jibe very well with our best accounts of language learning (see Bloom 2000 for extensive discussion of these issues). If one takes the internal representations to have the same content as the external units, and thinks this is so *because* the internal units were patterned after or caused by the external units, one has excluded from the picture the mental content necessary for the child to learn language. For example, it appears that the child uses pragmatic hypotheses, including suppositions about what other people are likely to do, in order to learn the names of things. The child can frame such hypotheses only if she has at her disposal a significant conceptual repertoire—with content fixed, not inherited from language.

Finally, even if we allow that the internal units operate by some kind of principle of deference, whereby they inherit their content from independently content-laden linguistic units, reasoning from that assumption to an extended mind seems perilous. The dependence in question would seem to support equally the inclusion of *many other minds* in the subject's mind. Insofar as the external units possess independent content, it is in virtue of the content of the mental states of ancestors, elders, and current-day speakers other than the subject. Language does not suddenly appear in the world, its content in place. If our subject's mind extends into the world because the content of her thoughts derives from the content of the external units that caused the development of some of her internal resources, then our subject's mind should also extend to encompass the minds of those ancestors and the like, the mental states in whom are responsible for the current external units' having the content they have. Thus, however exactly the dependence-reasoning is supposed to proceed, it seems unprincipled to include external linguistic resources as part of the extended mind, while excluding the minds that give rise to the content of those external linguistic resources; in both cases—moving from current subject to linguistic units and from linguistic units to other subjects—content-dependence is the issue.[12] But to include all of these other minds in the extended mind is a *reductio* of the view; cognitive science has no use for cognitive systems that include the dead and decomposed.

Alternative (3) offers a more roundabout route to content-dependence and from there to the extended mind. On this view, internal units are structured or processed in certain ways, and they, or their governing processes, take on that structure as an effect of the subject's interaction with external linguistic resources; and it is on account of this structure that the internal units possess the content they do.

This possibility can be fleshed out in a variety of ways. Think first in terms of a Fodorian language of thought (LOT) in which at least some of the terms are subject to an externalist semantics (for the various aspects of this picture and arguments for them, see Fodor 1975, 1987, 1990, 1994, 1998). Fodor's claim that the system of mental representations is innate (Fodor 1975, 1981) strikes many authors as implausible, largely because these authors resist the idea that our concepts could, in any sense, be present at birth. So far as I can tell, however, this results largely from misunderstanding (Rupert 1996, chap. 4, 2001). Fodor's conception of innateness is very weak, requiring only that there is no cognitive psychological explanation of the acquisition of our many innate concepts (where what counts as such an explanation is defined restrictively, in terms of learning by hypothesis testing). This does not preclude there being innate concepts the acquisition of which occurs, for humans, under only very constrained conditions. This view allows that many concepts—even innate concepts—are *difficult* to acquire; the triggering conditions for acquisition might elude most of us for some time, maybe for life (Fodor 1998, pp. 156–161).

The difficulty of acquiring certain concepts can be made clearer by attending to the conditions of concept acquisition: at least part of what is required to acquire concept C is that the subject come to have a mental representation with the content c. Assume that coming to have a mental representation with such content is largely a matter of coming into the right causal (or nomological, or historical) relation to the property or individual c. A mental representation's coming to stand in such a relation may require, at least for the typical human, much mediation (Fodor, 1987, pp. 121–122). It might be that, in some cases, the structure of external linguistic resources provides a model of some sort—a compositional or inferential model—after which internal processing can be patterned, eventuating in the acquisition of the concept in question.

This offers us a way to make sense of Carruthers and Boucher's remark that language is obviously a prerequisite for the acquisition of such concepts as electron (Carruthers and Boucher 1998a, p. 2).[13] Furthermore, the view makes sense even on the assumption that the mental representation electron is atomic (that is, not a structured representation that has further mental representations as components). For even if it is atomic, it is very likely that closely connected to it are complex mental representations of sentences containing the word "electron" (in the case of English speakers). To acquire a mental representation that has the content *electron*, the mental representation electron must come into the right causal (or other content-making) relation with the property of being an electron; but until the subject reads about electrons or has a model of the atom explained, it is very unlikely that she has any mental representation bearing the content-making relation to electrons. On this view, the very arrangement of external units catalyzes the acquisition of such concepts as electron, by way of mediating the content-fixing causal dependence-relations within the subject as well as between the subject and the extraorganismic world.

Understood in the preceding fashion, (3) takes us no closer to the extended mind, for it merely asserts a causal or historical dependence of the content of certain mental representations on the presence of external linguistic structures (and possibly representations of such structures). Perhaps, though, we might try invoking a more robust aspect of linguistic structure as the ground of (3). For example, it is plausible that mathematical language provides processing guidelines that indirectly fix the content of those mental representations disciplined to follow linguistically given guidelines (Bloom 2000, chap. 9)—perhaps because mathematical concepts (and perhaps this applies to logical terms as well; see Fodor 1990) are subject to an inferential-role semantics. Part of what one learns when learning mathematics is how to *proceed*, in counting, adding, and solving various other sorts of problems, and one learns this by learning to internalize certain relations that hold among external linguistic structures (patterns of recursive combination, for example). If the patterns of relations holding among bits of language cause certain internal processes to be far more likely to occur in the subject, and these processes help to determine the content of the subject's relevant mental representations, then language plays a central role in the determination of mental content, in at least some important cases.

This interpretation of (3) still amounts to little more than a causal or historical dependence claim; if there is anything more to the position, it pertains to the content of the external structures: that the external structures have the same content as the internal ones. The basis for the attribution of such content, however, seems to be the contribution of other minds in creating linguistic structures with the right patterns. Thus, either the present interpretation of (3) asserts that linguistic structure has caused the subject's brain to process internal units in a way that confers on those units particular contents—a straightforward claim of causal-historical dependence that in no way advances the language-based inference—or the present interpretation of (3) asserts a kind of content-inheritance. On the latter view, the content-dependence extends equally to the minds of those who first began using mathematical language in a way that gives it its content, thus inviting the charge of a gratuitous bloat in cognitive systems.

4 Language and Cognitive Processing

In this section, I shift focus away from content to the processes that lead from one content-laden state to another, from one set of capacities to a new set, and from a task-situation to the responses given in that situation. Our best explanations of how the relevant internal cognitive processes come to take a certain form might invoke the subject's interaction with external linguistic resources; and this relation might be so intimate as to render the external linguistic resources parts of human cognitive systems, and thus human minds.

Clark, following the lead of Dennett and others, has done the most to develop this line of thinking (Clark 1997, 1998, 2004, 2006). In what follows, I consider three kinds of argument Clark has used: one emphasizing the internalization of dynamical structure, one on the role of external language as an active control structure, and the last on the way in which language facilitates higher-order thought.

A subject's experiences of external, linguistic structures can have lasting effects on the way in which she solves problems. For instance, when introducing rules of inference, some logic instructors use as examples particular natural-language applications of the rules, to which these instructors then refer repeatedly in the weeks that follow. These natural language instances might—if they do their job—stick in a student's head to the extent that, when the student has to work on a proof on her own, she replays internal representations of the sound-forms produced by the instructor or visual images of the sentences constituting the instructor's example. In some cases, such mental processing might follow an internalized causal dynamics; in the cases at hand, the process is more likely to be merely temporal. The student replays the sound of the instructor's voice, order intact, and her reasoning follows the structure provided by the mental representation of the instructor's voice.

Although the preceding story, and many more of its ilk, seems psychologically realistic, it lends no support to the language-based inference. Dependence and systems-based considerations must again be given their due. It might be that learning to recognize the sex of chickens requires interaction with chickens, but that does not make the chickens a part of the chicken-sexer's mind, even if some mental images of chickens persist in the mind of the chicken-sexer and guide her future determinations. Furthermore, even if there is some useful sense in which the external language is, during coupling or periods of one-way dependence (during a logic lecture, say), part of a short-lived cognitive system, there is no reason to include it as part of the cognitive system in the sense in which that system is a realization of the persisting mind. Complex, ordered mental representations of words may become part of the persisting system, but this gives us no reason to think the causal "instigators" become part of the system. External language is not, after all, ever literally *in* the organism.

There is a further reason for skepticism here. In many cases of language-dependent skill acquisition, the subject learns a generalization, something that applies beyond the training cases. The best logic students understand the idea behind, for example, hypothetical syllogism (these are the students who, for example, do not have to ask whether it matters in which order two premises of a hypothetical syllogism appear in a natural deduction proof). The nature of generalization is, of course, poorly understood. Nevertheless, flexible intelligence does not exist without the capacity to generalize. In the cases at hand, it involves at the very least knowledge of what in general to look for when comparing a proposed solution to a new problem with the auditory representation of the instructor's examples. Bear in mind that in the typical case, the observed problem has little in common—linguistically speaking—with the instance originally given by the lecturer. The stored mental representation of the instructor's examples would thus seem to act more as trigger, allowing the student access to the mental representation of a general rule, than as a template that guides processing.

Sometimes Clark emphasizes the role that external linguistic resources play as an active control structure (Clark 1997, pp. 195–196; 1998, pp. 173, 181). Such a structure might be produced by the subject herself (talking herself through a problem, for example), or it might be something more like a list of written instructions given to the subject. When this occurs, there exists a distinctive kind of coupled system (or a system that exhibits one-way dependence): the external linguistic units play a central role in computation, the guiding role played by important aspects of the *program* in a standard computational system.

We now face the same sort of choice we faced above in the discussion of content-dependence, version (1). Surely for the external code to do its business, it must have effects on the organism. Thus, a more conservative model competes with the extended view; according to this more conservative model, the organismically bounded cognitive system makes ongoing use, bit by bit, of external instructions. The considerations of section 2 speak in favor of this approach.

Two further points might be added, though, in support of the conservative taxonomy of cognitive systems, considerations that apply specially to the proposal at hand. First, in some of the parade cases of external linguistic control—children talking themselves through complex tasks, for instance—there is an independent argument for the internal representation of the instructions: the child must have these internally encoded, else she would not be able to produce the external linguistic instructions, her own spoken words. This makes it all the more plausible that vocalization merely strengthens the role of an internally represented code, giving *it*, the internal code, control over the computational process. At the very least, this observation counteracts a tendency to think that the external linguistic units exhaust or nearly exhaust the representational resources at work (cf. Rowlands 1999).

Second, note that many advocates of the extended mind are sympathetic to connectionist models (and not merely as models of the implementation of classical theories of cognition—see Fodor and Pylyshyn

1988). If, however, this is the correct account of the human organism's cognitive architecture, the language-based inference faces further difficulty. Connectionist views claim that the cognitive system consists of simple interconnected units, their connection strengths, and various rules for the activation of those units and for the alteration of the connections holding between them (there are many variations, but this is the general picture—see Rumelhart, Hinton, and McClelland 1986). Distinctive of such models is the inseparability of data and process. There are no encoded instructions stored at memory addresses, waiting to be called up for execution. To the extent that they are present in a connectionist system, such things as concepts, programs, and data structures are *implicit* in the system's processes—that is, built into patterns of connectivity, connection strengths, and activation profiles. In contrast, external linguistic units are discrete, repeatable, and have local causal efficacy (Clark 2004, p. 723); these external units would seem to function, *qua* control structures, like commands in a traditional program. Thus, advocates of connectionist theories of the human organism's role in cognition face another principled reason to draw a theoretically important distinction between the organismic cognitive system and external linguistic units.

The third proposed processing-based route through the language-based inference appeals to the way in which external language facilitates higher-order thought. This approach itself comes in two flavors, one internalist, the other externalist. The internalist approach claims that external language provides the subject with augmented computing power and new cognitive strategies by offering to the subject fixed mental units that serve as stand-ins for her own thoughts, units which can then be the object of further reflection and manipulation. External language contributes discrete orthographic and auditory units, after which internal representations are patterned by straightforward causation. Because those bits of external language express prior thoughts of the subject, and because the internal copies inherit that content, it becomes manageable for the subject to think *about* the thoughts expressed by the sentences internally copied.

This internalist route does not seem promising. Humans greatly value the abilities acquired in the manner just described, and it is difficult—perhaps even nomologically impossible—for humans to acquire these skills absent the causal contribution of language. Such observations do not, however, constitute responses to the various concerns I have raised about systems-individuation and dependence reasoning.

The externalist option returns our attention to coupled systems and systems that exhibit one-way dependence. Clark frequently points out the extent to which our cognitive achievements are rooted in iterated interaction with various bits of external media, including language (Clark 1997, pp. 206–207). This is partly a matter of external storage,[14] but in the present context, it is more a matter of the extent to which we actively engage with the external linguistic units that codify our previous thought processes. Here I think Clark blends the pursuit of multiple goals. He wants partly to dispel the hubris and the accompanying skin-bag prejudice of those who think they do it all themselves. Dispelling this hubris and prejudice hardly entails that the mind is extended, however. It is quite consistent to say both "I could not have written this paper without my notes" and "my notes are not part of my mind." It would be interesting to know what explicit dependence premise gets us from the first claim to a denial of the second.

In addition, Clark is moved by the *extent* of dependence, the thought being that our cognitive lives and achievements depend on the scaffolding of language in such a deep way that the connection becomes essential or constitutive. The sheer number of times one interacts with bits of language when, say, writing a substantive paper boggles the mind. Do not the external bits of language thereby become part of the cognitive system writing the paper? Is there something about the cumulative and complex nature of the case that outweighs the weakness of dependence-reasoning?

It seems to me that there is not. Take one instance of a writer's use of her notes. The previous thoughts she recorded in those notes surely were her thoughts just prior to the time she wrote them; they were, apparently, not the thoughts of an extended system. Reviewing her notes now reminds her of those prior thoughts and helps her to hold in mind a complicated structure of mental representations, even if only a complicated structure of pointers that make more readily accessible material held in long-term memory (Ericsson and Kintsch 1995). Why should this make the external reminder part of her mind, though, especially when the explanation of the relevant phenomenon—the formulation of a new or additional thought—decomposes into the subject's prior contribution of non-extended content and the current causal contribution of the external symbols? Furthermore, why should the nature of the explanation change simply because the process recurs, say, two hundred times, rather than occurring only once? Think of how the process began. The subject contributed the content to the notes she made initially, when she set out to write her paper; apparently she can have *those* thoughts without notes. If she can make further notes of the thoughts catalyzed by the first-stage notes, then clearly she can have those second-stage thoughts independently of the second-stage notes she uses to write down those thoughts. In fact, she can have those second-stage thoughts independently of the first-stage notes; it is not as if she must stay in constant contact with the first set of notes in order to have the ideas that are then expressed in the second set. Reiteration introduces no extended aspect into the explanation, nothing beyond content-dependence and causal interaction.[15]

A proponent of the extended view might also be impressed by the ubiquity of language in the human environment; language is always there, contributing to cognition. The sort of ubiquity required does not seem to hold, however. It is one thing to say that some bits or other of language are frequently in the subject's environment; it is another to say that there is some particular subset of external linguistic resources that is constant in the subject's environment—enough so as to become part of her mind. Language is frequently in the air, as it were, but it is not that any particular bit of language—say, a particular set of notes—is ubiquitous in the typical subject's environment. What is ubiquitous is the subject's ability to engage with language, whatever bits of language happen to turn up in her environment (with some limitations, of course; she might know only one language).[16]

In this chapter I have returned repeatedly to two points. The first concerns scientific methodology. We must make judgments about the properties of interest to a given discipline, and about the systems that instantiate those properties—often these judgments are built into the *explananda* of the discipline. They are to some extent negotiable, but in the case at hand, negotiations favor conservatism in our identification of the cognitive systems relevant to the mind's location. Second, dependence-reasoning should, in general, be rejected. When properly understood and applied, these two points speak strongly against any inference from the admittedly enormous importance of language in our cognitive lives to the conclusion that the human mind extends beyond the boundary of the organism.

Acknowledgments

My thanks to Edward Averill and Douglas Kutach for comments on an earlier draft of this chapter. Thanks also to Aaron Meskin for helpful discussions of some of this material.

Notes

1. This qualification is meant to preempt confusion that might arise from equivocation on "cognitive system." One way of thinking about systems is very liberal:

anything that is of any causal importance in a particular context counts as part of the system of interest in that context. This liberal view does not, however, license any inference from extended cognitive systems to an extended mind. Hereafter, I omit this qualification, except where the temptation to equivocate seems especially strong.

2. Cf. Adams and Aizawa's observation that "the mere causal coupling of some process with a broader environment does not, in general, thereby, extend that process into the broader environment" (2001, p. 56). For more detailed discussion, see Adams and Aizawa 2008, chap. 6.

3. For a discussion of coupled systems as cognitive systems, see Clark and Chalmers 1998 and Clark 1997, on what Clark calls "continuous reciprocal causation." Regarding nontrivial causal spread, see Wheeler and Clark 1999. See also van Gelder 1995.

4. Compare Wheeler's example of a system that exhibits nontrivial causal spread, the system involving a robot that locks onto a white triangle on the wall (Wheeler 2004, pp. 703–705); the robot is sensitive, in an ongoing fashion, to the triangle's reflectance of light, but the state of the triangle does not depend on the changing states of the robot. Of course, the robot's movement affects the values of the robot's input sensors, by changing the robot's position relative to the triangle; this, however, is a fact about the robot's internal processes.

5. Wilson argues that human cognitive-*cum*-computational systems are often wide—i.e., include parts beyond the boundaries of the organism. Furthermore, he takes this to bear on the question of an extended mind: "Wide computational systems thus involve *minds* that literally extend beyond the confines of the skull into the world" (2004, p. 165, emphasis added), which would seem to entail that the individual is extended rather than organismically bound.

6. Clark and Chalmers's (1998, reprinted in this volume) discussion of portability, as well as their criteria for extended states, seems partly motivated by a concern for persisting systemic integrity.

7. Consider a related worry. Often in perception, and in action based on perception, humans think about or perceive the same things with which they are interacting; if the cognitive system is individuated liberally, these things are part of our minds, because our perception depends on them. But this leads to a kind of idealism that should give us pause: humans do not, on the basis of perception, interact with the objects perceived; rather, certain parts of the human mind interact with other parts of the mind!

8. These authors all seem to accept that representation consists in a mind–world relation(s) tied in some way to reference, truth conditions, accuracy, aboutness, or correctness of fit. The discussion in the main text is appropriately ecumenical, yet there are limits to what will count as representational content. Robert Wilson's view of content as exploitative and enactive (Wilson 2004) most likely falls outside

those limits. Wilson allows external states, such as the rigidity of bodies in the environment, to play a role in computations—this is part of the reasoning that leads him to endorse extended cognition. At the same time, though, Wilson asserts that there is no computation without representations (2004, p. 177), which makes it a bit difficult to pin down his notion of representation. What does the state of a rigid body represent? What is it a representation *of*? Something more helpful might be suggested by Wilson's talk of enactive representation: "Representation is not something implanted in individuals but something that individuals do by exploiting the rich structures of their environments in cycles of perception and action" (ibid., p. 178). Wilson claims his view is not behaviorist (ibid., p. 184), but he also seems to want representation to play its standard sort of role, representing "objects, properties, events, and propositions" (ibid., p. 222). What is there, on this account, to representing *that P* other than behaving in certain ways in certain circumstances; i.e., what is there to make Wilson's view nonbehaviorist? Nothing, it seems to me; but if it is not behaviorist, it seems eliminativist. It is not clear, then, how much of what I say below about content applies to content as Wilson conceives of it.

9. See, e.g., the discussion of reading comprehension studies—using measures of literal memory for details and also inferences drawn from them—in Gathercole and Baddeley 1993, p. 228. Differences in performance on such tasks is best explained by differences in various subjects' construction and maintenance of internal structure, for the reading material has been taken from the subjects at the time the capacities are tested.

10. It does not help to cast matters epistemically, in terms of what investigators would need to know in order to understand fully a given phenomenon (see Rupert 2004, pp. 395–396).

11. There is good reason to reject the Sapir–Whorf hypothesis in its stronger forms (Bloom 2000; Goldin-Meadow and Zheng 1998; Carruthers 2002), but many important questions about the relation between thought and language remain open (see Majid et al. 2004, and the essays in Carruthers and Boucher 1998b and Gentner and Goldin-Meadow 2003).

12. A counterfactual test does not help to isolate language from users other than the subject; there are no nearby worlds where external words have their content but that content does not derive from minds.

13. I adopt the following orthographic conventions: terms referring to properties or kinds, in the abstract, as well as terms that refer to mental contents, are set in italics; concepts, considered as mental particulars, are set in capital letters, where a given concept's label (horse, for instance) derives from the content we assume to be carried by that mental particular.

14. For concerns about extended memory, see Rupert 2004.

15. Driving the language-based inference in such cases might be an inference from "the final paper consists of the (non-extended) author's thoughts" to "there was a single time when the author had, clearly in mind, all of the thoughts expressed in the paper," taken together with the view that the author simply could not have had the entire structure of the paper in mind at once. But this would be a mistake. First off, the inference is bad. The attribution of written work to a non-extended author does not entail that the author ever had the entire work in mind at a single time. (Jack built a house, but he did not build it all at once.) Second, much of the work reviewed by Ericsson and Kintsch (1995) suggests that human memory is really quite impressive. This is especially clear in cases of expertise, which is the sort of case we are addressing when we talk about professionals writing papers and books. Note, too, that impressive memory capacity is not merely a freak-show trick mastered only by a few (contrary to what some of Clark's remarks suggest—Clark 2003, p. 74); the experimental work reveals such skill among everyday people operating in their own domains of expertise, for example, servers in restaurants.

16. Dennett makes the further suggestion that experience with language transforms the architecture of the cognitive system, by causing the formation of virtual machines in the connectionist wetware of the human brain; the structure of external language itself causes some of the thought processes of language-users to take the form of serial operations on discrete units (Dennett 1991, pp. 224–225). If Dennett is right about the effects of language on language users, this a testament to the transformative power of language use, not an argument for including language in the physical system that realizes the mind. Many factors have profound and lasting effects on children's development—parents' political attitudes, for example. But if one takes seriously the idea that the mind *has* a location—because, say, one wishes to adhere to naturalistic and materialist scruples—this transformative effect carries us no distance toward extended minds. The physical part of the parent's brain that carried her political attitudes has not literally become part of the physical system that is the child's mind.

References

Adams, F., and Aizawa, K. (2001). The bounds of cognition. *Philosophical Psychology*, *14*, 43–64.

Adams, F., and Aizawa, K. (2008). *The Bounds of Cognition*. Malden, MA: Blackwell.

Bahrick, H. P. (1979). Maintenance of knowledge: Questions about memory we forgot to ask. *Journal of Experimental Psychology. General*, *108*, 296–308.

Bahrick, H. P. (1984). Semantic memory content in permastore: Fifty years of memory for Spanish learned in school. *Journal of Experimental Psychology. General*, *113*, 1–29.

Ballard, D. H., Hayhoe, M. M., Pook, P. K., and Rao, R. P. N. (1997). Deictic codes for the embodiment of cognition. *Behavioral and Brain Sciences, 20*, 723–742.

Bloom, P. (2000). *How Children Learn the Meanings of Words*. Cambridge, MA: MIT Press.

Brooks, R. (1999). *Cambrian Intelligence: The Early History of the New AI*. Cambridge, MA: MIT Press.

Butler, K. (1998). *Internal Affairs: Making Room for Psychosemantic Internalism*. Boston: Kluwer.

Carruthers, P. (2002). The cognitive functions of language. *Behavioral and Brain Sciences, 25*, 657–674.

Carruthers, P., and Boucher, J. (1998a). Introduction: Opening up options. In P. Carruthers and J. Boucher (eds.), *Language and Thought: Interdisciplinary Themes* (pp. 1–18). Cambridge: Cambridge University Press.

Carruthers, P., and Boucher, J. (eds.) (1998b). *Language and Thought: Interdisciplinary Themes*. Cambridge: Cambridge University Press.

Churchland, P. M. (1998). Conceptual similarity across sensory and neural diversity: The Fodor/LePore challenge answered. *Journal of Philosophy, 95*, 5–32.

Clark, A. (1997). *Being There: Putting Brain, Body, and World Together Again*. Cambridge, MA: MIT Press.

Clark, A. (1998). Magic words: How language augments human computation. In P. Carruthers and J. Boucher (eds.), *Language and Thought: Interdisciplinary Themes* (pp. 162–183). Cambridge: Cambridge University Press.

Clark, A. (2003). *Natural-Born Cyborgs*. Oxford: Oxford University Press.

Clark, A. (2004). Is language special? Some remarks on control, coding, and co-ordination. *Language Sciences, 26*, 717–726.

Clark, A. (2006). Language, embodiment, and the cognitive niche. *Trends in Cognitive Sciences, 10*, 370–374.

Clark, A. (2007). Curing cognitive hiccups: A defense of the extended mind. *Journal of Philosophy, 104*(4), 163–192.

Clark, A., and Chalmers, D. (1998). The extended mind. *Analysis, 58*, 7–19. Reprinted as chapter 2 of this volume.

Clark, A., and Toribio, J. (1994). Doing without representing? *Synthese, 101*, 401–431.

Dennett, D. (1991). *Consciousness Explained*. Boston: Little, Brown.

Dennett, D. (1996). *Kinds of Minds: Toward an Understanding of Consciousness*. New York: Basic Books.

Elman, J. (1995). Language as a dynamical system. In R. F. Port and T. van Gelder, (eds.), *Mind as Motion: Exploration in the Dynamics of Cognition* (pp. 195–225). Cambridge, MA: MIT Press.

Ericsson, K. A., and Kintsch, W. (1995). Long-term working memory. *Psychological Review, 102*, 211–245.

Fodor, J. (1975). *The Language of Thought*. Cambridge, MA: Harvard University Press.

Fodor, J. (1981). The present status of the innateness controversy. In J. Fodor, *Representations* (pp. 257–316). Cambridge, MA: MIT Press.

Fodor, J. (1987). *Psychosemantics: The Problem of Meaning in the Philosophy of Mind*. Cambridge, MA: MIT Press.

Fodor, J. (1990). *A Theory of Content and Other Essays*. Cambridge, MA: MIT Press.

Fodor, J. (1994). *The Elm and the Expert*. Cambridge, MA: MIT Press.

Fodor, J. (1998). *Concepts: Where Cognitive Science Went Wrong*. Oxford: Oxford University Press.

Fodor, J., and Pylyshyn, Z. (1988). Connectionism and cognitive architecture: A critical analysis. *Cognition, 28*, 3–71.

Gathercole, S. E., and Baddeley, A. (1993). *Working Memory and Language*. Hillsdale, NJ: Lawrence Erlbaum.

Gentner, D., and Goldin-Meadow, S. (eds.) (2003). *Language in Mind: Advances in the Study of Language and Thought*. Cambridge, MA: MIT Press.

Gibbs, R. (2006). *Embodiment and Cognitive Science*. Cambridge: Cambridge University Press.

Goldin-Meadow, S., and Zheng, M. (1998). Thought before language: The expression of motion events prior to the impact of a conventional language model. In P. Carruthers, and J. Boucher (eds.), *Language and Thought: Interdisciplinary Themes* (pp. 26–54). Cambridge: Cambridge University Press.

Grush, R. (1997). The architecture of representation. *Philosophical Psychology, 10*, 5–23.

Grush, R. (2003). In defense of some "Cartesian" assumptions concerning the brain and its operation. *Biology and Philosophy, 18*, 53–93.

Houghton, D. (1997). Mental content and external representations. *Philosophical Quarterly, 47*, 159–177.

Hurley, S. (1998). Vehicles, contents, conceptual structure, and externalism. *Analysis*, *58*, 1–6.

Kelso, J. S. (1995). *Dynamic Patterns: The Self-Organization of Brain and Behavior.* Cambridge, MA: MIT Press.

Lakoff, G., and Johnson, M. (1999). *Philosophy in the Flesh: The Embodied Mind and Its Challenge to Western Thought.* New York: Basic Books.

Majid, A., Bowerman, M., Kita, S., Haun, D., and Levinson, S. (2004). Can language restructure cognition? The case for space. *Trends in Cognitive Sciences*, *8*(3), 108–114.

Port, R. F., and van Gelder, T. (eds.) (1995). *Mind as Motion: Exploration in the Dynamics of Cognition.* Cambridge, MA: MIT Press.

Rowlands, M. (1999). *The Body in Mind: Understanding Cognitive Processes.* Cambridge: Cambridge University Press.

Rumelhart, D., Hinton, G., and McClelland, J. (1986). A general framework for parallel distributed processing. In D. Rumelhart, J. McClelland, and the PDP Research Group, *Parallel Distributed Processing: Explorations in the Microstructure of Cognition*, vol. 1: *Foundations* (pp. 45–76). Cambridge, MA: MIT Press.

Rupert, R. (1996). The best test theory of extension. Ph.D. dissertation, University of Illinois at Chicago.

Rupert, R. (2001). Coining terms in the language of thought: Innateness, emergence, and the lot of Cummins's argument against the causal theory of mental content. *Journal of Philosophy*, *98*, 499–530.

Rupert, R. (2004). Challenges to the hypothesis of extended cognition. *Journal of Philosophy*, *101*, 389–428.

Segal, G. (1997). Review of Robert Wilson, *Cartesian Psychology and Physical Minds: Individualism and the Sciences of the Mind. British Journal for the Philosophy of Science*, *48*, 151–156.

Spivey, M., Richardson, D., and Zednik, C. (forthcoming). Language is spatial, not special: Using space for language and memory. In L. Smith, K. Mix, and M. Gasser (eds.), *Spatial Foundations of Cognition and Language.* Oxford: Oxford University Press.

Thelen, E., and Smith, L. B. (1994). *A Dynamic Systems Approach to the Development of Cognition and Action.* Cambridge, MA: MIT Press.

Treisman, A. (1998). The perception of features and objects. In R. D. Wright (ed.), *Visual Attention* (pp. 26–54). Oxford: Oxford University Press.

van Gelder, T. (1991). Classical questions, radical answers: Connectionism and the structure of mental representations. In T. Horgan and J. Tienson (eds.), *Connection-*

ism and the Philosophy of Mind, Studies in Cognitive Systems, vol. 9. Dordrecht: Kluwer Academic.

van Gelder, T. (1995). What might cognition be, if not computation? *Journal of Philosophy, 92*, 345–381.

Varela, F., Thompson, E., and Rosch, E. (1991). *The Embodied Mind: Cognitive Science and Human Experience*. Cambridge, MA: MIT Press.

Wheeler, M. (2001). Two threats to representation. *Synthese, 129*, 211–231.

Wheeler, M. (2004). Is language the ultimate artefact? *Language Sciences, 26*, 693–715.

Wheeler, M. (2005). *Reconstructing the Cognitive World: The Next Step*. Cambridge, MA: MIT Press.

Wheeler, M., and Clark, A. (1999). Genic representation: Reconciling content and causal complexity. *British Journal for the Philosophy of Science, 50*, 103–135.

Wilson, M. (2002). Six views of embodied cognition. *Psychonomic Bulletin and Review, 9*, 625–636.

Wilson, R. (2004). *Boundaries of the Mind: The Individual in the Fragile Sciences*. Cambridge: Cambridge University Press.

15 The Extended Mind, the Concept of Belief, and Epistemic Credit

John Preston

Introduction

In their 1998 paper "The Extended Mind,"[1] Andy Clark and David Chalmers present two closely related theses. The first, *active externalism*, they plausibly detect playing a growing role in cognitive science research, as well as in its philosophy (p. 29, n. 2). It says that when humans are appropriately linked with external entities, the whole arrangement constitutes a cognitive system in its own right (p. 29). The "boundary" between the intelligent system and the world, Clark says elsewhere (Clark 1997, pp. 213–214), is more plastic than supposed by those who take it to be formed by skin and skull. Although genuinely cognitive systems may be confined within the brain and body, they may just as well be spatially extended beyond them.

Clark and Chalmers then distinguish this view, framed in terms of the technical concept of a cognitive system, from a second view, which I take to be *the extended mind thesis*, that some, if not all, of a subject's mental phenomena are constituted partly by features of that subject's environment. In particular, they run the extended mind thesis for *beliefs*, concluding that these can be constituted partly by features of the environment, and therefore that "the mind extends into the world" (p. 33). Clark also wants to argue, along the same lines, for *persons* and *selves* being thus extended, although he resists the thesis for individual *consciousnesses* (Clark 1997, pp. 215–217).

These few remarks already raise a host of issues. Here, I seek to challenge the particular version of the extended mind thesis that Clark and Chalmers run for beliefs. This doesn't imply that I have to reject the extended mind thesis for *all* mental phenomena.[2] I'll confine my argument to *human* beliefs, mainly because Clark and Chalmers do so, too. The idea that our beliefs are constituted by features of our environments, I shall argue, isn't sufficiently supported by the argument Clark and Chalmers give, and represents a serious distortion of certain important aspects of the concept of belief.

1   Otto, Inga, and the Appeal to Natural Kinds

The belief version of the extended mind thesis has it that one's beliefs can be constituted partly by features of one's environment. (Note that whatever *constituted* means, it can't be taken in the way some social scientists understand it: it doesn't just mean "caused.")[3] To support this we're asked to consider Inga, whose faculties are in good fettle, and Otto, who suffers from Alzheimer's disease and relies on information in the environment to help structure his life. Otto carries with him a notebook in which he writes down new information that he comes across. His notebook, we're told, "plays the role usually played by a biological memory" (p. 33). In a particular case, he walks to 53rd Street because he wants to go to the Museum of Modern Art and sees, from his notebook, that the museum is on 53rd. According to Clark and Chalmers, Otto believed the museum was on 53rd Street *even before* consulting his notebook, since the notebook plays for him the same role that memory plays for others:

Clearly, Otto walked to 53rd Street because he wanted to go to the museum and he believed the museum was on 53rd Street. And just as Inga had her belief even before she consulted her memory, it seems reasonable to say that Otto believed the museum was on 53rd Street even before consulting his notebook. For in relevant respects the cases are entirely analogous: the notebook plays for Otto the same role that memory plays for Inga. The information in the notebook functions just like the information constituting an ordinary non-occurrent belief; it just happens that this information lies beyond the skin. (pp. 33–34)

Clark and Chalmers do something to deflect potential attempts to argue that this case fails to fit the everyday concept of belief. Unfortunately, in doing so they also explicitly say they don't care about standard use of the concept:

In all important respects, Otto's case is similar to a standard case of (non-occurrent) belief. The differences between Otto's case and Inga's are striking, but they are superficial. By using the "belief" notion in a wider way, it picks out something more akin to a natural kind. The notion becomes deeper and more unified, and is more useful in explanation. (p. 35)

This, I think, is a deeply unsatisfactory move to make at this point. Whether or not the concept of belief as it stands picks out a natural kind, proposals to alter the concept should be resisted.[4]

Using the concept of belief in a new, wider way, even assuming that it would retain its identity as a concept of *belief*, promises an easy but shallow victory. "Explanations" may prove easy to come by, but there will be no guarantee that they make contact with the phenomena one is supposed to be explaining. And it's the *explananda* that Clark and Chalmers are messing with here, not just the *explanans*. If one can violate the constraints which currently govern concepts like belief and mind, beliefs and minds might turn out to be unrecognizable to those who use those terms correctly in nontechnical contexts. This is entirely acceptable when forging a technical scientific concept to be used in constructing scientific explanations. There, how the term is used in nontechnical contexts (if indeed it has such a use) shouldn't constrain what scientists want to mean by it. But when dealing with a commonsense, everyday concept which figures centrally in what cognitive science has to explain, it has to be inadvisable. To retain the connection between cognition and everyday psychological abilities and achievements as pretheoretically conceived is *essential*, because among the ultimate *explananda* of cognitive science are phenomena picked out by perfectly ordinary cognitive concepts like belief, knowledge, memory, perception, and so on.

2   The Commonsense Alternative and the Issue of Simplicity

Clark and Chalmers seek to make hay not just from the fact that active externalism is becoming popular among cognitive scientists, but also from the fact that alternative views are, in their opinion, needlessly complex. The commonsensical alternative to their view is, of course, that Otto's notebook is an aid or tool that he uses in cognitive contexts, not a component of his extended mind. And the usual way of explaining his situation is that until he consults his notebook he doesn't yet believe that the answer to the question "Where's the museum?" is "on 53rd," but he does (or might) believe that his notebook contains the answer to that question.

It's true that this is more articulated than Clark and Chalmers's way of describing the situation. But conceptual considerations take preference over simplicity here: if either active externalism or the extended mind thesis conflicts with our psychological concepts, it is thereby impugned as a foundation for (or account of) the study of cognition.

A proposal for conceptual change can't answer questions about our existing concepts, and can only sweep existing conceptual problems under the rug. So I shall henceforth ignore the idea that the meaning of terms like "believes" should or even could be fixed by cognitive science. What I propose to do is put forward what I think are the relevant facts and present a conclusion which illuminates the exact status of Otto's situation.

3   Otto's Situation

Clark and Chalmers think that because that situation satisfies the following conditions, Otto can be said to have believed that the museum is on 53rd Street even before consulting his notebook:

Otto's notebook plays the role usually played by one's memory. He constantly uses it; it's "central to his actions in all sorts of contexts, in the way that an ordinary memory is central in an ordinary life" (p. 34).

The information "is reliably there when needed, available to consciousness and available to guide action in just the way that we expect a belief to be" (p. 34).

The "essential causal dynamics" of Otto's situation are the same as that of Inga's. Otto's belief plays the same explanatory role as Inga's. The relevant external features play an active role and have a direct impact on behavior (p. 34).

Inga's access to the information is at most only slightly more reliable than Otto's (p. 36).

Inga's access to the information is at most only of slightly better quality than Otto's (p. 36).

Upon retrieving the information in question from his notebook, Otto automatically endorses it (p. 38).

Otto has consciously endorsed the information contained in the notebook at some time in the past, and it's still there as a consequence of that endorsement (p. 38).

One might have reservations about some of these claims, and some of them will emerge below. Notice at this point, though, that these conditions do supply a far richer background to claims about Otto's cognitive abilities than the one very thin condition that Clark and Chalmers officially require when they discuss active externalism. That condition is simply that for coupled systems to be cognitive, reliable coupling is neces-

sary, and that one is reliably coupled to resources as long as they are generally there when required (p. 31).

In order to present Otto's situation as one of believing one might, however, go even further. Whether or not Clark and Chalmers care, Otto
seems to satisfy certain other constraints which support their idea that he
had the belief in question even before consulting his notebook. Among
these are that:

Otto isn't *surprised* to find out that he believes that the museum is on 53rd St.
Otto doesn't need to *interpret* what's written in his notebook.
On consulting his notebook Otto would sincerely and non-self-deceptively
avow that he thinks that the museum is on 53rd St.

Clark and Chalmers ignore these aspects of Otto's situation. Part of whatever plausibility is had by the claim that Otto already believes that the
museum is on 53rd, though, derives from them. The example trades on
the familiarity of these conditions being fulfilled, and if one explicitly
considers it without these conditions, the claim about Otto's belief is even
less plausible. But the final suggested condition brings me to the main
objection to Clark and Chalmers's conclusion about Otto that I propose to
consider here: the issue of what Otto himself could and would say.

4   The Issue of "First-Person Authority"

It's a crucial component of both active externalism and the extended
mind thesis that cognition can involve resources existing and processes
taking place outside the head. No doubt this is so. That is, there can be no
objection to the idea that a person's cognitive skills, capacities, and abilities can be, and in many cases *must* be, initiated, developed, honed, or
manifested using resources such as language, paper and pencil, abaci, diaries, notebooks, computers, and a host of others. But this acceptable thesis
is a *genetic* thesis about cognitive phenomena, not a thesis about what
such phenomena *are*.[5]

As we've seen, Clark and Chalmers suppose the extended mind thesis
to apply not just to cognitive processes generally but paradigmatically to
belief. But belief is (along with meaning, intention, suspicion, supposition,
expectation, hope, and apprehension) one of the mental phenomena about
which we have *first-person authority in utterance*. One has a sort of cognitively
primitive authority over what it is one thinks, means, intends, expects,
and so on. When it comes to belief, this is the fact that, for the heart of each

person's belief system, the massive central core of one's thinking that so-and-so is the case, one just *can say*, with authority, what it is one thinks or believes in a way that brooks no contradiction by others (or even by oneself at a later date).

There are certainly tricky questions about the *extent* of this authority. It's clearly not shaken by insincerity or slips of the tongue. But in order to count as being able to say what it is one believes, does one have to be able to respond immediately to a request to say what it is? Does everything one would claim to remember being the case, no matter how hard it may be to recall, count as something one believes? Can one make a slip, retract it, have another stab, and have it still count? What about cases of self-deception?

To most of these questions, the outlines of answers can be given.[6] Take an example from the last category: on finding out that Martin, who purports to be an Arsenal fan, is absolutely elated that his least-favorite team, Spurs, won the cup final, we might all agree that he was wrong in saying that he wanted Arsenal to win, even though he said it sincerely and considered the matter attentively. Cases like this can indeed be taken to involve desires and beliefs. But the desires and beliefs in question are *unconscious* ones, where there's no presumption of first-person authority.

My claim, then, is that people do have a limited but real first-person authority about what it is they believe. Here, sincerity suffices for truth. However, the sorts of real-world resources and processes which, according to the extended mind thesis, can partly constitute one's beliefs aren't ones about which we can have first-person authority, on pain of our being authoritative about contingent matters of fact concerning the "external world." Consider the contents of Otto's notebook, for example. Of course, upon being asked, Otto is the authority on whether what's written in his notebook is indeed what he believes. But he isn't authoritative about the contents of the notebook *before* he has consulted it. He can't avow what-he-believed-before-consulting-his-notebook at times prior to his consulting it, which is what matters to the claim that he already believed it. So even though he isn't *surprised* to find it out, Otto does have to wait and see how things are in the "external world" (i.e., his notebook) before finding out what he believes. However, in ordinary cases of belief, I suggest, there's simply *no such thing as* "finding out what one believes." (That phrase can only mean *making up* one's mind.)

The conjunction of the extended mind thesis with first-person authority would wrongly imply that Otto is authoritative about what's written in his notebook, which is, of course, a contingent fact concerning the "external world," that is, not the kind of thing one can be authoritative about at all. So the extended mind thesis for belief has to flout first-person authority (whether or not ordinary ["passive"] externalism does so).[7]

Clark and Chalmers might respond in one of several ways. They might reply that there's no relevant difference between Otto's case and Inga's in respect of authority, since one could likewise render her incapable of saying what she believes (by interfering with, e.g., the bits of her brain subserving memory). This, though, would be a case of *changing* what she believes, or of *eradicating* her beliefs.

Alternatively, they might respond that Otto does have the requisite first-person authority *when considered together with his notebook*. This move would reflect the fact that, for most purposes and given the reliability of his notebook's presence, Otto is as good an informant as Inga. However, it gerrymanders the existing way of distinguishing between thinkers and their environments. That way does not, *pace* Clark and Chalmers, lead inexorably to a vision of the "naked mind." But it does insist that the *person* is what does the thinking, the cognition. These concepts, of thinker and environmental props, are again everyday ones, concepts that people come to deploy just a result of being competent speakers of a natural language, not in virtue of knowing anything about cognitive science. Since this move to alter them is of a piece with the idea of providing a new, wider, natural kind concept of belief, my remarks on that apply here, too.

A different move would be to say that if we accept active externalism, Otto has the requisite first-person authority because the cognitive system in question already *encompasses* his notebook. This suggestion, however, has two drawbacks. First, it isn't really to the point, since first-person authority pertains to *truth*, not to knowledge. I think we should resist the temptation to construe first-person authority as a kind of "self-knowledge," let alone a kind of "privileged access" to, or a priori knowledge of, (some of) the "contents" of one's own mind. Second, it changes the subject, from Otto to the cognitive system of which he's part. The idea of first-person authority attaches to *cognizers*, not to cognitive systems of which such beings are components. Clark and Chalmers may want to claim that the cognitive system of which Otto is a component has first-"person" authority over what it believes. It certainly doesn't follow that Otto has that authority, or the belief in question. But the issue (and Clark and Chalmers's original claim) concerns whether *Otto* has the belief, not merely whether, as it were, the belief is within and accessible to the cognitive system of which Otto is part. To respond to the objection from first-person authority along these lines, Clark and Chalmers have to establish that cognitive systems can be credited not just with beliefs, but also with the ability to say, authoritatively, what it is they believe.

5   The Functional Equivalence Claim

Clark and Chalmers claim that "the 'essential causal dynamics' of Otto's situation are the same as that of Inga's" (p. 34). But in what respect(s) are Otto and Inga functionally equivalent? Are they so in respect of their mental capacities, which are what's at issue?

Certain aspects of the situation suggest that no such equivalence obtains. What the cognizers in question would and could *say* (so crucial in assessing *human* cognition) should count as a very significant factor in answering questions about their cognitive capacities. As long as he's untainted by "functionalism," or reliabilist epistemology, if asked whether he *knew* that the museum is on 53rd, prior to consulting his notebook, Otto would undoubtedly say that he didn't. And it's not that he had at that point some inkling about the location, but wasn't confident about it. The location just didn't come to his mind at all. So if asked whether he *thought* or *believed* that the museum is on 53rd, prior to consulting his notebook, he should and would reply likewise. Clark and Chalmers's position involves riding roughshod over these sorts of responses.

Suppose, though, that Otto doesn't respond in the way I think he would and should. Suppose he says he did believe that the museum is on 53rd, even before consulting his notebook. What happens when he and Inga are each asked *why* they believe that this is where the museum is? Inga might make one or more of any number of replies, like "I just remember it," "I remember going there," "I recall seeing it," "Someone told me," "I saw its address in the paper," "It's opposite the Design Store." Otto, though, can *only* truthfully reply "That's what's written in my (very reliable) notebook." Doesn't this suggest that his "belief" is far more impoverished than Inga's? The idea that *this* belief of Inga's and Otto's "belief" fall under the same natural kind is implausible.

A further failure of mental isomorphism is that the information in Otto's notebook has to enter his mind *through perception*.[8] The information "in" Inga's memory (even assuming that's the right way to conceive things) doesn't.

Unaided, Otto can't remember or say where the museum is when asked (that's why he has to refer to his notebook). Inga can do both. Clark and Chalmers might seek to deny this by insisting that Otto can indeed remember *with the help of his notebook*. But this just means that Otto *can't* remember.

It's not that Otto's notebook helps him to remember where the museum is. Rather, it's because he can't remember where the museum is that he needs to consult his notebook.

Otto and Inga, I suggest, are functionally equivalent only in respect of their gross behavioral capacities and only when these are conceived within a very restricted temporal frame. If the functions they carry out during that time are described in purely behavioral terms, Otto and Inga may be isomorphic, to a certain very limited extent. (They aren't even *behaviorally* identical in other respects: Inga unhesitatingly turns left out of the subway exit, whereas Otto just draws a blank, and has to consult his notebook.) Looking at them in a wider context, though, what they have in common is behavioral, but cognitively superficial. In this respect, Clark and Chalmers's functionalist view is revealed as too behavioristic, conceiving of functional equivalence only in gross behavioral terms.

6 Unconscious Belief?

If Otto doesn't really believe that the museum is on 53rd, in the ordinary sense of that phrase, is his case perhaps one of *unconscious belief*? There are certainly some parallels with what Freudians might mean by that expression. Call the statement that the museum is on 53rd St. "*q*." If Otto were to follow Clark and Chalmers in judging that he believes that *q* (assuming, for a moment, that one *can* judge that one has a specific belief),[9] this judgment would be based on the same *sort* of considerations as other people use to find out what he (unconsciously or otherwise) believes: publicly available evidence. And, as with an unconscious belief, Otto's commitment to the judgment that he believes that *q* doesn't imply that he's capable of offering some *direct* defense of the statement that *q*, in the form of evidence or argument (having Alzheimer's, this may well be one of the things he can't do). However, *unlike* an unconscious belief, Otto's commitment to the judgment that he believes that *q* does imply that he regards it as plausible, on the basis of his notebook's past reliability, that *q*. He certainly wouldn't, as the unconscious believer of the Freudian kind does, candidly *deny* what he's supposed unconsciously to believe. He could and would offer an *indirect* defense of it, citing the fact that it's written in his notebook, together with his notebook's past reliability. And although ascribing an unconscious belief to a person is no evidence for the truth of that belief, the inscription in Otto's notebook *is* (weak or modest) evidence that the museum is on 53rd (given the meticulous way in which his notebook is compiled).

All this shows that Otto's isn't a good case of belief (a good case with which to *teach* the concept, for example), whether ordinary *or* unconscious. It's more like the following. On asking one of my colleagues what he thought about a certain philosophical issue, he replied "Let's see," and lunged for the nearest copy of his recently published book. In such cases, an expression of what one "believes" has an "external" existence. Just as in the case of unconscious belief, one takes a *sort* of third-person stance toward one's own commitments,[10] although the sort is different in each case. Here, to talk of what one believes is to talk about what one *believed* when one wrote, and one uses the external resource to *remind* oneself what this was. To indicate one's own previously written product and say "Here's the state (or a record of it), so *that* must be what I believe" can only be a joke. Politicians can do this sort of thing when adverting to the party line as their "official position," but in doing so, of course, they don't reveal what they *believe*, but bypass the issue entirely.

7 Memory

As we've seen, Clark and Chalmers claim that Otto's notebook plays the role usually played by a person's memory. In particular, it plays the same role for Otto as Inga's memory plays for her. He constantly uses it; it's "central to his actions in all sorts of contexts, in the way that an ordinary memory is central in an ordinary life" (p. 34). Clark and Chalmers want to say that just as Inga had her belief, non-occurrently, before she consulted her memory to retrieve it, Otto believed the museum was on 53rd even before consulting his notebook. This, I would urge, involves putting too intellectualist a construction on the concept of memory.[11] If asked what you think about a certain topic, you may be in a position to answer immediately, informatively, and unaided. Where you are, you standardly have first-person authority over your utterance. But is it right to describe such cases as cases in which you remember what it is you believe, *and* in which you do so as a result of having consulted your memory? Does Inga, for example, have to remember that she believes the museum is on 53rd? (Note that this is separate from the issue of whether she remembers that the museum is on 53rd.) And if she does, does she have to consult her memory in order to remember it?

Ordinarily, there's just no such thing as remembering what one believes. That is, present-tense expressions of the form "I remember what I believe," "I don't remember what I think," "She remembers what she thinks," "She can't remember what she thinks," and so on, standardly have no use. If one can't at the time say what one thinks, but later comes to be able to say, one would usually be said to have acquired the belief (for the first or the nth time) at that later point. If we *do* describe the person in this sort of case as remembering (or being able to remember) what he or she thinks, it certainly shouldn't be supposed that remembering of this kind always involves the mental operation which Clark and Chalmers apparently think is central to all belief· consulting one's memory. Being able to remember (in this new, wide sense) need not involve consulting one's memory at all. This isn't to say that one never consults one's memory: there are occasions on which that phrase would be appropriate. But Inga doesn't have to "consult" her memory in the way Otto does have to consult his notebook. Clark and Chalmers's claim that the two are on a par in this respect is flawed.

If, on the other hand, there were a sense in which remembering that p necessarily involved consulting one's memory, Inga's case *needn't* be a case of remembering (or being able to remember) that p. There's no reason to think (to dogmatically insist) that any such consultation goes on in cases where one *just says* what one thinks.

Medical science tells us that Alzheimer's disease causes one to lose one's memory. Doctors would undoubtedly say that this is what happened to Otto. Cognitive science shouldn't deny this, but Clark and Chalmers do, on its behalf, if they really suppose that Otto's carrying a notebook is a way of restoring his memory.[12] Otto's notebook is no more a cure for his Alzheimer's than a hearing-aid is a cure for hearing impairment, or a prosthetic limb a cure for having had one's leg amputated. All are aids or tools for alleviating impaired function.

Clark and Chalmers (p. 35) assert that it would beg the question to think that *where* the information is located is relevant to whether it counts as cognitive. However, if our concepts are such that it *does* make a difference where the information is, then to argue, as Clark and Chalmers do, that the respects in which Otto differs from Inga aren't "important and relevant," or "deep," is already itself to do violence to those concepts. We distinguish between parts of one's body, implants—that is, things implanted in one's body (artificial hips, knees, hearts, certain hearing-aids, and other implants, cybernetic or otherwise)—prosthetic additions to one's body (artificial limbs), and tools or aids to one's bodily functioning (spectacles, hearing aids, walking sticks, Zimmer-frames). Should cognitive science seek to plow under these distinctions? One very good reason why it shouldn't derives from the idea of the *integrity* of the body, which is a crucial and central aspect of our conceptual scheme. (A related idea is that

Otto is no longer functioning, psychologically, as a human being *should* function.) *Pace* contemporary forms of functionalism, our concept of the body is partly *normative*, not purely structural, and not such as to be captured in *purely* causal terms. What *could* be more important or deep than this concept which, whether Clark and Chalmers like it or not, plays a vital role in the distinctions between body parts, implants, and tools?

8   Epistemic Actions and Epistemic Credit

One final aspect of Clark and Chalmers's views on epistemic concepts bears examination in this context. They take over from David Kirsh and Paul Maglio the phrase *epistemic actions* to refer to actions that alter the agent's physical environment so as to aid and augment cognitive processes (such as recognition and search). The contrast here is with *pragmatic* actions, which alter the agent's physical environment for the sake of attaining some physical goal.

I think we ought to agree about the existence and importance of epistemic actions. But Clark and Chalmers go on to claim that epistemic actions demand the spread of epistemic *credit* (p. 27). What does this mean?

It might most naturally be taken to mean that we should distribute the credit for an epistemic achievement over the whole arrangement of person-plus-environmental supports, judging that the *cognitive system* in question believes, knows, and so on.[13] But this obviously conflicts with how we *do* assign credit using central epistemic concepts, like knowledge. Under many conditions relevant to assessing what a subject knows, we judge them not to know but to have *cheated* if they use certain external resources. Even when such resources are allowable (as in Clark and Chalmers's game of Tetris case), the credit still goes to the person, not the arrangement. We say things like "She did the calculation with the calculator," "She knew how to do the multiplication (viz., using the calculator)," "He knows how to do long division," "She drafted her article on her laptop computer."[14] Cognitive phenomena can sometimes be credited to systems, but in such cases the attributions can, and *must* (to be literally true), be cashed out in a way that gives the credit to the relevant *cognizer(s)* involved.[15] No advantage, only confusion, can accrue from taking the elliptical form of attribution literally.

Even without trying to give cognitive systems the credit for epistemic achievements, "spreading epistemic credit" is problematic. We distinguish between two kinds of informants: those who know whether *p* is the case, and those who, although they don't, do know how to find out whether it is. And this distinction can be extremely important in certain circumstances. For example, if you were sent to find out whether *p* from someone who's supposed to know whether *p* (Otto, perhaps), your expectations would be rudely disappointed if they needed to consult external resources which didn't happen to be available at the time. Of course, you'd be equally disappointed if they didn't need to consult such resources, but simply couldn't recall whether *p*. But in this case the prospective informant (Inga, maybe) would be said to have *forgotten*, and therefore no longer to know, whether *p*.[16] Even this weak reading of the epistemic credit thesis threatens to erase the distinction, replacing it by a difference in degree between people who have their knowledge "at their fingertips" and people who have to expend considerable effort to bring to bear what they (already, on this account) know.

To retain the connection between cognition and everyday psychological abilities and achievements, which I've argued is essential simply because cognitive science is an attempt to explain such things, cognitive scientists and their attendant philosophers have to respect certain constraints on the use of psychological concepts. One of these is simply that the abilities and achievements in question are credited to people (or other organisms), not to brains, and at best only derivatively to the arrangements in which organisms and their brains are embedded.

Acknowledgments

This chapter was mainly written during my time as a visiting researcher at the Center for Consciousness Studies, University of Arizona. I'd like to thank Dave Chalmers for helpful discussions there, my colleague Hanjo Glock for helpful comments, and audiences at Tucson, the Universities of North London, Hertfordshire, and Reading for helpful feedback. Thanks are also due to the Leverhulme Trust, who awarded me a research fellowship to work on this material.

Notes

1. Unless otherwise noted, page references are to this essay as it appears in this volume.

2. I suspect that *experiences*, which Clark and Chalmers suppose "may be determined internally" (p. 33), are better candidates for being partly constituted by environmental features. We identify experiences, after all, in terms of what they are experiences *of*, and this is usually something environmental.

3. Clark and Chalmers's use of "determined" as an alternative to "constituted" (see, e.g., the quote from p. 33 in the previous note) is unhelpful in this respect.

4. I also suspect that Clark and Chalmers's vision of what could constitute a natural kind will be severely and inappropriately restricted by their commitment to philosophical naturalism.

5. Alternatively, when active externalism is in question, it may be a *conceptual* thesis about cognitive systems or cognitive processing. Here, since the concepts of a cognitive system and cognitive processing are theoretical ones, somewhat less constrained by our ordinary concepts of cognition, there's more room for maneuver. I began to address this in Preston 2006.

6. See Hacker 1997, pp. 293–294.

7. For arguments that it does so, see McKinsey 1991; Glock and Preston 1995.

8. Adams and Aizawa (2001, p. 55) also put forward this objection, saying that Otto's "memory recall" involves cognitive-motor processing and visual processing not found in Inga's genuine memory recall. I agree with their underlying point, even while denying that Inga's case need involve memory (see below).

9. Arguably, one *can* judge or believe that one believes that *p*, but *only* in cases like unconscious belief, or where one takes a third-person stance toward one's own commitments.

10. See, e.g., Hamilton 2000, p. 27.

11. Clark and Chalmers's distinction between "occurrent" and "non-occurrent" beliefs also misconstrues the difference between beliefs and occurrent thoughts, although I don't have space to go into this here.

12. For this point, I'm grateful to Hanjo Glock.

13. I take it that a thesis about *epistemic* credit applies to knowledge as well as to belief.

14. This suggests that active externalism might be even less plausible as a thesis about the paradigm cognitive concept, knowledge, than about belief. [I[

15. This, I have argued, makes sense of John Searle's "Chinese room" scenario. See Preston 2002, pp. 29–31. Cognitive "systems" like libraries can of course be said to contain knowledge, but they can't be said to know, believe, etc.

16. Clark and Chalmers's clause stating that the resources be reliably present doesn't deal with this. I'm not now considering the thesis which credits cognitive systems with epistemic achievements, but only the idea that epistemic credit should be spread to a person not just in virtue of his or her ability to answer a question, but in virtue of his or her ability to discover its answer.

References

Adams, F., and Aizawa, K. (2001). The bounds of cognition. *Philosophical Psychology*, *14*, 43–64.

Clark, A. (1997). *Being There: Putting, Brain, Body and World Together Again*. Cambridge, MA: MIT Press.

Clark, A., and Chalmers, D. (1998). The extended mind. *Analysis, 58*, 7–19. Reprinted as chapter 2 of this volume.

Glock, H.-J., and Preston, J. M. (1995). Externalism and first-person authority. *Monist, 78*, 515–533.

Hacker, P. M. S. (1997). Davidson on first-person authority. *Philosophical Quarterly*, *47*, 285–304.

Hamilton, A. (2000). The authority of avowals and the concept of belief. *European Journal of Philosophy, 8*, 20–39.

McKinsey, M. (1991). Anti-individualism and privileged access. *Analysis, 51*, 9–16. (Reprinted in P. Ludlow and N. Martin [eds.], *Externalism and Self-Knowledge* [pp. 175–184], Stanford: CSLI Publications, 1998.)

Preston, J. M. (2002). Introduction. In J. M. Preston and J. M. Bishop (eds.), *Views into the Chinese Room: New Essays on Searle and AI*. Oxford: Oxford University Press.

Preston, J. M. (2006). Is your mobile part of your mind? In K. Nyiri (ed.), *Mobile Understanding: The Epistemology of Ubiquitous Communication* (pp. 67–77). Vienna: Passagen Verlag.

Contributors

Professor Fred Adams Department of Linguistics and Cognitive Science, University of Delaware, USA

Professor Ken Aizawa Centenary College Louisiana, USA

Professor David J. Chalmers School of Philosophy, Research School of Social Sciences, The Australian National University, Australia

Professor Andy Clark School of Philosophy, The University of Edinburgh, UK

Dr. Stephen Cowley School of Psychology, The University of Hertfordshire, UK

Professor Susan Hurley (deceased) Formerly at the Department of Philosophy, The University of Bristol, UK

Professor James Ladyman Department of Philosophy, The University of Bristol, UK

Dr. Richard Menary Philosophy Programme, The University of Wollongong, Australia

Dr. John Preston Department of Philosophy, The University of Reading, UK

Professor Don Ross Department of Philosophy and Department of Finance, Economics and Quantitative Methods, University of Alabama at Birmingham, USA, and School of Economics, University of Cape Town, South Africa

Professor Mark Rowlands Department of Philosophy, The University of Miami, Florida, USA

Associate Professor Robert D. Rupert Department of Philosophy, The University of Colorado at Boulder, USA

Professor David Spurrett Philosophy, University of KwaZulu-Natal, South Africa

Professor John Sutton Macquarie Centre for Cognitive Science, The University of Macquarie, Australia

Dr. Michael Wheeler Department of Philosophy, The University of Stirling, UK

Professor Robert A. Wilson Department of Philosophy, The University of Alberta, Canada

Index